GHETTOSTADT

GHETTOSTADT

ŁÓDŹ AND THE MAKING

OF A NAZI CITY

Gordon J. Horwitz

THE BELKNAP PRESS OF
HARVARD UNIVERSITY PRESS

Cambridge, Massachusetts
London, England
2008

Maps 1 and 2 are from *The Chronicle of the Łódź Ghetto, 1941–1944,*
ed. Lucjan Dobroszycki, trans. Richard Lourie et al.
(New Haven: Yale University Press, 1984).

Library of Congress Cataloging-in-Publication Data
Horwitz, Gordon J.
Ghettostadt : Łódź and the making of a Nazi city / Gordon J. Horwitz.
p.   cm.
Includes bibliographical references and index.
ISBN-13: 978-0-674-02799-2 (alk. paper)
ISBN-10: 0-674-02799-X (alk. paper)
1. Jews—Persecutions—Poland—Łódź—History.   2. Holocaust, Jewish
(1939–1945)—Poland—Łódź.   3. Łódź (Poland)—Ethnic relations.   I. Title.
DS134.62.H67   2008
940.53′1853847—dc22   2007050934

In memory of Marcia L. Kahn

Contents

Prologue   *1*

1 Autumn 1939: Conquest   *8*

2 A City without Jews   *30*

3 The Enclosure   *62*

4 The Ghetto Will Endure   *91*

5 The Ghetto and the City of the Future   *113*

6 Banishment   *143*

7 Departure, Worry, and Disappearance   *159*

8 "Give Me Your Children"   *192*

9 Who Shall Live and Who Shall Die?   *232*

10 Numbered Are the Days   *266*

Epilogue   *311*

Notes   *325*

Acknowledgments   *383*

Index   *385*

GHETTOSTADT

Prologue

On a late-summer morning in 1941 a camera crew from the Ufa film studio in Berlin arrived in Litzmannstadt, formerly known as Łódź, the newly renamed and annexed Polish city then undergoing dramatic redevelopment into a modern metropolis of the Third Reich. The filmmakers had come to continue their work on a documentary designed to highlight the city's transformation. Checking into the downtown Savoy Hotel, the team began filming at the first location of a twenty-five-day tour that would take them to more than forty sites in and around Litzmannstadt. That day, according to the shooting log, "was sunny, with big, bright clouds."[1]

The crew set up their cameras at a spot by the water's edge in the Erzhausen district, a southern quarter of the city through which coursed the gentle headwaters of the meandering river Ner. Here, turning northward, the waterway briefly widened and spilled into a long basin, forming a small lake. At this site, long neglected yet deemed suitable for recreation, a new bathing beach was under construction. Stones were being laid in the riverbed, and improvements to the embankment and its surroundings were under way; trees were being transplanted and nearby meadows tended.[2] To judge by the quaint designations given to newly christened streets and byways of the area, the recently installed German city fathers envisaged a place of enchantment. Visitors approaching the lake from the west could enjoy a walk down fabled side streets named for Rumpelstiltskin, Cinderella, Hansel, Little Red Riding Hood and the Wolf, and the Brothers Grimm. Those nearing from the east might wander along other streets invoking Snow White and Sleeping Beauty. Faun Street led directly to the water. Along a shoreline promenade strollers had a choice of turning north, in tandem with Gnomes Way, or directly south, on or close by Erlking Way.[3]

The new regime was eager to promote filming of the work being done at the water's edge, for images of such improvements were ideally suited to highlighting the film's central theme of the renovation and modernization of the city under German guidance and administration. In the coming days, the crew would travel with their equipment to local parks and squares, new and remodeled housing, street renewal and demolition sites, bureaus and camps for ethnic German settlers, factories, city hospitals, the Health Department, a mortuary, a stockyard, a gasworks, renovated theaters, a music school, a stadium, and a festive assembly of Hitler Youth, altogether completing by the time of their departure "over 2,000 meters" of film shot both indoors and out. During the course of their stay, the film crew would share portions of the ongoing results with the mayor and local officials, for whom private showings of unedited footage were presented at a downtown theater.[4]

On the surface the filmmakers presented a picture of a modern city, progressive, orderly, and clean. In many respects it was to be like any other, a center of industry and commerce, culture and recreation. And yet at its core, the theme of this presentation was mean-spirited and cruel, for this new city, as the film was determined to demonstrate, was to be a Nazi city, and by definition a city without Jews.

The metropolis to which the Nazis laid claim had emerged rapidly, a boomtown of nineteenth-century industrial development. By the end of the second decade of the nineteenth century little more than a Polish village of fewer than eight hundred people, by 1914, spurred by the revolution in textile machinery and mass production, the city had grown to more than 478,000 inhabitants. Encouraged by the then-ruling Russian imperial administration to settle here and invest, German entrepreneurial talent played a critical role in the city's early economic development. Indeed, German textile barons would establish the first of the city's great factories for the production of woolen and cotton goods. As the city's industrial base grew, so too did its workforce. From the countryside Poles arrived in ever greater numbers. In parallel with that same mid-nineteenth-century in-migration, Jewish industrialists, merchants, small manufacturers, and petty tradesmen and their families were drawn to the city as well. Between 1825 and 1862, however, with the exception of all but a privileged and wealthy few, the Jews were by law confined to a cluster of residential streets beside a ramshackle market square north of the city center. Over the course of the century, the numbers of Poles and Jews quickly overtook those of German heritage. By 1931 the city's population had grown to almost 604,000, of whom according to linguistic criteria 357,000, or 59 percent, were Poles; 192,000, or 32 percent, were Jews; and 54,000, or just under 9 percent, were German. With the size of the overall population still rising, in 1939 the estimated number of Jews had grown to well over 200,000, constituting one-third or more of all residents in the city.[5]

To a Nazi regime intent on staking claim to the lands in the East, this demographic imbalance was to be rectified speedily and by all available means. Secured by German arms, reshaped by German planning and technical expertise, the city was to be remade inside and out. German migrants were encouraged to settle here. Compelled to yield to German demands, many of the city's Polish residents would be shipped away, some to locales farther east, others transported back to Germany to work as laborers for the Reich. Those who remained were banished from residence in the city center; they would serve strictly as a labor force for local industry. But the Jews would be removed forever from the life of the city. To the new rulers the prospect of their continued presence was as intolerable as it was unthinkable. At the time of the filmmakers' visit the Jews of Łódź were safely isolated from the remainder of the population, confined to a ghetto. Inadequately supplied, subject to deadly assault if they dared to cross its guarded perimeter, they labored for the German war economy until such time as, by means not yet determined, they would disappear altogether, never to return.

Precisely how this disappearance was to be effected was not altogether clear in that summer of 1941. Farther to the east, German killing squads were slaughtering Jews across a broad front from the Baltic to the Black Sea, but the death camps were not yet constructed, though they would be very soon. Their creation would mark a historical divide, introducing into the world a phenomenon so unexpected and outrageous in design and execution as to exceed the then-understood limits of organized human cruelty.

On the eve of the war to come, then, the Jews of Łódź could not have foreseen the ultimate fate that awaited them. To be sure, given the rise of the National Socialists across the border in Germany and of extreme nationalists on the right wing of the Polish political spectrum, in the 1930s the city's Jews were increasingly subject to verbal threats in the local press and became the target of sporadic, violent anti-Semitic assaults. In 1934, in a stunning victory, anti-Semitic parties of both Polish and ethnic German composition briefly assumed a dominant position on the Łódź city council, subjecting Jews to further harassment.[6] But even these isolated attacks, however menacing, remained light-years distant from the unimaginable events to follow.

Long before the Nazi invasion, the Jewish community of Łódź, organized to promote and defend Jewish interests, had been not just numerous but well organized and strong. A highly developed network of religious institutions, social welfare organizations, educational establishments, political parties and associations, commercial enterprises, and institutions of public health offered its members broad material, intellectual, and spiritual support. Successful Jewish merchants, none more celebrated than the nineteenth-century cotton magnate Izrael K. Poznański, contributed generously to the founding of Jewish hospitals, shelters for the poor, schools, and orphanages. Some of the buildings he funded and commissioned would assist in shaping the look of the city. Under the patronage of its most successful industrialists and merchants, Jewish architects had been commissioned to design several of the city's most impressive mansions, banking houses, and hotels. In addition to smaller houses of prayer, four magnificent, ornately crafted synagogues towered high above the streets below. Most impressive of all, a product of the 1880s, in the very heart of the city stood the Great Synagogue, outwardly "combin[ing] Romanesque and Moorish elements" with an "interior . . . richly decorated in the oriental style, with multi-colored mosaics and paintings covering the walls and the vaulting."[7] Beginning in 1892 a great walled Jewish cemetery was completed, the wooded pathways and avenues of its nearly one hundred acres decorated with headstones of remarkably stylish design. In 1900, when Izrael Poznański was laid to rest, he would occupy a family tomb that was encircled by columns and buttresses and whose interior structure's high dome was decorated with a glass mosaic depicting palm trees beside gentle waters.[8]

The prewar cultural life of Łódź Jewry was lively and inventive, nourished by an active Yiddish and Polish-language daily press, Jewish literary circles, Jewish artists, and an active Jewish cabaret and theater. Famed Jewish poets of the era such as Moshe Broderson, Julian Tuwim, and Yitzhak Katzenelson were inextricably linked to the life of the community, as were painters, among them Maurycy Trębacz and Arthur Szyk, Yiddish theatrical performers such as Szymon Dzigan and Mose Pulawer, and emerging talents, including the young photographer Mendel Grossman. In music, Dawid Bajgelman and Teodor Ryder composed and conducted local orchestras. The renowned twentieth-century pianist Artur Rubinstein was born in Łódź and knew it as a child. His parents were also laid to rest in the large Jewish cemetery.[9]

Jews were a visible part of city life. Along with the city's gentile residents, they walked and shopped on Piotrkowska Street, the great avenue that was home to the city's finest shops, hotels, cafés, and restaurants. On a visit to the city in the 1920s, the Austrian Jewish writer Josef Roth, walking that same avenue, commented on the stunning beauty of young Jewish brides strolling arm in arm with their merchant husbands.[10]

However successful its great families and broad middle class, the Łódź Jewish community was largely a community of the poor. One had only to travel a few long blocks north of the elegant establishments on Piotrkowska Street to find them. Many resided there in a district known as Bałuty, a setting of dilapidated housing, neglected pavements, flooded gutters, noisy, crowded, and narrow thoroughfares lined with factories, warehouses, and bustling open-air markets. Here the look of things was grittier. The district had a downscale feel, and its ill-regulated, impoverished surroundings, though home largely to the hardworking poor, also bore a reputation as the neighborhood of roughnecks, illicit traders, and petty gangs. Wandering the district in the 1920s, the Berlin novelist Alfred

Döblin marveled at the crowding and the raucousness but also the lively energies of the zone.[11]

Bałuty was a garment district. To walk the streets was to be aware of textile work in all its variety. In small-scale operations, often localized by buildings or blocks, fabric was cut, sewn, stitched, fitted, and pressed. Manufacture, visible to passersby through nearby windows, spilled from homes and workshops into the streets. Carts filled with pyramided bales of cloth crisscrossed the narrow thoroughfares; on market squares stalls were set up; hawkers called out to potential customers to come and examine their wares; boys marched past with baskets filled with warmed bagels and pretzels to sell.[12] In spite of the local color, Jews, like all others who could afford to do so, moved to more respectable areas of the city as soon as they could. A shop or residence on Piotrkowska Street occupied one of the city's most stylish addresses, while Pieprzowa, or Pepper Street, just south of the square known as Bałut Market, was considered one of the city's most impoverished and forlorn.[13]

The heart of the daily experience of the Jewish community was marked by family and friendship. Personal memoirs of these years evoke summertime excursions and hours spent in city parks and the nearby countryside. Lives were open-ended then, possessed of numerous potentialities and trajectories into the future. Thoughts of the city stirred recollections of the Yiddish theater, a meeting after school under the clock tower of city hall, visits to the zoo, or open-air concerts in the park, a father coming home from work and reaching into his pocket for the candies he would distribute to the children in the courtyard. Before the war, many Jews from this city traveled widely both within Poland and abroad. Some went as far as Palestine, sampling an alternative life, before heading back. Trains were a favored mode of transportation then. And at summer's end, families greeted the return of relatives who had vacationed in the countryside or in other lands such as Austria.[14] Cherished furnishings filled Jewish homes, objects reflecting both the warmth and protection of family life and an awareness of possessing a place in the world. Recollecting these things would nourish the memory of those who, in later years, looked back on all that was lost.[15] In photographs, mothers and fathers appear beside or holding their young sons and daughters, friends stand next to one another in the snow, pupils are seated with their teachers. Jewish children at summer camp lift their arms for calisthenics, follow the arc of a volleyball in the air, hold hands and dance in a circle.[16] A memoirist speaks of remembered articles of clothing—"a white tennis suit, white tennis shoes, white socks"—once worn by an admired friend. Thoughts of her loved ones and companions from before the war would bring to mind fondly evoked details of how they appeared in life, an intimate catalogue of tanned limbs, bright faces, dark eyes, and long lashes. She would recall as well how her young brother once proclaimed his intention to "conquer the world."[17] Lives were being lived, futures anticipated. The story of so many lives was as yet unknown.

For what was about to happen to the Jews of Łódź there was nowhere to go for guidance. In no bookshop or library of 1939 would they find historical or literary discussion of what would become their fate. For them there were neither books nor films to familiarize them with the scope of the tragedy to come, nor ways to ponder a threat so unprecedented. The memoirists, historians, poets, artists, and filmmakers who, in the course of the late twentieth century and beyond, were to apply their talents to this theme were children at the time, or not yet born. There was no *Night*, no *Destruction of the European Jews*, no *Drowned and the Saved*, no *Shoah*, no *Schindler's List*.[18] Auschwitz existed as a place on the map of merely local and parochial interest.

Documenting the city's historic transformation, the filmmakers who had come to Łódź were busily crafting a narrative entirely shaped by a Nazi vision. In addition to highlighting impressions of the future city, the film script called for a tour of its pre-Nazi past, full of the basest anti-Semitic stereotypes. At a critical juncture the caricature of a Jewish face was to be seen hovering menacingly over the city. Against the backdrop of fearsome heavens, appearing small, then growing ever larger, was the date "September 1939." Simultaneously, the sound of a Stuka dive bomber was to be heard from afar. At first only faintly perceptible, the sound of its engine would grow louder and louder and louder until it attained the level of a terrifying howl.[19]

1

Autumn 1939

CONQUEST

As pleasant a late-summer day as one might wish for dawned over west-central Poland on Friday, the first of September, 1939. For this day, so like those exceptionally "cloudless" and "bright" days to follow, was marked, we are told, by a sky altogether blue and clear.[1] The danger, emerging unexpectedly from the heavens, materialized within seconds. On that September morning, people looked up and could hardly believe their eyes.

In the countryside just north of Łódź, a great urban center, second-largest city in Poland, home as well to the second-most populous Jewish community in the country, a group of Jewish mothers accompanied by their children were enjoying a restful outing in the nearby Chełmy Forest. The sound of aircraft overhead was reported to have drawn the children out of the woods to get a better view; to their "great joy," the "airplanes descended," flying "so low that the youngsters, merrily welcoming their appearance, could see the pilots" inside. Then the aircraft opened fire. Alerted to the sudden danger by the sound of their children's screams, the mothers came running; gathering them quickly, they fled homeward while the planes sped after them in pursuit. Many were wounded, and one of their number, a child from Łódź, was killed.[2]

Immediately to the south, in the city that morning factory whistles were activated, sounding a general alert. Citizens cleared the streets, shut their windows, and scrambled down stairways to reach the protection of cellars and shelters. Downtown the sound of a plane was heard overhead, followed by a single explosion. When the assault broke off, people reemerged, many at first riveted in place, staring as rescue vehicles raced through the streets. Radios were switched on, tuned to repeated confirmation that the nation was under attack. At the offices of the *Nayer Folksblat,* a Yiddish daily headquartered at 21 Piotrkowska Street, the very heart of the city, telephones started ringing and employees rushed back in to answer the calls. Nearby, the streets swarmed with people, some heading directly home, others toward shops to gather needed provisions. Only with the sounding of a new alarm did the streets empty again, as individuals raced about, cautiously "hugging the walls" of buildings, dashing for safety "from one entryway to the next." It was dangerous to step out into the open. Witnesses watched in horror as a young man attempting to run across a downtown street was instantly struck and killed by a streetcar that had suddenly rounded the corner at furious speed. Three aircraft appeared overhead, at first lazily circling in formation. Then yet another explosion was heard, as before. Only hours later did people emerge once more and pour into the streets, continuing to make their way home before nightfall. Only moments before having again to seek out the safety of their shelters, residents "counted heads" to determine just "who [was] present" and "who still missing."[3]

In spite of the initial shock, as well as the continuing threat from the air, on this day and in days to follow Łódź would be spared the worst. But by the middle of the coming week, in the face of the continuing German advance, ultimate prospects for the safety of the city, and for the country as well, appeared increasingly grave. Hoping to bolster defense of the capital, on the night of September 5 the Polish government ordered men between the ages of sixteen and sixty to evacuate the city and proceed to Warsaw. Fearful that their additional presence would only hinder the military, the authorities instructed women and children to remain behind, though many chose to join the "mass exodus."[4] For many the decision would prove fatal. Along the route, columns of refugees were cut to pieces by German attack from above. So violent was the effect of the strafing that many recovered bodies consisted of little more than tattered remains. In Łódź, surviving relatives turned to hospitals and Jewish welfare agencies for information about the fate of loved ones. Inevitably "terrible scenes" took place as people examined posted lists of victims. Others, still left uncertain, made their way to the cemetery—to which the remains of the slaughtered had been delivered by the "hundreds"—in the hope of achieving resolution even in the face of their worst fears.[5]

Following a night marked by artillery bombardment, on Friday, September 8, advance German formations entered the city.[6] On the roundabout at the top of Piotrkowska Street, at Plac Wolnośći—Freedom Square, symbol of Polish independence—the conquerors were rewarded with offerings of bread and salt from the hands of their thankful local ethnic German brethren. That night there were impromptu festivities as the conquerors were treated to "a ball, with fireworks, with music and dancing."[7] In the heart of the downtown district, the city's premier establishment, the Grand Hotel on Piotrkowska Street, was "bedecked with garlands of flowers" while "civilians—boys, girls—jump[ed] into the passing military cars with happy cries of *'Heil Hitler!'*" One heard the sound of "loud German conversation in the streets." The city and the skies above it securely in the hands of the occupier, its long-darkened "streets" were at last "lit for the night."[8]

On the afternoon of September 13, following his arrival at a nearby airfield and a brief motor tour of the scenes of recent fighting and meetings with divisional commanders in the field, Hitler rode into Łódź. Along a route overseen by soldiers, SS, and military and auxiliary police, crowds of local ethnic Germans, their arms raised in salute, excitedly observed the passing of the motorcade and cheered the unexpected appearance of their deliverer. All went smoothly, though a correspondent accompanying the motorcade noted that it had been forced to "a brief standstill" owing to road work being done by "hundreds of Jews," many "still clothed in caftans and greasy little East European caps. . . . Ethnic German auxiliary police are supervising their work—the first productive work," the report insisted, "that these Eastern Jews have ever done in their life."[9]

A terrible autumn was to follow. The world of Łódź Jewry was turned upside down. It was nightmarish. To recall the events long afterward is to be reminded of the inadequacy of language in gaining psychological purchase on such outbursts of cruelty as would characterize these initial assaults on human dignity, human life, and human limb. The German victory was understood to have granted license for open attacks on Jews wherever one might find them: in the streets or even rousted violently from their own homes, to be hauled away for the carnivalesque enjoyment of the mocking citizenry and soldiery who would gather round to watch or to participate in the spectacle. Such outrages, now being staged in the streets of Łódź (as in countless other locales, large and small, throughout occupied Poland), were long a hallmark of the regime: while one Jew would be paraded about inside a cart for sport, others, hitched to the rigging like beasts, were made to pull it.[10] Another unfortunate soul was hung by the back of his coat amid the branches of a tree, his legs dangling high above the ground.[11] It was deemed amusing to force Jews to undress in public: bareheaded, barefooted, forcibly stripped to their undergarments, and made to dance before jeering crowds in the street or, similarly, made to remove their clothes and then lined up at gunpoint for the staging of a mock execution.[12] For a Jew, suddenly overnight "no neighborhood or time of day was safe."[13] In one instance Jews walking down the street were hit over the head by someone wielding a blunt instrument from a passing truck. When, recognizing what was happening, others disappeared indoors, the tormentor, descending from the vehicle, simply went into a building and dragged a Jewish man from his workbench. Leading his victim to the truck, the brute "took the man by the collar and with a heave threw him into the vehicle," treating him like a beaten dog.[14]

Under the pretext that they be made to work, Jews were also "pulled from streetcars and *droskies* [horse-drawn wagons]" and taken away to perform all manner of supposed labor assignments whose real purpose was "to humiliate the Jews with all sorts of menial, filthy, and totally useless jobs." Local Jew-haters quickly saw the possibilities of the moment: "Not only did the authorities (in or out of uniform) engage in this, but also civilians: a janitor or a schoolboy, an urchin, even a nine-year-old child dragged a Jew to work or just pointed him out." Such local assistance proved especially useful to those German occupiers less skilled in immediately identifying as Jews those who, by virtue of possessing less distinguishing features or dress, "avoided recognition because of their looks."[15] Senseless, often Sisyphean tasks—such as hauling heavy furniture or stones up and down a staircase for hours on end—were popular forms of abuse.[16] The richest of degradations involved the staging of rituals that were scatological or misogynistic in overtone: "Cleaning toilets with bare hands, scrubbing floors with fingernails were daily occurrences. Women were told to take off their underwear and use it to clean the floors, the windows, and toilets."[17]

Understandably wishing to avoid, whenever possible, the dangers associated with appearing in public spaces, Jews sought refuge indoors. But if the streets were unsafe, so too were the now instantly violable interiors of Jewish homes.[18] For amusing as it proved for many to exercise their aggressions against the Jews in public, exposing to sport and punishment and pain the flesh and bone and dignity of helpless human beings, in the lawlessness of the hour it was a simple matter to realize that the Jews' material possessions were now there for the taking. Among the first targets of opportunity were residences left unoccupied by Jewish citizens who had fled the city during or in the immediate aftermath of the invasion. Fellow Jews, impressed into serving as movers, were compelled to empty these "abandoned" residences of their most valued contents, hauling away "furniture, carpets, radios, crystal, books, fabric, clothing, furs," cash, and jewels, and loading them into vehicles parked outside, waiting and ready to receive the loot.[19] Covetous acquaintances, in one way or another familiar with particular Jewish households, were quick to spot their chance to stake a claim. A Jewish physician recalled how one day a distant, materially less fortunate former schoolmate from decades past unexpectedly arrived at his home. Entering and making himself comfortable in a chair, the visitor made a show of surveying the family's furnishings and insolently insisted that the physician's father, who owned the building, deed the property to him.[20] A Jewish married woman, the mother of an infant son, later recalled how an illiterate Polish handyman who had been hired on numerous occasions in the past to perform household repairs to her home suddenly reappeared at her door. Asserting his new identity as ethnically German and announcing his status as "trustee" of the family's property, the man laid claim to their residence and possessions.[21] Throughout the autumn, under the pretext of searching out possessions now illegal for Jews to own, German military personnel and SS were wont to knock heavily on doors at any hour of the day or night, entering in search of whatever might be had. Sometimes the plunderers walked away with only razors and blades, handkerchiefs, medical equipment, radios, or typewriters, but above all the hunt was on for luxury articles and valuables. In the process, cabinets and closets were emptied, pocketbooks opened, upholstery ripped apart. Not infrequently these invasions were accompanied by beatings on the spot, or the brandishing or firing of weapons with the intent to terrorize, to wound, or to kill.[22]

Such wild and unregulated seizures marked the initial days of the occupation with a lawless frenzy that would never altogether cease. But the era of unbridled sport and mockery was gradually to be channeled in a more orderly and supervised direction. Within the first weeks, the occupation authorities undertook to establish formal institutional arrangements designed to regulate the acquisition of Jewish assets, laying the groundwork for the quasi-legal confiscation of Jewish-owned or occupied residences, furnishings and household effects, cash holdings and financial instruments, business inventory, factories, and real estate. Under the relentless pressure of these military and civilian administrative decrees, in a matter of weeks and months the commercial holdings, accumulated savings, and household possessions of prosperous Jews, as well as the modest means available to the Jewish middle and lower-middle classes and the Jewish poor, were funneled into German hands.

First, accompanying a September 18 ordinance establishing a currency rate of two Polish złoty to the German Reichsmark, came word of severe restrictions placed on Jews accessing privately owned financial assets. Henceforth "Jews were not allowed to withdraw more than 500 złoty a week from their bank accounts" and simultaneously barred from otherwise keeping, in their homes or elsewhere, cash in excess of two thousand złoty.[23] Then at month's end came an official declaration that so-called abandoned property—private residences and businesses, many having been left behind by Jews fleeing the city during and following the hostilities—were now forfeit and taken into German possession. Eyeing existing inventory in advance of their seizure, in mid-September the military authorities instructed the Association of Combing Mills to survey stocks of Jewish-held "raw materials." Once removed, items worth an estimated 1.8 million marks were seized. As the confiscatory regime expanded, a newly created Trustee for Raw Materials (Treuhänder für Rohstoffe), following the same pattern, instructed Jewish textile manufacturers, shipping firms, and shop owners to list their current inventories and proceeded to take over all such reported supplies of raw materials and finished articles on hand or completed since September 10. By November, two additional agencies destined to play an expanding role in the ongoing acquisition and sale of Jewish property and possessions, the Main Trusteeship Office East (Haupttreuhandstlle Ost, or HTO), charged with the liquidation of Jewish factories and commercial enterprises, and the Łódź Trade Society (Lodzer Warenhandelsgesellschaft, or LWHG), specializing in the ongoing removal and disposition of Jewish business inventories and output, had stepped to the fore. Additional ordinances that autumn—making it illegal for Jews to engage in commerce involving "textiles and leather goods and raw material" or in "road transport," or, to cite but one example of restrictions placed on Jewish professionals, barring Jewish doctors from attending non-Jewish patients—made it increasingly difficult for Jews in Łódź to earn their livelihood and maintain an independent existence.[24]

The Jewish community organization, or Kehilla—the principal institution to which, in circumstances of need, members of the community had in the past been accustomed to turn—also suffered terrible material and organizational losses. Its funds, as well as those of allied Jewish charitable and welfare agencies, had become subject to seizure, and, signaling a crisis in the community's leadership, many who had run the community council and its offices had fled the city—among them community president Leib Mincberg—leaving the community without direction. Into the breach stepped others. On September 12 new elections to the community board were held. Selected for the presidency was the Kehilla's current vice president, Leizer I. Pływacki, an important figure, like Mincberg, in the locally dominant Agudah movement.[25] Simultaneously advancing to the now vacant vice presidency was another locally well-known, energetic, though hardly congenial community activist, Mordechai Chaim Rumkowski. A man of ambition difficult to overlook, albeit not particularly well regarded or trusted, Rumkowski had long served on the board as a minority representative of a Zionist faction. In office he had developed a reputation as disputatious, long-winded, fiercely independent, and strong willed. Rumkowski craved authority, saw no reason to abandon it, and, it was said, reveled in his moments in the limelight. He was, after all, a man who liked to put himself forward, and when given the chance, he gladly took the floor to speak, commanding attention.[26]

Only a month later, anxious to firm up lines of authority and establish a reliable administrative channel for directing orders pertaining to the Jews of occupied Łódź, on October 13 the newly occupied city's chief civilian officer, Stadtkommissar Leister, Commissar of the City of Łódź, selected Rumkowski to head the Jewish community, conferring on him the title of Eldest of the Jews, simultaneously instructing him to appoint a council to assist him in his upcoming tasks. The arrangement was broadly in conformity with a key occupation directive, issued in September by Reinhard Heydrich, chief of the Security Service, calling for the establishment in large and medium-sized cities in the newly conquered territories of councils of so-called Jewish Elders, whose task it would be to cooperate unconditionally in carrying out German instructions affecting the Jews.[27]

For better or worse, Rumkowski now emerged as the man of the hour. The circumstances surrounding his selection by the new German civil administration to head the council remain shrouded in conjecture. Much is made of Rumkowski's long-standing ambition to lead and to wield authority, reinforcing the likelihood that he would have been eager to step forward and make his availability and readiness to serve known to the Germans. At the community headquarters, where the Germans had stationed representatives, he would certainly have drawn notice. Solomon Uberbaum, a man "associated with Rumkowski before the war" and who later "worked for" the council, reported: "He used to come to the *Kehilla* building every day. When the Germans came in and asked, 'Which one of you is the Elder here?' he made a striking impression. An elderly Jew. Gray hair. So they said: 'You will be the Elder.' That's what they say, and it could be the truth."[28] Others, too, recalled his cutting an imposing figure. By one account he was of greater-than-average stature, "a head taller than everyone else, a six-footer," with an impressive mane of "abundant gray hair" reputedly complemented by an impressive face that "was always suntanned, even in winter," and who, when dressed in "high, black, shiny boots, riding breeches, and a short jacket," strode with "a vigorous gait. He looked like a leader." Impressions do vary, however. Isaac Rus, son of a former community leader, Benjamin Rus, and long familiar with the man, later described Rumkowski as only "of medium height, perhaps somewhat taller," and "somewhat stooped," altogether creating the image of "an old man" whose appearance seemed to him to have remained remarkably unaltered over the years: "He looked in 1944 just as I had known him in

1929; nothing had changed."[29] Rus was convinced that only days prior to Rumkowski's formal selection as head of the council, Stadtkommissar Leister had already singled him out for special consideration. When a delegation of Jewish representatives, Rumkowski among them, arrived at city hall seeking authorization to meet with the Stadtkommissar, "Leister took their documents and wrote on them in turn: 'Permit the bearer of this document to come to me.' When he came to Rumkowski he said: 'You don't need this. You have a better paper!'" According to Rus, "Rumkowski blanched; his companions nearly fainted. . . . Some five or six days afterwards a letter from Leister announced that Mordechai Ḥaim Rumkowski was now the Elder of the Lodz Ghetto."[30]

However remarkable and, to some, even suspicious the circumstances prompting the Germans to turn to a man of such problematic stature as Rumkowski, the matter of his appointment may have been rather more straightforward. Not long after Pływacki's own advancement to president of the Kehilla, he, like his predecessor, fled the city, "leaving Rumkowski as the highest official representative of the Jewish community." It was in this capacity that in the weeks leading to his appointment he and associated community officers had been in frequent contact with local German officials.[31] So it was that in the fall of 1939 this man, now aged sixty-two, of at least distinctive appearance—that thick head of hair, though by now fully white, his undisputed signature characteristic—came into his own. Long considered a marginal albeit noticeable figure in Jewish communal government, by virtue of merely having remained put Rumkowski had placed himself within reach of securing the position of communal leadership, and with it the attendant powers and deference accorded to office, which he had long coveted—in short, a position commanding respect and offering the prospect of accomplishing great things for the Jews of Łódź in their hour of need.

Rumkowski, self-involved though hardly self-critical, was, to say the least, a man of contradictions: a sentimental man and a skillful organizer, but at the same time a striver, a vain man, overbearing, domineering, quick-tempered, and vindictive, on the verge of old age yet still "energetic," mentally alert, forward looking, sensual, a seeker of power.[32] Drawing strength in longevity, in the seventh decade of his life Rumkowski was looking to new challenges, still ambitious to make his name in the field of Jewish social welfare and, ultimately, as a leader, a man whom people would respect and admire. He was born in March 1877 in rural Belo-russia; his modest education consisted largely of a few years spent in a Jewish schoolroom, or *cheder,* and "four or five years" of primary educa-tion. In the years prior to the First World War he had some success in the textile business, but revolutionary upheaval in Russia put an end to his holdings. He came to Łódź after the war, ultimately becoming an insur-ance agent and finding a niche in the world of Jewish social welfare. He had been invited, in 1920, to assist in running summer camps for Jewish youngsters, institutions supported through funding by the New York–based Jewish Joint Distribution Committee. From this modest beginning he succeeded in making a name for himself in managing homes for Jewish orphans in and outside the city of Łódź, in addition to his service in Kehilla governance.[33]

In 1926, on the occasion of the death of the prominent Łódź philan-thropist Yosef Urison, Rumkowski suggested the expansion of a newly es-tablished summer home for Jewish children on the city's outskirts in Helenówek into a year-round facility. He considered an adjacent tract of farmland which had recently become available ideal for the creation of an experimental farm where youngsters might learn valuable agricul-tural skills in preparation for their future independence, whether in Po-land or in Palestine. Indeed, as Rumkowski, claiming acquaintance with the highly respected philanthropist, forcefully argued, such a vision for Helenówek accorded perfectly with what he expressed as the departed man's unfulfilled wish. It would be an altogether fitting tribute to him that this site—to be named in his honor Beit Yosef, or the House of Jo-seph—be transformed into a model orphanage and outdoor training cen-ter. Yet, apart from the expense of acquiring the additional acreage, others hearing of the scheme thought it at the very least unwise, if not preposter-ous, to consider situating a year-round colony of Jewish youngsters in the countryside, where they would reside away from the city in the midst of a potentially hostile non-Jewish population. But Rumkowski was adamant, and because the plan struck a responsive chord among those eager to honor Urison's good works on behalf of the community, he succeeded in inspiring like-minded supporters to back this seemingly radical idea, mak-ing it a reality. The success was quintessentially Rumkowskian: asserting himself where others might hesitate, confidently proposing sweeping and ambitious projects, carrying others along with his enthusiasm, benefiting the Jewish community, and all the while reaping honor and position that might advance his career.[34]

A decidedly praiseworthy image of life at Helenówek emerges from a 1931 report composed by a university student from Warsaw who, on visiting the facility in association with an educational project, described in glowing terms the impressive facilities and attractive setting. Making his way to the site, located a quarter hour's walk from the nearest regional tramway stop from Łódź, he proceeded along an unpaved country road, delighting not only in the discernibly "healthy air" of the surroundings but remarking favorably as well on the several attractive villas and little houses set amid lovely greenery that lined the way. Upon his arrival he found before him the orphanage's main building, two stories in height and "majestically" fronted with "beautiful, spacious terraces." It was situated at the end of a tree-lined path, and appeared to the student an attractive country "villa" worthy of comparison to "a mansion."[35]

A tour of the facility's main building revealed it to be thoughtfully equipped with its own theater and recreation room, as well as study and classrooms, a dining hall, a dormitory, and dental and medical facilities. Downstairs were to be found a kitchen, food storage area, and even a bakery capable of daily turning out a "supply of fresh baked goods" for the orphans and staff. Two outbuildings housed vocational training classrooms as well as additional "dormitory rooms for staff [and] older youngsters as well as a prayer house." An additional structure, impressively supplying its own electricity, included a laundry, various workshops for sewing and shoemaking, and a bathing facility. A "large greenhouse for the cultivation of flowers" was scheduled for completion later that year. On the nearby farm, fruits and vegetables, as well as milk, were produced for consumption by residents of the home.[36]

The institution received high marks, too, for its ability to more than adequately feed and clothe its charges, then numbering about one hundred throughout the year, most between the ages of two and fourteen, rising to two hundred in the summer months. Its attention to hygiene was demonstrated by the fact that at a time when influenza had been widespread, "not a single child came down with the flu" at the home. In a setting of orderly informality, the visitor from Warsaw found above all a "pleasant and familial atmosphere" in which the children could be observed playing games, working on their lessons, or reading in the library.

"I saw healthy and merry youngsters," he reported, not at all weak but rather "toughened physically and spiritually."[37]

In this era prior to the use of antibiotics, such attention to the physical well-being of the young was of the essence. An outdoor home such as the one Rumkowski had helped establish offered an outstanding setting for containing communicable illnesses and promoting healthy development. In June 1926 a physician, Dr. David Rozenzweig, in an article for the journal *The Orphan* underscored the kind of sensible measures then being undertaken to minimize the spread of disease among those living communally. Above all he stressed the importance of creating an environment favorable to the health of mothers, infants, and most especially schoolchildren and orphans, recommending close monitoring of youngsters to detect and respond to symptoms of the onset of tuberculosis. In addition to recommending that youngsters be taught to avoid close contact and that children with known contagion be isolated, Dr. Rosenzweig thought that summer colonies and other facilities for orphans were ideally suited to promoting the health of children. Simply stated, the basic elements required for ensuring the health of the young were ready to be marshaled: "To assist us, we have but to appropriate the forces of nature: light, air, sun, and water—they are all, thank God, weapons still within our grasp."[38] Indeed, the doctor's prescription was an ideal complement to Rumkowski's Zionist-inspired enthusiasm for promoting self-reliance by leading the young, from the most tender of ages upward, to farm the land, thereby assisting them in acquiring not only practical skills with which later to earn a living but also a positive lifelong relationship to the outdoors and to nature. Such a vision was expansive, outward directed; it would lift the young out of the confines of the city into an environmentally cleaner, more morally sound, and professionally promising and worthwhile existence.[39]

Such glowing prospects notwithstanding, by the end of the 1930s the Helenówek home was to become the object of attentions of an altogether unexpected order when rumors began to surface alleging that Rumkowski had engaged in sexual misconduct with some of his charges during his tenure as director. Such explosive accusations remained at best only tentatively explored and wholly unresolved at the time, though it is clear that influential contemporaries lent them credence, and similar allegations would continue to arise in later years.[40] The elusive nature of such rumors may be gleaned from an account by Dr. Edward Reicher, a dermatologist who had been a neighbor of Rumkowski's in the 1930s. He recalled Rumkowski telephoning him on one occasion requesting that he examine a young girl from the Helenówek orphanage who had been suffering from an undiagnosed ailment. Scheduling a consultation, Dr. Reicher determined that the girl, eight years old, had contracted gonorrhea. Such cases, the doctor indicated, were at the time by no means rare; transmission of the disease to youngsters from impoverished homes was frequently attributable to the not uncommon practice of several members of the same family sharing a single bed.[41] As a precaution, Dr. Reicher informed Rumkowski of the ongoing danger of the further spread of the disease within the communal setting of the orphanage—where, he explained, the sharing of sheets, towels, and sanitary facilities might offer opportunity for further outbreaks. He advised that all the children in the orphanage be examined and that those found to be infected be sent to a hospital for treatment. Rumkowski, however, struck the doctor as noticeably agitated and unequivocally urged otherwise, tearfully insisting that all might be cared for quite admirably in the orphanage's own infirmary. Acceding to this forceful request, Dr. Reicher agreed to attend the youngsters at Helenówek, and over the course of several months of twice-weekly visits, he successfully cured a total of three cases of venereal infection. He was impressed with both the quality of the medical facilities and the diligence of the staff as well as the general orderliness of life in the institution. All the same, in light of later-emerging rumors of Rumkowski's misconduct, Reicher sensed that the true reason Rumkowski had wished to have the children treated on-site rather than in an outside facility was to shield himself from accusations of abuse and the attendant disgrace.[42]

Thus Rumkowski, entering this most critical phase in his career, was a man still under a cloud of suspicion. Yet he had otherwise developed a sturdy record of accomplishment on which to draw in defense of his honor and good name. Now, in this hour of crisis, the community had far more pressing matters to attend to, and the moment offered Rumkowski an opportunity to prove his indispensability and worth. Even more, it offered the promise of winning prestige and a measure of power. With that he might not only do good, serving his people in their time of need, but also wield enough authority to stifle any dark allegations.

That autumn Rumkowski hurled himself into his new tasks. The hungry, the poor, the weak, the sick, the homeless, the imprisoned, and, as ever, the young were to be the objects of his energies and concern. With promised deliveries to the Jewish community falling short, he won permission from the city authorities to send representatives into the provinces to purchase flour with which to bake bread. Concurrently, he persuaded Jewish bakers to advance the community funds to support the effort and placed orders for periodic delivery of specified quantities of bread for community orphanages, public kitchens, schools, homes for the aged and the mentally and physically handicapped, maternity clinics, a community hospital, and communal offices. In addition, he secured supplies of milk for downtown orphanages and infant care facilities and, further cajoling Jewish contributors, appealed for help in clothing orphans for the approaching winter. He ran soup kitchens where, that fall alone, thousands of meals were daily provided to schoolchildren and to the needy. Exercising rights granted him by the city commissioner, he requisitioned essential classroom space for Jewish pupils. So that the Jewish poor might wash, he requested supplies of coal from the city to heat a community-run public bath. Rumkowski saw to meeting ongoing expenses associated with maintenance of the downtown Poznański Hospital as well as medical charges levied against the community for the treatment of sick children and wounded Jewish soldiers. He located and borrowed needed typewriters for the Jewish community offices. For Jewish inmates held in detention, he secured bread from a local bakery at community expense. Even the dead commanded Rumkowski's attention, which resulted in a request to the city commissioner for the removal to a Jewish cemetery of the body of a Jewish soldier "mistakenly" laid to rest in a garrison burial ground.[43]

Working tirelessly and inventively with diminishing resources, Rumkowski did well, proceeding according to long-established and honorable traditions of Jewish social welfare. His was an act of rescue amid the storm. Yet given the additional outrages accompanying the first weeks of his energetic tenure as head of the Jewish community, one would doubt whether the new German masters who appointed him cared much one way or the other.

Late on the morning of Tuesday, November 2, Minister of Propaganda and Enlightenment Joseph Goebbels, arriving by air for a brief Polish tour, landed at Łódź. In town for discussions with party leaders and a per-

sonal tour of conditions in newly occupied Poland, Goebbels was anything but impressed with what he found. "Lodz itself is a hideous city," he
wrote, summarizing in his diary his altogether unflattering view of the
place. Undoubtedly referring to a visit to the heavily Jewish-populated
Bałuty slum quarter, he was rich in scorn: "Drive through the Ghetto. We
get out and inspect everything thoroughly. It is indescribable. These are
no longer human beings, they are animals. For this reason, our task is no
longer humanitarian but surgical. Steps must be taken here, and they
must be radical ones, make no mistake."[44] Not that Goebbels revealed
himself any better disposed toward Warsaw. "This is Hell," he wrote upon
subsequently arriving in the ruined former Polish capital. "The populace
is apathetic, shadowy. The people creep through the streets like insects. It
is repulsive and scarcely describable."[45] On the following day, already
back in Berlin, Goebbels met with Hitler, conveying such impressions
firsthand. "In particular, my description of the Jewish problem meets with
his complete approval," he wrote of the meeting. "The Jew is a waste
product. More a clinical than a social problem."[46]

Filled with loathing, replete with disgust, the minds of the leadership
recoiled at the sight of such beings—human, after a fashion, but altogether, on close inspection, in their eyes disturbingly creature-like too.
Searching for a solution, such minds tracked effortlessly along lines that
foresaw work ahead for the surgeon, if not the sanitation man or the ex-
terminator.

The Goebbels visit would coincide with yet another outrage. Only a
day before, on November 1, at the Astoria Café on Piotrkowska Street, located in the heart of downtown and an establishment popular with local
Jewish actors, writers, politicians, and educators, armed men entered,
fired at a chandelier hanging from the ceiling, seized the personal documents of those present, and ordered them to appear early the next morning at a Gestapo bureau on Zgierska Street. Upon their arrival, the men
were subjected to beatings, following which the Gestapo assembled them
into groups and transported them to an improvised site of execution in
the vicinity of a church building in the nearby Łagiewnicki Woods. At
this location fifteen of them were shot before open graves shoveled by six
of their number who had been forced to serve as gravediggers.[47] Then, on
the night of November 10 the first of the four main synagogues of Łódź
that would be destroyed over the coming days was set ablaze. At roughly
the same time, nearly all the members of the newly established Jewish

Council, or Beirat, were inexplicably taken away to an improvised concentration camp set up inside a factory north of the city in Radogoszcz. They were horribly tortured, and all but a handful were shot or beaten to death. Days later, on November 14, all Jews of the city—"irrespective of age"—were ordered to outfit themselves with identifying armbands of grotesquely specified "Jewish yellow" color, which they were to wear at all times in public. The directive fastidiously specified as well the precise location of their placement—"just below the armpit"—making them sound both psychologically painful and physically uncomfortable to wear. Simultaneously, Jews were subject to restriction in their movement about the city and to severe curfews. In particular, Piotrkowska Street, home to many of the better-situated Jewish households and finest shops, was henceforth altogether and at all times out of bounds. Moreover, daily between five o'clock in the afternoon and eight the next morning, all Jews, with the exception of those bearing official passes, were confined to their residences and made invisible to the public.[48]

The men of the Beirat had no sooner been dispatched to their destruction than Rumkowski set about seeking replacements for them. None could have looked with favor on the receipt of an invitation to assume so dubious and so dangerous a distinction. For his part, Rumkowski was not one to entertain pleas to be excused from serving on the council. When Dr. Reicher, one of the unwilling recipients of a summons to join the new body, dared to demur, he found himself subject to the force of Rumkowski's wrath. Reicher had sought to convey to Rumkowski that, in view of his complete unsuitability for organizational tasks, he would prefer to serve in the accustomed role of "a mere physician." Rumkowski, who had glowingly referred to Reicher's future role as comparable to that of "minister of health" and expansively described all that he expected to accomplish for the ghetto, flew into a rage. As Reicher remembered the scene, Rumkowski then addressed him as follows: "You species of imbecile, just what are you thinking? Do you think you can just do what you like?" More browbeating and invective was to follow. "This is war and we are like soldiers, we have to carry out orders, obey without condition and fulfill our tasks unconditionally—or die! If you do not do what I, the president of the Jewish Council, order [you to do], I will crush you like an ant. And if you, you shameless vermin, ever have the audacity to invoke our relationship at the orphanage, you will be sent to a place from whence no one returns alive!" Now proclaiming Reicher "too much of a coward" to assume the directorship of health services, Rumkowski immediately assigned him instead to become head of the department overseeing infectious disease in the ghetto. It was a dangerous enough position, as Rumkowski more than hinted, indicating that in this role he would be "solely answerable to the German authorities." Reicher, admittedly intimidated, felt as if he were being spoken to by "a lunatic," and, responding in a clinical manner, adopted a soft-spoken demeanor, hoping in this way to calm Rumkowski, rather as he would a patient given to such outbursts, though with little success. The episode concluded only when, as the doctor noted, "he showed me the door."[49]

While Rumkowski was free to attend, as determinedly as he might, to the pressing needs of his Jewish brethren in occupied Łódź, German authorities at the highest levels were busy developing plans for reshaping the ethnic makeup of their new sphere of influence in the East. Initial measures directed toward restricting the freedom of Jews and excluding them from public life were but one element in a far broader and more ambitious demographic project. Satisfying as it was to savor the forced submission and ruin of local Jewry, even closer to Nazi hearts lay the parallel endeavor centering on the colonization and repeopling of the newly conquered lands. This would entail clearing the cities and countryside of the annexed territories of Poles and Jews and replacing them with people of German stock, lured to the region by the promise of a prosperous and dignified existence as citizens of the expanded Reich. Many of these settlers, referred to as the Volksdeutsche, or ethnic Germans, were to be drawn from homesteads deep within the newly broadened territorial sphere of Soviet Russia, the improbable ally with which Germany shared the division of the spoils in a defeated and partitioned Poland. By agreement with the Russians, Germany had additionally won for the ethnic Germans— drawn, primarily, from the formerly eastern Polish territory of Volhynia and from the Baltic states—the right to emigrate from Soviet territory and, crossing the divide separating the two occupying forces, to unite with their fellow Germans and begin new lives.

The initial plans to remake the demographics of the incorporated lands, laid out during the first weeks of the occupation, had been sweeping indeed. To make room for the new arrivals, and most especially to free up

farms, businesses, and homes for their occupancy, these ambitious projections anticipated the rapid forced evacuation of as many as a million
Poles and Jews residing in the newly annexed Reich provinces, or Gaus, of
West Prussia, Posen (Warthegau), and East Upper Silesia, to the unincor-
porated, German-controlled zone in central Poland known to the Germans as the Generalgouvernement. In the face of mounting technical difficulties, however, the planners soon found that their reach had exceeded
their immediate grasp. Through the first week in November, the ultimate administrative disposition of the city and immediate vicinity of
Łódź, geographically wedged between the incorporated Gau of Posen
(Wartheland) to the west and the Generalgouvernement to the east, had
been left undetermined. Desirous of immediately creating space in a metropolitan area for the first wave of largely urbanized German immi-
grants from the Baltic region, on November 8, Germany annexed Łódź to
the Wartheland. It was now to become officially a city of the Reich. Yet
given the goal of immediately ridding the annexed lands and their cities of
Jews, the incorporation of Łódź, a city with such a sizable Jewish ethnic
component, meant that a way was going to have to be found to expel a
substantially larger number of Jews from the Wartheland right away. In
spite of initial optimistic projections for the swift expulsion of "600,00
Jews and 400,000 Poles from the eastern Gaus," this proved an increasingly doubtful proposition.[50] In consequence, on November 28 Reinhard
Heydrich, compelled to accede to what for the moment appeared within
the realm of the possible (yet without in the least abandoning the wider
goal of clearing the area of unwanted populations), announced that as a
preliminary or "short-term" solution only some eighty thousand Poles and
Jews, and solely those residing in the Warthegau, were to be transferred
during the first half of December 1939.[51]

Indeed, this December operation, involving sweeps of both the countryside and urban centers in the province, would center heavily on Łódź
and its Jewish community. In this initial roundup of eighty thousand, of
whom some fifteen thousand were targeted for removal from Łódź, it was
"above all politically suspicious and intellectual Poles [who] were to be
evacuated." As it turned out, the desired quota of Polish candidates for expulsion simply could not be achieved, and so the Jews, more readily
identifiable and accessible to seizure, were made to fill out their allotment
as well. Through a combination of appeals to the Jewish leadership to as-

sist in recruiting persons willing to evacuate and the engagement of local police and uniformed auxiliary forces to clear Jews from their homes in a selected residential area in the north of the city, the operation went ahead. Even then, in a deportation procedure marked by insufficient and unreliably assembled rail transport, to say nothing of the deplorable crowding and primitive conditions awaiting those climbing aboard available cars, the organizers by their own rough calculations fell far short of their expected goal, in the end expelling just under ten thousand.[52]

From the German perspective the results had proved unsatisfactory, but local authorities gained valuable experience applicable for future operations. Terrifying to those affected, the operation undoubtedly offered the community and its leaders a preview of the kind of forced evacuations they might experience in the future. Jews elsewhere in the city took note. The worst hit had been Jews residing in a targeted sector near the Old Market area. Families living in buildings along several streets there had been brutally ejected from their homes with little if anything in hand.[53] With so many Jewish homes consequently abandoned, it was not long before bands of thieves entered now empty neighborhoods and buildings to make off with whatever was to be had inside.[54] The assault touched off something of a panic, as Jews by now desperate to depart the city of their own volition hired farm wagons to take them to other communities. Places on the heavily laden carts were hard to come by, and people were paying as much as "hundreds of złoty" for a seat. In miserable sub-zero weather, "caravans" consisting of "hundreds of carts" headed out into the countryside loaded with their cargo of household effects and desperate Jewish women and children, their newly attached yellow stars visible front and back, exposed to the elements.[55] Only later, as word spread that the Germans had called a halt to the expulsion, did many who had not yet departed remove their things from carts still being readied, leaving the drivers to return, empty of their expected cargo, to the outlying areas from whence they had originally come. At the same time, some of the Jews who had left in the earlier transports managed to make their way back to the city. A notable element of relative calm seemed to follow in the wake of the cancellation of the immediate danger.[56]

However disturbing the revealed tactical shortcomings of the December operation, local authorities in Łódź had already taken the first steps toward an altogether methodical approach to removing the Jews from the city. The December action, involving the removal of only a small fraction of the city's Jewish population, was but a preliminary step in a far more extensive undertaking aimed at cleansing the province of all Jews. With this clearly in mind, Regierungspräsident Friedrich Uebelhoer, governor of the Kalisch district—the Warthegau administrative sector to which responsibility for Łódź had been assigned—seized the initiative. Without losing sight of the wider goal of total removal of the Jewish population in his sphere, Uebelhoer foresaw the necessity of carefully planning for the creation of a restricted quarter, or ghetto, to which the city's Jews would be confined in advance of the ultimate determination of their fate.[57]

There were, he noted, a host of practical considerations. Since the Jews were no longer permitted to earn their livelihoods freely as before, if they were not to be left to starve and fall prey to uncontrollable outbreaks of disease that might harm the general population, they were going to have to be fed. It was expected that the city would be responsible for delivering provisions to the ghetto in exchange for payment in the form of surrendered currency and convertible valuables, textiles, and other movable goods. This was a matter to be coordinated between the city and designated representatives of the Jewish community. To contain contagious illnesses, disinfectants, medicines, and medical instruments would have to be supplied, waste removed, and the dead buried, all matters touching upon the responsibilities of local public health agencies. Also, the establishment of a closed Jewish residential quarter would set in motion a massive population transfer, affecting occupancy and ownership of residential and commercial properties both inside and outside the ghetto. Therefore, from its initial conception and first stage of planning, the ghetto was expected to demand the attention and participation of municipal bureaus.[58]

As a result, on December 10, 1939, the date when Uebelhoer formally presented his plan to coordinate the creation of a ghetto in Łódź, his first practical task was the creation of a working group *(Arbeitstab)* that, in addition to representatives of the party, security police, and SS, would include others from municipal departments responsible for food, health, housing, and finance, and the local chamber of industry and commerce. Just as the ghetto could not exist without the cooperation of these agencies, the German planners understood, too, that within the ghetto the Jews were to bear responsibility for coordinating agencies to perform key tasks on their own behalf. Consequently, Uebelhoer planned to charge the

Jews with the task of organizing an internal bureaucracy with departments
for distributing delivered stocks of food and fuel, maintaining public
kitchens, and overseeing matters related to housing. They would also have
to assemble a staff of physicians and auxiliary care personnel as well as supervise ghetto hospitals and clinics. They would be charged with securing
drinking water, removing garbage and waste, maintaining cemeteries, coordinating payment for supplies, controlling internal security and combating fires, overseeing residential and collective housing, and conducting
statistical surveys of the ghetto population, recording its size and registering its demographic fluctuations.[59]

At this date the geographic contours of the proposed zone were yet to
be sketched in ultimate detail. Uebelhoer's initial conception, however,
proceeded from the assumption that all Jews in the city would be restricted to occupying one or the other of two as yet broadly defined,
partially specified zones. The larger of these, centering on the area of
greatest but by no means exclusively Jewish settlement, comprised that
sector "north of the line" marked by the newly renamed Novemberstraße
(formerly Listopada Street) in the west through Freiheitsplatz (Plac
Wolności) at the apex of the city's principal avenue, and extending along
Pomerschestraße (Pomorska Street) to the east. Here, according to his estimate, more than two thirds of the Jewish population was thought to reside. In this initial scheme, later modified, Jews residing south of this line
and who were capable of working were to be moved into barracks, collectively fed according to rations established by the municipal food department, and organized into work columns supplying a reserve of heavy laborers for city demolition projects. The remainder of the city's Jewish
population residing in this southern area were to abandon their residences
and move north of the divide to settle in the ghetto. Upon their departure, Jews were to hand over the keys to their homes to caretakers, who,
under police supervision, were obliged to secure the properties on behalf
of a city agency, the Municipal Bureau of Lodgings and Real Estate, that
was authorized to take possession of surrendered Jewish properties. To
discourage potential acts of material sabotage, "severest measures" awaited
Jews who dared to inflict "malicious destruction" in response to the forcible abandonment of their homes. Jews found unsuitable for heavy labor,
like those who in the course of working on the labor columns became
unfit to continue, were to be relocated to the ghetto. There Jews deemed

fit to work were to be organized for internal assignment, and possibly, pending later decision, transferred to barracks for external tasks as well.[60]

With this, Uebelhoer presented an initial outline for the creation of what would become known as the Łódź ghetto. Yet from its inception the ghetto was conceived not as an institution of lasting duration but rather as a temporary expedient. "It goes without saying," he wrote at the time, that this was "only a transitional measure." At some point in the not too distant future the Jews of Łódź would disappear altogether. Or—putting the matter in grotesquely emphatic terms redolent of the imagery of disease with which the local leadership would repeatedly refer to the Jews and the ghetto—the Regierungspräsident concluded that at an as yet indeterminate time and by a method of his choosing, the "pestilent boil" that was Łódź Jewry would be "burned off," leaving "no trace."[61]

The cleansing was about to begin in earnest. It would track along the pathways of the demographic (removal of the Jews and peopling of the city with settlers of German ethnicity), the biological (lifting from the general population the threat of contagious illnesses), the economic (expropriation of Jewish assets), and the aesthetic (a thoroughgoing redevelopment and remaking of the appearance of the city). Each called for methodical planning and execution. Unlike in the first weeks of the occupation, it became less and less acceptable for unauthorized individuals to assault Jews in spontaneous, unregulated, and independent actions. The process now was to be carefully planned and supervised; lines of authority were to be strictly delimited; responsibility for making preparations and carrying out defined tasks was to be appropriately assigned. Already traumatized by a season of torments, internally subordinate to a stern yet to the Germans outwardly cooperative leader, the Jews could be counted on to comply, or—if still in need of further intimidation—be made to do as they were told.

2

A City without Jews

For the Jews, increasingly harassed, hemmed in by onerous restrictions, and subject to sudden expulsion from their homes and banishment to distant locales, a new and dangerous period of uprooting and displacement had begun. It was their misfortune to be a source of opportunity for others. As tirelessly as the regime worked to effect the Jews' speedy removal from their midst, it opened arms of welcome wide to others on whom unexpected fortune seemed at last to be smiling. For by now another wandering folk, ethnic peoples of Germanic stock, had begun to pour into the region from Volhynia in the Soviet-occupied zone of Poland to the east, from Galicia to the south, and even from the faraway Baltic states of Latvia and Estonia to the north. Encouraged by the German government to abandon their homes and return to the Reich, they moved to German lands where new homes and a new life were promised. Increasingly the focus of official attention, the resettlers were immediately granted rights of citizenship, given shelter, and promised training and jobs, farmsteads, and shops or businesses. The welfare of their hardworking heads of household, their aged relations, and most especially their careworn mothers and infants were matters of deepest official importance. Indeed, viewed through the eyes of the regime, the newcomers were everything the Jews were not, existing within that circle of commonality to which the empathy of good-

will and of those better situated was supposed to extend. Their integration into the community was welcomed, and their suffering was to be
relieved.[1]

Already by the turn of the new year, thirty transports bearing more
than twenty thousand ethnic Germans from Volhynia and Galicia had
reached Łódź. For them, this city had become the terminus of a lengthy
westward journey by rail, some boarding from their point of origin, others
only after an arduous trek across the line of demarcation separating the
German and Soviet zones. Upon their arrival the newcomers were assigned to one of forty-five temporary housing sites located in commercial
or residential properties within the city or elsewhere in the region. Some
were put up in summer resorts. Many were immediately unloaded near a
large reception camp able to accommodate "comfortably" up to 3,500
people at once, while trainloads of more that a thousand passengers at a
time were processed on the grounds of a textile factory in the large nearby
suburb of Pabianice. While many of the new arrivals would ultimately
make their homes in Łódź or elsewhere in the region, others were sent on
as quickly as possible to reception areas in locations inside the prewar bor-
ders of the Reich.[2]

At Pabianice, where a giant rail platform several hundred meters in
length had been constructed at the main station to facilitate their disembarking from the trains, resettlers were directed to a sports field, the site of
their initial processing. Here each received a room assignment, along with
an identification number matching the one attached to his or her personal
belongings. The newcomers were then directed indoors, where, over the
course of two to three hours, men and women were led in separate groups
to a newly installed 120-head shower facility, where they were able to wash
for the first time after their long journey. As they showered, their clothing
and bags, previously set aside, underwent disinfection in special "heated-
air" enclosures before being returned to their owners, now drying off and
cooling down. By this time, according to an observer, "one often hears it
said: 'That did a world of good. Now I know that I am a human being
again.'" Awaiting them were newly established quarters, consisting of simple but attractively arranged housing in renovated, high-ceilinged factory
space outfitted with basic furnishings, plumbing and drinking water, and
"newly whitewashed" walls. A modest sixty-bed hospital, stocked with
medicines and staffed by physicians and nurses, saw to their medical

needs. For education and amusement, living spaces included recreation areas and were provided with newspapers and radios. As a hidden feature, yet altogether bespeaking thoughtful regard for the residents' well-being, a built-in "automatic sprinkler system" protected the residential area in the event of fire.[3]

With the city and the region opening their precincts to receive fresh settlers arriving from the East, strengthening by their numbers the Germanic claim to the land, mighty demographic forces had been set in motion. One was meant to sense, indeed, that as a citizen of this rapidly evolving city, one was witness to a renewal of epochal proportions. And this social alteration, involving not simply an ingathering of peoples of welcome ethnic stock but the removal of the Jews, together constituting the centerpiece of a project of wider import, had about it something of the workings of a force of nature.

Even in the depths of winter the newly Germanizing city, referred to now as Lodsch, revealed unmistakable indications of these changes. Among the first of these to draw attention were newly installed signs signaling the transformation of Polish place-names into unmistakably German ones. The city's commanding north-south boulevard, Ulica Piotrkowska, more recently Petrikauerstraße, was henceforth renamed Adolf-Hitler-Straße; Kościuszko-Allee, immediately to its west, was christened Hermann-Göring-Straße; and the names of intersecting thoroughfares recalled luminaries from the world of Germanic statesmanship and war: Bismarck, von Moltke, and General Karl Litzmann, the last in tribute to the officer who had led German forces to victory in a nearby battle during the First World War. Two of the city's great downtown squares, formerly Plac Wolności (Freedom Square), site of the old city hall, lying at the northern terminus of what was now Adolf-Hitler-Straße, and Plac Reymont, its endpoint to the south, became known, respectively, as Deutschlandplatz and Frießenplatz. It was thought to be a matter of note that neither the cold nor the driving snow of mid-January could keep the curious from gathering at the intersections to view some of the newly posted street signs, their white lettering distinctively set against a background of blue, clear evidence of the developing transformation of the urban landscape.[4] Visible too, and from afar by night, was another sign marking the opening, under new management, of a renamed theater, now known as the Theater der Stadt Lodsch, premiering on the evening

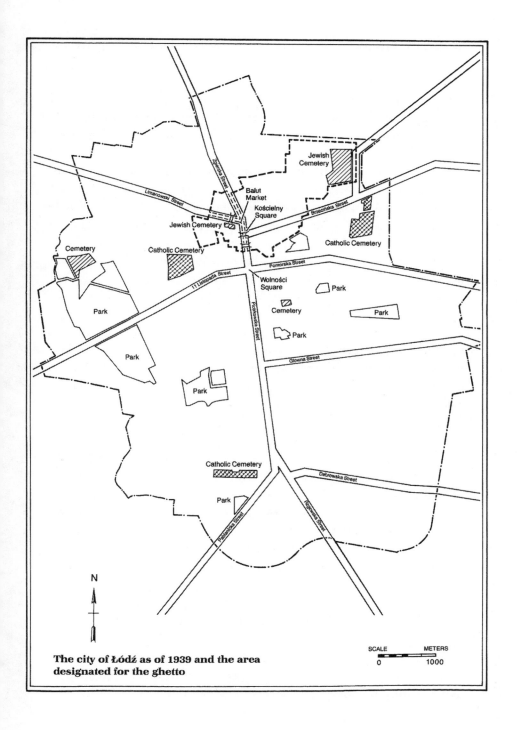

The city of Łódź as of 1939 and the area designated for the ghetto

Jewish Cemetery

Balut Market

Kościelny Square

Limanowski Street

Zgierska Street

Brzezińska Street

Jewish Cemetery

Catholic Cemetery

Catholic Cemetery

Cemetery

Catholic Cemetery

Pomorska Street

11 Listopada Street

Wolności Square

Park

Park

Cemetery

Park

Park

Piotrkowska Street

Park

Głowna Street

Park

Park

Catholic Cemetery

Park

Dąbrowska Street

Pabianicka Street

Rzgowska Street

N

SCALE   METERS
0   1000

of January 13 with a performance of Lessing's lighthearted eighteenth-century comedic work *Mina von Barnheim*. Graciously conducted on a tour of the facility at intermission by its resident stage designer, Wilhelm Terboven, a reporter remarked favorably on the recent application of "bright colors throughout." Replacing what were described as the once prevailing "dark, even gloomy tones" of the interior, the new design was "unusually clean, friendly, festive."[5]

In spite of these promising improvements, commentators could not suppress a conscious awareness of the undeniably inferior status of their structurally and aesthetically challenged metropolis. *"Lodsch wants to be beautiful!"* a leading writer for the *Lodscher Zeitung* proclaimed in the New Year's Day edition. "That won't happen overnight. Certainly not. But with some love, something can be made out of our neglected city. It need not necessarily become a second Munich or another Darmstadt. But Lodsch can become a city that is clean and has its own look." The daunting tasks facing the new city administration, however, were plain to see. "When we look at our streets we are seized with horror," the writer continued, noting that "the day on which the Lodsch water main is put into operation will be one of the most important days in the history of our city. Without a doubt schools will be on holiday and all the bells will ring. That this day may dawn soon indeed is an additional New Year's wish."[6]

Great hopes for the success of the city's renewal rested on the experienced shoulders of Wilhelm Hallbauer, who, arriving in Łódź from the port city of Wilhelmshaven, where he had overseen a program of urban expansion, assumed the post of director of a building department in a city that was now the sixth largest in the entire Reich. His new position, given the enormity of the tasks of urban modernization and social renewal that lay ahead, presented great challenges but also potentially immense rewards. Altogether disparaging of what he saw as the prior neglect and mismanagement of the city's infrastructure in every area of critical importance—from streets to sanitation to housing—Hallbauer envisioned the development of a new and modern metropolis refashioned according to the latest principles of planning, construction, and civil engineering. But the city's modernization was not conceived independent of the new social arrangements at the forefront of the regime's thinking. Above all, Hallbauer presented his plans as part of the great scheme of historic population changes then under way, matching urban improvements to the broader vision of a Germanification of the city and the region.

There was much work to be done. According to Hallbauer, even by the standards of large cities, with a population density of 11,500 persons per square kilometer Łódź was extraordinarily crowded, far more so than cities of comparable size inside the Reich. He cited statistics indicating that over 60 percent of the city's population lived in cramped single-room dwellings. These were not, by and large, freestanding rural-style abodes, Hallbauer reminded the public, but units boxed inside sizable three- and four-story residential structures built around deep inner courtyards, often some two hundred meters in length. To reach one of these crowded dwellings one typically traversed long, dark corridors. About half of these one-room apartments were dependent for natural light on inadequate northern exposures. To Hallbauer, these deplorable circumstances were but a further indication of the city's woeful history of haphazard development, caused by the neglectful oversight of previous imperial Russian and Polish city administrations, resulting in rapid but unregulated residential and industrial growth. Poorly paved streets and sidewalks were one obvious shortcoming in need of immediate correction, but the scandalous inattention to basic principles of sanitation and health was especially troubling. A glaring example was manifest in the gross inadequacies of the city sewage system, typified by pollution from industrial runoff from factories deliberately situated near available streams, by deficient domestic plumbing, and by the general failure to create a central water supply system capable of safely meeting the basic needs of so large a population. Not infrequently, he noted by way of example, shallow wells serving even residences in the downtown area as a principal supply of drinking water were located dangerously close to receptacles for containing human waste.[7]

Under enlightened German administration, however, all this was going to change. As part of the ingathering of the "diaspora," as he termed it, of Germanic settlers, the city's population was undergoing radical alteration. While most of the Polish population of Łódź, the base of its factory workforce, would remain for the foreseeable future, though restricted in their areas of residence, the Jews were slated for initial confinement to the ghetto, then eventual removal. Łódź, as the last great outpost on the far frontier of the Reich and a "bulwark" of German settlement in the East, was a city whose material redevelopment was unthinkable without reshaping the demographics of its inhabitants.[8] What with the modernization of the city's water system and above- and below-surface infrastructure, the relocation of Jews and Poles, and impressive new, exclusively German residential settlements to the west and northeast of downtown, Hallbauer and his team of city planners saw themselves embarked on nothing less than a series of changes whose benefits would be enjoyed by Germans for generations to come.[9]

It hardly required stating that this envisioned city of the future was to be a city without Jews. In his earliest demographic projections Hallbauer had already taken account of their removal from the scene. Estimating that if but one third of the former Jewish population were replaced by new inhabitants of German stock, the overall urban population would likely stabilize at a suitable level of some 600,000 residents.[10]

Indeed, not only did the Jews have no role to play in the future of the city, but also their relocation and removal was deemed critical to the health and safety of the general population. Given the unquestioned assumption that infectious cases of spotted fever originated in the area of heaviest Jewish residential concentration, spreading from there to other sections of the city, the establishment of a ghetto was deemed a rational and effective measure with which to respond to what was seen as an immediate physical threat to the citizenry. It was further argued that not only must the Jews be strictly confined to their existing primary residential area, but also, as a precaution against further contagion, even Jews currently residing outside this supposed hot zone of infection, with which they were assumed to be in contact, were to be uprooted from their homes and confined there as well. In the wake of their exodus, the homes that Jews would be compelled to abandon elsewhere in the city would be freed up for occupancy by local Germans and their ethnic brethren arriving from the East, as well as those relocating to the area from within the Reich. Poles dislodged in the process of establishing the ghetto, while banned from residing in areas of the city center redistricted for exclusively German occupancy, might also be assigned accommodation in forfeited Jewish dwellings elsewhere, primarily in the city's southern districts.[11]

For the local German medical establishment, isolating the Jews from the general population and establishing a strictly enforced territorial quarantine, or ghetto, was deemed a matter of utmost urgency. Affirming a view shared throughout the leadership cadre at both the national and local

levels, city health officers considered the Jews little more than an unwanted foreign people who, found to harbor harmful and even deadly
contagion, had too long resided dangerously within their midst. Circulating throughout the city, they were said to have shed disease-causing
agents among the unsuspecting and vulnerable population. City planners
reckoned their removal, then, a prudent and decent thing undertaken in
defense of the common good. In response to the threat, by decree and by
force the Jews were now to be kept at a safe remove, corralled into isolation, and eventually expelled. In the eyes of the authorities, a ghetto,
by successfully forming an impermeable barrier separating this collective
breeding ground of contagion from the wider commonwealth, was the
very device to bring this about.[12]

Seen in this light, the case for confining the Jews to a ghetto appeared
self-evident. Asserting that incidences of spotted fever had been determined to center precisely in the heavily Jewish northern sector of the city,
advancing from there to other sectors of the metropolitan area, one medical officer warned of a growing danger to the general public. Without
strict intervention to prevent their coming into contact with others, the
Jews were sure to continue to serve as carriers infecting anyone who
crossed their path. It was not surprising, he said, that disease flourished
among Jews, "a race lacking a sense of cleanliness," long accustomed to
living "under the most primitive hygienic conditions." It surely was "no
wonder" to discover their "homes and persons" to be "generally infested
with lice." As a practical matter, it simply would not suffice to rely on a
more loosely regulated and unreliable system of controls in which Jews,
subject only to routine disinfection of entire residential blocks, might be
permitted to come and go as they wished. "In this state of affairs the sole
remaining hygienic measure promising success in combating the epidemic
must be to avoid under all circumstances any contact with the Jews, for, as
far as anyone can judge, only in this way is the transmission of lice to be
ruled out." The establishment of a ghetto was, consequently, an "irrefut-
able necessity," and not just for the confinement of those who already
lived within the epicenter of the outbreak, but for "*all* Jews resident in
Lodsch." Restricting the entire Jewish population to a single area—preferably within the city's "northern district," the area of heaviest Jewish population density—was essential in order to "hermetically" seal off "all [the]
paths which scientific experience indicates the epidemic could take."[13]

Planners, seeking to maximize the effectiveness of the undertaking, were already critically examining the experience of other cities with an eye to making improvements. They insisted on the necessity of enforcing the strictest possible enclosure in contrast to what they judged to be the inadequate precautions being undertaken to restrict access to the as yet unsealed Jewish residential quarter in Warsaw. There, the lack of sufficient manpower to guard the area had led to easily bypassed barriers and a consequent disregard for regulations forbidding entry into the district by the general population. Indeed, restraining wire had been trampled or even removed. That a large-scale epidemic had not broken out under these circumstances was to be regarded as nothing more than "blind luck."[14]

Even as they proposed to tighten the perimeter, health planning officials acknowledged that, as a matter of course, it was to be expected that the ghetto's heavy population density would be accompanied by "an increase in morbidity." Consequently, critical defensive measures, if only in the interest of stemming the immediate threat to those guarding the district, would have to be undertaken. Thus a restricted *Bannmeile,* or inviolable neutral zone, would surround the district. Unauthorized entry by Jews into the zone was to be met with deadly force. Additionally, they conceded, the ghetto was going to have to be equipped with medical facilities in order to contain as far as possible the spread of infection. This would necessitate the establishment of a hospital of at least "300 to 350 bed" capacity, dedicated to combating infectious outbreaks, as well as a second hospital for noninfectious illnesses. These facilities were to be staffed exclusively by ghetto physicians and medical assistants. Medicines were to be available for purchase at any of four ghetto pharmacies which were projected initially to serve the needs of the community. Necessary disinfectants were also to be supplied.[15]

Crowded ghetto housing would impact sanitation too. Experience had shown that in the Jewish sector of Warsaw it was not uncommon to have as many as "3 to 5, even 7 families living in one room. Buildings which previously counted up to 100 residents now [contain] 800 to 1,000 and even more inhabitants. Similar circumstances will have to be reckoned with in Lodsch as well. In this situation it is clear that latrine facilities will have to be expanded and that, in view of the considerable daily yield of feces, a regular emptying of the cesspools will have to be systematically carried out." The hope was to come up with a system that was "neither expensive, nor requiring extensive preparations, but in the process offers adequate protection against the spread of infectious diseases." A related area of concern was the suitability of the district's water supply, subject as it was to pollution from surface and sub-surface sources. Consideration was given to setting up taps at the ghetto's edge, providing at least a provisional supply of nonpotable water from firefighting resources, necessitating boiling before use, until the district could be served by a link to the city water system.[16]

However it was decided that Jews be permitted to conduct commerce, most specifically in order to pay for the provision of foodstuffs, it was essential that products exiting the ghetto be subject to disinfection to ensure that goods making their way from the ghetto were "free of lice." Once again, extreme care was be taken at the point of exchange to avoid any direct physical contact with the Jews. "It goes just as much without saying that in interaction with representatives of the Jewish community, to be kept as limited as possible, necessary caution must prevail. Contact is in any case to be avoided. The installation of suitable rooms for the passing of delivered goods will prove necessary."[17]

To avoid the dangers of transporting the Jewish dead to burial sites outside the assigned district, burial would take place in the old Jewish cemetery located inside the ghetto. Existing grave markers, to a large extent already having "fallen down," were "to be lifted out or leveled." Throughout, in the implementation of these measures, the rule was to be that "under no circumstances should the principle of total isolation be violated." In this way the city might look ahead to "the well-founded prospect of limiting spotted fever in Lodsch to its source and in so doing to protect the general public from the spread of the epidemic."[18]

In regard to their own assumptions about the concentration and spread of tuberculosis, however, authorities were confronted with the need to explain the inconvenient anomaly that local rates of infection and mortality for this disease were actually lower among the Jews than among the gentile population. Constituting, by German estimate, approximately 30 percent of the population of Łódź, the Jews had accounted for only 13.5 percent of its deaths from tuberculosis. Indicative of the speciousness with which such arguments were framed, the authorities were quick to deny any suggestion that the Jews' lower death rate might have to do with any inherited superiority in fighting off the disease. Rather they insisted that the cause of the Jews' greater immunity could be attributed to their having been vastly underrepresented in the ranks of physical laborers, the category of the overall population heaviest hit by the ailment. "Barely 30 percent" of Jews, it was noted, earned their living through heavy labor, while some 72 percent of the general population were workers, a category that accounted for just over 87 percent of those afflicted with the illness. Many of these persons were also victims of the woeful inadequacy of local housing, of which, according to a survey of some ten thousand residences, nearly four fifths consisted of single-room dwellings where persons suffering from active tuberculosis infection typically shared their limited space with four to six others, or even many more. To the extent that Jews, by contrast, succeeded in "living not from their own labor but from that of other[s]," they had managed to evade dangers to which they would be just as susceptible if only they were exposed to the same conditions. "One sees, then, that in relation to tuberculosis as well, the Jewish moneybag has made the Jewish race 'more resistant.'" New measures, the public was assured, would tackle this problem by eliminating the kind of housing in which illness bred. Soon, "rich and poor will have equal share in the blessings of medical science."[19] Left unmentioned, however, was why it was then judged a matter of the common good to uproot those Jews whose superior occupations and living standards had so clearly contributed to their better health in order to crowd them as well into a ghetto where conditions would more closely resemble those decried by the planners as so favorable to the spread of disease.

Concerned above all to confine expected outbreaks to the ghetto, early in January officers of the city Health Department, working in close consultation with representatives of the Regierungspräsident, the Gestapo, and the city Building Department, pressed ahead with plans to establish as rapidly as possible an infectious disease hospital in which to quarantine Jews who displayed signs of contagion. On December 29 the Jewish community had been directed to undertake measures necessary for creating such a facility within two days after the beginning of the New Year. The project called for the conversion of an existing factory on Wesola Street, well within the projected zone of the ghetto, adjacent to a Jewish psychiatric hospital and located conveniently near an old Jewish burial ground that would serve as a site for the rapid disposal of the dead. To increase the isolation of the structure, along the front of the building a fence two meters high was to be installed, and where appropriate, windows were to be sealed; inside, existing machinery was to be disassembled and removed, making way for the installation of three hundred beds; latrines to accommodate the expected requirements of the facility were to be dug immediately. But as his workmen fell quickly behind schedule and necessary materials were slow to arrive, Rumkowski was summoned first to the offices of the Health Department, and then, on the department's initiative, before a representative of the Security Police to hear threats that further delay would result in the imposition of mounting fines against the community and the potential arrest of individuals on charges of "sabotage of the struggle against contagious diseases."[20]

In its single-minded mission to make the ghetto a reality, the Health Department, under the direction of its aptly named director Dr. Schnell, proved to be an agency in a hurry indeed. By the morning of January 13, in a joint review of outstanding issues pertaining to progress toward the creation of the ghetto, Schnell stressed that "in light of the sharp rise in the incidences of spotted fever in January of this year the deadline could not be delayed too long." Dr. Schnell had a further concern, however, indicative of continued uncertainty about whether the ghetto, once established, really was to be of only brief duration. While at last expressing confidence that the three hundred beds for the Wesola Street hospital would be installed within a week, he deemed that "for the planned, temporary period of the ghetto's duration it is sufficient, but for the longer term it is too small." Consequently, the Health Department pressed for a redrawing of the proposed boundary of the ghetto, favoring the creation of a corridor facilitating inclusion of the city's main Jewish medical facility, the Poznański Hospital on Sterlinga Street, within the Jewish district as well.[21] While this recommendation was later abandoned as impractical, it was agreed that Jewish physicians be supplied with instruments from the Poznański facility and that four existing pharmacies capable of supplying medical facilities and the ghetto population "remain open" inside the district. At this time as well the Regierungspräsident announced that Polish labor was now deemed sufficient to accomplish vital tasks; there was no longer any need for housing a separate Jewish workforce in the city. Henceforth, even Jews deemed fit for heavy labor were to be sent immediately to the ghetto along with the rest of the Jewish population.[22]

At this preliminary stage, then, the Health Department, acting in concert with allied agencies in the offices of the Regierungspräsident, the Security Police, and the housing and building departments, was eager to ensure the containment of diseases inside the ghetto, if only to protect the health of the wider population. To be sure, the Jews, narrowly confined to the ghetto, were expected to suffer outbreaks of disease. But their immediate physical extermination appears not to have been the initial goal of the public health establishment, which was considerably less obsessed with destroying the Jews than with seeing to it that they not pose a health threat to the general population. Given their prejudiced assumptions, the reasoning of the health officials was that Jews must be geographically isolated until such time as they could be removed altogether. But so long as they remained, they should be given the minimal resources necessary to combat the outbreaks that, paradoxically, were now more likely precisely because they were forced to live under conditions of crowding and deprivation.

While city and regional leaders, working closely with experts in the city departments responsible for health and construction, and in consultation with police and security officials, devoted their attention to the remaining details of the ghetto, definitive measures were set in motion. On January 24, preliminary to the formal public announcement of the establishment of the ghetto, local authorities began a limited transfer of Jews to the zone. On that date "a telegram arrived at the community building from the German police precinct number 5," headquartered in the northern Bałuty district, summoning Rumkowski to an urgent discussion. As he was just then engaged in an "audience with the mayor," two of his trusted subordinates, Henryk Neftalin, a young Łódź attorney, and Dora Fuchs, a German-speaking secretary, were dispatched in his stead. At the precinct headquarters the managing officer, Warnke, informed them that, in response to grave considerations of public health, the Police President had issued the order for the immediate transfer of a number of Jews residing elsewhere in the city to the heavily populated Jewish district in his area. They were to be conducted, under police escort, to precincts 5 and 6, from whence they would be settled in what was now being referred to as a *Seuchengebiet,* or zone of quarantine.[23] In the course of this discussion Rumkowski at last appeared. Hearing the news, he quickly ensured his staff's participation in the impending operation.[24] He accordingly charged

Neftalin with remaining at the precinct to work out further details and see to it that all available community employees were rounded up at once and made ready to assist. Already time was pressing. It was then three o'clock in the afternoon, just two hours before curfew, and according to Warnke the first of the columns of transferees could be expected "at any minute." Neftalin received from the officer a precise overview of the dimensions of the affected zone, in the process making sketches for further use, as well as a number of passes to be issued to community employees who would be engaged in assisting in the transfer.[25] Quickly dispatched to the district to begin surveying for any available space to accommodate the newcomers, these employees had hardly begun their assignment when the first group of Jews being marched north, laden "with small suitcases or other bundles," began to arrive at the police precincts, awaiting assignment to their new residences.[26]

At the same time, Rumkowski obtained permission to coordinate the transfer from the offices of the community building at 19 Południowa Street, where his housing bureau, "newly established" and hastily assembled, now set to work operating from a "large hall" inside. While those moving to the district were henceforth directed straight to the community headquarters rather than to the police precincts, the police continued to play a key role, supervising the formal registration of new arrivals and then escorting them by groups to the district. To fulfill these tasks, the police established a presence in the Jewish community building. Warnke assigned a lead officer and twenty patrolmen, ten each from precincts 5 and 6, to take up positions in "two rooms in front" of the building.[27]

For those arriving at Południowa Street to undergo administrative processing, the wait to see the housing officials was lengthy and arduous. The line leading to the Housing Department's makeshift upstairs quarters snaked down the stairs and out of the building into the winter cold of the courtyard. Members of the housing staff did their best to alleviate the general discomfort by distributing rolls and hot refreshments to those waiting in line.[28] After completing the processing, the new arrivals were at last assembled into columns; carts were provided to transport the elderly and the bedridden. They were then led north under German police guard and, accompanied by housing officers, taken to "collection points" located in school buildings inside the Bałuty district. Here they waited yet again, attended by community officials, looked after by doctors, and provided once more with sustenance—typically coffee and bread, "sometimes . . . a meal"—yet still markedly ill at ease. Many revealed signs of nervous strain while awaiting transfer to their new residences.[29]

Setting to work at short notice, the newly established housing office did its best to adapt to the rapidly increasing pressure to find apartment space. Much to the relief of officials scrambling to assist the new arrivals, Rumkowski quickly succeeded in locating suitable units along Zgeriska Street, site of the recent evacuation of Jewish residents during the forced population transfer in December. As might be expected, however, a host of emerging difficulties arose. During initial inspections of potential housing in the assigned quarter, department officers neglected to take account of essential details regarding the state of plumbing and available furnishings, oversights leading to subsequent confusion and complaint. Moreover, the department found itself forced to contend with the demands of relatives, as yet unaffected by the transfer, who stepped forward, insisting that their relations' now abandoned properties and possessions be given over to them. In consequence, a special administrative section had to be formed to sort through these claims. Additional complications resulted when it was discovered that a number of persons looking for places to live in the assigned district had succeeded in bypassing the department altogether and obtained housing permits directly through the police precincts. Uninformed of these external arrangements, housing officers would find themselves assigning people to apartments that were discovered to have been already claimed or occupied by others. Given the pressures of the moment, similar mix-ups resulted from the officials' occasional failure to record accurately their own assignment of particular units in their inventory. Complicating the resolution of such matters were instances in which people who had taken up residence in an apartment could not produce evidence one way or another as to whether they had done so legitimately.[30]

Only days prior to what would be an official declaration of the ghetto's formation and the extension of transfer to include all Jews residing in the city, the director of the city's Health Department boasted of his bureau's efforts to isolate the Jews and thereby stem the tide of infectious disease. Speaking to a correspondent for the *Lodscher Zeitung*, Dr. Schnell reminded the public that infectious illnesses were to be traced to an identifiable local source: "Again and again we have occasion to determine that as a rule the Jews are carriers of epidemics. One cannot be warned urgently enough against contact with Jews." Dr. Schnell outlined some of the extensive "tasks" his division was undertaking. Among its key responsibilities, and in conformity with its focus on "the human being" as a "biological personality," was its commitment to creating a universal catalogue detailing for all the residents their individual "inherited and racial-biological" characteristics. Promotion of public health was, of course, a matter not only of inventorying human material but of promoting enlightened practices and serving the basic medical needs of the community as well. Undoubtedly seeking to lead by example, the department's tuberculosis station was outfitted with the "the most modern equipment." A tour of its "bright, friendly rooms" revealed dressing cubicles, separate areas for taking and developing x-rays, a laboratory, and examination rooms with "divided entryways" to guard against infectious transmissions. A separate dental clinic for schoolchildren, "in which naturally," it was stated, "only German pupils will be received and treated," featured its own "modern x-ray apparatus for dental diagnostics," a heat lamp, and "an oxygen device" said to be useful in curing certain gum ailments. "Here the greatest stress is placed on scrupulous cleanliness." Altogether, concluding on an upbeat note, the newspaper reported that the city's "hygienic care" was "in the best of hands," and "from the standpoint of health as well," Łódź could look forward to "a beautiful future."[31]

At last, on February 8, Police President and SS-Brigadeführer Johannes Schäfer officially proclaimed the creation of an enclosed residential district for the Jews, defining its projected perimeter, establishing procedures for movement into and out of the zone, and laying out the duties and responsibilities of those to be displaced by its creation.[32] The establishment of the ghetto meant not only that Jews living elsewhere in the city were going to be forced to move to the ghetto, but also that all ethnic German and Polish residents of the newly demarcated zone were going to have to leave. Consequently, procedures regulating the flow of large numbers of persons headed in opposite directions were complemented by regulations governing the orderly transfer of rented apartments as well as residential and commercial properties, personal possessions, and stocks of inventory. Whatever disruptions and inconveniences this might entail for non-Jews living in the district were subordinated to the chief administrative goal:

Jews residing outside the zone were to abandon their homes and properties and take up alternate residence in the closed district.

The operation was to commence on Monday, February 12. Movement
was not to be random but was regulated by the day and hour according to
precise timetables issued weekly by the police. For Poles slated to move
out of the ghetto area and for Jews who were moving into it, the timetables specified when all persons subject to the decree were to report for
removal. In advance of upcoming transfers, all persons residing in specified sectors identified by street and, where appropriate, by building number as well were ordered to report to designated neighborhood collection
points, from whence they would proceed on foot or, if deemed too weak,
by alternate conveyance, supervised by a designated block leader, under
guard, and "in closed formation." According to the initial implementation regulations, beginning at eight o'clock each morning and every two
hours thereafter through six in the evening, 150 Poles at a time would be
led away from the zone now designated exclusively for Jewish settlement.
On a simultaneous schedule, Jews from elsewhere in the city, assembled into groups of three hundred, would set out under armed escort
northward toward the ghetto. Prior to departure, both Poles leaving their
homes in the ghetto district and Jews theirs elsewhere in the city were required first to secure their residences and keys, then present their block
leader completed forms inventorying the size and remaining contents of
their abandoned residences and any commercial property and goods in
their possession. Poles were required to supply change of address notification for the records of the local police as well. While under way, and then
while awaiting ultimate assignment of new quarters, persons were forbidden to leave the columns. Guards were freely authorized to employ their
weapons in the event of perceived "resistance" or "defiance" of orders.
Prior to exiting the zone, Poles, along with the possessions they carried,
were required to "undergo disinfection conducted by representatives of
the city Health Department." Ethnic Germans residing in the district, under orders to leave as well, were granted the privilege of making multiple
trips in and out of the area in order to secure their belongings; while in
each instance their removed possessions were to be disinfected, they themselves were required to undergo disinfection only upon their first and last
departures. The general pattern, then, was to coordinate as closely as possible the movement of Poles, advancing sector by sector out of the ghetto

district, with the regulated entry of Jews arriving from elsewhere in the city into areas the Poles had abandoned. Reporting to the municipal housing authorities, ethnic Germans were to be assigned residences in newly available apartments in the city center, while Poles would have to take up residence in newly designated Polish areas.[33]

In response to the police order, Jewish housing office employees raced into affected neighborhoods in advance of the impending evacuations, contacting the families to be resettled and telling them where to assemble and form columns for their march to the ghetto. Hoping to ease the sometimes overwhelming burdens associated with imminent departure, they assisted families in packing, arranged for carts and stretchers to accommodate the aged and sick, and even pitched in by carrying items for at least a few of those weighted down with luggage as they struggled along the route of march. All the same, the transports were marred by inevitable disorder as so many people, quickly proving unable to keep up under the burden of having to carry their own belongings, tired and fell out of line. The Germans had warned that this was the very thing that would result in violence, as indeed it did, with guards assigned to the transports typically enforcing order by striking out with the butts of their rifles. Nor did it help matters that too frequently space on board some of the carts specifically set aside for those too frail to make the journey on foot was taken by others who, though evidently "strong and healthy," refused to budge.[34]

Many compelled to leave seemed incapable of gathering their things and heading out the door. In one particularly grievous instance the head of a large household, obviously at his wits' end, in tears and beyond the reach of persuasion, "beat himself about the head with his fists, [and] hurled himself to the floor," proclaiming himself unwilling "to leave his apartment under any circumstances." Only with difficulty, "half willingly, half through the use of force," was a housing official able to lead the man out and place him on a cart.[35] Others, not knowing where to begin the overwhelming task of gathering up whatever possessions they could, in the end had to leave their homes without taking a thing. Empty-handed departures were occasioned not merely by confusion but by force, for some evacuations were accompanied by brazen cruelties: armed men appeared at doorways brandishing guns and demanding that residents get out immediately and leave everything behind. Yet many did succeed in saving what they could, hastily selecting and packing a portion of their

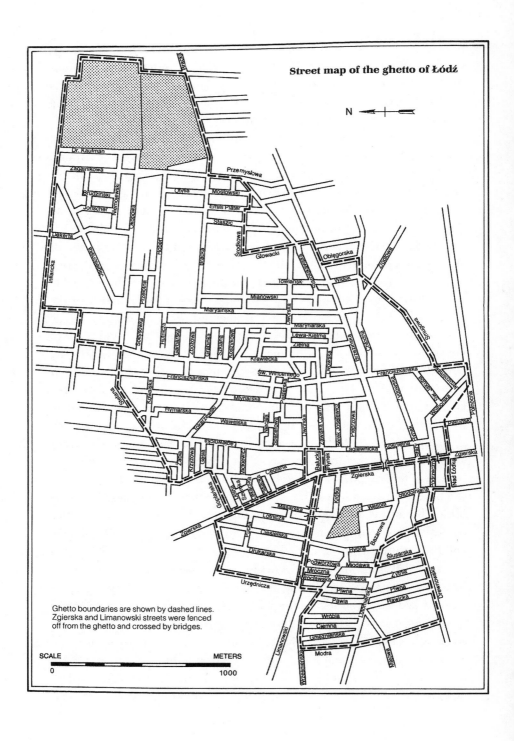

Street map of the ghetto of Łódź

N

Ghetto boundaries are shown by dashed lines.
Zgierska and Limanowski streets were fenced
off from the ghetto and crossed by bridges.

SCALE   METERS
0   1000

belongings, though often this entailed little more than the basics: some undergarments and extra clothing, as well as sheets, pillows, and blankets, heaped, when available, onto hand carts and sleds, which they hauled themselves, and atop which were to be seen seated small children who, oblivious to the reason for this sudden uprooting, asked of anxious and bewildered parents the unanswerable question, why were they moving? Adding to the misery of the terrified and dispossessed was the audible mockery of gentile neighbors, onlookers to this exodus that led past the familiar thresholds of apartments long resided in, down stairways and stairwells, through courtyards, and into the streets. Polish youngsters ran after the sudden exiles, too, barking insults.[36]

With the issuance of the general order to remove all Jews to the newly established residential district, the Housing Department relocated to the ghetto as well, moving from space inside the community building on Południowa Street to quarters on the site of a municipal bus station at 13 Lutomierska Street. Conditions there, too, left much to be desired. For one thing, the place was "cold, damp, anything but cozy, and very run down." Outside, where "day after day" crowds gathered in the cold of the station's "spacious courtyard" awaiting entry into the building, the setting was even more unpleasant. Inside the bureau a kind of barely controlled bedlam reigned. On those occasions when the director, presiding from a table in "a little room in the back," did have time to meet personally with members of the public, he frequently found himself attempting to deal with several all at once. Given the stream of interruptions, he seemed unable or unwilling to concentrate on or understand what these petitioners were saying. Employees were constantly rapping at his window with various queries to which he responded by issuing "all manner of chaotic instructions [*wydawał jakieś chaotyczne dyspozycje*]." In brief, the scene was one best described as that of "crowds in the yard but in the small, packed rooms of the Housing Department—shouts, screams."[37]

The de-Judaizing of the city core had been under way less than a month when, still dissatisfied with the pace of the operation and piqued by instances of Jews apparently evading removal, the Germans staged a sudden downtown assault. On the terrible night of March 6–7, "Bloody Thursday" as it came to be known, they hauled people from their homes on the city's main avenue, Adolf-Hitler-Straße, shooting "about 200" of them in the course of the raid. Others were speedily hauled away to stag-

ing areas elsewhere in the city and terrorized. Some 150 more were taken
to a nearby woods and shot.[38] This incident, singular even in the general
context of menace that had characterized the forcible transfer of Jews to
the ghetto district, looked very much like a reversion to those dramatic
outbursts of violence marking the initial wave of assaults the previous autumn. Indeed, violence against the Jews was continuously in the air.
Sometimes its expression was geographically diffuse, sometimes limited to
isolated instances of unpunished popular acts of spontaneous torment; yet
at any moment, and seemingly unexpectedly, it might flare, as it did now,
into concentrated, directed outbursts of indescribable savagery. For all the
attention to careful multiagency planning and adherence to precise timetables for the orderly movement of populations, the events of the night of
March 6 were a reminder that the violent energies given free rein during
the first weeks of the occupation in the late summer and autumn of 1939
had by no means been exhausted. As if in conformity to a kind of kinetic
law, those same violent impulses and energies, though momentarily re-
strained when tightly wound around precise administrative procedures,
were just as easily released into another form, and with great force.

Returning on foot from the ghetto district late that night, a housing office employee had just reached the corner of Listopada and Zachodnia
streets, lying just south of the ghetto district, when, in his words, "from a
distance I heard screams, groaning, the sounds of beating and torment."
He "immediately returned and reported to Neftalin about the approaching Jewish transport and the conditions under which the Jews were being
escorted. The Order Service [Jewish police] were notified to take up posts
at the border of the ghetto and receive the transport." The newcomers
had suffered a merciless attack. "The group arrived from the city in a
condition worse than desperate. People were literally frantic, beaten,
wounded. . . . Women as well as men wailed and cried." Offering assistance, he and his colleagues in the housing bureau helped bring them to
the safety of an assembly point inside the ghetto. People were "in a state of
total breakdown, as if after some kind of horrible psychic shock." At one
o'clock that morning another wave of unfortunates arrived "in the same
condition as the first." Doctors attended to their injuries. Many of the
wounded had been struck by rifle butts and slashed by bayonets. A final
group, "in a state even more deplorable than the one preceding it," made
it to the ghetto at ten o'clock the next morning.[39]

Where was Rumkowski? Leon Hurwicz, a contemporary and a ghetto resident whose diary reveals him as one of Rumkowski's severest internal critics, found the man oddly disengaged at the very moment when these brutalities were occurring. He recalled that while a number of people, badly beaten and in desperate straits, came and gathered in the courtyard of the community headquarters seeking "solace" from the Jewish leadership, Rumkowski remained locked away in a meeting discussing educational matters. When, soon thereafter, he summoned his council into late-night session, its members, "their hearts beating" with anticipation as they anxiously awaited news of the situation, were disappointed to discover that Rumkowksi had called them together only in order to consider the allocation of residences to people who had won his favor. In Hurwicz's view, it was as if the terrible recent events preying on everyone else's mind simply "did not touch him."[40]

In the face of so uncontrollable an outburst of violence on the part of the authorities, it ought not to have been unexpected that Rumkowski would direct his attention to matters over which he was still able to exercise some control. Even now, apart from the matter of securing his power and arranging its organizational bases, it was the care of orphans that drove the energies of the chairman. They had been the focus of his career, his point of contact with the community, and, though this was open to question, the source of his claim to its respect. That frantic spring, amid trying efforts to lead his people to their designated home in Bałuty, amid endlessly pleading with the authorities and overcoming the strained logistics involved in saving this or that piece of movable community property—among them school benches for the children and an x-ray machine and other medical instruments for use by ghetto physicians—and the attempts to free up buildings in the Jewish quarter for use, it was the survival of the orphanages that he wished, perhaps above all, to ensure. Repeatedly during his tenure as head of the ghetto, Rumkowski would be portrayed as pleased by the organization of these affairs, refreshed at the very sight of his children hard at work on their indoor and outdoor projects, attending to their lessons in school, spooning thick soup from their bowls, dancing in circles.[41]

The terrifying night of the Bloody Thursday assault had hardly passed when at last the time came for the orphans from two of the community's downtown residences to make their way to the ghetto. In a sympathetic

account of the founding of the ghetto orphanages, composed in the
ghetto in 1942, it was reported that many were initially upset about a
move to the unknown district until Rumkowski "encouraged them with
the promise to watch over them in the future as well." On March 12
they finally moved into their new quarters, a spacious two-story building
located just behind Bałut Market at 10 Dworska Street. In time the structure would be amply outfitted with "a newly organized kitchen, a common dining room, and a playroom for the little ones on the main floor,"
and bedrooms for the girls on the first story and for the boys on the second. In addition the new ghetto facility would come to house, on the
girls' floor, a quarantine and doctor's office and a space for sewing. Close
by, "a large courtyard with a garden" would offer the youngsters "ample
opportunity to be able to breathe in the fresh springtime air." In April,
prior to the sealing of the ghetto, Rumkowski would succeed in moving
in additional orphans, residents of two remaining city homes: a religious
orphanage for boys run by the community on Pomorska Street, resettled
into "a little house" next door on Dworska Street, and a girls' home,
"Przytulisko," afforded new quarters on Franciszkańska Street, at number
85, attractively "enclosed by a large field which the children cultivated
with great enthusiasm."[42]

Springtime neared, and with it came great changes. Many were the signs
of the city's metamorphosis. At the end of March, on Good Friday, a date
coinciding that year with the 108th anniversary of Goethe's death, *Faust*
premiered to a full auditorium at the main city theater. It was the kind of
production of Germanic classics deemed by the *Lodscher Zeitung* to be
properly supplanting what the reviewer dismissed as trivial entertainments
formerly performed at this same venue, notable among them "works of
Jewish jargon," now thankfully abandoned.[43] No such creation even mer-
ited comparison to *Faust,* which embodied nothing less than "the crystal-
lization of our purest racial thoughts and feelings."[44] For those seeking
lighter fare, the newly Germanizing city offered ample diversion: the Casanova cabaret had recently opened, offering evening spectacles such as
dance numbers, ranging in style from the "fashionable" to the "fanciful"
and the "acrobatic," as well as the sounds of a "house orchestra" and a pi-
ano player named Harry.[45] The Hohenstein puppet company was in town

too; its wooden marionettes were praised as so remarkably lifelike that one hardly noticed that skillful artists were animating remarkable performances in which, as if all on their own, the dummies came to life, one running its fingers over the keyboard of an accordion while a whole ensemble danced in time to a waltz.[46]

On April 11 the city received a new name; by proclamation of the Führer, henceforth Lodsch was to be known as Litzmannstadt, a tribute to the Great War commander General Karl Litzmann, who, in addition to his honored status as the hero who had led German forces to victory on a nearby field of battle, had gone on to distinguish himself as a loyal supporter of the Nazi movement.[47] Fittingly, the city's premier guest establishment, located in the heart of downtown, the Grand Hotel on Adolf-Hitler-Straße, announced that it would henceforth be called the Fremdenhof General Litzmann. Of course downtown streets, in addition to bearing the names of Germanic heroes and Nazis both living and dead, proudly bore those of creative artists—among favored composers, Handel, Haydn, Mozart, Schubert, Schumann, Johann Strauß, and Wagner each had a thoroughfare dedicated in his honor[48]—as Łódź more than ever took on the look and feel of a city of the Reich. The decisive difference, noticeable above all to those who knew the city well, was that at last the Jews had disappeared from the urban scene. "What business have the Jews here! The time is long since past that they were forbidden to set foot on these and other thoroughfares, and woe to the criminals should they ever dare show their faces here again," noted a travel feature seeking to highlight recent changes.[49] Those renamed avenues were thought more orderly and peaceful now that young newsboys, known for loudly hawking newspapers everywhere, were banned from the streets. Their presence was said to have been attributable to exploitative Jewish commercial enterprise. It was deemed "easy" enough to bid them "farewell" from the urban scene. "Their time is past. Past, like everything connected with Judaism."[50] Gone as well from the cityscape were what were described as badly maintained, scratched-up, and unsanitary horse-drawn cabs once steered throughout the city by ragged Jewish coachmen. For all their superficially quaint touches, such old-fashioned conveyances, though still driven by Polish drivers, were judged in bad repair and altogether in need of a thorough cleaning inside and out.[51]

Litzmannstadt was not alone, of course, in celebrating the passing of that era when Jewry dared leave its mark upon the city and the land. From the Gau capital in Posen came word of a recent planned renovation: a synagogue was to be torn down to its foundation and converted into a public swimming pool. Three mounted Stars of David, sheet-copper constructions of which the largest measured some two meters high, had been pulled from the structure. The planned facility, soon to "serve the health" of the public, contributing to its general "zest for life," offered tangible evidence of the ways in which "something negative" was on its way to being "transformed into something positive."[52]

Fresh from the announcement that henceforth the city would bear the name of Litzmannstadt, Warthegau Gauleiter Arthur Greiser and his entourage headed out beyond its precincts on a whirlwind tour of regional settlements of ethnic German settlers and their families. Anticipating his arrival, a reporter stationed at a crossing just outside Zgierz, the nearby town that was to be his first stop, watched as a speeding uniformed motorcyclist of the transport corps (NSKK) pulled abruptly to a halt and, signaling the number of minutes until the Gauleiter's arrival, thrust ten fingers in the air. One drew confidence, the writer commented, from the organizational certainty of such gestures, much as one did from the clearly legible new signs along the roadway, posted only the night before, pointing the way: "To Litzmannstadt." Greiser was depicted as warmly received everywhere, expansive in his well-wishes and promises for the settlers, in turn accepting heartfelt expressions of praise for the regime that had brought them to freedom and with it the hope of prosperity. To especially worthy settlers he distributed cash premiums, and from unwed young women he elicited a promise: once married to eligible German men, they should keep him informed about the many children they were sure to bring into the world. Fittingly, Greiser was said to have been especially solicitous toward the littlest of Germanic youngsters he encountered along the way.[53]

Without objecting in principle to the necessity of creating the ghetto, those wishing to influence the drawing of its boundaries made their voices heard, requiring an official response. On March 11, 1940, for example, representatives attending the Fulda Conference of Bishops, objecting to the planned inclusion within the boundaries of the ghetto of the towering red-brick Church of the Virgin Mary, or Marienkirche, situated in the heart of the Bałuty district, appealed to the office of the Reich minister for ecclesiastical affairs in Berlin. Noting the church's status as both a city "landmark" and a site of importance to the local German Catholic population, they suggested that moving the border of the ghetto by a distance of only 150 meters might resolve the problem. The matter was ultimately referred for consideration to the Reich Commissariat for the Strengthening of Germandom and the Litzmannstadt branch of the Security Service (SD). In delayed response, in late May, with the ghetto by then a reality and the Marienkirche still fenced inside, the SD rejected the appeal, arguing that the church was situated in a district that even prior to the war had been one in which Jews constituted a majority of the population. Moreover, "the number of Catholics of German ethnicity" in the once 45,798-member, largely Polish-speaking parish "was not significant," amounting to "between 600 and 700 souls." By May the SD would deem the matter of the disposition of the church resolved, declaring: "The establishment of the Jewish ghetto is already completed and the ghetto sealed from the rest of the city. The Marienkirche is closed until further notice, probably until the dissolution of the ghetto."[54]

Exercising greater influence, ethnic German property owners long resident in the city, and with material interests at stake in the process of creating a Jewish enclave, continued to appeal to the authorities to redraw the boundaries of the assigned district in order to exclude their holdings from the territory of the ghetto. In an effort to make some headway against the tide of these petitions, municipal building director Hallbauer, recognizing that the projected density within the ghetto, already averaging some eight persons per room, was approaching intolerable limits, circulated an explanatory leaflet to the public underscoring the unavoidable necessity of creating the ghetto within boundaries that included their holdings. Hallbauer sought to remind the citizenry that establishing the ghetto was an undesirable yet essential precondition for the containment of epidemics and for the revitalization of the local economy, in which there could be absolutely no "personal contact with the Jews." He explained that the ghetto had to expand to include areas populated by persons of German ethnicity because of "the unfortunate fact that during the Polish era a large number of Germans lived and resided in the midst of these Jews." Still, owners were to be reassured that this expansion would not result in an "expropriation." Quite to the contrary, not only had they been permitted to carry away their possessions, but they were also entitled to receive equivalent compensation in the form of properties and businesses elsewhere in the city; any loss of steady income resulting from the transfer was to be fully compensated as well. German owners were assured that, with the dissolution of the ghetto and the removal of the Jews, all properties forfeit for the duration of the ghetto's existence were to be sanitized and, should the owners opt to reclaim them, placed once more at their disposal. Any "material damages" owing to Jewish occupation would be repaired or financially compensated, "even in the event of a total loss." Appealing to patriotic sentiment, the leaflet urged local property owners to "show necessary understanding," for in comparison to the sacrifices Germany's soldiers were being asked to make on behalf of the nation, theirs were limited and of restricted duration, likely only "a matter of months." Owners were to rest assured that in the drawing up of the present boundaries, "all authorities of the state, the city, the economy, and the party have been involved, thereby guaranteeing that, at the moment, there is no better solution for reaching the necessary, greater goal."[55]

By the beginning of April, with the installation of barbed wire nearly complete and only weeks remaining before the official sealing of the ghetto, Rumkowski too was pleading for modifications to the ghetto perimeter to enhance the district's size and if possible to delay its total enclosure.[56] Arguing that the danger of the spread of tuberculosis was especially acute during April and May, he sought from the mayor a two-month postponement in the placement of wire and fencing along narrow walkways so that when the sick were removed from ghetto dwellings they would not be brought into unnecessary contact with passersby. In this context he underscored that "there are in the territory only very few streets with fresh air which the people urgently require for the maintenance of their health." In addition, he requested that he be given access to a number of still unused properties that could be of great help to him in seeing to the medical needs of the population. Arguing the limitations of an available 175-bed ghetto hospital on Drewnowska Street, Rumkowski brought to the mayor's attention the existence of one such essential structure that was still off-limits, an immense public health insurance facility, the Chasa Chrorych building at 36 Łagiewnicka Street, with estimated space for "some 400 beds." Arguing for its inclusion in the available building stock of the ghetto, he noted that not only would it be suitable for transferring facilities from the downtown Poznański Hospital, but also it would add much-needed patient capacity while, in distinction to the more crowded Drewnowska Street facility, permitting essential separation of key medical departments for gynecology, pediatrics, surgery, and even a ward for the treatment of prostitutes. In a further bid to modify the dimensions of the district, though ever formally courteous in the wording of his requests, Rumkowski petitioned for enlargement of the ghetto up to the cemetery situated in a remote corner of the zone's Marysin quarter. This was necessary "in order to avoid possible quarrels with the other inhabitants," a reference to ongoing harassment by unruly non-Jewish neighbors.[57] Indeed, there had been repeated disturbances in which funeral processions going to the large walled cemetery had been "constantly subject to invectives" and stoning by gentiles who still resided on the streets along the distant route.[58] That the cemetery remained a focal point of local troublemaking the authorities well knew, though it was less than clear whether they cared one way or another who was responsible. On April 16 Police President Schäfer noted that "a number of gravestones had been overturned" and the cemetery walls had been defaced. Nevertheless, attributing the damage to "children playing," he merely ordered Rumkowski to clean it up and instruct the Jewish police to prevent similar occurrences in the future.[59]

Looking ahead to the impending necessity of sustaining the Jewish population over time, Rumkowski suggested to the mayor the broad outlines of a plan to garner revenue from the employment of a significant contingent of skilled Jewish workers. He estimated that some eight to ten thousand persons—to be drawn from a list of tradespeople, including shoemakers, saddle makers, leather goods specialists, tailors, undergarment seamstresses, hat and cap makers, plumbers, carpenters, painters, bookbinders, and paperhangers—could be made available for the purpose. He specifically proposed that in exchange for the delivery of the necessary raw materials, these ghetto craftsmen, working on-site in workshops and at wage rates determined by the authorities, would create and then return to the authorities a host of finished articles suitable for sale. In turn, the ghetto would be granted compensation, either in the form of wage payments, which Rumkowki could then pass on to the workers, or through provision of foodstuffs of equivalent value for feeding the ghetto population. Hoping as well to guarantee an end to the kind of arbitrary seizures that had so plagued the Jewish community since the first days of the occupation, Rumkowski requested an ordinance be issued forbidding outsiders to enter the ghetto for the purpose of "[pulling] people off the street for work." In addition, he asked permission from the German authorities to collect rents in ghetto residential buildings, consideration being given to the fact that, in any event, many inhabitants would be too impoverished to pay and hence would have to be excused from this obligation. Rumkowski would, however, undertake the responsibility for making repairs. Also, in the interests of attending to the security and health of the ghetto's residents (through maintenance of a Jewish police force, through critical welfare assistance to "the poor and the needy," and through measures designed to "protect the population from illness" and to serve "all other needs of the Jewish population"), Rumkowski did not hesitate to broach the prospect of "an appropriate subsidy" with which the authorities might help him manage his growing budget.[60]

In proposing a comprehensive program of employment to be built around a core of experienced Jewish labor, Rumkowski had succeeded in engaging his German masters on the plane of reasoning where the authorities' self-serving interests intersected with the immediate requirements of the beleaguered community Rumkowski sought to preserve. Whatever else the Jews might be in the opinion of anti-Semites, those who had their eye on the local economy also saw in the Jews an exploitable factor of production in the form of trained, inexpensive labor from which money could be made. Even amid the unrestrained cruelties of the first weeks of the occupation, when unofficially sanctioned mistreatment of the Jews was given free rein, the notion that the Jews could be made to "work" for their masters was an underlying supposition. But in the longer term, both public officials charged with administering the ghetto and private entrepreneurs who saw in its creation opportunities for expansion and the generation of revenues were thinking along lines similar to those Rumkowski was proposing.

As one local German manufacturer, Günter Schwarz, owner of a major textile plant in Litzmannstadt as well as an affiliate enterprise in the nearby town of Brzeziny, wrote at the end of March in a lengthy memorandum of his own, experienced Jewish laborers constituted a native resource that might profitably be employed in the interest of meeting current demands and putting the regional textile industry on a new footing. Conceding that prior to the war "the clothing industry in the Wartheland was almost exclusively in Jewish hands," he argued for its rapid reconstruction in strict accordance with "National Socialist principles." That transformation was under way, the manufacturer noted: "With the approval of influential authorities we have completed preparations and have already begun making uniforms and clothing of all types" through "the exploitation of available, experienced Jewish craftsmen." At the same time, while "the fastest possible replacement of Jewish craftsmen by retrained German [craft workers]" was desirable, such retraining would take at least several months. Until then, and indeed "as long as the Jews live off the food we provide, they will also have to work profitably for Germany." By Schwarz's estimate, taking into account not only a core of "nearly 17,000" existing skilled Jewish workers but also those who might yet be trained or otherwise incorporated into the workforce, the potential pool of labor in the Litzmannstadt ghetto was huge, "reaching well over 100,000" in number. Assuming the necessity of first "relieving" the ghetto, he advised making provision for shifting highly skilled workers to so-called factory ghettos, where, once more safely cordoned off from contact with the outside, they would continue to serve German industry. In what appears to be a reference to the projected dissolution of the ghetto as a whole, he thought it advisable that the remaining force of skilled laborers be held back, to be "transported at the very end" of the operation or, alternatively, "separated by occupational category and housed in enclosed camps where their occupational knowledge can be put to further use."[61]

Dispossessed and exiled, on the eve of the district's closure many ghetto residents nonetheless found reason to welcome those few hopeful signs that, at long last, and only in comparison to the terrors and uncertainties of the preceding months, a measure of calm and even security might be found within the isolation of their new surroundings. As warning signs posted at the ghetto perimeter made unmistakably clear, unauthorized entry by outsiders was strictly forbidden.[62] At least they seemed spared for now from the kind of random seizure for work or assault on the streets that had characterized the early days of the occupation.[63] Moreover, and much to the relief of the Jewish mourners whose funeral processions ill-disposed gentile neighbors had seen fit to pelt with stones, Rumkowski did succeed in his appeal to extend the boundaries of the ghetto to include the streets leading to the Jewish cemetery in Marysin. In this way, even the Jewish dead might enjoy the prospect of lying undisturbed. As for the living, it was said that "little by little conditions settled down, [and] after the tempestuous days in the city there followed [a period] of calm and easing of tensions." In fact, "the ghetto appeared greener." Ghetto building administrators, charged with seeing to the cleanup of property in their care, had brought about noticeable improvements in the general look of things. Patches of new grass and little gardens made their appearance, and along Lutomierska Street, amid further greenery, even "small benches had been arrayed."[64]

"In the last days of April" Passover arrived, and Rumkowski saw to the distribution of unleavened bread so that the community might properly celebrate this important festival, ever a marker of approaching springtime and above all of Jewish remembrance of Israel's bitter sojourn in Egypt and its ultimate delivery from bondage. For his part, Rumkowski chose to spend his Passover meal in the company of the newly settled orphans, sharing with them a multicourse ritual repast of "*matzoth* made of pure corn meal, fish, eggs, [and] special holiday dishes." The occasion was said to have been "a source of great, lasting joy for all and proof that in this new epoch, which the entire Jewish population awaited, the orphans had not been forgotten."[65]

The new epoch was at hand. According to schedule, brooking no delay, on the night of April 30 the ghetto would be sealed. The date was one of some portent. As the local newspaper reminded its readers, the dark hours leading to the first of May had long been known in folk tradition as Walpurgisnacht, signaling the moment when spring, battling one last time against the grudging retreat of winter, established its dominance. This was the night when all manner of devilish creatures gave themselves over to a final fling, and when even now, if only symbolically and in isolated rural communities, the people still, as in distant medieval times, sought to keep such malicious spirits at bay. The paper reported that in towns in Thuringia and the Harz region, recalling an earlier time, little girls, costumed in cone-shaped paper hats, took to roaming about like witches to be hunted, and boys on hobbyhorses rode out to the edge of the fields to post guard; citizens saw to it that broomsticks were hidden away and billy goats were gathered and locked in a barn lest the demons, seeking transportation, find them and journey forth on their terrifying errands.[66]

The Jews of the city were at last banished from their homes and assembled in a mournful place of confinement. From this place there was to be no unauthorized entry or exit. A fenced boundary, fearsomely patrolled, marked the perimeter of the ghetto's constricted boundaries. The immediate fate of the Jews now lay firmly in the hands of municipal German planners. To them fell responsibility for overseeing the ghetto. However long it should endure, they would see to it that it was exploited to their own best advantage. Above all, in their view, with the creation of the ghetto, Litzmannstadt had taken an essential step toward realizing its great potential. At last free of the harmful presence of Jews residing in their midst, the city's increasing German citizenry could breathe more easily now; their unrestrained energies and talents would know no bounds.

3

The Enclosure

By the beginning of spring, the initial phase of the operation was complete: uprooted and confined, banished to a crowded, fenced-in quarter on the city's northern edge, the Jews had vanished from daily life. No more were they to be seen on the streets and in their shops, in their offices, and in their homes. No more were gentile neighbors encountering them opening the doors to their apartments, chatting in stairwells, or congregating in the courtyards. Jewish businesses, Jewish schools, Jewish hospitals, Jewish restaurants were a thing of the past. Yet for the German administrators, however much pride they took in the ghetto's establishment, it remained an institution of temporary duration and secondary importance to the greater goal of total removal of the Jewish population to some distant location.

Ghetto records indicate that as of May 1, 1940, an estimated 163,777 souls had been confined to the district, far fewer than the city's prewar Jewish population in excess of 200,000, yet assuredly for German planners a reflection of losses attributable to the initial waves of flight, expulsion, and physical destruction. But given the pinched dimensions of the zone, a mere four kilometers square, to which so many Jews had been densely restricted, the figure was sizable indeed.[1] Deprived of their independence, unable to earn their livelihood as before, the Jews were going to have to be provided with food and other basic necessities. The authorities could simply leave them to starve, fall ill, and die, in principle hardly a matter of administrative concern.[2] But that option posed the potential of igniting a widespread epidemic capable of leaping the boundary of the ghetto and harming the general population. One thing was certain. If the ghetto was to be supplied, one way or another the Jews must ultimately be made to bear the costs of their own upkeep. With this essential principle established, the ghetto commenced operation under the heavy hand of German institutional supervision.

From the outset the ghetto presented to the municipal leadership two immediate and related questions: how much would it cost to maintain the ghetto, and could the captive Jewish community cover the expense? Surveying the experience gained during the first weeks of its operation, on May 27, 1940, Litzmannstadt mayor Karl Marder laid out a preliminary estimate of current and immediately pending financial burdens imposed by the existence of the ghetto and the means by which they were to be met. He concluded that, at least preliminarily, the costs of ghetto maintenance, amounting to some RM750,000 for the first month, appeared altogether satisfactorily limited and manageable. Yet, he warned, such estimates were likely to prove an unrealistic gauge of future outlays. Indeed, by his reckoning such low initial maintenance costs were but a reflection of the capacity of ghetto inhabitants to live for the short term off supplemental resources of food and other supplies. Their availability was expected to be of brief duration. In consequence, the city and its agents responsible for supplying the ghetto would have to reckon with steeply rising budgetary demands. By June expenses were expected to mount to some RM100,000 per day, totaling as much as 2 if not 3 million Reichsmarks for the month, and set to double to a daily estimated expenditure of RM200,000 by the second half of July.[3]

Such accelerating demands necessitated intensified efforts to draw vast quantities of capital from the ghetto. Marder identified several potential sources. It was commonly assumed that in moving to the ghetto the Jews had succeeded in retaining quantities of hard currency. In the mayor's estimate, this amounted to some 5 million Reichsmarks. As a means to compel inhabitants of the ghetto to surrender the money, Marder looked ahead to the introduction of a special internal ghetto currency, which, in enforced substitution for the Reichsmark, was to become the sole permissible commercial instrument circulating within the enclosed district. In direct exchange for delivery of Reichsmarks collected from the ghetto population, Rumkowski was to be issued substitute quantities of this scrip for general distribution. Pending resolution of rival SS claims, the mayor also set his sights on recovering personal articles of value, including "jewelry, precious metals, [and] diamonds, in addition to textiles and leather," either through direct confiscation or by purchasing them in the new currency. In what was destined to become an additional source of income, Marder took note of efforts under way to draw from the wages of Jewish labor by employing Jewish artisans in boot making, furniture manufacture, and ready-made textile production. Jews were also to be set to work producing recyclable stone products, breaking apart streets to be taken out of service and demolishing structures as part of a wider project designed to create a firebreak, or clearing, between a portion of the ghetto perimeter and the city. Exploiting the goodwill of relatives and friends of ghetto residents, the German administration prepared to gain direct control over funds already flowing in to the beleaguered residents of the ghetto in the form of donations from abroad. During the first month alone some forty thousand Reichsmarks in contributions had been transferred to the Jewish community by way of outside banks and savings institutions. To solidify control over such funds, financial institutions both foreign and domestic were to be informed that henceforth all such contributions were to be sent directly to a downtown account, held at the Litzmannstadt City Savings Bank, through which the municipality managed the financial affairs of the ghetto. In a further example of the lengths to which he was prepared to go in pursuit of all possible sources of revenue, Marder spoke strongly in favor of collecting even on outstanding sums still owed by "ethnic Germans and other debtors" to Jewish residents in the ghetto.[4]

Initially, the responsibility for daily oversight and administration of ghetto affairs fell to a newly established subsidiary department of the Main Office of Food and Economy (Ernährungs- und Wirtschaftsamt Hauptsetlle), a municipal bureau headquartered downtown in a building at 21 Hermann-Göring-Straße charged with supervising the provisioning of the city. The bureau's executive officer was Johann Moldenhauer. At the beginning of May, Hans Biebow, at age thirty-seven a young, commercially successful business owner from Bremen just arrived on assignment

to Litzmannstadt, assumed the directorship of the Food and Economy
Office's Ghetto Division, then comprising a staff of twenty-four members, though rapidly expanding, more than doubling in size to fifty-eight
by later that month.[5]

Both Moldenhauer and Biebow were intent on running a tight ship, an
attitude expressed in directives demanding of bureau employees outward
displays of loyalty, efficiency of communication, attention to personal
cleanliness in the workplace, strict respect for lines of authority, and careful monitoring of the comings and goings of office personnel. Employees
were reminded of restraints on their personal interaction with the surrounding Polish population; most especially, even work-related contacts
with the Jews in the ghetto were to be kept to an absolute minimum and
restricted to a select circle of departmental employees and workers. In all
official settings employees were to demonstrate their allegiance. "I expect
of all members of my staff—the women included—that the [raising of]
the German salute provide [visible] expression to their inner deport-
ment," Moldenhauer instructed. Taking note of a decree from the minister of the interior against outward displays of affection toward Polish
women, Moldenhauer cautioned his staff against similar improprieties.[6]
As of June 18, 1940, a central in-house telephone exchange, staffed by two
women, linked departments of the Food and Economy Office, including
its Ghetto Division, both internally and with outside parties. In the interest of maintaining a no-nonsense, businesslike demeanor, both operators
and office staff were directed to be at all times brief and professional. In
their communications with clients, switchboard operators were to be "always objective and polite." In the event the telephoning party failed to behave in the same manner, or when a conversation became too involved,
operators were to "remain calm and to the point," at their discretion directing such problem calls "to the bureau director or the relevant department head."[7]

Cleanliness and hygiene in the workplace were paramount virtues. A
team of ten cleaning women, four of whom were specifically assigned to
Ghetto Division offices located on the second, third, and fourth stories of
the building, saw to the general upkeep.[8] In addition, beginning the following winter, each week on Monday mornings at eleven o'clock, runners
were to circulate through the offices on each floor collecting soiled hand
towels and distributing fresh ones—each towel being assigned for the ex-

clusive use of no more than two individuals at a time.[9] With like regard
for cleanliness, and a nod to thrift as well, in August 1940 a dozen female
staff assistants would petition, asking that each be afforded a change of
work aprons in order to protect their clothing from undue "soiling."
"Daily sedentary work and handling of carbon paper," they argued, was
resulting in undesirable stress on fabrics. "Nowadays it is demanded of
each and every *Volksgensosse* that he be gentle with his clothing and treat it
with care so that wear and tear is not too great and raw materials are
spared."[10] As of June 3, 1940, working hours for employees of the Ghetto
Division were set at 7:30 in the morning to 4:30 in the afternoon. To discourage venturing off the premises during breaks, staff, with the exception
of those assigned to tasks in the field, were strongly urged to take their
midday meals on-site. For their convenience, first a canteen, and then, beginning on September 30, a well-equipped communal dining facility located on the building's third floor, were placed at their disposal. In compensation, at least materially, for sacrificing the privilege of dining at local
eateries, each employee was to be provided, for the sum of sixty pfennigs,
with what was officially described as a "very well prepared lunch" that was
"fully adequate for a meal."[11] In an indication of efforts to promote workplace solidarity as well as to suggest suitable types of off-duty recreation
for employees, at the end of the third week in June members of the
Ghetto Division were encouraged to take part in a special workplace-
sponsored Sunday outing. Those interested in the "mystery trip" were
urged to attend an informational session to be held in the main bureau's
common room on the Saturday afternoon before the event.[12]

From these modest beginnings, over time ghetto management would develop an organizational structure dominated by Biebow as director, assisted by two principal deputies responsible for general supervision of all
operations related to maintaining the ghetto and its captive workforce and
population. Oversight of these tasks fell to four principal business subdivisions regulating labor creation and manufacturing, monetary conversion
of goods removed from the ghetto, financial administration, and central
purchasing. Overseeing ghetto manufacture of textile, wood, and leather
products, the labor creation and manufacturing bureau additionally attended to contracts concluded with ghetto suppliers and clients, chief

among them the German military, for which the ghetto sewed and refurbished uniforms, as well as a host of manufacturers and retailers in the private sector, primarily in the ready-made clothing and furniture trades. The division additionally monitored prices and wages, storage of textile articles, and the sanitizing of processed raw materials and finished products prior to their removal from the ghetto for storage in the city or direct shipment to purchasers.[13]

The Warenverwertung, or merchandise utilization department, was the key body within the agency devoted to the lucrative liquidation of items of Jewish-owned silver, gold, jewels, furs, textiles, clothing, household contents, and crystal, whether acquired by confiscation or through administered purchase. The division oversaw both wholesale and in-house retail-level sales of these articles and ran a downtown warehouse for storage of confiscated goods at 39 Hermann-Göring-Straße, near Ghetto Division headquarters. In addition to its responsibilities in the areas of insurance, transport, and personnel, the unit supervised product transfer facilities and oversight of incoming raw materials as well as outgoing finished products.[14]

A third principal division, financial management, operating through a central bookkeeping department, oversaw the main cash desk and accounting matters related to transactions involving foreign currency, handled incoming voluntary monetary donations intended for Jews from relatives and acquaintances beyond the ghetto, processed invoices, and compiled statistics; the division also headed a main registry with responsibility, among other things, for the mailroom and building management. Rounding out the administrative tasks, a department of central purchasing saw to the procurement of foodstuffs, including bread, meat, milk, vegetables, and potatoes, supplementary to an array of items for personal use, including medications, medical instruments, and other supplies. It included a sub-directorate, situated at the point of transfer in the ghetto, for oversight of bookkeeping tasks as well as those related to the receiving, weighing, distribution, and disinfecting of wares at this primary location, and later, on completion of facilities at the railhead beyond the ghetto's northern boundary in 1941, the loading and unloading of goods at the ghetto station.[15]

While the Food and Economy Office and its subsidiary Ghetto Division attended to the administrative and commercial oversight of the dis-

trict, responsibility for ghetto security fell to three principal institutions—
the Schutzpolizei (Schupo), or uniformed German police; the Secret State
Police (Gestapo); and the Criminal Police, or Kriminalpolizei (Kripo)—
each of which immediately established a presence within the ghetto. It
was the primary responsibility of the uniformed police, operating from
the area headquarters of their sixth precinct, a modern structure situated
opposite the entrance to Bałut Market "on the corner of Limanowskiego
and Zgierska streets," to mount armed guards and to patrol the outer perimeter of the ghetto. Posted at intervals of fifty to one hundred meters,
police guards, organized into two special ghetto battalions,[16] reinforced
late in 1940 by the addition of armed police reservists from the Reich,
were authorized to shoot to kill without hesitation anyone suspected of attempting to breach the boundary of the ghetto.[17] If the Schutzpolizei were
the dreaded, ever visible instrument of the regime, the Gestapo was the
institutional embodiment of its veiled intelligence. Already decisive in directing the fate of the inhabitants of the ghetto, by April the Gestapo was
exercising its oversight through the local administrative subdivision of its
bureau for Jewish affairs, occupying for this purpose two rooms inside the
sixth precinct headquarters building. Closely allied to the Gestapo within
the security regime, the Kripo operated as a detective force specializing
above all in halting illegal trade between the ghetto and the outside and in
rooting out and seizing hidden Jewish valuables, whether left behind in
the city prior to the closure of the ghetto or, most especially, concealed
in ghetto apartments and storage areas.[18]

On May 10 the Police President issued a special directive for the Criminal Police Department to detach a twenty-man contingent to the ghetto
for the purpose of "combating smuggling and halting unauthorized movement in and out of the ghetto." Like members of the Gestapo branch office, initially lacking independent office space of their own, Kripo officials
assigned to the ghetto were compelled to work from the premises of the
sixth precinct bureau as well. Although this placed the Kripo unit in the
unenviable position of relying, as it were, solely on the sufferance of another institution, the bureau's growing responsibilities cried out for the establishment of its own independent facility. "In the 3 days during which
officials were active it was determined that the task of the Criminal
Officials is enormous," a Kripo inspector noted. This was evidenced not

only by the "large number" of persons already caught smuggling or "unlawfully" attempting "to leave or enter the ghetto through the wire" but also in the quantities of goods and foreign currency already seized in the course of searches. Given the poor, even "primitive" state of the interrogation facilities then available to them on-site, Kripo agents found themselves shuttling informants and suspects between the ghetto and departmental headquarters in the city. The removal of such persons posed a serious hygienic risk, for at the moment the facility used for disinfecting people leaving the ghetto was still operating under restrictions confining access to Germans. In order to bypass this difficulty, as well as spare individual agents from having "to make long trip[s] to the ghetto over every little matter," a freestanding and well-equipped branch office within the ghetto was desirable.[19]

Indeed, the inspector noted, there existed a suitable location for a separate Criminal Police bureau in an as yet unoccupied parish building at 8–10 Kościelny Street, located just behind the now vacant Church of the Virgin Mary, which had recently been cleaned "from top to bottom" by a team of Jewish workmen. An inspection revealed that while the six rooms on the entrance level were in rather bad repair and "somewhat damp," the seven upstairs rooms—"4 large and 3 small"—as well as others in the attic, would prove quite adequate to house the criminal branch and make possible the orderly conduct of routine office work. Additional improvements, including the installation of a cloakroom and toilet, locks on the doors, furniture (taken from confiscated inventory), and telephones would follow. Another item of importance was a cellar with two rooms and outfitted with barred windows, which would serve as a temporary detention facility. It was expected that the bureau's duties would be such as to necessitate early morning and late evening as well as nighttime patrols. For this reason it was preferable for men assigned to the unit to "live in the vicinity of the ghetto." It was recommended that some of the unmarried men, if not others as well, should be afforded residential space in the building so that they could be on call in the event of any nighttime emergencies.[20] Accordingly, the ghetto bureau of the Litzmannstadt Kripo quickly established its quarters in the parish building. The outward modesty of this two-story structure, its red-brick façade quaintly matching that of the towering church in whose shadow it stood, belied its new purpose. As ghetto residents soon came to understand and fear, the bureau, its officers relentlessly engaged in torturous interrogation of those suspected of harboring valuables, was a house of pain.[21]

In tandem with the organizational expansion and development of this impressive German managerial and security apparatus, Rumkowski too succeeded in building a sizable administrative network of his own to oversee, under strict German supervision, the multiple tasks essential to the maintenance of the ghetto population and the functioning of the ghetto economy. Examination of graphic representations of ghetto departments and divisions dated February and May 1941 reveals his administration to have remained especially attentive to addressing the same broad spectrum of responsibilities traditionally associated with the social welfare tasks of the Jewish community. To see to the requirements of those universally regarded as most in need, the ghetto established separate bureaus for supervising the housing and care of orphans, the elderly, and the homeless, for whom, respectively, the ghetto welfare division managed a central orphanage, an old-age home, and a shelter. An associated welfare bureau supervised the disbursement of relief payments to those deemed unable to work. In addition, the ghetto Health Department oversaw an impressively inclusive medical network of no fewer than five hospitals, a nursery for the care of infants, four outpatient clinics, two ambulance stations, and seven pharmacies. The principal facility, Hospital I, centrally located just north of Bałut Market at 34–36 Łagiewnicka Street, included specialized internal medicine, surgery, gynecology, pediatrics, optometry, neurology, urology, dermatology, and ear, nose, and throat departments. The main hospital also housed x-ray and electrotherapy divisions. The Health Department established a bacteriological laboratory as well. Occupying a place of central importance in the lives of the population, the ghetto Food Supply Department controlled the receipt, storage, and distribution of foodstuffs, maintaining for this purpose a monitored ghetto-wide system of distribution centers for the disbursement of heavily rationed essentials, above all vegetables, bread, milk, and, when available, horsemeat, as well as tobacco products and coal. Assisting in the feeding of the population, a Department of Kitchens would oversee collective dining facilities offering eligible ghetto residents the opportunity to consume prepared meals away from home.[22]

Supervision of ghetto housing affairs fell to separate bureaus within the larger Finance and Economy Division with responsibility for regulating the allocation of residential space, collection of rents and taxes, oversight of building superintendents, accomplishment of renovations, and removal of garbage and waste. Monitoring utilities was the responsibility of separate gas and electricity bureaus, while twin purchasing offices specialized in collecting used materials and valuables still in the hands of the ghetto population. Most significantly, a ghetto bank, initially subordinate to the purchasing agency for used articles and clothing, served as the institution through which ghetto residents received payment in the form of internally circulating currency in exchange for voluntary—and, in many instances obligatory—surrender of independently held quantities of valuables such as hard currency, jewelry, household furnishings, raw materials, even used clothing, above all furs and fur pieces. Once collected, articles had then to be packed and transferred, either in their existing state or after any necessary refurbishment in ghetto workshops, to the possession of the German ghetto supervisory agency for subsequent sale or monetary conversion.[23]

Vital to the ghetto's very survival, and essential to providing the income necessary for meeting its expenses and proving to the Germans the ghetto's indispensable contribution to the wartime economy, was the central workshops bureau. Under its guidance the ghetto maintained a network of factories and workshops. Referred to locally as *ressorts,* these design, manufacture, and assembly facilities specialized above all in turning out finished textile articles for both the German armed forces and domestic retailers. Led by its dominant tailoring branch, which contained a dozen individual subdivisions by February 1941, the central workshops bureau additionally coordinated the production of a diverse assortment of hats, gloves, shoes, knitwear, undergarments, leather goods, rubberized coats, quilts, carpeting, and metal products.[24]

In an expression of Rumkowki's wish to serve the young while at the same time maintaining continuity with prewar Jewish life, a ghetto School Department, headquartered at 27 Franciskańska Street, coordinated a comprehensive educational system. Built around a network of schools staffed by experienced Jewish teachers, it offered organized classroom instruction at both elementary and secondary levels, also providing dedicated facilities for those who preferred a religious-oriented curriculum and for youngsters with special needs as well.[25]

Each of these institutions, the product of Rumkowski's energetic promotion of the health, welfare, and occupational development of the community, contributed vitally to its collective survival. Together they constituted the administrative expression of a genuine, as yet not altogether unfounded communal hope that, even in such hard-pressed circumstances, the residents of the ghetto possessed enough energy, talent, faith, and fortitude to persevere. By demonstrating the Jews' responsible conduct of their own affairs and their contributions to the war effort, Rumkowski, the Jewish administration's singular director, a man already attentively gauging the outer limits of the possible, staked all on mollifying the Germans and blunting their inclination for doing harm.

At the same time, recognizing that he needed to showcase his ability to maintain public order, Rumkowski saw to the creation of an internal security establishment as well. Central to this network was a ghetto police force, the Jewish Order Service, or OD (Ordnungsdienst), founded during the previous winter, whose task it was to patrol the district day and night, enforce curfews, monitor internal approaches to gates and perimeters, guard storehouses, supervise lines at distribution centers, search out contraband, combat theft and other crimes, and arrest violators of ghetto regulations. Under the command of departmental headquarters, centrally housed at 1 Lutomierska Street, the ghetto police operated out of five numbered precinct houses. In addition, there was a Special Section, or Sonderabteilung,[26] dedicated to the search for and seizure of concealed valuables, an investigative branch, and a sanitation control department. Central as well to upholding its system of security, the ghetto also ran its own court, staffed by professional Jewish judges, prosecutors, and defense attorneys. Although the court was involved in passing civil judgments, including the adjudication of divorce proceedings, its primary function was to render verdicts in criminal matters, with judges empowered to sentence the guilty to terms of incarceration. For this purpose the court operated a detention center, the Central Prison.[27]

At the very summit of the administrative complex stood the ghetto's Central Secretariat. Known too as the Headquarters Department, or Zentrale, this critical bureau included Rumkowski's main office, housed, as of May 7, 1940, directly on Bałut Market, as well as a host of principal subdivisions clustered nearby. From these commanding administrative heights Rumkowski surveyed the vast apparatus of the ghetto's welfare, labor, and security network, formulated internal policies, oversaw staffing and employment, and coordinated production. Maintaining a continuous line of communication with departments and agencies throughout the ghetto, and working through its subsidiary Presidential Department, the Secretariat conceived and issued for their attention a stream of directives, in turn receiving from them information on their activity and progress. Sharing offices with the Presidential and Personnel departments, a Secretariat for Petitions and Requests fielded personal appeals from ghetto residents seeking assistance, whether in the form of supplemental rations, improved housing or employment, or admission of aged relations into the ghetto old people's home or for children to the orphanage or care facilities. The main cash desk, the burial division, and administration of the ghetto cemetery were assigned to oversight of the Central Secretariat as well.[28]

Surviving internal photographs afford brief glimpses of top Jewish staff members in their office environs. Posed snapshots reveal them to be well dressed, with male employees typically attired in suits and ties, the female staff trimly outfitted in skirts and blouses or dresses. Background details suggest as well an impression of orderly surroundings, the offices furnished with sturdy desks and chairs, cabinets, shelving, wall maps depicting the boundaries of the ghetto, and, resting on desktops, letter holders, ink blotters, document stands, typewriters, and telephones.[29] It is striking, yet revealing of the regard for such hardware, to note several staff members, especially the women, posing with telephone receivers held to their ears. No doubt the telephones, devices restricted to official bureaus and factory offices, were a cherished symbol of importance and authority. But on occasion a different impression is conveyed. One woman is smiling while a skinny-legged little boy in shorts, seated in her lap, can be seen holding what in relation to his relatively underdeveloped proportions is an oversized receiver.[30] Some officials decorated their workspace with ornaments. Bernard Fuchs, director of the labor office, was photographed writing at his desk, on which sat a metal airplane with a propeller.[31] In addition to the privilege of working in a cleaner setting than that of the workshops, and the not inconsiderable rewards of higher status and pay, these employees also gained the psychic benefits of enjoying a daily setting of relative normality and routine.

Recognizing from the start the unavoidable necessity of establishing a restricted zone for regulating on-site supervision of the ghetto, the Food and Economy Office's Ghetto Division established a presence on Bałut Market—Baluter Ring, as the Germans called it—a commercial square centrally located just off Zgierska Street in the heart of the enclosed Jewish quarter. Beginning in May 1940 and throughout its existence, from this field location Biebow and a select team of staff members, initially numbering ten persons, conducted the day-to-day tasks of administering the ghetto. For this purpose they would occupy a second set of offices installed within a newly built wooden barracks erected on the site. In thoroughgoing conformity with the goal of financing ghetto operations solely through the acquisition and conversion of available Jewish assets, a newspaper report informed the public that an important transfer complex—its working space rigidly compartmentalized into zones designed to ensure that during the course of important exchanges of goods entering and leaving the ghetto "no Aryan will come into contact with the Jews"—was being assembled from wood removed from nearby, formerly Jewish-owned vacation properties.[32] Signifying the importance the German administrators placed on establishing a close and continuous supervisory channel of authority to the Jewish internal leadership, Rumkowski, whose first ghetto headquarters had originally been located in a corner building on Plac Kościelny, moved in response to the German summons into barrack offices on the square as well, accompanied by his headquarters staff. Admission to this sensitive site, surrounded by wire, its gates monitored by sentries, was strictly regulated. Neither the general ghetto population, nor unauthorized outsiders, nor any but a restricted circle of personnel from the Food and Economy Office's Ghetto Division were to be granted access without express police permission.[33]

Routine operations began at Bałut Market on May 6. From then on the working day typically would commence with an 8 AM conference between representatives of the Ghetto Division and Rumkowski, this being his opportunity to go over his immediate requirements for maintenance of the ghetto and discuss forthcoming payments. By the following morning Rumkowski would have formalized the previous day's oral requests, at this time submitting them in writing, typed on standardized forms. At the

morning conferences Rumkowski also delivered any funds to be handed
over to the German authorities, which were then promptly transported to
the Litzmannstadt City Savings Bank for deposit, the bank in turn mail-
ing the appropriate credit slips to operational headquarters on Hermann-
Göring-Straße. At Bałuty Market, delivery vehicles laden with goods and
foodstuffs from suppliers would roll in; civilian drivers then handed over
to Ghetto Division personnel an inventory of items on board their vehicles, the German staff in turn reviewing their paperwork and supervising
delivery. The contents of vehicles bearing packaged goods would then be
transferred onto ghetto carts; conveyances also hauled bulk items such as
"coal, flour, groats, onions, and the like." Before the carts could pass beyond the transfer area into the ghetto, a change of crew occurred whereby
outside drivers were replaced by ghetto teamsters, who then drove the
wares to designated delivery sites inside the ghetto. They would have just
ten minutes to unload the wares before driving back to Bałuty Market,
where the original drivers, stationed at the entrance gate awaited their return. Back at headquarters on Hermann-Göring-Straße, current deliveries
and invoices were reviewed against contracts for accuracy, with appropriate crediting of suppliers' accounts paid promptly—on the same day if
possible. At that location as well the Purchasing Department would maintain oversight of food deliveries, checking to ensure that available stocks
of provisions remained adequate to satisfy the presumed requirements of
the ghetto population. The bookkeeping department monitored bank
statements and, through the creation of three distinct card files, kept tabs
on suppliers, assortments of goods, and creditor as well as debtor accounts. In May the division was already working toward the creation of a
schedule enabling "a daily overview of the various goods delivered," the
purpose of which, revealingly stressed at the time, was "to prevent the
oversupply of the Jewish population."[34]

During its initial weeks the ghetto mobilized for labor, with the tailoring
and carpentry operations in the lead. To be sure, the beginnings of the labor system were modest; it would take many months before a widespread
network of workshops, later to prove so essential to the functioning of the
ghetto economy, was fully up and running. Yet Rumkowski's efforts in
their creation, reinforced by the will and organizational talents of ghetto

craftsmen, were increasingly winning approval from German authorities as well as local commercial establishments eager to engage skilled Jewish labor. Responding to the call, tailors reported with their sewing machines, and master carpenters long resident in the district donated space and tools and set to work.[35] During the first month, in fulfillment of an initial contract arranged through the Ghetto Division's Labor Procurement Department, ghetto tailors "completed, in all, 519 coats for women and girls and 33 pairs of boys' trousers."[36] Pressing ahead with production, on May 27 Mayor Marder, Food and Economy Office director Moldenhauer, and Biebow consulted with individual representatives of Litzmannstadt ready-to-wear merchants and the Chamber of Industry and Commerce. For an agreed price, and in exchange for finished articles, the commercial representatives declared themselves willing to deliver to the ghetto necessary quantities of raw materials, including "fabric, accessories, and linings."[37]

As a follow-up to these discussions, Rumkowski, brought in to review technical details of production, introduced three of his experts in the field, who promised outstanding results with a confident guarantee of rapid delivery.[38] In June the mayor passed along to Rumkowski a request from a city manufacturer seeking to locate Jewish craftsmen specializing in creating wooden molds used in hat making. A city shoe store, seeking to reestablish former ties with Jewish suppliers, requested ghetto labor for manufacturing footwear. Rumkowski replied that "in his labor department are registered 800 qualified boot stitchers" who were "capable of producing from 400–500 pairs of bootlegs a week."[39] By the end of May, carpentry operations were said to be awaiting the arrival from Posen of expected shipments of wood.[40] Commencing with internal ghetto projects and the remodeling of articles of furniture earlier confiscated from Jewish owners, ghetto carpenters and other skilled craftsmen quickly proved a favored resource on which government agencies came to draw in outfitting newly established German administrative bureaus in the city, among them, by early June, the offices of the Ghetto Division, and by later in the year, among others, police headquarters (which received, according to one listing, ghetto-supplied desks, office chairs, typewriter tables, shelving, file cabinets, and wastepaper baskets).[41]

Launching the labor program represented a promising start, yet as Rumkowski frankly admitted, there were problems he was still at pains to overcome heading into the summer. On June 12 he would submit a review of popular sentiment and general progress to date, indicating in broad terms his success in providing for the immediate needs of the ghetto population and winning its confidence and cooperation. The task had not been easy. To begin with, during the first two weeks he had been forced to confront obstacles to ensuring fair distribution and stability of prices for basic foodstuffs. This had proved especially troublesome in the distribution of bread, the one indispensable commodity that, in the absence of adequate supplies of wider staples, people found increasingly central to their diet. Unfortunately, as a result of the loss of former Jewish bakeries in the city, remaining bakeries in the ghetto were too few to satisfy the ghetto's requirements. Long distribution lines—worrisome because injurious to morale and a potential flashpoint for disorder—testified to underlying difficulties. Rumkowski was aware that unscrupulous individuals had aggravated the crisis, manipulating available quantities of scarce commodities in a bid to raise prices. Counteracting their efforts, though, he claimed success in having seen to the delivery of additional quantities of flour to ghetto bakeries, at the same time compelling producers to bake more bread without delay. Ever with an eye to demonstrating his ability to satisfy the population and maintain order within his precincts, Rumkowski pointed with some pride to his having provided shelter for all. Even the ghetto poor could count on a roof over their heads. He had recently been able to assure them that those unable to pay would be freed from the necessity of paying rent—a promise he was in the process of making good on. Indigent residents who fell ill could count as well on access to a panoply of ghetto medical services through hospitals, clinics, and home care visits and to medicines and services rendered "free of charge."[42]

Rumkowski kept an especially cautious watch on the mood of the ghetto's working population. In the first days after the closure of the ghetto, unemployment had been a source of evident discontent, and Rumkowski took wary note of the sight of idle Jewish workers milling about and congregating in the open. But while even into June such gatherings had not ceased, the ongoing development of the first workshops had provoked a fortuitous turn away from political questions and toward consideration of the emerging "labor system" and the "the new conditions essential to life in the ghetto." To encourage that trend, he had taken to making speeches, hoping in this way to elaborate on issued directives while consciously steering the public away from politics by offering "new themes" for their consideration. If he could issue but one plea to his German over-lords, it would be that the current work program be expanded even fur-ther. For Rumkowski, labor offered the prospect of generating the income he needed to feed his people. Achieving that, surely he would succeed in establishing "total calm" and securing the people's "trust."[43]

There was, however, a further concern. Conditions in the overcrowded district with its already substandard sanitary infrastructure remained de-plorable, inevitably contributing to outbreaks of precisely those conta-gious diseases the Germans remained anxious about and determined to keep in check. Dysentery quickly proved the greatest killer that spring. Cases were rising dramatically, leaping from 56 reported instances in May to an astonishing 2,195 in June, resulting in a combined total of 243 deaths.[44] Yet even these figures represented but the tip of the iceberg, for, including an accounting of mortality from all causes, no fewer than 433 persons would die in the ghetto in May and another 888 in June. Dysen-tery was to prove especially cruel, striking hardest small children up to age eight, 99 of whom were included in the reported two-month death toll, and the elderly over age sixty, of whom, according to official count, 92 had died by the end of June.[45]

With instances of contagion on the rise, issues of sanitation and waste removal became a leading topic of concern to the German authorities, as ever alarmed when it came to outbreaks of infectious diseases bearing the potential to affect the entire city. In consultation with Rumkowski and his medical advisers, municipal public health officers, with the approval of ghetto management and the Gestapo, undertook practical steps designed to alleviate the growing potential for outbreaks at what they deemed to be their source. With the warm summer months approaching, they focused their concern on rapidly rising volumes of garbage and human waste inad-equately stored and accumulating in courtyard receptacles that were near the point of overflowing and gave off an overpowering stench. The prob-lem was deemed especially acute because uncollected waste had been detected in crowded ghetto residential buildings located just inside the fencing along city thoroughfares intersecting the ghetto.[46] Responding af-firmatively to the recommendation of a ghetto physician, Dr. Ludwik

Falk, the city medical officer, Obermedizinalrat Dr. Merkert, took the lead in obtaining exceptional police authorization to permit carefully supervised, temporary opening and closing of sections of fencing in front of some 160 buildings bordering the affected roadways. This was deemed the most efficient way to enable loaded Jewish sanitation carts to exit the courtyards of those buildings and immediately proceed toward their destination, a dumping ground located in a remote section of the ghetto, during lightly trafficked late night and early morning hours.[47]

With these efforts under way, late on the night of July 18, Biebow, accompanied by the director of Gestapo operations in the ghetto, Albert Richter, undertook an on-site inspection of the procedures.[48] That night, along a stretch of ghetto properties inside the fence along Zgierska Street, waste removal was slated to begin at 11 PM. Contrary to all expected procedures, the two encountered evidence of an exasperating lack of preparedness and coordination, signs of serious oversights attributable to both German and Jewish administrative failings. Inquiring of a guard as to whether he had been informed that Jewish police and sanitation personnel were permitted to approach the fence in order to exit with their carts, Richter learned that in fact the guard's superiors had given him no such notice. The man asserted instead his unequivocal readiness to employ the usual force to counter anyone approaching the perimeter. It was just as evident that neither the residents nor, most especially, caretakers who should have been at the ready to admit the sanitation crews had been told that their buildings were slated for nighttime sanitary clearance. As a result, men from the Jewish Order Service had found it necessary to pound repeatedly on doors in order to compel the custodians to emerge and open the gates. While regular Jewish police were present, the Jewish Sonderpolizei, who should have been on hand in order to lend assistance, were nowhere to be found; a check revealed that their headquarters had been left unoccupied without explanation at the time of the operation. Inexplicably absent as well were the skilled Jewish laborers and supervisors who would have been necessary for the proper dismantling and repair of the fences. In the face of these shortcomings, for once Biebow was sufficiently piqued to question, with a detectable note of sarcasm, the reliability of Rumkowski's vaunted reputation for efficient compliance with German directives.[49]

Biebow observed ghetto sanitation personnel closely as they went about their tasks. He asked them pointed questions, later pondering technical solutions to the problems they encountered and suggesting a number of improvements. He noted glaring, unacceptable deficiencies in their tools and equipment. Given that three of the five vehicles lacked necessary vacuums and pumps, in emptying their contents ghetto sanitation workers had been forced to approach the cesspits while lying on their stomachs, their heads just above the surface, reaching over the top to scoop the muck into buckets. Once filled, these had to be passed along by hand, the slop inevitably overspilling the rims and dirtying the courtyards. Judging the procedure "totally inadequate" and "on hygienic grounds intolerable," Biebow deemed the acquisition of pumps essential and wanted either the city Building Department or the Raw Materials Procurement Office to look into providing the necessary devices. Biebow additionally wondered whether it might not be possible to outfit the men with carbide lamps to help them see what they were doing. As matters stood, defective lighting alone rendered their tasks "enormously difficult." In any event, the courtyards would have to undergo thorough cleaning. For this purpose he thought it advisable for Rumkowski to see to it that caretakers were supplied with the necessary brooms and pails of water, in addition to quantities of disinfectant.[50]

It was bad enough that, once under way, the loaded, leaky carts rolled along the streets leaving behind a disagreeable and unsanitary trail of muck. Driving on ahead of the carts in order to await their arrival at the dumping site, Biebow and Richter further learned that the sanitation workers went about their job incautiously and, even when acting with good intentions, seemed overmatched by the primitive nature of technical arrangements at the end of the line. "Whether out of lack of understanding or for reasons of convenience—that will have to be determined—instead of using the approach roads the wagons drove straight across the fields," with the result that they sank into the rain-soaked ground. Biebow speculated that "had we not been present, the drivers probably would have emptied the tanks wherever they found it most convenient. Only when asked why they did not drive right up to the pit did they explain that they feared that their wagons would roll into [it]." One could see why. Biebow suggested that to prevent such an eventuality "a type of ramp or rise" be constructed, preferably outfitted with a thick board to prevent carts from slipping back as they backed up toward the edge. No detail seemed too minor to escape Biebow's attention. His instinct for order keenly engaged on behalf of even the most disagreeable of assignments, he contemplated a further improvement: "Perhaps the installation of a gutter would be advisable as well so that the fecal matter actually goes where it is supposed to, rather than be left to lie in front of the pit or cling to the sloping terrain." One more item drew his attention: the short handles of the implements with which the men were forced to work when "closing and opening the tanks ought to be lengthened, because otherwise the person who opens the valve prior to emptying [the container] is totally covered in filth [*sich total beschmutzt*]." The result: "a new source of danger with regard to the transmission of dysentery." In this instance Biebow thought "[it] should be an easy matter for a locksmith to fashion an extension piece, removable as needed." He was insistent about the necessity of spreading a good deal of disinfectant around the unloading site. But "in spite of continuous delivery of considerable quantities," none was to be found there. Closing this altogether negative assessment of the night's inspection, characterized in his view by failings "up and down the line," he felt compelled to conclude that until matters were rectified, "one will hardly succeed in rolling back the dysentery epidemic to a minimum, as the interests of the city of Litzmannstadt would demand."[51]

On the evening of July 22, making his own inspection, Rumkowski discovered that at 9 PM seven filled sanitation wagons had been turned away and prevented from emptying their loads at the distant disposal pit because guards at the scene were threatening to shoot if the wagons did not depart that instant. As a result, the full, stinking carts then had to be driven all the way back to the corner of Łagiewnicka and Brzezińska streets, just east of Kościelny Square, which was exactly where Rumkowski found them parked and contaminating the vicinity, the nighttime air heavy with a "frightfully oppressive" odor. "I therefore proceeded straight to the sixth police precinct," he wrote in describing the incident, "and an official proceeded from there to the pit in order to apprise the guards that the manure carts have to be emptied at the pit, and they were not to interfere with the *Aktion*." That solved the immediate problem, but time was lost, delaying once again the carts' availability for scheduled waste removal operations that night.[52]

Attending to such matters, though surely unpleasant, was a necessity. Both the quality of life and the prospect of improving the health of the ghetto population very much depended on mastering the challenges posed by the district's substandard sanitation. In this area at least, Rumkowski's desire to protect and promote the general health of the community in his care continued to coincide with the interest of the German managers and municipal health establishment in stemming the tide of contagion.

Yet Rumkowski was eager to make the ghetto not just bearable but a place where, though within the narrow bounds of his autonomy, Jewish life might find a home and even thrive. The future of the Jewish people was its young, as he had always known, and with the approach of summer he foresaw the opportunity, even here, to do all in his power to continue his life's work on behalf of the welfare of Jewish children. That admirable goal, of course, was hardly his alone, and his success in caring for them owes much to the energetic efforts of Jewish educators who helped organize and staff the newly established ghetto school system, already serving a total of 11,783 preschool, elementary, and high school pupils enrolled for the 1939–40 school year. Instruction was divided among 163 classrooms located in seventeen buildings. Pupils were additionally afforded hygienic and medical examinations, as well as meals prepared in school kitchens. Teachers, too, took it upon themselves to identify those youngsters in need of proper clothing and shoes, undertaking collection drives and distributing to them whatever they could.[53] At the end of June 1940, responding to an initiative emerging from the ranks of ghetto educators as well, Rumkowski announced the commencement of a program of open registration of youngsters wishing to enroll in special summer colonies, recreational camps where, under watchful supervision by adult staff, they would be fed regular, nutritious meals prepared in kitchens on-site, bathed, given haircuts, and issued fresh articles of clothing. These colonies were organized that year into rotating sessions. The facilities were of two varieties: one in which the children, quartered in dormitories, remained overnight during their stay, the other, referred to as "children's convalescent homes" *(Kindererholungsheime)* or "half-colonies" *(Halbkoloinien),* in which participating youngsters, arriving by eight o'clock each morning, would return to their families at the conclusion of the day, generally at six. That first season, lasting from July to October, the great majority of those cared for in the half-colonies were among the ghetto's very youngest residents: 5,403 were between the ages of three and seven; of the remaining 890 day visitors, all but five fell between the ages of eight and fourteen. Those admitted to the overnight colonies, situated in the semirural Marysin quarter and open year-round, were on average somewhat older. Here, beginning in August and September 1940, a total of 1,212 boys and girls, the majority approximately ten to thirteen years old, received accommodation. By December over a hundred full orphans (children lacking both parents) would be recorded among the residential colony population. Their numbers would rise more than fourfold by late the following summer.[54]

Rumkowksi was justifiably proud of these initial accomplishments in the field of social welfare. He was all the more determined to carry on the task of organizing with as much autonomy as might be achieved within the administrative bounds of his emerging relationship to his German masters. The limited extent of the room in which he could maneuver in order to achieve his goals was by now well established, but perhaps in his view not entirely fixed. From early on in the life of the ghetto, Rumkowski, by nature a man quick to take offense, proved alert to personal slights or signs of disrespect directed toward his person or his office. On occasion he displayed a remarkable willingness to challenge lower-ranking German agents when they acted in a way he considered out of line. If they talked down to him or issued an order he thought likely to countermand essential tasks of higher priority, he let both Biebow and the Gestapo know about it. Rumkowski was not incorrect in thinking that the good working relationship he had thus far established with the German administration, based on dutiful cooperation and an early track record of accomplishments, would afford him a positive hearing. As a result, if a police officer behaved disrespectfully toward him or brushed off his questioning an impossible directive, Rumkowski would report the man, and at least initially, Biebow was prepared to back him up.

Such had been the upshot of an unpleasant encounter Rumkowski endured in the course of a heated discussion with a German police sergeant on July 11. Summoned that afternoon to the sixth precinct headquarters, Rumkowski was ordered by Hauptwachtmeister Jäger to have at the ready on July 15 a complement of wagons for the purpose of hauling to Bałut Market the belongings of some Poles who had managed to remain within the ghetto district, and who were at last about to be resettled. Objecting to the demand, Rumkowski tried to explain that these carts were already fully engaged in the critical work of conveying essential food supplies to his warehouses, and from there to numerous distribution centers through-out the ghetto. In addition, he noted, carts were already reserved for nightly sewage removal. Rumkowski told the sergeant that under the cir-cumstances, the instruction was impossible to carry out, arguing that "the Poles could surely take their things to Balut Ring by themselves." With that, however, Jäger accused Rumkowski of being "insolent," of resisting an order, and of "issuing insults." Licking his wounds, Rumkowski turned to higher-ranking officials for support. "As you are well aware," he wrote, "during the entire period of my activity I have received no reproaches and the authorities know that I carry out the orders correctly and 100%. I think, therefore, that I have not earned such insults and sharp rebukes. This incident is unfortunately not the first, and I permit myself, then, to bring this to your attention."[55]

Indeed, Biebow for one thought it "in the long run insufferable" that police officers should treat Rumkowski as they did, noting that on the day of the incident "the Eldest of the Jews was so upset that for once he was barely capable of taking on and carrying out" his assignments. In Biebow's opinion, Rumkowski was altogether justified in his assertion that

> he endeavors to carry out punctually everything he is charged with accomplishing, and indeed one has to acknowledge the zeal and the effort which he gives to the accomplishment of all tasks. . . . So that he not suffer diminishment in his authority, I consider it expedient for the Police President to instruct the police officers [*Wachbeamten*] on Balut Ring that they should in no way allow themselves to be drawn into further insults directed against the Eldest. In my view, no patrolman or sergeant has the right to confront the Jews, and espe-cially not the Jewish Eldest, in such a way or manner that, instead of working to my department's advantage, leads in a considerable de-gree to its detriment.[56]

In a sign of his growing confidence in winning the protection of his German superiors, Rumkowski boldly confronted another German po-liceman who had been making trouble for ghetto residents. Prior to the

installation of wooden pedestrian overpasses, those who had to cross intersecting city streets in order to get from one sector of the ghetto to
another had been compelled first to pass through guarded wooden gates;
this required waiting patiently until a crowd gathered behind them and
German traffic officers finally gave them permission to proceed. In consequence, people had been left vulnerable to minor abuses—forced, for
example, to break into a run on command rather than being allowed
to proceed across the roadway at a normal pace. Learning that a German traffic policeman had been ordering ghetto "pedestrians—including
women and children" to cross on the double,[57] Rumkowski went to investigate the matter for himself. Confirming the mistreatment, he confronted the officer, pointedly asking him "why he did not let the pedestrians walk across the street normally." The policeman abruptly ordered
him to go away. Rumkowski persisted. "After I told him that I am 'the Eldest of the Jews' and therefore have the right and the duty to inquire,
he answered me in an insulting manner and said I should leave immediately." This Rumkowski did, but not before taking down the officer's
badge number, specifically noting it in a report on the incident which he
then directed to the Gestapo, "politely" requesting an investigation into
the matter.[58]

Notwithstanding Rumkowki's occasional challenges to the authority of
lesser-ranking officers—and a few minor victories—when acting within
their acknowledged sphere and operating with the backing of allied institutions governing the affairs of the ghetto, the police proved fully capable
of enforcing their will. It bears noting that during the first months of their
confinement, many ghetto residents—some undoubtedly prior inhabitants of the district, others newcomers to it from elsewhere in the city—
had managed to retain their pet dogs. These beloved and loyal companions sharing with their owners the fate of confinement in the ghetto were
the first to experience collective selection, removal, and physical destruction at the hands of the Germans. In conformity with an increasingly familiar pattern, the authorities issued the decisive edicts in response to
official concerns for the protection of public health and safety. In this instance the police claimed that rabies had struck the population of domestic animals in the ghetto. It was an assertion that Rumkowski attempted

to counter, indicating that apart from one animal, originally classified in June as a suspected carrier yet subsequently vaccinated and found to be free of the illness, not a single case of rabies had been discovered in the district.[59] The claim carried no weight with the police. The operation went forward, though it began harmlessly enough. In the first week of July the German police initially demanded a ghetto-wide accounting of both animals and their owners. Pursuant to that demand, on July 2 Rumkowski issued an order that all dog owners appear at the office building at 4 Plac Kościelny, Room 1, no later than Thursday, July 4, for the purpose of registering their animals. The ghetto was in turn to submit to the authorities lists indicating each owner's name, place of residence, and the breed and sex of any dogs in his or her possession. A simultaneous directive, however, demanded that, because of the outbreak of rabies, all dogs in the ghetto were to be outfitted with muzzles and led about at all times on a leash. One woman, Salomea Szmulian, residing at 22a Zawiszy Czarnego, registered her mixed-breed Maltese, while Chawa Feingold, three doors down the street at number 28, did the same on behalf of her fox terrier. Both Motel Solewicz and Szlama Cweig, fellow tenants at 100 Franzciskańska, owned watchdogs. Majer Perle, residing farther down the street at number 47, had a dachshund, while Zacharia Gorszkiewicz, Perle's neighbor across the street at number 49, had a mongrel. Watchdogs seem to have been popular; Josef Zelkowicz, the journalist and writer, living at 36–38 Goplańska, registered one. Surviving canine inventories list at least three hundred pet dogs of a variety of breeds, including, in addition to those already mentioned, bulldogs, Dobermans, wolfhounds, terriers, numerous mixed breeds and strays, rat-catchers, and one Pekinese.[60]

As ordered, Rumkowski duly forwarded information gained in this initial canine census, along with supplementary lists compiled with the aid of a required follow-up conducted in the residences by building administrators. Then, on July 18, the police issued a further demand: Rumkowski was to see to it that every dog in the ghetto be brought in by its owner for a direct inspection to take place in four days, on the morning of July 22. He was told quite pointedly that he was to be held "personally responsible" for adherence to this deadline and for ensuring that the inspection was conducted without incident. Pursuant to this demand, and without offering any public explanation of what they might expect, Rumkowski

issued general notification that all owners would be compelled to bring in
their dogs, muzzled and leashed, by nine o'clock on the appointed morning to a rear courtyard at 8 Kościelny Street, accessible from an entrance
on Brzezińska Street. Owners were further informed of their obligation to
pay at this time a fee of two marks per dog. In this too the police warned
Rumkowski that it would be his personal responsibility to hand over the
entire sum to a police official at the conclusion of the inspection.[61]

This was, however, no ordinary inspection. The dogs were being led to
their destruction. The truth was contained in a German police ordinance issued on August 14 and officially revealed to the Jewish population through a general announcement, issued in Rumkowski's name and
posted in the ghetto on August 27, stating: "Due to a prevailing outbreak
of rabies in Litzmannstadt, on July 22, 1940, the dogs that were in the
ghetto were put to death. The killing of these dogs ensues pursuant
to considerations dictated by the sanitary police." At that same time
Rumkowski stressed once more that possession of a dog was strictly forbidden, demanding that any dogs remaining in the ghetto be brought to
the Criminal Police building on Plac Kościelny no later than eight o'clock
on the morning of August 29. Anyone found still harboring a dog after
the deadline would be subject to severe punishment. Strays discovered
roaming the premises of a residence were to be handed over by the house
committee to "the nearest precinct of my Order Service" forthwith. His
announcement made no pretense of the fate awaiting the dogs that had
escaped the July *Aktion*. He concluded with a stern directive charging "all
tenants living in the building" with co-responsibility for the "delivery" of
the dogs.[62] Lest any pets, potentially rabid or otherwise, should find their
way in from the outside, even Litzmannstadt city residents were informed
that occupants of the ghetto were expressly forbidden to keep them. A
newspaper announcement of the Police President's order explicitly warned
the public: "Persons, whatever their nationality, who attempt to smuggle
dogs into the ghetto will be severely punished."[63]

German security officials had declared that dogs should be registered,
then issued the order that they be delivered. When his appeal for recon-
sideration of the edict was rejected, Rumkowski had passed on the order
to the ghetto community, demanding in turn unquestioning cooperation
in the surrender of the animals. However sad an occasion for their owners,
the *Aktion* had led to no loss of human life. It was still too soon to foresee

a day when the Germans would insist on the surrender into their possession not of dogs but of people.

On the afternoon of Wednesday, May 29, a high-powered delegation
headed by Hitler's chief of staff, Philipp Bouhler, director of the Führer
Chancellery in Berlin, and two leading associates, among them Reichs-
amtsleiter Viktor Brack, arrived in Litzmannstadt for two days of informational meetings with city officials. In a series of presentations Bouhler
and his distinguished entourage were provided an overview of a range of
prospects and accomplishments centering on efforts to modernize and remake the former city of Łódź, special attention being devoted to urban
reconstruction, hygiene, and demographic changes. A viewing of displays set up at city hall by building director Hallbauer helped illustrate
some of the principal themes; later an evening lecture by Dr. Schnell, director of the city health program, focused "on questions of racial and
population policy." The following morning the guests were taken to see
the ghetto. A tour of the city followed, as well as an inspection of nearby
camps for ethnic Germans in Pabianice and Waldhorst, affording Bouhler
an opportunity to speak with numerous residents. Among additional
stops that second day were a horse breeding stable and the local branch
of the Reich Propaganda Office, where Bouhler had occasion to meet with
Regierungspräsident Uebelhoer and vice president Moser, and view a selection of filmed presentations highlighting aspects of the city's development.[64]

Departing the city later that day, Bouhler settled in for the train ride
that would take him from Litzmannstadt to Berlin. After passing the rail
junction at Kutno to the north, the train headed due west as darkness fell.
A local editor from Litzmannstadt, aboard for the journey, succeeded in
gaining Bouhler's consent to an interview, though recorded for publication only in a brief summary. Bouhler told him "that, coming from the
Generalgouvernement, he had visited our city, above all in order to study
on the spot some of the urgent problems [facing] the region, namely the
Jewish question and, in connection to that, the ghetto." Bouhler additionally "expressed his joy that in relation to matters of hygiene and other
things as well in Litzmannstadt everywhere men are at work who know
what they want, who apply themselves totally to [the development of] the

German East and are focused upon it with energy and drive." Following a discussion of the challenges and opportunities facing the ethnic German settlers, Bouhler expressed his expectations for Litzmannstadt's future success.[65]

The Jews were gone from the city streets, but one could not quite get them out of one's thoughts. They had been for so long so very much a part of the daily scene, their disappearance did not go unnoticed or unrecalled. Sometimes the mere sound of a particular phrase sufficed to bring them unexpectedly to mind. One day at the end of June a writer was startled to hear, coming from the street below, what he thought to be the unmistakable sounds of a Jewish peddler who had once walked the neighborhood. "Curious," he went out onto the balcony to investigate. The Jew, a dealer in used articles, would often pass beneath the windows, a "dirty sack on his back," crying out for people to come sell their old clothing and assorted castoffs in exchange for small sums he offered. But no, upon taking a good look, the writer could see that this was not that man but a non-Jew, unmistakably "Aryan" and, to judge by his interaction with neighbors below, thoroughly comfortable in his native German. Evidently the new tradesman had not only taken the place of the now absent rival but also had uncannily imitated his predecessor's Yiddish-accented greeting. A local curiosity, to be sure, though in the writer's estimation a phenomenon to be dismissed as little more than one "last, displeasing vestige of a past era!"[66]

But then real Jews were sometimes spotted in town, some drifting in illegally from elsewhere or making a clandestine escape from the ghetto. Leading an illicit existence, if they were discovered in hiding or moving about surreptitiously without wearing identifying markers, they were brought before a summary court and sentenced to a term of imprisonment. On June 19 the public was informed that the court had convicted "a Jew and three Jewesses" of having left the ghetto. They were additionally charged with failing to wear the Star of David. They received punishments ranging from eight to ten months in prison. In the first week in July it was reported as well that a Jewish woman, said to have been a professional prostitute of some ten years' experience, had reached Litzmannstadt from Warsaw after illegally crossing the border into the Reich

and was living unlawfully in the city and continuing to exercise her trade.
Apart from quite naturally failing, like other Jews revealed to be living an
illegal existence, to wear the identifying Star of David, she was additionally found to have neglected to submit to required medical examination.
The court sentenced her to fourteen months' incarceration. On July 17 it
was reported that a Jewish woman, also escaped from the ghetto, who had
taken up residence with unnamed "acquaintances" in the nearby town of
Pabianice, had been caught attempting to make her way to Löwenstadt
(Brzeziny) in the company of another Jewish woman from the ghetto.
The two were convicted and received sentences of eight months for their
crime. More unusually, a Polish woman, reported to have taken up residence inside the ghetto in order to live with a Jewish man, and in consequence forfeiting her right to reside elsewhere, had been sentenced to a
term of eight months for leaving the district illegally.[67]

The underlying message was clear: the Jews were passing from the
scene, and not a moment too soon. Adolf Kargel, a prominent local
feature writer for the *Litzmannstädter Zeitung*, highlighting the many
changes the city was undergoing in the new era of National Socialism,
glibly welcomed the disappearance of the Jews from a nearby town: "Today Alexandrow is one of the few cities in the vicinity of Litzmannstadt
that is already fully free of Jews. The oriental ghost has turned to dust."[68]

4

The Ghetto Will Endure

At the end of July the traveling Althoff Circus came to town, raising its tents at Blücherplatz, accessibly situated west of the city center near the main railway station. True to advance publicity promising "People! Animals and Unique Sensations!" the troupe offered a rich and varied spectacle: "Truxa" the tightrope walker; hilarious clowns playing music on oversized instruments; and a variety of animal acts featuring elephants, lions, tigers, and monkeys. For the finale of the successful opening night premiere, a playful troupe of seven bears paraded into the ring. Their trainer, armed with a whip, was at the point of commencing the performance when all at once, without warning, one of the bears attacked his assistant, a young man of twenty-one. The other beasts quickly joined in the frenzy, viciously mauling the unfortunate victim before the eyes of horrified spectators. Only the quick-wittedness and courage of the animal trainer and the circus owner, armed with a whip, some clubs, and an iron pitchfork, managed to gain the upper hand and rescue the badly injured youth. The young man was rushed to a city hospital, where surgeons, liberally applying stitches, successfully treated his wounds.[1] It had been a moment of stunning terror, an incident that suggested the fragility of even the most finely calculated powers of precision and control. Order and equilibrium had to be restored, and at the circus that evening, they were.

Similarly, in the city itself the regime promised its citizenry renewal in spite of unforeseen hazards. An era of chaos and disorder had ended, a new one of order and stability, and no less of beauty and design, had commenced. Yet even in the face of the best preparation and planning, tragedy, even senseless loss of life, might erupt with little notice. Everyone knew immediately who was to blame. Rather like the unpredictable creatures removed from the wild, the Jews, even now, long after being confined within their ghetto, were thought capable of destabilizing the equilibrium of daily life and causing mortal harm. Not only did they remain the presumed breeding ground of menacing contagion, but also the legacy of their supposed destructive handiwork proved an additional source of danger. On August 8, only a week after the tragedy at the circus, on Gartenstraße, where a dilapidated residential building was being demolished, there occurred a terrible accident: the structure collapsed, crushing workmen beneath billowing dust and heavy debris. The mishap was attributed to the alleged carelessness of an unnamed Jewish architect. One of the laborers—a man with a wife and family, the public was reminded— had died as a result. This was said to be yet another instance in which the blood of decent men and women was on the hands of the Jews.[2]

Yet all in all, the face of the city was thought to be changing for the better. In this remade city there was much to do, much to experience and see: remodeled athletic facilities provided opportunities for swimming, tennis, track, and bicycling.[3] Indeed, that August Litzmannstadt played host to a regional Hitler Youth sporting competition, attended by Gauleiter Greiser, Regierungspräsident Uebelhoer, and other local dignitaries.[4] A major recreational project was under way that summer as workers, busy at a location south of the city center, laid the groundwork for construction of a water park.[5] Other city parks offered quiet relaxation, a place to stroll or to enjoy a moment alone on a bench with a newspaper.[6] The regional tramway, too, provided a convenient means to explore outlying woods and hiking destinations.[7] Most promising of all, Litzmannstadt was now on the map. Increasingly, entertainers arrived, making the city a stop on their tours of the East.

Amid the general picture of a rapidly improving, hardworking, but also recreationally, culturally, and aesthetically developing city, the ghetto persisted. It had not gone away, and in spite of the best of its planners' prior intentions, there was little likelihood of its immediate disappearance. That was a problem, because the attendant costs of keeping so large a population confined and maintained, even at a level of minimal subsistence, were becoming increasingly untenable. The ghetto was running out of money to pay its bills. Something was going to have to be done to rectify the imbalance, for as surely as one season followed the next, the cold of the coming autumn and winter was certain to raise the costs even higher.

By the fourth month of the ghetto's existence, the Jews were fast approaching the limits of their available resources. To be sure, every possible source of revenue was pursued to the fullest, including workshop production; the collection of rents, fees, and outside charitable contributions; and the acquisition of personal articles of value, whether extracted from the ghetto population in exchange for cash (albeit now only in the form of internally circulating ghetto currency) or seized as a result of the relentless activities of the Kripo and the now active Sonderkommando unit of the Jewish police. Combined, these had enabled Rumkowski to meet the ghetto's ongoing obligations through the month of July. Yet by the end of August such sources were no longer providing sufficient funds to prevent the community from falling into arrears. The emerging shortfall, in excess of a quarter-million marks, was glaring. In a frank assessment, reviewing the financial state of the ghetto Biebow conceded that the community had been so thoroughly squeezed of available resources that even the continuing seizure of convertible raw materials and portable wealth still thought hidden among the Jewish population was, by itself, unlikely to prove sufficient to meet the monthly budgetary expenses entailed in supplying and feeding the residents. In so concluding he cited Rumkowski's own estimate that "already 70% of the Jewish population possess no additional cash," making them "a burden on the Jewish community." Even while reserving judgment on the full accuracy of so high a reported percentage of the population deemed fully destitute, Biebow nonetheless considered the estimate plausible, since, as he understood matters, early on the community's wealthier individuals had largely succeeded in fleeing the city. Given the increasingly "hopeless situation facing the Jews," he thought that for the average ghetto resident the chief preoccupation remained "as much as possible to hold one's head above water," each person "anxiously" husbanding whatever remaining private resources were in his possession and consequently "thinking not in the least of sacrificing himself for the good of the general population."[8]

Despite being generally contemptuous of the people over whom he held sway and who, by his own assessment, had proved deficient in the virtues of mutual sacrifice, in such desperate material circumstances Biebow nonetheless viewed warily the consequences of allowing matters to deteriorate. With the approach of winter threatening a food crisis and an attendant outbreak of the ever-feared epidemic with the potential to leap the boundaries of the ghetto, the population could not be left to starve. A previously discussed government loan, to be issued through the Main Trusteeship Office East's Litzmannstädter Warenhandelsgesellschaft, was now considered a looming necessity. On the surface, such a tender appeared to violate ghetto management's principled commitment to maintaining the ghetto without recourse to state resources. But in fact even these funds, amounting to a six-month loan in the amount of 3 million marks, to be repaid by the Jewish community at a rate of 4.5 percent interest, derived from the proceeds of confiscated Jewish-owned assets.[9]

In the meantime, with the ghetto proving incapable of covering its obligations, its administrators attempted a harsher tactic, instituting a temporary halt to food shipments over the course of several days. This reduced the ghetto's expenses to RM726,000 for the month of September, but by month's end the ghetto was still showing a deficit of RM566,000. The effort was of little use. By October 14 the debt had advanced to just short of RM800,000 and was climbing ever higher. This was, incidentally, a matter of concern not just to the Food and Economy Office and the ghetto, for outside suppliers, many of whose firms had limited reserves of cash, and whose bills had come due, were awaiting payment. Under the circumstances, by the middle of October ghetto management felt compelled to request of the Regierungspräsident the immediate infusion of the sum of 2 million marks to meet the current shortfall in revenue as well as to provide a limited financial cushion going forward. In addition, with an eye to placing orders for vegetables in advance of the onset of cold weather, the managers urged that an additional 3 million marks be placed at their disposal.[10]

Even in advance of receiving the loan, compelled to respond to the immediate crisis of poverty, hunger, and the prospect of unrest, on September 20 Rumkowski announced the establishment of public support payments to enable in particular the nearly 100,000 residents who, by his estimate, were now without any other means to do so, to purchase basic food rations through the community. This was an ambitious goal, amounting to a cost of some 1 million marks per month. Indigent working-age adults, numbering some 60,000, would each receive a monthly stipend in the amount of 9 marks; youngsters up to the age of fourteen, some 15,000 in all, a grant of 7 marks per month; and dependent persons over sixty years of age, amounting to some 7,000 individuals, would receive stipends of 10 marks each per month. Approximately 15,000 additional persons, including children in ghetto colonies, orphanages, and infant care facilities, as well as residents of the old age home, would otherwise be furnished with institutionally provided meals for the month. Once registered, eligible recipients would receive their welfare payments, distributed to their residences by the ghetto postal service. As a further concession to the increasingly dire financial straits of the general population, those on welfare were "exempted from rental payments." Ghetto residents were also reminded that subsidized midday meals—offered at price levels of 15, 20, and 25 pfennigs per seating—as well as inexpensive breakfasts, were available at public community and building committee–organized kitchens.[11]

The challenges to meeting the ghetto's obligations were mounting. Nor were they likely to be of brief duration. By the autumn of 1940 it had become increasingly difficult for those responsible for managing the ghetto to avoid having to acknowledge that it was to endure longer than originally foreseen. "Since one may no longer reckon with an immediate transfer of the Jews from Litzmannstadt, those measures, formerly undertaken and more provisional in character, must now be transformed into lasting ones," the city maintained in its October monthly report.[12] In consequence, a "productionist" strategy was to be pursued with all due speed.[13] The broadest possible exploitation of ghetto labor was thought to be the most effective way to generate income to cover the costs of maintaining the community while minimizing reliance on government-arranged subsidies to meet its monthly obligations. The emerging policy demanded an elevation of the administrative profile of the bureau responsible for ghetto provisioning and labor from its status as a subsidiary branch of the city's Food and Economy Office to that of an autonomous division reporting directly to the mayor. The Food and Economy Office's Ghetto Department, under Biebow's ongoing directorship, was henceforth to be known as the Ghetto Administration (Gettoverwaltung), a separate municipal entity internally designated as Stadtamt (City Bureau) 027. Plans were to go forward for its eventual occupation of separate office space and for the expansion of its ranks from the current base of 109 employees and workers to a projected staff of about two hundred.[14]

In order to expand the ghetto's base of manufacture, Jewish officials were authorized to enter available workshops situated within the confines of the ghetto for the purpose of inspecting and starting up any machinery found useful to production. The necessary approval of German agencies currently in control of stocks of raw materials usable for such production was to be forthcoming. In addition, arrangements were to be made to allow for the employment of Jewish labor outside the ghetto. Although the Police President cautioned that he had not as yet even the minimum of personnel to spare for guarding such contingents, he agreed nevertheless to apply for additional manpower to meet the requirement. It was recommended, however, that for the most part Jewish heads of families be selected for external work assignment, as such individuals were deemed less likely to pose a flight risk. Administrative preparations for ensuring additional sources of income to support ghetto operations were also in progress. Henceforth "gold articles and jewelry extracted from the ghetto were to be sold on the open market." Hoping to create an additional source of income, the Ghetto Administration was to assume jurisdiction over outlying smaller ghettos in the Regierungsbezirk, organizing labor projects for Jews in these areas with an eye to gaining surplus revenue for ghetto operations in Litzmannstadt.[15]

Equally essential, by the end of October the Ghetto Administration achieved resolution of its claim that valuables and textiles seized in Criminal Police operations inside the ghetto should be transferred without equivocation to its possession. It had been a source of longstanding irritation for ghetto management that the Kripo, broadly asserting its right to maintain possession of articles it deemed evidence of a crime, had continued to hold property confiscated from Jews. It was essential to the Ghetto Administration that nothing of value be withheld, for when sold, these items constituted a significant source of revenue to support ongoing ghetto maintenance. Now at last, in exchange for recognition that it alone had responsibility for conducting such searches and seizures in the ghetto, and the right to designate who might carry out seizure of Jewish movable property in the city as well, the Criminal Police conceded that all such confiscated goods should be turned over to the Ghetto Administration. In turn, the administration declared itself disposed to meet the request of the Criminal Police, first, that each of its men be provided with outerwear and suits as well as pay supplements equivalent to those of city workers employed in the ghetto; and second, that Criminal Police employees should be granted the right to purchase at a discount selected articles from stocks of confiscated items.[16]

A policy had crystallized, a way had been determined. The ghetto was going to be increasingly a revenue-generating enterprise. There was necessity in this as well as logic. Although no extras would be lavished on the Jews, the city was resigned to supplying the essentials, as long as payment was forthcoming. But the ghetto should receive just enough to keep the Jewish workers fed and the workshops humming. By October as well the Germans had hit upon a formula of provisioning: residents of the ghetto were to be supplied only with a bare minimum of rations conforming to standards established for feeding inmates in German penitentiaries.[17] The Jews of the ghetto would work, they would produce, and they would yield up the remainder of their portable wealth. Gold, silver, crystal, furs, cottons and woolens, everything worth acquiring or refurbishing was to be collected, stored, and then sold to provide for their upkeep. The Jews would be made to give and give, and the Germans would take from the ghetto whatever of value was there for the taking; increasingly that entailed whatever could be made or remade in ghetto workshops, then collected, warehoused, and sold.

Temporary expedient though it remained, the ghetto was to go on a while longer. How much longer no one could say, though surely into the coming year. It would be, all the same, an unwanted thing, an embarrassment, an eyesore, something to be swept away at the first opportunity. Until then, it was not to be permitted to be a drain on the resources of the city, which would have to suffer its presence for the time being. Its continued existence was not to interfere with greater tasks.

For the ghetto community, the acquisition and delivery of food remained essential to life: every quantity was precious, and even more so as winter approached. To assist the weakest members of the community, Rumkowski announced a new schedule of welfare payments, extending support for an additional forty days from October 20 to December 1. In addition, the new schedule offered slightly more generous supplements, particularly for the elderly, now categorized by age groups ranging from sixty-one to seventy, seventy-one to seventy-nine, and eighty years and older, with individual disbursements correspondingly rising the more senior the individual's age bracket.[18] In mid-November, Rumkowski announced his intention to distribute for consumption over the winter months an additional ration of cabbage and, most important, fifty kilograms of potatoes per person in order to supplement over the longer term the standard monthly allotment of basic commodities such as salt, rye flour, groats, sugar, oil, and coal. Intended to last from December through February, these additional supplies were to be kept in people's homes. Quantities of other items for long-term storage awaited further announcement. To cover the costs of the winter distribution, however, a one-time charge of twenty marks was to be levied on each resident; for welfare recipients, that amount would be subtracted from their monthly subsidies in four installments, beginning in December. Workers and community staff employees, being entitled to the distribution as well, would find a like sum deducted from their monthly pay packets, in three installments for those earning up to sixty marks per month, in two installments for those earning more. Persons neither drawing welfare nor receiving wages or salary would be charged one time and in full.[19]

In the end, however, the promised winter ration of potatoes largely failed to materialize. All Rumkowski could do was to remind the city Health Department that the productivity of his workforce remained imperiled by the failure to receive adequate quantities of bread and fats. He noted that in spite of this privation, workers commonly refrained from consuming portions of their own meager rations in order to share whatever they possessed with members of their families. Rumkowski urged, as a step toward improving the bread supply, alleviating the ghetto's dependence on deliveries of bread manufactured in the city by once more directly supplying flour to the ghetto.[20] In this way he could at least reopen recently closed ghetto bakeries and manufacture bread for the ghetto population on-site, independently of outside providers. This would permit him to reduce his welfare rolls while creating renewed employment for a thousand unemployed bakery workers, on whom some three thousand additional family members were dependent. At the same time he could supplement the budget by providing a source of revenue derived from the sale of ingredients to ghetto producers and, in the wider sense, better serve the nutritional requirements of the community and, most particularly, its labor force. This was especially important in so far as the Ghetto Division of the Food and Economy Office, the Gestapo, and the city Health Department had themselves confirmed that some of the bread currently supplied by city merchants was of such inferior quality as to constitute in itself an ongoing bodily threat; Rumkowski spoke of "bread harmful to health," whose mere consumption had resulted in outbreaks of stomach ailments.[21]

From the beginning of the ghetto's existence, provisioning had been unstable and subject to the uncertainties of supply and demand. Initially, the Jewish administration had relied on people obtaining basic necessities from locally licensed ghetto shops. While food supplies were ultimately dependent on whatever the Germans would deliver, in exchange for revenue extracted from the ghetto, this unfortunately left room for price manipulation, as unscrupulous profiteers could buy up large quantities of articles, await the exhaustion of available supplies, and then sell desperately needed items at vastly inflated prices. In response, a solution was attempted: food would be collected and distributed through residential building and block committees, under the assumption that trusted representatives, themselves subject to local oversight, would provide greater efficiency and control of the market. This too, experience showed, did not eliminate cheating, and had the secondary disadvantage that individuals and families, dependent on these agents, could not pick up their food by themselves.[22]

In the autumn of 1940 an alternate system, based on ration coupons, was developed. Over the course of November and December, and subject to subsequent technical modifications in 1941, the coupon system would thereafter constitute the principal mechanism for distributing scarce supplies of food to the ghetto population.[23] While retaining the entitlements to higher pay and rations for those employed in offices within the Jewish administration and in skilled positions in ghetto workshops and factories, the new system promised a modicum of equity in the distribution of critical essentials. This is not to deny the persistent insufficiencies, in both quantity and quality, of the bread, milk, and produce necessary to sustain the health of the workforce and the general ghetto population; but the coupons offered the best hope of avoiding, though never eliminating, market tampering and exploitative practices.

On Rumkowski's order, on November 5 the provisioning department initiated a ghetto-wide registration whereby chairpersons of house committees, working closely with property managers, consulted residential registries and completed forms documenting all occupants residing in their buildings. This information in turn provided the groundwork for compiling a centralized master file, comprising separate listings for each individual ghetto resident, on which basis ration cards were issued and monitored. Each card was to be valid for presentation solely at designated neighborhood grocery, bread, and milk distribution centers, dispersed by sector throughout the ghetto.[24]

In preparation for the issuance of the cards, 150 ghetto students in their final year of high school were brought together in a school assembly hall at 76 Franciskańska Street, where, over the course of only ten days, they would complete the laborious process of filling out by hand bread and foodstuff ration cards for the entire ghetto population. The completed cards were then grouped according to residential sector and stored in anticipation of the moment when Rumkowski would issue the order to commence distributing them. On December 15 a team of 563 distribution agents fanned out across the ghetto, entering its residences, handing out the cards, and collecting signatures, as well as noting any irregularities and then reporting on the operation's success.[25]

Back at the provisioning department, the bookkeeping division, supplemented by a team of some twenty employees on loan from the ghetto registry (Meldebüro), spent several days working after hours investigating cases pertaining to undistributed cards. They successfully identified persons who had changed residence between November 5, the date of the baseline residential survey, and December 15, the day when cards were delivered. Most of those who had failed to receive their cards were tracked down at their new addresses. Their cards were then selected for routing by way of internal ghetto post.[26]

While the Jewish administration mobilized for a new method of distributing scarce provisions, with the approach of winter the drive to strip ghetto residents of personal property and valuables proceeded apace. To the authorities this process was hardly to be viewed as the organized theft that it was, but rather was seen as legitimately laying claim to residual Jewish wealth. Value extracted from the acquisition and further sale of Jewish property was earmarked for deposit in a ghetto account—a so-called *Ernährungskonto*—on which the Ghetto Administration was free to draw in offsetting regular expenses associated with upkeep of the Jewish quarter. Textiles—in the form of raw materials, semi-finished products, or used articles—whether salable in their current state or upon refurbishing, as well as furs, constituted one major category; valuables, in the form of convertible gold, silver, and other precious metals, jewelry, and foreign currency, were another. By autumn it had been agreed that, upon receipt, items that were ready for sale were to be directed immediately to a Ghetto Administration city warehouse. Items in need of reworking would first pass through ghetto workshops. Upon registration, and when ready for conversion, reworked textile goods were sold to the Litzmannstädter Warenhandelsgesellschaft; articles containing precious metals and stones, including "diamond rings, gold pocket and wristwatches, silver bowls, and the like," were to be professionally assessed and made available for commercial sale within the Warthegau, or alternately transferred to the Gold- und Silber-Scheideanstalt in Berlin in exchange for payment.[27]

It was not long before desirable goods streaming into the Ghetto Administration warehouse began attracting independent buyers. Lured by the prospect of purchasing items of value, "all sorts of people" had begun showing up, often on their own and without prior authorization from ghetto management at the premises of its warehouse for Jewish property on Hermann-Göring-Straße. Unopposed in principle to the sale of certain items to eligible members of the public, Biebow would not tolerate transactions occurring outside proper channels. To ensure tighter oversight, on October 28 he ordered Hermann Straube, the administrative officer responsible for the facility, to turn away anyone coming to the warehouse for the purpose of making a purchase who did not present written authorization. Undocumented clients were to be directed instead to the main office. In addition, to avoid unnecessary "nuisances," Straube was "under no circumstances" to offer special consideration to interested purchasers employed by the ghetto management staff.[28] The following month, November 1940, the warehouse on Hermann-Göring-Straße would report having served 235 customers, resulting in a retail turnover of RM7,361.[29]

In addition to concerns over unregulated sales, ghetto management was alert to suspicions that outsiders or even workers in its employ might be engaging in outright theft from its storage areas, vehicles, and offices. It was recommended that a regulation be issued that additional locks, activated simultaneously by trusted employees, be installed at the entrance to the main warehouse. A similar dual lock and key system, requiring two persons to be present simultaneously for operation, was recommended for safes containing valuables inside the facility as well.[30]

Outside the official channels of directed interchange and commerce, smugglers conducted their own clandestine trade in Jewish-owned wares. Profit was the most obvious incentive. As one local ethnic German who was willing to benefit from the illicit traffic in smuggled goods would later recall, "I saw it from the point of view of a businessman." The Jews "couldn't nibble on a ring, but if they could get a piece of bread for it, then they could survive for a day or two." So "if I got something in my hand for 100 marks and it was worth 5000 marks, then I'd be stupid not to buy it. . . . You don't have to be a businessman—that's what life's about."[31]

Quick to exploit any points of weakness, brazen even in the face of potential capture, determined smugglers continued to ply their trade. Guards were on the lookout, and the Criminal Police were constantly on their trail, but sentinels were as yet too thinly distributed to halt the traffic along isolated stretches of the ghetto perimeter. A principal locus of concern was a poorly secured southwestern sector that was "almost nightly" a scene of such activity. Difficult to patrol, particularly after dark—individual guards were having to cover as much as five hundred meters of weakly constructed fencepost and wire border at a time—the location enclosed an open area of weeds and grass close by an empty residential property lying just outside the perimeter. One night Kriminaloberassistant W. Neumann stationed himself nearby to observe the tactics of the smugglers as they went about their tasks. He watched as they emerged from a corner location to take up positions in the unoccupied building. From there they signaled by flashlight to Jewish smugglers inside the ghetto. With that, their Jewish confederates emerged to retrieve items, left either "in the open terrain or at the rear entrances to the buildings." Neumann requested realignment of the fencing to exclude the empty field that was the site of such activity. As an afterthought, he mentioned that Polish residents living nearby might gratefully benefit from the freeing up a newly accessible "garden area" resulting from the change.[32]

Writing for the pages of a ghetto youth publication, *Kol Hechazit,* a girl who signed herself Szoszana F. meditated on the darkness of those restless autumn nights when even the light of moon and stars lay hidden in clouds. No force being great enough to challenge the autumn wind, "all sought the shelter of their burrows."[33] Confined to so fragile a home as the ghetto, shut off from the world, one might yet take solace from a reminder of one's link to the still vital, diverse, and numerous community of world Jewry. Hoping to keep spirits high, that November the same journal featured a piece by the French author Edmond Fleg, a fantasy fulfillment of the promise of Jewish liberation, homecoming, and fruitful increase. A man lies down to sleep, and then awakens to discover before his eyes an image of the Jews at the moment of their exilic crossing of the Red Sea in their flight from bondage in Egypt. What strikes him most are their features in all their variation, a wonder of difference visible in the variety of shapes of their lips, their noses, the many colors and textures of their hair, the array of colors reflected in their eyes.[34] Another article meticulously surveyed the numbers of Jews throughout the world, counting, by continent and by nation, those millions residing in the lands of the Americas, Europe, the Middle East, Asia, and Africa.[35] Even in the ghetto, one felt a part of this wider community, of a globe where elsewhere Jews lived in freedom. Once a multitude had crossed over by way of the parting seas; today Jews resided on all continents. There was still a place for Jews on this earth. And most important, it was possible to take comfort in their number.

True to its Zionist orientation, *Kol Hechazit* of course sought to keep alive most especially the hope of eventual travel to the Land of Israel. One knew that far beyond the ghetto lay the palms and sands of Palestine, and that one day, God willing, one might join those fortunates residing there. The ghetto, however, was not the globe. For the foreseeable future, journeys would remain confined to the province of the spirit.

Isolated and enclosed, the ghetto could only dream of establishing contact with the world beyond the reach of its seclusion. Integrated and expanding, by contrast, the city welcomed all who bore glad tidings of the extended Nazi realm that was its model and inspiration. A year after its "liberation," Litzmannstadt was proving an increasingly important stopover for those traveling the length and breadth of the newly peopled lands of the East. Touring youth were an irresistibly popular focus of attraction.

On Monday, November 11, an admittedly quite privileged set of young German travelers, members of a celebrated boys' choir from Regensburg affectionately known as the "Domspatzen," or Cathedral Sparrows, had slipped into town and, after a memorable single evening's performance, just as quickly departed on the final leg of their continent-wide "little world tour." Demonstrating remarkable vocal inventiveness and range, the young singers awakened in the audience rapturous appreciation and sustained applause, particularly in response to a soprano solo of unusual grace.[36] Another popular November evening concert occurred at the Sporthalle with an orchestral performance of the overture to Mozart's *Don Giovanni*. It was said to have all but transported listeners back in time to "the Biedermeier and Rococo era of Old Vienna."[37]

Otherworldly evocations aside, the new authorities, so eager to create a metropolitan ambience even in this remote outpost of German civilization, discovered in musical performance confirmation of the city's developing sophistication, pointing the way toward its full participation in Germany's unrivaled mastery of the arts. Litzmannstadt would demonstrate its place in this great tradition. That November a festive evening ceremony marked the reopening, now under German direction, of a city music school located in the rich setting of the former Palais Poznański on Danzigerstraße. Local dignitaries spoke, and a trio performed before assembled guests. Addressing visitors in the company of the new director of the institute, Gerd Benoit, Mayor Marder expressed the hope that its establishment would contribute to "the German lifestyle and German spirit" of the city.[38] Self-consciously associating itself with achievement in the musical arts, the local regime perceived the usefulness of music in shaking off the city's underlying crudeness and provinciality. That the Jews and the Poles were even now ceaselessly blamed for all the city's past and present limitations hardly sufficed. In evoking and drawing inspiration from the transformative power of music, Litzmannstadt's political elite sensed its spiritual potential as a new Nazi city.

That November as well, during the course of his visit to Litzmannstadt the Nazi minister of education,[39] Bernhard Rust, gave expression to the harsh realities that must rule the new age. Dropping in on a *Gymnasium* class then engaged in a study of the prologue to Goethe's *Faust,* Rust took it upon himself to convey what he interpreted to be the work's central lesson: "He alone wins freedom and life who conquers it each day." Later the minister expounded on his favorite theme: life as a constant test and struggle in which there is no pity and certainly no mercy for the weak or the unwilling: "God has given to the world great diversity in its evolution, and it is through *selection* that the living should evolve." One cannot, however, remain passive. "There is absolutely nothing on earth that is guaranteed by the Creator. Eternal remains the law that to the strong all is rewarded," but "the weak must give everything away."[40]

Convinced of their civilizing mission to cleanse and repair and make habitable a city characterized by deplorable neglect, the new rulers acted on the unquestioned assumption that in the interest of urban improvement, Jews simply could not be permitted to dwell any longer among the general population. This assumption had necessitated their separation and removal to the ghetto; presumably lacking in sound hygienic habits and thereby endangering the health and safety of the public, they would have to be fenced into their sealed residential quarter lest, like menacing creatures of some subspecies, they escape to spread contagion as before. The cage-like nature of the arrangement, fittingly evoked since it was designed to house a people repeatedly stigmatized as biologically inferior and a magnet for vermin and attendant diseases, testifies to the interest the regime had in questions of humanity's relationship to lesser but related species. The state-controlled press found the topic worthy of note, and at year's end readers of the *Litzmannstädter Zeitung* learned of a correspondent's visit to the Munich Zoo, where experimental research was being conducted into the remarkably human-like behavior of the orangutan. For purposes of scientific study, the creatures had been placed in an unusual setting, equipped with civilized comforts, in what was described as "a colony of single-family dwellings, meeting and exercise halls, parks, and swimming pools." Orangutan families were additionally outfitted with "individual bedrooms" furnished with beds, as well as chamber pots for the young and even flush toilets for the adults; a special apparatus ensured the simulation of darkness, providing the twelve-hour cycle of rest the animals required. Recognizing that the orangutan was susceptible to precisely the same diseases, both common and exotic, as humans, the researchers had installed glass partitions that hermetically shielded the creatures from contamination by the numerous spectators who came to observe them. Among the remarkable findings of the experiment was that the animals exhibited the ability to burst spontaneously into song. The orangutan—the term, readers were told, meant "forest man"—had a "painfully exact" internal anatomical resemblance to human beings. In the face of present evidence, confronted with what appeared to be "the near relation of this life form," the reporter hesitated even "to call [it] an animal."[41]

Citizens of Litzmannstadt, who might be expected never to have had occasion to encounter such unusual creatures in the wild, had only to stroll as far as the Helenenhof Park, an outdoor recreational area situated just beyond the ghetto's southern perimeter, to encounter some of the most unusual and intriguing specimens of the animal kingdom on display. An illuminated sign, visible upon approach, invited visitors to enter and view a menagerie of creatures from faraway lands, among them Berber lions, as well as tigers and jackals, an Indian elephant, rhesus monkeys, Tibetan camels, Egyptian donkeys, Arabian dromedaries, even cockatoos and other parrots. There were black and red foxes, too, and wolves that frightfully "howled in the park by night." But citizens were to rest assured: these wild beasts were "in safe custody," securely confined to their cages and compounds.[42]

In truth, the distant world of the jungle, of which the creatures wintering in the park were such tangible representatives, remained a topic of endless fascination, awakening the public imagination to contemplation of only too recent German colonial encounters with subtropical lands. These places continued to evoke not only the possibility of coming upon fearsome wild animals but also the danger of contracting fatal illnesses; they were places too in which one might explore the bounds of human moral behavior. In spite of, and often precisely because of, the perils met in such realms, Africa and the tropics, distant frontiers and lands apart, were thought alluring to adventurers, misfits, and outcasts. Here, beyond the reach of civilized law, such restless souls could expect to find a special kind of freedom in which to maneuver and to survive.[43]

The arrival within the year of German settlers from the perilous regions of the East underscored the existence of savage frontiers much closer to home. The fate of those engaged in vital struggles for survival had already found reflection in even grander cultural spectacles. On November 30, in advance of their appearance at the local premiere of their new feature film *Enemies (Feinde)*, leading actress Brigitte Horney and her co-star Ivan Petrovich walked through the entrance of their downtown hotel into the waiting company of publicity agents and press who had gathered in expectation of their arrival. The film's anticipated showing provided yet another occasion to highlight the oft-recalled plight of the ethnic German settlers, "pioneers" whose bravery in the face of hardship and persecution was by now already being transformed into a cinematic epic. From this perspective it was not the Jews but the Germans who were the victims of terrifying persecution. In the East, vicious gangs, motivated by envy and a thirst for violence, and unrestrained by the authorities, had been loosed upon ethnic Germans of the Polish borderlands. Fleeing for their lives, whole families had been forced to abandon their homes and take to the road on perilous marches west toward Germany, taking with them into exile only what few belongings they had the strength to carry.[44]

On a practical level, heavy work was well under way to create proper homes for the thousands of ethnic settler families still being moved into the city. Attention was drawn to the Herculean efforts of the Haupt-treuhandstelle to clean and renovate former Jewish and Polish apartments in a northern quarter of the downtown area. There, in a zone recognizable by the many red-framed placards marked "confiscated" affixed to buildings throughout the vicinity, some two thousand artisans and skilled workers labored intensively, remodeling units to raise them to what were considered habitable German standards. A journalist touring the housing noted, "We examined apartments which, in the Altreich [Germany proper], would hardly have been used for accommodating cattle: half-decayed beams and floors, scratched-up walls, and filthy kitchens testified to the so-called style of home furnishing of the former inhabitants of these buildings." The tour provided yet another opportunity to remind the public that these unsanitary hovels and their irresponsible inhabitants had been "a breeding ground of contagious diseases." Furthermore, "the Jewish architects of these buildings paid no attention to hygienic requirements. Almost all of them divided a section of the kitchen with wooden walls in order to install [a privy]." Now, thanks to the importation of vast quantities of "wood and pasteboard, tar and pipes, oven tiles and painting supplies," some 2,500 units had been made ready for Volhynian and Galican Germans.[45]

From such descriptions one could hardly fail to conclude that the Jews and the Poles had lived like animals. Indeed, by their alleged indifference to elementary standards of domestic hygiene they had opened house and home to all manner of material decay. Readers whose attention was drawn to this state of affairs could feel little more than disgust for the former inhabitants. The sensation was further heightened by reports pointing out that by living in such conditions, the residents had attracted all manner of infestations. Readers were asked to imagine all the vermin—the rats and roaches—that had lived comfortably in their midst. One of the city's leading building officials, Oberbaurat Keil, forced earlier in the year to confront just such a nuisance upon moving into his own Litzmannstadt apartment, proved tenacious in combating the problem. Committed to doing everything in his power to eradicate pests from residential properties, he experimented widely with insecticides. Trumpeting his success, that autumn he claimed to have fumigated some ten thousand residential units, now declaring "the once heavily infested quarter south of Deutschlandplatz" to be at last "free of bugs" (wanzenfrei).[46]

Relentlessly testing chemicals for their utility in cleansing city housing, Oberbaurat Keil was not alone in attending to the effects of noxious gasses. For ghetto management the handling of gas had become a matter of increasing concern. For purposes of disinfection, warehouse textiles exiting the ghetto were now passing through the sterilization facility located on the southern edge of the quarter near the Old Market Square. A team of ten workers had been assigned the difficult task of sorting, arranging, and finally hanging up items in preparation for disinfection. It was considered an odious job, for it was associated not only with the risk of infection arising from handling what were considered to be potentially infection-ridden articles, but also with unpleasant side effects resulting from exposure to poisonous substances employed at the facility. Already employees had developed symptoms such as nausea and vomiting. In order to help settle their stomachs, the crew had been supplied with milk to drink. Noting their hardship, Stadtoberinspektor Quay was sufficiently moved to recommend that the men be granted a small boost in salary. The evident danger to their health involved in handling the products was surely worthy of at least minimal additional compensation.[47]

Unsparing in his empathy for the queasy stomachs of the administration's disinfection crew, Inspector Quay took a more crude approach to the employment of Jewish labor, noting that "The *working* Jew—viewed from an ideological perspective—constitutes for us a form of exploitable capital which, when organized for large-scale operation, is comparable to a machine that can only be brought up to full speed when adequately greased." In this context, adequately greasing a working Jew meant seeing to it that he had at least enough to eat to keep going. This had been a topic of continuous discussion among German authorities, little concerned though they were with the needs of the nonworking ghetto population, but by autumn increasingly eager to drive the productivity of skilled labor as the ghetto cranked up production. One of the ghetto's main tailoring shops, employing some three to four hundred Jewish workers, had been forced out of service for two days on December 1 and 2 precisely because of the "exhaustion" of the workforce. A day later, in another shop, "some 20 Jewish tailors fainted in the presence of the director of the textile department." In light of the evident physical weakness of some of the ghetto's most highly valued workers, Quay stressed the importance of installing communal kitchens for the exclusive benefit of skilled and heavy laborers directly in the factories where they worked. In this way one might help ensure that they alone, as the ones for whom the additional rations were exclusively intended, would become their sole consumers, preventing necessary workers from sharing their supplements with others. This might "relieve the state of unprofitable subsidies for the upkeep of Jews felt in any case to be a scourge."[48]

Within the ghetto as a whole, apart from the usual debilitating scarcities of food, the season was shaping up to be one of a decidedly diminishing prospect of warmth. An ominous sign came when, under German order, on December 17 Rumkowski was compelled to issue a proclamation demanding that residents hand in all fur items by the first of the year. The ghetto bank was given the task of collecting the articles, assessing their value, and issuing payments in ghetto currency. Internal ghetto estimates indicate that "over 5,000 items passed through the hands of specialists on the busiest days. . . . As to the quality of the fur pieces sold, nearly 50 percent fell into the very shabby category, 30 percent were middling, and barely 20 percent were good."[49]

With an eye to acquiring for themselves a portion of the desirable loot, favored agencies and leading officials had already taken supplementary items of clothing and outerwear in advance of the approaching winter season. As early as November policemen had come to Biebow with requests for fur coats, a matter that, when brought to the mayor's attention, received the latter's full approval, though he insisted that priority be given in the issuing of the coats to "those . . . who are actively working with the Ghetto Administration."[50] For their part, the mayor and his wife selected an assortment of custom goods. Overseeing special orders, Biebow's deputy Friedrich Ribbe, in correspondence with Hermann Straube, the director of the Jewish goods storehouse on Hermann-Göring-Straße, sought to follow up on a recent request of interest to the mayor. On December 2 it was reported that the mayor's wife had taken possession of a quantity of "various fabrics" from the warehouse. Ribbe wished to know if, as requested, this delivery had included "1½ meters of dark blue coat material" intended for "a 2-year-old child" as well as "2¼ meters of dark fancy-dress material with light-colored bands."[51] Early in December on two occasions the mayor's wife had additionally acquired fourteen meters of "black artificial silk." In the wake of the latter transaction Ribbe had found himself in possession of remainders he wished Straube to examine for the purpose of estimating their worth. That month, too, perhaps as a gesture of reciprocal courtesy, the mayor in turn approved Biebow's own purchase, at a cost of RM200, of a recently produced overcoat, to be worn "primarily on business trips and journeys."[52] The coat, of black cloth and featuring an otter collar, was trimmed with monkey fur.[53]

The Christmas season had arrived, and the city prepared to mark its coming. By December 12, following the appearance of a large shipment of 2,500 Christmas trees, fortunate citizens were spotted carrying their beloved fir trees home through the city streets. For the enjoyment of the general public as well, two decorated trees were fixed in place at opposite ends of Adolf-Hitler-Straße. The one on Friesenplatz, situated at the lower end of the boulevard, would have stood roughly at the point where, during the previous February, some of the first columns of Jews had assembled and set out on their police-ordered march toward the ghetto. The other official tree adorned the roundabout at the head of the boulevard just outside city hall on Deutschlandplatz, just south of the ghetto. With the onset of darkness, for the first time the trees' glowing lights, symbolic of "one of our oldest and most beautiful holidays," were lit, creating "a festive mood" perceptible "even from afar."[54]

Year's end brought occasion for government agencies to survey their developing record of hard-won accomplishments. Looking back, Police President Albert[55] expressed nothing but the highest regard for his men; they had fulfilled their tasks under the most trying of circumstances. With pride he noted their contributions to the previous December's massive resettlement, meeting trainloads of arriving Baltic Germans and overseeing as well the accompanying expulsion of the Jews to free up space for the privileged newcomers. No matter that the weather had played havoc, the police fulfilled their duties. Under punishing circumstances, forgoing sleep and battling forbidding conditions, they had continued to supervise the arrival of resettlement trains. Waylaid by the elements, trucks carrying additional police sent to relieve overworked colleagues had in turn broken down, not infrequently getting stuck in the snow, forcing policemen to trudge to their assignments by foot on sometimes hours-long journeys through "severe frost and icy winds." Albert also praised the Criminal Police, and above all the men assigned to the ghetto, where they had to labor "under the dirtiest imaginable conditions, placing at risk their own health as well as that of their families."[56]

No review of the city's efforts was complete without reference to the establishment of the ghetto. At a late December assembly in the Sportpalast, government and party dignitaries, among them Regierungspräsident Uebelhoer, and military officers gathered to honor the efforts of the mayor and his city administration in their efforts to reshape Łódź into the newly Germanized and rechristened city of Litzmannstadt. In an atmosphere enlivened by the reading of poems and musical contributions by members of the local symphony, Mayor Marder considered the many obstacles overcome in launching the city's revival. Amid a lengthy summation of the year's activities, the removal of the Jews from the general population, the establishment of the ghetto, the management of its economy, and the recent development of its workforce were duly underscored as being among the most notable achievements. It had been no light task to undertake the provisioning of a population of 160,000 Jews with all manner of "foodstuffs, medicines, fuel, and so forth," but at least they were being put to work. As for the renovation of the city center, through the first difficult months of the year local workers had had their hands full trying to "clear away the filth and stink" from city streets and courtyards, but by spring and summer even Germans had felt comfortable enough to move into downtown sectors previously thought unlivable. The removal of "Jewish and Polish signs" and "rusted shop gates and rickety shutters" had gone a long way toward making the downtown area a presentable place for commerce as well. With the opening of theaters, schools, hospitals, dental clinics, and disinfection installations to serve the citizenry, as well as housing for municipal employees, Litzmannstadt was well on its way to improving the urban infrastructure.[57]

While the mayor trumpeted the creation of the new Nazi city, in the ghetto the Jews, excluded from the presumed blessings of the new era and marked for eventual removal, were left to scrape by on ever-dwindling resources. Already their brief experience of life in the ghetto had been a calamity. During the eight months of its existence, from May through December 1940, 6,851 people were recorded as having died in the ghetto, 928 in the month of December alone.[58] As the first ghetto winter commenced, no end to this suffering was in sight.

5

The Ghetto and the City
of the Future

For both the Germans, intent on refashioning the city in their own image, and for the Jews, desperate in the face of all hardships to make the ghetto a place of survival, the year 1941 would bring an increasing measure of confidence. All the same, the outlook and prospects of the German overlords and their Jewish captives could not have been more divergent. While the German rulers proudly trumpeted Litzmannstadt's demographic transformation and progress toward modernity, the Jews, in their eyes an unwanted holdover from the past, remained sealed away, properly isolated from the life of the city. Confirmed in its status as the institution charged with managing the ghetto and its economy, the Ghetto Administration was expanding, growing stronger and in the accomplishment of its mission increasingly self-assured. The organs of the German security establishment, bolstered by fresh reinforcements, tightened control over the ghetto inside and out, finding fulfillment in the unfettered exercise of their authority.

In spite of ongoing strains and pressures associated with shortages and the punishing cold, come the spring and summer the Jewish leadership too, surveying the development of ghetto industry, cultural institutions, and care for the young, reflected optimistically on the success of its conscious strategy to ride out the crisis of war by working hard for the Germans, and in so doing preserving life even within the confines of the ghetto. That was not to be immediately achieved. Months would pass before Rumkowski could bask for a time in the glow of hard-won if grudging acceptance of his leadership, all the while touting a number of limited achievements. Until then, a season of biting misery awaited the general population of the ghetto. Stripped of all but the barest of coverings, meagerly warmed, meagerly clothed, and meagerly fed, the Jews hung on to the world as if by a shoestring. For when the second winter of the war was upon them, it found them physically weakened, materially bereft, and increasingly at the mercy of circumstances they seemed powerless to alter.

The winter of 1940–41 proved harsh, with temperatures averaging below freezing, and since Christmas the snows had been heavy. Forced out into the frigid temperatures to work and to gather supplies, the residents of the ghetto were prey to painful missteps on the ice, to bodily exhaustion from hunger and frost, and, ultimately, to a painful death.[1] For many, exposure to the elements occasioned a complete and systemic physical collapse. Some keeled over in the streets, others in their homes. "People drop," it was said, "as quietly as doves."[2] On January 17 the bodies of three middle-aged men, two in their early forties, one in his mid-sixties, each a victim of the twin scourges of hunger and cold, were found in the open; that same day another ghetto resident, victim of a heart attack, died ascending the Zgierska Street bridge.[3] People were dying of cold indoors as well. On the morning of January 6 two young men were found dead, "frozen in their dark little rooms," each leaving behind "emaciated, half-dead wives and children." The wives, themselves "already standing on the edge of the grave," appeared incapable of summoning an emotional response to their husbands' passing.[4] On January 7, 110 people, including twenty-two children, were rushed to the hospital "barely alive. All of them are so weakened and frozen that they didn't know where they were and what was happening to them."[5]

While Litzmannstadt was being remodeled and reborn as a place of welcome and comfort to an expanding ethnic German population, a city revitalized by new buildings and housing estates, the ghetto was being literally torn apart, plank by plank, from within. For in the absence of necessary quantities of coal to heat all the workshops, offices, and residences that served as meager shelter for the Jews, Rumkowski gave the go-ahead for the demolition of designated sheds and outbuildings to provide a ration of wood. However well intentioned, his plan was improvised and riddled with mismanagement. What had been conceived as a means to distribute a precious commodity in an orderly way quickly devolved into a chaotic struggle, compelling the weak once more to battle the strong in a desperate effort to procure their promised allotments.[6] Out of dire necessity furnishings too were being chopped to pieces and burned to heat cold ghetto flats and fuel stoves for cooking. Typically, bed frames and other furnishings were dismantled and the scraps fed to the flames. The poor were then reduced to sleeping on loose pillows, sheets, and covers laid on the bare floor.[7]

A common sign of the drastic need to seize hold of anything that might be burned for warmth was the sight of crowded masses of the desperate burrowing in the soil, rummaging about refuse pits in search of any remaining bits of flammable debris. Most prized of all were discarded chips of coal and dustings dumped on the outskirts of Marysin long before the war. Children were not the only ones found here; adults as well lowered themselves into the pits, where they dug and picked at the ground in search of combustible bits and pieces. People who had to hike through Marysin on their way to visit the ghetto cemetery thought the sight of scavengers reduced to rooting about in the dirt a disgrace. The children ought to have been in school, not digging through garbage, their skin exposed and covered in soot and grime.[8]

For Rumkowski the harsh start to the year was a worrisome matter, for shortages had indeed unleashed bitterness, much of it directed his way. In January the carpenters, demanding higher rations and pay, had gone on strike, occupying the workshops. Declaring that he could meet such demands only at the expense of reducing what was left for the population as a whole, Rumkowski refused to budge. This was a test of wills, and his authority was under challenge. He called in the Jewish Order Service. They entered the workplace where the strikers had holed up, removing them bodily and closing the premises. The men were vulnerable. Without work and pay, they and their families would be completely deprived of a livelihood, such as it was. Rumkowski had triumphed, at the same time demonstrating to the Germans his internal mastery and ability to restore order. All the same, he needed the services of skilled labor and was anxious to put the men back to work—but on his terms. They would get a temporary food supplement. He would see what he could do.[9]

The ghetto, its subsistence all but totally dependent on whatever the Germans deigned to ship in for its use, was subject to the perilous swings of a weak and unreliable supply mechanism. For his own part, having constructed his budget in large measure on the prospect of developing income from ghetto labor, Biebow understood only too well that if ghetto workshops were to continue to bring in the income essential to meeting monthly expenses, then Jewish workers simply had to be minimally fed. What to him seemed especially galling was that supplies of food to the ghetto remained insufficient to achieve even the level distributed to prison inmates. In spite of a willingness to do their jobs, ghetto workers were proving incapable of summoning the bare physical capacity to fulfill their tasks. Moreover, the shortage of coal was directly impacting production as well, as the already underfed laborers, unable to bear the strain of working in the cold, were failing to appear for work. Early that year Biebow would express his concerns in conference with a representative of the district government and officials within the Gau supply establishment; his entreaty met with a sufficiently positive response for him to expect alleviation of the shortfall in food. He also obtained the city's promise to set aside for the ghetto a small portion of its available coal. These as well as subsequent promises to meet the ghetto's basic requirements would prove, to Biebow's ongoing consternation, short-lived.[10]

The effort to ensure adequate supplies for the ghetto workforce mattered to Biebow all the more since, heading into the new year, management had reported favorable signs of forward momentum. At the beginning of the year, the Ghetto Administration's Lagerverwaltung on Bałuty Market had reported "remarkably strong" production in the textile sector. A significant factor in this activity was the delivery of raw materials from the German military to be reworked into finished products in ghetto workshops.[11] At the very moment when ghetto residents were compelled to break apart their remaining furniture for fuel, the ghetto was increasingly a supplier of furnishings for German offices and homes. By the end of 1940 the ghetto carpentry works were turning out desks, typing tables, shelves, and filing cabinets, among other items, as well as kitchen furniture, sofas, easy chairs, and small quantities of bedroom and dining room sets.[12]

To accommodate stepped-up production, at the beginning of February 1941 the transport capacity of the ghetto underwent significant enhancement when its new freight rail facility—the Bahnhof Radegast—opened for operation. Supplementing Bałuty Market as a vital point of entry and exit for foodstuffs, raw materials, and finished products manufactured in ghetto workshops, in that first month of operations the station serviced sixty-seven wagonloads of foodstuffs as well as two more containing shipments of rags. Although completion of the Radegast station still awaited a reliable telephone link and installation of lighting necessary for nighttime unloading, as well as stepped-up provision of carts and labor, the new facility promised an expansion of ghetto commerce. In addition to the impressive quantities of work undertaken for the military, by February the Gettoverwaltung's textile division reported having exceeded the million mark in the circulation of goods related to contracts from clients in the private sector.[13]

As the winter progressed, there emerged a few visible signs that, for all the troubles suffered by the community in the initial weeks of the new year, conditions were ameliorating slightly. Mortality had declined: February's total of 1,069 deaths, an appalling figure to be sure, was nevertheless a step down from the 1,218 recorded in January, marginally undercutting the record total of 1,366 who had died the previous July when dysentery still raged. At the beginning of March a "gradual improvement" in the supply of foodstuffs, including increased provision of flour, had permitted renewed production in ghetto bakeries and a modest hike in daily bread rations.[14] And yet this good news was not to last. By March 13 provisioning had declined and the distribution centers were closed, casting the population once again into a disheartened mood.[15]

The ghetto remained tense, minimal improvements being hardly sufficient to alter the daily struggle with death and its harsh realities. On March 5 Młynarska Street became the site of a mass demonstration as some seven hundred persons gathered to demand improved rations and an end to supplemental distributions for privileged members of the community administration. "The crowd sent up hostile shouts against the Community authorities. A series of appeals in Polish and Yiddish were posted condemning the ghetto's own government." The Jewish police arrived, "dispersing the demonstrators in about fifteen minutes," though not without resorting to violence. "Several of the civilians were badly roughed up, and two members of the Order Service received wounds."[16] Another sign of ongoing trouble was the "increase in criminal offenses." Arrests for crimes other than theft and "resisting orders" had risen in February to 486 from 344 in January.[17] Even the recent, minor decline in mortality was meager solace to the families affected, for whom the battle against death was never-ending. Parents of sick youngsters were especially on edge. One father, desperate to save his young daughter, told by the doctors she must by all means be taken to the hospital yet unable to get access to a hospital bed, marched into the hospital office to demand that she be accepted for treatment. Instead, he was taken away to Czarnieckiego Prison. Mournfully, his wife, insisting that his outburst was understandably brought on by his concern for the survival of their daughter, pleaded for his release in advance of his impending trial.[18] Another desperate parent was arrested for failing to report the death of "his only son, a 7-year-old boy." The man had concealed the child's death "in order to use his only son's bread and food coupons. . . . He is now in prison awaiting the sentence of the court," the *Chronicle* recorded on March 1, adding the sad comment that "the mother has been left at liberty in view of her mental illness."[19]

However desperately the Jews struggled to hold on to life, the Nazis remained a fearsome menace. There could be no doubt that the power of life and death over the ghetto and its future lay firmly in their hands. Nor could one overlook the persistence of irrational hatred toward the Jews of the ghetto, as well as the use of violence in enforcing their permanent removal and isolation.

For now the Jews were going nowhere; local security and public health agencies in particular zealously saw to it that their confinement was as tight and narrow as possible. No unauthorized individuals were to enter or leave the zone. Neither should there be the least unauthorized contact between the residents of the ghetto and the citizenry. It remained a serious infraction to walk anywhere near a ghetto fence. The Kriminalpolizei, working closely with police sentries—since November 28, 1940, the guard had been reinforced by the men of the 101st Police Battalion out of Hamburg—kept a careful watch on the snow-covered perimeter.[20] Sentries were usually quick to take aim and fire at anything suspicious that moved within range. On January 9 a young man on his way to visit a friend was ordered by a guard to take off at a run, then was "shot from behind."[21] On January 16 smugglers were fired at; one of them was killed "on the spot," while the others fled into the ghetto.[22] Through the winter and beyond, guards routinely took aim at will. On the evening of March 12 a sentry fired two bullets into a thirteen-year-old boy, Wolf Finkelstein, killing him brutally. The youth had approached the wire to watch a passing streetcar. Alerted to the incident, his parents, pale-faced with terror, came tearing out of their apartment, running to the scene. Finding the boy dead, the parents "pleaded with the sentry to shoot them too." Only the forceful intervention of Jewish policemen, physically removing them, spared them from the granting of that horrible wish.[23]

Ever on the alert for signs that once again the Jewish district might emerge as a source of pestilence to endanger the good citizens of Litzmannstadt, the city Health Department, anticipating the onset of warmer temperatures and an "immense increase" in cases of dysentery and typhus, raised growing alarm over failures of hygiene. Matters were only worsened by the fact that, because toilet doors, seats, and even roofs had been dismantled for their wood, outhouses were left partially exposed.[24] In spite of specific orders that disinfectant be sprinkled on, around, and most especially inside the toilets—as well as in street gutters—Health Department inspections revealed inexcusably little evidence that this had been done. Expressing exasperation, Stadtmedizinalrat Dr. Nieberding implored the Police President "to force" upon "the Jew" compliance with mandatory sanitary regulations. It was, he argued, a matter of complete "indifference to us how many Jews" died of contagion, but he would not stand for "endanger[ing] the rest of the city." Regrettably, he noted, "the pathogens do not come to a halt at the ghetto fence."[25]

Long absent from the life of the city yet far from forgotten, the Jews remained an object of intense and abusive regard. Readers of the *Litzmannstädter Zeitung* were repeatedly encouraged to reflect on the outrageousness of the Jews and the harm they purportedly inflicted on innocent people. Such contemplation would show just how much of a godsend it was that at last the Jews were gone from the city forever. On Friday, Janu-

ary 17, *The Eternal Jew,* a notorious documentary purporting to reveal in
lurid detail the truth about world Jewry, enjoyed its Litzmannstadt premiere. A local reviewer noted with pride that it was "precisely here in our
city that a large portion of the photographs" included in the film originated. The most sensational imagery was employed to recall how the Jews
had proved skillful in the art of deception and disguise, masking their true
appearance. One was to beware the Jew who was clean-shaven and well
dressed, for beneath the "smoking jacket," the "dress shirt[,] or elegant
business suit" of even the most cultured among them lurked hidden the
same backward, vermin-ridden, yet cleverly scheming "eternal Jew" of the
ghetto. Even Jewish children were suspect. Unlike German boys and girls,
who took to the outdoors, so athletic, their skin appealingly tanned by the
sun, Jewish youngsters preferred the dark of the indoors, shying away
from the light, devoted to imitating their elders, at a young age already
practicing their skills of trade and corruption. To see the Jews in this revealing light was to learn that they must and would ultimately disappear.
The review concluded with the Führer's chilling assurance: "We will see to
it that Europe is freed of this scourge forever!"[26]

To that sentiment Wilhelm Hallbauer, intensively at work on plans for
remodeling the city center, could only add his applause. Immediately after
being summoned to his new post in December 1939, he had made it clear
that, as a prerequisite to the city's modernization and the establishment of
security and order essential to its development, Litzmannstadt was going
to have to be emptied of unwanted peoples. Hallbauer was everywhere at
work: overseeing reconstruction of the city's infrastructure and plans for
its development, speaking before visiting delegations to the city, promoting a project of renewal to cleanse the city center of all but Germans while
simultaneously ridding the city of dilapidated housing and office space,
replacing it with remodeled or altogether new structures and housing developments, removing industry to the periphery, establishing green spaces,
and creating an entirely revised system of traffic and transport that would
more effectively link Litzmannstadt to the wider world. Working closely
with his Berlin colleague the architect Walter Bangert, he assisted in de-
signing the blueprint for the centerpiece of the projected redevelopment
of the city. The new "forum," as it was called in Bangert's original conception, was to be built around a new main passenger rail terminal, with the
addition of a nearby hotel, movie theater, government offices, assembly

hall, and parade square, all closely integrated with the adjacent Hitler-Jugend-Park. Beyond the new station and the existing municipal athletic stadium to the west was to rise an entirely new, modern residential neighborhood, the German West City development, to include new schools and twin Hitler Youth centers, with residential capacity for 22,000 residents. Several blocks to the east of the new assembly hall, an expanded cross-town corridor would link the new cultural center with Adolf-Hitler-Straße. In the initial stages, and as an economic necessity in wartime, renovation of existing housing stock would take momentary precedence over new residential construction. On February 1, with great pleasure, Hallbauer reported to Bangert that, building on the successful renovation of some eight thousand residential units in the previous calendar year, current and projected remodeling and construction was likely to achieve a total of thirty thousand units suitable for occupancy by Germans by the end of 1941.[27]

Yet even this commendable work would have been for naught were underlying municipal infrastructure not subject to a thoroughgoing overhaul. For this reason, throughout the past year streets and sidewalks had been torn up and repaved and pipes laid below ground. Because large portions of the city were still reliant on horse-drawn tankers for the delivery of water, conduits were being laid from nearby sources to enable water to flow automatically through city pipes. Accumulated refuse, a source of stifling odors evident even to those walking the streets of the city center at the onset of warmer weather the previous year, had already, in 1940, undergone significant clearance, delivering promised relief from future assaults on the public's sensibilities.[28]

By spring the Gettoverwaltung too was getting into the swing of renewal and renovation. Since its founding a year earlier, the bureau had continued to occupy space with the Food and Economy Office, the parent institution from which it had sprung. Administratively independent since the autumn of 1940 and still growing, that spring the Gettoverwaltung was making final preparations in advance of moving to its own headquarters on May 21. Remodeling at the site of the new building, centrally located just a block east of Adolf-Hitler-Straße in the heart of the downtown district, had been proceeding throughout the winter. On the eve of this important moment in the life of his organization, and undoubtedly infused with a bit of that official confidence in Litzmannstadt's future that filled the air, Biebow expressed to Mayor Marder his personal satisfaction in knowing that the Gettoverwaltung, in preparing its new administrative home, had made its own contribution to Litzmannstadt's renewal. "The senior managers of the Gettoverwaltung have made every imaginable effort to create an office" of high architectural standards, Biebow assured him. "When later the Gettoverwaltung is finally dissolved, the city will have at its disposal a building that can be occupied by a like authority for which, for purposes of representation, impeccable service quarters are a precondition."[29]

Also in May, the occasion of the appointment of a new Oberbürgermeister in Litzmannstadt, Werner Ventzki, provided a welcome opportunity for the local leadership to reflect with satisfaction upon the city's numerous achievements to date. On the first anniversary of the sealing of the ghetto, Regierungspräsident Uebelhoer boasted that in financial terms the ghetto had indeed demonstrated its efficiency, in the end costing the state "not a single pfennig." The Jews were paying for their upkeep through their own "material assets and labor." Gauleiter Greiser expressed astonishment at how things had been transformed for the better, not only in terms of the city's appearance but also in the settling of ethnic Germans on the land. "A new phase in the history of the city is beginning," he remarked. "For us the city of Łódź [Lodsch] as such already lies in the thick mists of the political and national past." Ventzki expressed full awareness of the momentousness "of this hour," proclaiming: "I believe that in their hearts and minds the people who come here can never be young enough. We require people who are free from too much experience, who are free of too many specialized, objective, and professional restraints, for otherwise they will not be up to the tasks" that "this land and this city" surely demand.[30]

There was so much that was new and changing, and the Nazi administrators and planners were eager to record it all. It was a particular challenge because the changes were so rapid that it would be difficult to document just how miraculously the emerging city differed from the one that had existed before. To illustrate the transformation, film was thought the ideal medium. That spring the city contracted with the commercial film division of the renowned Ufa film studios in Berlin to create a documentary, shot on location indoors and out, highlighting its achievements. In June a camera crew arrived to commence work. This was to be just the first of several visits, extending into the autumn of the following year. From the start of the filmmakers' activities it was evident that the city wanted to draw attention to many of the high-profile architectural and infrastructure projects that were tangible expressions of the new social order taking shape under the direction of the local Nazi planners. The Ufa team consulted with Oberbaudirektor Hallbauer and members of the Building Department and, in accord with the chief building director's wish, went out to inspect the city's first block-long redevelopment on Adolf-Hitler-Straße. During the course of the week's activities, they also filmed the city stadium and swimming pool. At Oberberbürgermeister Ventzki's urging, an early-morning presentation of unedited footage was arranged at a local cinema. Invitees included Oberbürgermeister Ventzki, Bürgermeister Marder, Oberbaudirektor Hallbauer and members of his staff, the city horticulture director, and representatives of the press.[31]

After a hiatus during a rainy August, early in September the Ufa film crew returned, equipped with a telephoto lens and improved lighting, for a longer working visit, devoting more than three weeks to intense daily shooting in and near the city. In addition to recording the progress being made on the new bathing beach beside the small lake in the city's southern Erzhausen district, they journeyed to a nearby hill to capture a panorama of the Litzmannstadt skyline. The crew made a point of supplementing their view of the city by filming as close to the ghetto as possible. Filming along its perimeter, they climbed onto a rooftop to capture a view of demolished structures, part of the city's ongoing efforts to construct a firebreak to protect it further from the isolated Jewish quarter. Reinforcing the film's thematic contrast of the old city of Łódź with the new city of Litzmannstadt, the cameras were directed at images of unsightly runoff and broken gutters in the ghetto's immediate vicinity. Because of a very bumpy ride that jolted the camera, the effort to film from a streetcar heading down Alexanderhofstraße (Limanowski) toward the ghetto proved less of a success. Elsewhere in the city they filmed on the street, but also from apartment windows and from moving automobiles. Visits to camps for German resettlers featured shots of food wagons, youngsters on a playground, and women in folk costumes. At the city's main hospital, under the watchful supervision of a doctor, shirtless male patients were shown stepping up to a device to be x-rayed. "Hold your breath, keep still," read a sign the filmmakers added to their visual record. Highlighting Litzmannstadt's burgeoning cultural institutions, they undertook interior and exterior shots of a new municipal theater. At the city music school, amid a setting of heavy curtains, an open doorway leading to a terrace and garden, columns, and parquet floors, children were filmed at their lessons. Since their September visit coincided with the city's hosting a Nazi convocation, the filmmakers recorded a colorful assembly at the Sportpalast, featuring marching Hitler Youth, orchestral and symphonic performances, speeches, fanfares, and the beating of drums.[32]

The film was a high-profile effort serving the interests of local leaders. They eagerly suggested points of interest and reviewed the images right away. That month, too, "invited guests" were privileged to view the film's progress at an additional special showing. As its title, *From Lodz to Litzmannstadt,* was meant to suggest, the contrast between the new city and the ghetto was central to its thematic approach. The many sites being filmed in and around the city were to serve as a perfect counterpoint, highlighting the future city of Litzmannstadt which had triumphantly supplanted the onetime city of Łódź, all but vanished and gone forever, a thing of the past.

Following a tumultuous winter a measure of stability returned to the ghetto, and Rumkowski took satisfaction in it. Undaunted by prior setbacks and the prevailing context of German threats, he sensed renewed confidence in his ability to preserve the ghetto and the lives of its inhabitants. He was honored with a sixty-fourth birthday celebration featuring, in addition to compote and stew, servings of "candy, sandwiches, wine," and liqueur; a glass was raised to his health, with the wish that he have the honor of living "to lead the Jews out of the ghetto back into the city" one day.[33] Ghetto industry was expanding with a new leather and saddle workshop, a paper products division, a metal works division, and a hatters' workshop.[34] Plans were even under way for staging a modest exhibition of products as a way of displaying before German officials the quality and range of ghetto industry.[35] On the whole, apart from ongoing shortages in the supply of coal to heat ghetto homes and factories, well into the spring the availability of food showed some improvement. At the beginning of May, even the open market price of bread, always a barometer for registering supply, temporarily declined, as did that for certain other foodstuffs.[36]

The arts were flourishing. There was music in the air: the popular Kitchen for Intellectuals, an institution founded the previous August, was undergoing expansion. It was a place where people of educated and professional background in particular liked to gather, even if, given the pressure of squeezing in up to four seatings an afternoon, clients were given only thirty minutes to finish their meals. The dining hall—built on the site of a former movie house—proved spacious enough to serve as the setting for musical performances. Dawid Bajgelman, an experienced conductor and composer, led the ghetto orchestra in accompanying locally renowned violin and choral soloists. Other entertainments were offered under the direction of the local actor and director Moshe Pulawer. Finally, a new ghetto postal center was inaugurated, representing a considerable upgrade in distinction to the cramped facilities with which the ghetto postal department and its clientele had had to contend up to then.[37]

Much like his counterpart Adam Czerniaków, head of the Jewish Council in Warsaw, a man who took a personal interest in creating recreational space for the ghetto children, that April Chairman Rumkowski was said to have been "searching for a location suitable for a playground where children could rest and play in the summer." He settled on an available site at 4 Brzezińska Street, arranged for the ghetto metal works "to install low, comfortable benches in the area." He also "ordered that grass be planted and a soup kitchen" created for the benefit of the "1,000 children [who] will make use of" the new facility.[38] However much Rumkowski remained scarred by his battles with internal opponents, with the noticeable pacification of the streets and the increase in incoming rations, he had reason to feel a certain optimism in regard to the effectiveness of his strategy for community survival.

Overriding all criticism, Rumkowski did his best to ensure that the community as a whole recognized him as the ghetto's indispensable guide and master of great achievements. At the beginning of March a ghetto newspaper, the *Getto-tsaytung,* was launched. This in-house publication, issued with the knowledge of the German authorities, was designed as a means for disseminating orders and decrees, and above all for countering those who would undermine the ghetto by attempting "to spread irresponsible ideas" that might lead to "chaos and disturbance." It also kept the public informed about important activities and events in the life of the ghetto, always with a positive spin, forever depicting Rumkowski as tireless in his dedication to promoting the common good.[39] Early in April, in a feature article, readers were taken to Bałut Market, the busy center of life in the ghetto. There one would find Rumkowski in his "modest office," conscientiously at work "from early morning until evening," dutifully "at his desk," poring over vital documents. Rumkowski was said to be a man "by nature" decisive, arriving at his decisions quickly, but only after thoughtful consideration of the matter at hand. He kept a close watch on the activities of his many subordinate bureaus and production facilities. Nothing of import that transpired in "his factories, workshops, offices, divisions, and the like" escaped his studied attention. Bałut Market, command post of ghetto operations, was at the very center of it all. It was also, readers were reminded, a tremendously busy place, the hub of the ghetto's daily commercial life.[40]

Rumkowski had been an indefatigable organizer indeed, and in this preliminary phase he had achieved numerous worthwhile accomplishments in the expansion of ghetto labor and in the area of social welfare. In May 1941, at the peak of his confidence, he traveled to Warsaw, paying a "state visit" to Poland's largest ghetto. He met with officials of the Warsaw Jewish community, including Czerniaków. In Warsaw Rumkowski carried himself with what others found a discomfiting assurance, presenting himself as a man who knew better than all the others how to organize and lead in these difficult times. Inside the Warsaw community offices, Rumkowski would talk about his achievements, praising the Sonderkommando, the special unit of the Jewish police in Łódź empowered to ferret out hidden valuables, and asserting that, in contrast to Warsaw, where the phenomenon was commonplace, "there are no paupers on the streets" of his district. When Warsaw officials reminded him of the high deathrate and declining birthrates in Łódź, Rumkowski would only concede that "there are many people with TB." Rumkowski's arrogance, for that was surely the way Czerniaków saw it, prompted the Warsaw leader to refer to him in his diary as "replete with self-praise, a conceited and witless man. A dangerous man too, since he keeps telling the authorities that all is well in his preserve."[41]

That arrogance was on display during Rumkowski's public address to former Łódź citizens now residing in the Warsaw ghetto. Rumkowski could not help but praise himself, noting his clear-mindedness and foresight. Referring to their origins in Łódź—not scolding them, only wishing they had remained and not fled—he reminded his listeners that he was the one who had seen what was coming and knew how to prepare. "I warned them many times," he said in reference to the Jews of Warsaw, "saying that all signs indicated Warsaw was on its way to becoming a ghetto. Nobody listened to me." Listing his achievements in the Łódź ghetto—"1) Work, 2) Bread, 3) Assistance to the Sick, 4) Care of the Children, 5) Peace in the Ghetto"—Rumkowski recounted how he had cleverly outmaneuvered and broken the back of a troublesome workers' movement in the factories, creating a prison for these troublemakers. In short, he had provided the preconditions for the establishment of a benevolent dictatorship in the "small kingdom" of his ghetto. "Dictatorship is not a dirty word. Through dictatorship I earned the Germans' respect for my work." He seemed especially pleased about the time he had shown the Germans just how tough he could be: "When the Germans were sitting in my office, the workers demanded to be heard. I let them in. I let them speak but toward the end I threw them out, in front of the Germans." To such toughness Rumkowski attributed his most cherished achievement: "The strictest autonomy governs the ghetto; no German would dare touch my prerogatives, and I shall never let any do so."[42] On returning to Łódź from Warsaw, Rumkowski resumed the boastful posturing which had characterized his appearance in the capital. "What, you are starving?" he challenged his community. "Go to Warsaw and you'll see what starvation means. With me you have the Garden of Eden, in Warsaw . . . [t]housands drop from hunger every day. With tears in their eyes the Warsaw Jews beseeched me to stay with them to become their Eldest and take over the leadership of the Warsaw community."[43]

Rumkowski's assertions notwithstanding, the situation in the ghetto was dire, and many of the Jews were indeed starving. Hunger was visible in the appearance of those who daily dragged themselves to work along the ghetto streets. At six o'clock each morning the army of slave laborers could be seen hurrying to work, undernourished and ill dressed, the worst off without shoes and basic attire, comparable to "homeless dogs," one diarist remarked. By the thousands they waited at the gates across the main roadways, impatient to cross, knowing that if they were only a minute late, they would forfeit even their meager ration of bread.[44]

As of May 22 there had been no new food distributions for two weeks. Suicides, aggravated by hunger, were on the rise. On May 26 it was reported that Renia Hecht, a thirty-seven-year-old mother of a three-month-old infant, had thrown herself from a third-story window. Another woman, forty-six years old, chose a similar fate. According to a note she left behind, she had killed herself out of despair over her inability to feed her three children. She cited their unbearable screams and their incessant pleas to be fed: "Mama, give us a little piece of bread." Her act appears to have been motivated in part by the faint hope of winning for her now orphaned children assistance from the community. "Let Rumkowski, who 'cares for' poor children so much, also take care of my children," she wrote.[45]

Searing grief over the loss of near relations, combined with bitterness over the indifference of ghetto leaders to whom he appealed for help, lay behind the desperate act of a young man, twenty years old, who at nine-thirty on the morning of the fifteenth of July leaped from a third-story window onto the pavement, where he lay "crushed" before "the eyes of hundreds of passersby." He had suffered grievously. "A day before Passover his mother died. Six weeks after Passover his only sister was shot, and finally his father became so sick that the doctors have given up hope." In a note he left behind, the young man heaped blame upon prominent ghetto leaders who, when he came to them for assistance, had denied it to him.[46]

Down only slightly from that winter peak of 1,224 dead in the single month of January 1941, there were 999 recorded deaths in May, followed by 930 in June, 897 in July, and 976 in August, in a year in which a total of 11,437 ghetto residents would die. Of this total some 2,134 deaths were officially attributed to malnourishment, ranking just behind the two leading causes of death, identified as heart disease (3,221 recorded cases) and tuberculosis of the lung (2,552 cases).[47] So great was the pressure to dispose of the dead that on May 17, while Rumkowski was still on his visit to Warsaw, three hundred bodies were awaiting burial at the ghetto cemetery. It was a sad scene there. Families waited all day just to spend time in the presence of their departed relatives, only to leave the cemetery knowing that the backlog of bodies would remain in limbo.[48]

In spite of all these difficulties, Rumkowski claimed to see progress and reason for hope that his organizational skills, combined with stern oversight, might succeed in rescuing most of the community from harm. He worked cooperatively with the Germans, even dutifully handing over iso-lated weapons found by the Jewish Order Service to the Criminal Police. Typically this involved surrendering a sword or pistol of uncertain origin discovered during dismantling of a structure or unearthed by someone digging in the ground. A number of gas masks, found in a school building inside the ghetto, were presumed to have been left behind by a Polish mil-itary unit that had temporarily occupied the premises. In duly receiving and registering the weapons, the Kripo took into consideration whether any of them were serviceable. When a handful of bullets were received from the Jewish police, its Gettokommisariat, remarking that they were of the same caliber as some of its own weapons, chose to add them to its arsenal.[49]

Scrupulously obliging, Rumkowksi remained single-minded in his de-termination to win the Germans' grudging acceptance of the ghetto as an institution necessary to the achievement of their own purposes. Unable to prevent widespread suffering, he nonetheless sensed that because the Ger-mans were increasingly reliant on Jewish labor, they would continue to find it in their interest to grant him the resources and the breathing room essential to stabilizing and even improving daily life for the residents of the ghetto. Perhaps too—and this was no small measure of Rumkowski's calculus—the Germans' growing interest in driving the labor program might serve to divert them from doing harm to the more orderly and so-ber pursuit of production and profit. For Rumkowski, therein lay his op-portunity for drawing his overseers into a plan that might lead indirectly to guaranteeing Jewish survival.[50]

Rumkowski had accomplished much for the ghetto, and the Germans were daily validating the soundness of the production strategy central to his goal. Fittingly, as the workshops expanded to fulfill their role as a reli-able producer of goods for civilian and military contractors, the ghetto was frequently visited by official German delegations arriving to inspect its ongoing economic operations. To their minds, the ghetto had been transformed into an increasingly successful industrial enterprise, its work-shops turning out an array of finished goods primarily for the German do-mestic clothing market as well as uniforms for the German armed forces. However desperate the conditions in the ghetto that spring, it continued to function precisely as Rumkowski wished. The Germans seemed pleased. Early in May, Gauleiter Greiser found occasion to pay the ghetto a visit. According to one account he met with Rumkowski at Bałut Market for "more than an hour," and afterwards toured the workshops with Rumkowski in attendance. Greiser reportedly expressed his satisfaction with what he found, remarking, "I would not have believed it if I had not seen it with my own eyes."[51] The next day a delegation of German journalists arrived by bus to make a similar inspection.[52]

Even more impressive delegations were to follow. On June 12 a telegram arrived announcing to local German officials that Heinrich Himmler, chief of the German police and of the SS and Reich Security, was to pay the ghetto a visit at five o'clock the following afternoon. On the day of Himmler's arrival, Rumkowski, undoubtedly much concerned about appearances, began preparing for the arrival in the ghetto of so influential a dignitary. He "acquired for his coachman a white cloak, and called for his carriage to be varnished anew." The Jewish police were arrayed at attention. Joining Rumkowski in the Jewish delegation were Aron Jakubowicz, Dora Fuchs, and an additional female employee. Rumkowski was outfitted for the occasion in a white Panama hat and white gloves; the women were "attired as if for a ball." The Jewish police, on guard against any possible disturbances, stood at attention as the Reichsführer's motorcade, consisting of "six elegant autos," appeared in the Bałut Market. A security official summoned Rumkowski to approach: "Eldest of the Jews, come closer, I want to introduce you to Minister Himmler." Rumkowski bowed, removing his hat and gloves, and approached. A photograph of the occasion shows Rumkowski standing beside the vehicle, a green BMW convertible with the top open, bearing license plate SS-1, with Himmler seated on the passenger side in front.

"How are things going for you in the ghetto?" Himmler wished to know.

"Everything is in the best of order, Herr Minister," Rumkowski replied.

"How does the food situation look?" was Himmler's next question.

"The workers have enough to eat."

"And do you feel healthy?"

"Thank you," responded the chairman of the Jews, and "with that ended the discussion at the Bałut Market." Himmler then accompanied party officers and officials as they drove off to visit a tailor shop and two carpentry establishments. "Greatly satisfied" with the inspections, the visitors told jokes, laughed with Biebow, and slapped him on the back. Meanwhile, the guests ignored Rumkowski, not even bothering to look at him the entire time. As the Germans drove back to Bałut Market in their cars, the Jewish leader, by now "completely forgotten," was left trailing after them in his carriage.[53]

Rumkowski, of course, was to them a subordinate being, an instrument of German policy. He served at their pleasure, and the ghetto community he guided would continue to exist only so long as his German superiors remained convinced that it served their interests. Thus far it had been Rumkowski's singular achievement to have demonstrated that those interests were indeed being served. The expansive program of production that, with his energetic support, Biebow and the Gettoverwaltung had championed was yielding noticeable results. Military orders for production in ghetto workshops were on the rise, as was a welcome increase in the ghetto's wage-earning, working population. Even Mayor Marder, otherwise inclined to complain that the existence of the ghetto had lost the city considerable commercial and taxable revenue while burdening it with additional outlays for rerouting and equipment for public transportation, street lighting, and police protection, acknowledged that the ghetto had by now achieved a level of economic viability. He had expected, he wrote Uebelhoer on July 4, 1941, that the ghetto would be dissolved by October 1 of the previous year, but that being unachievable, "its character" had so "fundamentally changed" that it was "no longer to be regarded as a type of holding or concentration camp but an essential component of the economy as a whole, that is to say, a large-scale enterprise *sui generis*."[54]

By the summer of 1941 the ghetto and its governors had succeeded in establishing a kind of fragile equilibrium. That the ghetto was not just still standing but indeed on at least a firmer footing with regard to productive capacity and self-sufficiency was for Rumkowski a minor triumph. Every meal served to the needy, every hour a ghetto child spent enjoying the out-of-doors or learning in a ghetto classroom, seemed proof that his cooperative strategy was working to the benefit of the community he served. To his German masters, the not inconsiderable contributions the ghetto was making in support of the wartime economy, once hardly imaginable, let alone desirable, were not altogether unwelcome. Whatever the future would bring, for now the ghetto appeared to have succeeded in justifying its continued existence.

All the same, there were no guarantees. The accommodation the ghetto administrators had made in acceding to the prospect of the ghetto's continued existence was to prove exceedingly tenuous. An insistent undertone of hatred toward the Jews continued to fill the air, as the rational impulse to exploit them coexisted uncertainly with the insistent fantasy of being rid of them one way or another. Locally, Litzmannstadt had big plans for the future. Neither the ghetto nor the Jews were to have a share in any part of it. Farther away, in Berlin, where both the city and its ghetto had become the object of increasing interest, decisions were being formulated that would have a vast impact on the ghetto, profoundly upsetting its stability.

Indeed, all the hard-won successes in developing the ghetto economy were gravely imperiled when, by autumn the community was compelled to absorb additional transports of Jews from the region and from the interior of the Reich. Because they were certain to strain the already limited resources available to maintain essential production, the prospect became a matter of deep and growing concern to the entire leadership cadre of the Gau, the district, and the city. It was especially worrisome to Hans Biebow, lower down the administrative ladder but closest to the point of impact. He immediately understood that such an influx was likely to overburden the ghetto's assiduously developed yet by no means stable system of production and subsistence. At worst the burden might lead to the kind of uncontrolled disorder he and his organization would be hard-pressed to master. In the first week of June, already aware of plans to transfer to Litzmannstadt as many as 100,000 Jews then residing in the smaller towns in the hinterland, Biebow urged the greatest caution. If so many Jews were to be shifted into a single location, it might be best to consider establishing an additional large ghetto rather than transferring them all to the one in Litzmannstadt. And if they had to be sent to Litzmannstadt, the ghetto would likely need to be expanded, but nothing should be undertaken prior to ensuring that all necessary additional resources required to accommodate the influx were securely in place. Otherwise the consequences, particularly in terms of the potential outbreak of contagious disease, would be "without a doubt, disastrous."[55]

Through the summer the prospect of such a transfer continued to threaten. From Berlin came additional pressures. An insistent Heinrich Himmler at last weighed in on the topic, insisting that, however disagreeable and inconvenient, the Litzmannstadt ghetto was to receive several additional transports of Jews, totaling in the end some twenty thousand in number. A further five thousand Gypsies were to be sent to the ghetto as well. On September 18 Himmler communicated the decision directly to Greiser, setting off a desperate effort by the local leadership in Litzmannstadt to put a stop to the plan. Mayor Ventzki, drawing on a lengthy brief prepared for him by Biebow, argued forcefully that, in essence, the ghetto was already at the limit of its capacity to house the existing population. Housing stock, long substandard and already overcrowded, was insufficient to accommodate an additional 25,000 residents; the only expedient remaining would be to "stuff" yet more persons into limited space, and even then it would prove necessary to shut down workshops in order to convert them into living quarters, a prospect that would be disastrous for the ghetto's ability to process goods for the military. The increasingly overcrowded dwellings only courted the possibility of a renewed outbreak of epidemics. As for the Gypsies, they were sure to reject orders and put up chaotic resistance. They might set fires in multiple locations; given the limitations of local firefighting capacity, there was no telling the destruction that could result. The conflagration might well leap the boundaries of the ghetto to imperil the safety of the city. Himmler would hear none of this. Litzmannstadt would have to manage as best it could.[56]

Excluded from the circle of these weighty deliberations, Rumkowski had reason to be satisfied with his success thus far in transforming the ghetto into an enduring refuge for his community. With the approach of autumn and the Jewish New Year, he could look back with pride on the expansion and functioning of ghetto factories, the creation of vacation homes for his officials, a summer of enjoyment for youngsters in the Marysin colonies, and above all the successful completion of a ghetto school year now coming to an end. In honor of Rumkowski's sponsorship, late that summer teachers and pupils were hard at work on creating a substantial album to be presented to the chairman on the occasion of the coming holiday. Over fourteen thousand signatures, the names of nearly every child enrolled in his schools, from the youngest to the oldest, were being collected. Arranged by class and set against a backdrop of original

sketched images of school and ghetto life, the album could only please the
vanity of this man on whom their well-being depended. Written beneath
the students' greetings were words of gratitude: "Today we children have
the privilege of thanking the great friend of children: for all that he has
given us he should live a long and happy life."[57] It was the end of summer, 1941. Two years after the German invasion of Poland, nearly fifteen
months since the sealing of the ghetto, a new year, 5702 by the Hebrew
calendar, awaited. No one, not even the clever chairman, was likely to
have foreseen the nature of the changes its arrival would bring.

In the midst of the New Year's celebrations Rumkowski was called away to
Bałuty Market, where the Germans informed him that thousands of Jews
from the provinces and from the Reich were to be sent to the ghetto, and
that their arrival was imminent. Only days later, on September 26, the
first of the newcomers, an advance contingent of nine hundred residents
of the northern Warthegau city of Włocławek (Leslau) and five of its
nearby towns, reached the ghetto by rail, disembarking at its transfer
station located just beyond the cemetery in Marysin. Their numbers
increased through further transports, in all 3,082 souls, preponderantly
women and youngsters—the men having been separated out for labor—
arrived from Włocławek in the coming days.[58] The experience of uprooting had proved traumatic for them. Ghetto residents looked on with concern, seeing the women, among them the elderly, and children led in
columns by the Jewish police to Bałuty Market for mandatory "disinfection" in a nearby bathing facility. Medical staff were on hand to assist, and
so were barbers, but to little avail; the women objected to the shearing of
their hair.[59] The settling in of the Jews from Włocławek was but a prelude
to the larger waves of new arrivals from the Reich to follow. From October 16 to November 3 came four shipments from Berlin, five from Vienna,
five more from Prague, two from Cologne, and one each from Frankfurt
am Main, Hamburg, Düsseldorf, and Luxemburg. In all, 19,953 persons—
8,263 of them male and 11,690 female, with 10,661 of the total over the age
of fifty—were uprooted from their former lives, loaded onto trains, transported east, and abruptly deposited in a distant ghetto in the unfamiliar
landscape of central Poland.[60]

A rude and disorienting welcome awaited them. Hustled from the train

cars, cursed by sentries, arrayed in columns, they trudged from the ghetto
station, passing first through the sparsely settled streets of the Marysin
quarter. Looking about, they found a drab and impoverished setting.
There could be no doubt: they had fallen far and fallen fast, geographically and socially a world removed from the one they had left behind.
"Where had they ended up?" asked Oskar Rosenfeld, a writer arriving
from Prague.[61] It was "impossible to say whether it was a city or a village."
The place was peculiar to look at, the scene unfolding before their eyes
one of horrid pathways, ramshackle structures, and nightmarish oddities:
"a few carriages, an emaciated horse tied to each," elsewhere "carts, small
carriages, drawn by young and old people rather than animals." Marching
under a "fog-gray sky, traversed by ravenlike birds," they made their
way, under guard, "through dung and morass" and "pools of sewage"
and "stinking refuse" to their destination: makeshift, crowded, unsanitary
quarters in ill-equipped school buildings whose dark, narrow hallways and
all but barren rooms were to serve them as collective quarters. It was difficult not to recognize the truth right away: they had been hurled from
their still relatively favorable material circumstances into a communal
limbo of dispossession. The places to which they were assigned proved altogether disagreeable: the only available toilets were outdoors, "the entryway . . . filled with sewage and water" (one had to watch one's step
coming and going), the living quarters dusty, scantily furnished, and overcrowded. People were now constantly in close, unwanted proximity with
one another. Night presented its own set of challenges. Since there was
not even a proper bed to sleep in, they counted themselves fortunate just
to lie on a wooden board with their bedding and belongings gathered
around them. Even then, "most people had to sleep on the floor. There
was not sufficient room for everybody to lie down and stretch out." The
unavoidable nocturnal stirrings of one's restless neighbors were a grating
chorus for all to hear: "Coughing, hissing, snarling, moaning, creaking of
wooden planks fill the emptiness of the night." People rising to use the latrines invariably disturbed the others; and the crowding meant that people had to step over one another, invariably, inadvertently but unavoidably stepping on or bumping into the other sleepers in the crowded room.
By day there was little for the newcomers to do but shift about, now and
then accidentally colliding with a stranger in the narrow confines of these
crowded rooms and corridors. Idleness was transformed into a never-end-

ing torment. "There [were]," Rosenfeld noted, "no books. No musical instruments except for a few harmonicas. No gramophone, no radio. No place to gather for a friendly conversation," only "constant movement. Scurrying, running, pushing, shouting, bawling, more pushing."

Food became a matter of increasing concern. Fortified by personal stores of cookies and other dry foods packed in their hand luggage for the journey, newcomers could draw on the kinds of extras unavailable to the general ghetto population. But in short order even these precious stocks dwindled. The ghetto community daily supplied a kind of coffee, though it consisted of little more than "brown water" suitable for temporarily filling an empty stomach, and servings of soup—typically a malodorous brew with mysteriously unidentifiable, reeking vegetable-like bits floating about. It was too wretched for newcomers still accustomed to food from real home kitchens and city restaurants to consume. Some passed on it—at first. That too would change with time. But for a while, even in their impoverishment, the new arrivals seemed infinitely rich in comparison to the general ghetto population, who hoped to share in their seeming good fortune. First came the children: imploring beggars who appeared at the windows, looking in, silent and sad, anxious to receive a handout—and, winning the empathy of many a newcomer, receive they did. Then came the traders. As any veteran ghetto resident well knew, the newcomers, gradually depleting their own portable stores of consumables yet hungry still, proved willing to exchange a blouse, a shirt, a dress, a hat, a pair of gloves, or a pair of shoes for food. Within the general population, those items, because they were particularly scarce, were prized, and not just for their warmth but for their value. Many an otherwise impoverished ghetto dweller, if willing to part with a portion of his community ration, profitably sold it to a still prosperous newcomer, receiving one of the coveted articles in exchange. In time, newcomers even took the initiative in stimulating the trade; they could be seen "roaming the streets," their arms laden with clothing for sale, looking to strike a deal. In this way many a new arrival unpacked what little personal inventory had been rescued and stored in suitcases and satchels and bargained it away for something to eat.

Even so, for many of the newcomers physical decline came rapidly, its signs swiftly visible. The ribs were there, all right, but since when did they manifest themselves so prominently? "The abdomen has been sagging," many newcomers discovered, and, most disturbingly, in probing about the midsection, people touched deep recesses of the body never before encountered in this way. Hunger affected the skin, resulting in "various kinds of eczema" and "boils that infect the surrounding tissue," potentially fatal, which the doctors had no means to counteract. Common ailments might include a headache—of the kind that, first sensed "in the back of the head," soon "spreads over the forehead and eyes"—or "pain in the shoulder blades and limbs." Insomnia too proved for many a common complaint. Lucky were those with access to sleeping medicines—"Shanodorny, Sedomit, Quadronok, Luminal, and Bromoral . . . on occasion even Veronal"—potions that promised welcome relief at night.[62] Many did not last long, though. Already, between October and December 1941, 399 of the newly arrived Jews from the Reich and Luxemburg would die in the ghetto; by the following June the number of dead would rise to 3,418.[63]

Concerned that the influx threatened to upset the hard-won organizational achievements of the ghetto's early months, Rumkowski tried to make the newcomers' stay as endurable as possible. He came to visit with them, to talk, to welcome them. He displayed a softer side. He let them know that he and the community wished them well. Extending a measure of communal tenderness toward the elderly, he promised that an old people's home would be created inside the ghetto.[64] Still, as the historian Isaiah Trunk would note, initially Rumkowski had some confidence that, on balance, the arrival of the newcomers might prove of some benefit. Rumkowski was inclined to accord the many academics and professionals among them a measure of outward respect and deference. He hoped, too, that from among their ranks would emerge many with the kind of physical strength and expertise that might contribute to the development of his expanding network of ghetto labor and industry. Unfortunately, far from being preponderantly made up of the young, the healthy, and the fit, their ranks were filled to a great degree with the aged and the dependent. But there were other disappointments as well. Rumkowski hated the ghetto's underground economy, and from the start of his tenure had waged a relentless struggle against the scourge of the internal black market. Now the newcomers were emptying their rucksacks and selling off otherwise nearly impossible to acquire articles—suits and ties and shirts and dresses and shoes, jewelry and furs and makeup and medicines—not to mention small but desirable luxuries such as brushes, combs, toothbrushes, and the like. But all these things, bought and sold or exchanged on the street, were not making their way into the community treasury. Rumkowski held it against the German Jews that many, in his estimation, were concealing their "furs and other valuable items." They should have handed them in. In addition, shirking work was to be "reckoned the greatest sin against the interests of the ghetto," and he found many of them failing in their duty in this respect as well. His addresses to them accordingly took on a tone of pique, and he was not above issuing veiled threats so as to push them into sharing more fully in the burdens of ghetto life. Speaking to a ghetto audience early in November, Rumkowski said of these new arrivals: "They think that they are the smartest, the best, the top of the crop. . . . They're making a big mistake." He issued a direct warning: "I'm telling you, watch your bones! In the event that you will not subject yourselves to my orders and decrees, I will have to calm you down. . . . I won't hesitate before the sharpest means, for that's why I have authority and power."[65]

Some of the newcomers were curious enough to explore their surroundings, in this way acquiring an even wider yet still disorienting glimpse of the city—or that part of the city to which they were confined—that for better or worse was now to be their home. Bernard Heilig, an accomplished young economic historian just arrived from Prague, related that his first walking tours of the ghetto had been "without doubt" the source of some of his "saddest impressions." He recalled "the overcrowded narrow streets," the many broken sidewalks, typically full of holes, with paving debris piled high. The sewage in the gutters was especially noticeable, since the wooden covers had long since been removed to be burned for fuel. The ghetto's "high wooden bridges," surely to a newcomer one of the district's more striking structural oddities, left him and others unsettled. "The density of traffic on these bridges," he related, "especially the large . . . one next to the church, seemed frightful to us, and it surely is, especially at certain times of day."[66] Alicja de Bunon, a fellow new arrival, pondered street signs, noticing German street names overlying others in Polish, but finding still others designating locales alphabetically: A Street, B Street, C Street. On frontages one still found lettering in three languages—Polish, Yiddish, and German—marking the persistence of a kind of meager private storefront economy. It constituted a little retail world of independent craftsmen, tucked inside the shadow of the larger, organized workshop economy. Behind an old store window the odd tea-room or restaurant came into view. An echo of the once busy commercial life of the Bałut, the characteristic "singsong" spiel of outdoor traders still filled the air, as did the unmistakable sound of people making their way over cobblestones in wooden-soled shoes. Shouting out to passing new-comers—their own characteristic pitch "Stars! Stars!" adding to the daily chorus—traders selling the Jewish Star of David patches called attention to the availability of their wares. Petty salesmen and saleswomen set up shop in the doorways or out in the open, their meager wares laid out on tabletops or portable stands sometimes consisting of no more than a box strapped to the seller. Children hawked little candies, candle sellers their "thin" candles for the Sabbath. A flea market took place at the Bałut's Old Town Square, "immediately in front of the detonated ruins of the great synagogue" on Wolborska Street, destroyed in autumn 1939; the market was a place to look for a pair of minimally refurbished shoes, though those on offer were pitiful specimens indeed.[67]

Looking about, the new arrivals were being looked at in return. Al-though at first they might not have known it, in the eyes of the general population these strolling newcomers, their outerwear fantastically desir-able, were an attraction. People stopped them in the street, sometimes just to exchange information, other times to ask if they might have something they would care to sell. Anyone in search of a solid pair of shoes could spot them on their feet. Almost like new they were, of a good brand—and none more in demand than those of the famed Czech manufacturer Bata. When *they* appeared on the streets of the ghetto, people got a good look: warm shoes, high shoes, made for winter, real "ski shoes," and "mountain boots," sturdy footwear many of the deportees had pointedly acquired for the journey in advance of their departure from Prague and the other cities of the Reich. How their owners were envied! It seemed that anyone with the means to do so was tempted to make the effort to initiate a purchase. Jewish Order Service men, assigned to duty in the newcomers' collective housing units, taking "the liveliest interest" in these articles, proved well placed to strike a deal.[68]

But apart from foodstuffs, enterprising members of the general popula-tion possessed something the newcomers desperately desired: a bed and a bit of privacy far from the wretchedness of the collective housing to which they had been assigned. The newcomers were approached and offers were pitched their way: would they like to take a look at "an apartment"? With but a few exceptions, the "apartment" was likely to be no more than a room or part of a room shared with others, perhaps a corner bed or just a sofa available for rent, either long term or just for the night. Some rooms were better than others, with superior stoves and furnishings. But above all the draw was the comparative luxury of being able, if for only a brief while, to escape the overcrowding and the indignity of their collective quarters in order to experience once again just a bit more comfort and privacy. To climb, just once more, into one's pajamas and slip beneath the covers of a clean bed would have meant so much. But this was a trade Rumkowski quickly put a stop to, denouncing the practice and putting teeth in the admonition that anyone offering unauthorized private lodgings to a newcomer was to be evicted. It was a sore point indeed; the newcomers wished nothing so much as to be granted a place of their own. Many thought eventually that was in the offing, and a wishful rumor made the rounds that residents of communal shelters were to be moved to private housing in their own designated sectors, the newcomers from Prague, from Berlin, and the other cities to reside in neighboring buildings, each cluster comprising its own separate "quarter" within the ghetto. That, like so much else they yearned for, was not to be.[69]

The dark and ramshackle district of the ghetto, the impoverished stepchild of the city, was more than ever an abject remnant of Łódź and its forgotten past. It was in the eyes of the new rulers fit only to serve as a point of contrast to the new "Litzmannstadt, City of the Future." Already they could see the new Nazi metropolis, the product of their imagination and their energies, rising up before their very eyes. Its streets and sidewalks repaired, its old apartments renovated and new residential buildings erected, its people fed, their health attended to: the new city was everything that the ghetto was not. And now, at year's end, the new city fathers trumpeted yet a further distinction that was a thoroughgoing expression of the regime's confidence in their overarching vision for the city and its potential for greatness.

By decree of the Führer, on October 21, 1941, Litzmannstadt was awarded the high municipal honor of being designated a location whose redevelopment *(Neugestaltung)* was to be furthered under provisions of a

1937 urban planning ordinance. This meant that Litzmannstadt was now to be ranked among an elite circle of privileged metropolitan centers, including Berlin, Munich, Nuremberg, Breslau, Dresden, Hamburg, Cologne, Linz, Salzburg, Königsberg, Posen, and Danzig, as a city whose redesign and modernization were to be accorded the highest priority. By this measure, Hitler had not only expressed Litzmannstadt's importance in his own eyes and those of the nation but also signaled to its officials the need for full cooperation in accomplishing his plans for the city's future. It was a further honor for Litzmannstadt's new Oberbürgermeister, Werner Ventzki, into whose hands Greiser entrusted municipal leadership of the project.[70] At the end of November the plans were unveiled in detail. This "magnificent project," when completed, would be for Germans of the future an expression of the legacy the Third Reich wished to leave behind. "There are moments in the life of a community when it seems even history must stop and hold its breath," one writer gushed. "Imagine—it takes only a little fantasy—we are standing in front of the Volkshalle, the building to our backs, then we look down [the length of] Ostlandstraße to the new town hall with its high tower, which will be a landmark of the city. Immediately in front of us we have the meadow of the Hitler-Jugend-Park. Behind us lies the new passenger rail station, linked via Ostlandstraße to the new freight station." In the immediate foreground "our glance rests upon the great representative structures of the state and the party as well as public buildings [designed] for general use." Nearby the Ludendorfstraße was to be "considerably widened and expanded into one of the central arteries of the new city."[71] A fantasy? Hardly. "The new Litzmannstadt is no utopia but very nearly reality." Attracted by the city's promise, people were moving to Litzmannstadt and, whatever their initial "hesitation," they were "putting down roots" in its "virgin soil." This was a moment of municipal exuberance. "Even in our wildest dreams we would not have believed in such possibilities." There was no question they would be realized. "We have our task; to the devil with anyone who tries to stop us."[72]

And so it was with great confidence that the plans for future development were presented to the town council and to the public. It would be the material expression of an ideology of racial exclusion, a powerful, visible statement that the new Litzmannstadt was a *German* city, a city for Germans and a German vision of the future: clean and healthy, attractive

to the eye, above all cultured and modern. In brief, it was a big city, mod-
eled after the greatest metropolises of the Reich, a newcomer, to be sure,
but for all that able like no other to represent enormous change. This was
to be a place where Germans would want to come and would want to stay.
Litzmannstadt was, quite simply, a city on the rise. The mountains of
cleared debris and the hundreds of kilometers of roadways already repaired were but one proof that the city's past was behind it and its future
was already taking shape. But even then, the project would go on and on,
a "living creation," following "its own laws of development," driven forward with truly impressive "élan" even now, but sure to be even greater
come "victory" and the peace to follow.[73]

6

Banishment

At the turn of the year 1942 the ghetto endured blizzard-like conditions that left "all the roads and squares covered in heaps of snow."[1] Adding to the miseries of nature came unsettling news. Ominously, on December 16 Rumkowski had been ordered to select twenty thousand residents of the ghetto for deportation, presumably to be sent to "smaller towns" to the east where food was more plentiful. But this was to occur in the dead of winter. In consultation with German superiors Rumkowski had succeeded in cutting the quota by half. Moreover, securing recognition of his "autonomy" and "authority," he had won for the ghetto as well the right to determine who among the population were to leave. To facilitate the selection and oversee their removal, Rumkowski had been granted the right to appoint a Resettlement Commission, to be headed by five trusted officers of his administrative and security establishment.[2] On January 4, addressing ghetto leaders at an assembly at the House of Culture, time and again he repeated that work alone ensured survival. It remained clear that he would cling to his labor strategy as the ghetto's single lifeline at all costs. Alongside the accumulation of goods and valuables, ghetto labor constituted the second of the twin "pillars" of his monthly budget, more than a third of which in 1941, he explained, had been given over to expenditures for social welfare. The workforce provided solid backing in the event that he needed to turn to the authorities for additional financial credits. Above all, the work program constituted the sole and thus far wholly successful means by which the German authorities had been convinced of the ghetto's usefulness. The Germans simply could not overlook such a contribution. "Indeed, from nothing we have created enormous establishments for productive labor, we have put the most varied enterprises and factories into operation. Today we employ an army of close to 50,000 people. Such a number of workers has to be treated seriously by everyone, including, first and foremost, those who make policy. Everyone here should realize that the policy makers I have just mentioned categorically demand that the ghetto be dedicated to work." For that reason, said Rumkowski, "from the beginning I have been striving to achieve one basic goal. That goal is to be able to demonstrate to the [German] authorities that the ghetto is composed exclusively of working people, that every able-bodied ghetto dweller has his own line of work." It was precisely because he had been successful in this respect that he was able to plead for amelioration of the harshest of decrees. "The authorities are full of admiration for the work which has been performed in the ghetto," he insisted, "and it is due to that work that they have confidence in me. Their approval of my motion to reduce the number of deportees from 20,000 to 10,000 is a sign of that confidence."[3]

As assuredly as Rumkowski held fast to his labor strategy, his rhetoric became heated when it touched on those in the community who dared undermine his efforts. He was quick to pour scorn upon unscrupulous traders, those "hyenas who serve as middlemen" who profited from acting as go-betweens in the illegal sale of goods within the underground ghetto economy. Nor did he spare from criticism those other "hyenas" among the ranks of the newcomers from Central Europe. They "are leading a life that is simply unforgivably frivolous. They still suffer from the mistaken belief that the present situation is already coming to an end and, under the influence of that delusion, are living from hand to mouth, selling off everything that they had brought here with them. Unfortunately, the present situation will go on and on."[4]

Pleading for cooperation, hoping that rather than compete among themselves, workshops might learn to share scarce resources, he appealed to common interests, insisting, "We are a single, united community here in the ghetto," and, in a bit of misplaced swashbuckling bravura, "Here it is one for all and all for one." Always searching for new ways to inject life into his dreary theme, toward the end of his oration Rumkowski exhorted the leadership once more, proclaiming: "A plan on the threshold of the new year! The plan is work, work, and more work!"[5]

As Rumkowski pounded into his listeners the message that, come what may, they must work, work, work, the ghetto orchestra, stocked with fresh talent from abroad, continued to offer redeeming moments of escape and relief for a careworn public. Three days after he spoke, the ghetto symphony, maestro Teodor Ryder at the podium, entertained with a selection of "works by Massenet, Beethoven, Humperdinck, and Puccini," and "the well-known Prague [in fact, Viennese] pianist [Leopold] Birkenfeld enchanted the public for a third time with his performance of Chopin's masterpieces: Variations in B Major; Nocturne in D-flat Major, and the Scherzo in C-sharp Minor." Well aware of the jarring contrast, however, the ghetto chroniclers did not hesitate to note that on that same day, "thirty-six-year-old Chaim Kirsztajn (of 4 Żydowska Street) died at 11 o'clock, in the gateway of the building at 8 Żydowska Street. The doctor summoned from First Aid determined the cause of death to be exhaustion."[6]

It had been, after all, a hard beginning to the new year. Death had taken no holiday, and as this still young man's all too common death would attest, no sooner had the mortality registers for 1941 been closed than fresh ones were opened and began filling fast. The death rate for the first two weeks of the first month of 1942 was averaging "46 per day," the ghetto's internal log, the *Chronicle*, noting as well that no fewer than 216 ghetto residents had died over a single stretch of four days between January 10 and 13. The usual trio of fatal maladies, "exhaustion, tuberculosis, and heart disease," accounted for the bulk of this agonizing toll.[7]

Faring even worse, and suffering especially badly from the effects of a typhus epidemic raging through their quarantined quarters, the Gypsies who had arrived at the same time as the Central European Jews in the autumn were dying off in even greater numbers. Some four hundred of the five thousand who had been shipped to the ghetto had been lowered into the ground in a dedicated sector of the Jewish cemetery in December, their dead carted away "in sideless hauling wagons especially constructed for that purpose. The wagons are enclosed by planks and covered from above with tarpaulin." Perhaps no less ominously, the others, "taken away in trucks," were removed from the ghetto to an unknown destination. By early January it was noted that their fenced-in enclosure, situated just inside the ghetto perimeter, "is practically deserted now, [and] will no doubt be entirely eliminated by the end of this week."[8]

January 13 was the date for those first summoned for deportation to report to the initial "assembly point at 7 Szklana Street. There, from 9 o'clock in the morning until 9 in the evening the formalities of registration proceed[ed] uninterrupted, performed by teachers and by officials from other departments summarily mobilized for the job." As part of this initial processing, people surrendered their ration cards, and declarations were accepted pertaining to elderly or sick relations who had not been capable of reporting, thereby setting in motion follow-up inspections conducted by ghetto physicians, who, in this preliminary stage of deportations, were given leeway to assign those judged unable to report to a care facility. From Szklana Street the deportees were transferred to one of three other centers, located in a "building adjacent to Central Prison at 6 Czarniecki Street, in Marysin, and in the school at 25 Młynarska Street." Among those arriving for the first transports, each deportee was handed, as promised, a travel supplement of ten marks and was fed "a normal bread ration, soup with meat, and coffee." Winter clothing and footwear were made available from ghetto stores; by the end of January deportees had received in all "some twelve thousand pairs of warm underwear, earmuffs, gloves, stockings, socks, and clogs" issued "right before" departure, along with "half a loaf of bread and sausage for the road."[9]

Such minor accommodations aside, it was clear that individuals responded to these summonses with dread. As ghetto postal carriers fanned out across the community to deliver the warrants, people fell into wild fits of anxiety. Loud wailing and tears accompanied receipt of the orders. Under the circumstances, many parents were hard-pressed to deal with their agitated children; some of the women, at their wits' end, literally "tore their hair out." In their desperation, people turned whichever way they could in search of contacts who might conceivably have sufficient influence to cancel the summons or strike their name from the list. It would prove a distant prospect at best for any but those possessing the highest connections.[10] One accepted and legitimate channel, however, remained open to all, even if in practical terms it proved little more than an illusory lifeline: a written appeal to the officers of the Resettlement Commission.

Foremost in the commission's sights were those labeled marginal to ghetto society or deemed harmful to its interests. Included in such categories were the unfortunate outsiders from the provincial community of Włocławek who, only months ago, had been so rudely uprooted and shunted to Łódź, but also, most especially, those individuals who had acquired criminal or otherwise adverse records during their time in the ghetto. Rather pointedly, "prostitutes and other 'undesirable elements'" were to be included in the lists and deported along with members of their families. Whether because of guilt by association or for the sake of administrative convenience, often those with whom they shared their residences were listed for expulsion as well. During the approximately seventy-two-hour interval between receipt of their summonses and the time they were to present themselves for removal, deportees were granted the dubious privilege of offering "their furniture and household effects" for sale to representatives of ghetto "carpenters' shops." In what appears to have been a concession to those still hopeful of eventually returning from their journey, people slated for departure were informed that "furniture [might] be left for safekeeping in the carpenters' shops instead of being sold." Moreover, in what in other times might have been regarded as a customer-friendly gesture, though in this instance was more likely designed merely to ensure that furnishings of any value would be surrendered into the community's hands rather than privately bartered or sold, deportees were told that "where sets of furniture are involved, the parties concerned may request that the experts performing the appraisals be sent to their apartments, in which cases the carpenters' shop will itself remove the furniture it purchases."[11]

Those who wrote to the commission knew that their lives hung in the balance, and some did not hesitate to say so directly, even as they respectfully appealed for sympathy in hope of gaining exemption from transport. Petitioning on January 11, 1942, on her own behalf and that of her daughter and son, all of whom had been summoned for deportation, one sixty-year-old woman pleaded: "Have mercy on us, and do not make us homeless and even poorer than we already are! Bear in mind that if you deport us you will be killing 3 people."[12] Temar Braun, wife of a man who had been sent to labor outside the ghetto and mother of a child of two and a half who had just been diagnosed with a lung disease, similarly chastised the commission: "How is it then possible that I and my child should leave our home? You are condemning my sick child to death."[13] Forty-five-year-old Szmul Ackermann foresaw that should he, his wife, his sister, and her two-year-old child be forced to depart as ordered, his aged parent would be placed in immediate danger. "What is going to become of my elderly seventy-two-year-old mother, who is sick and cannot leave her bed?" he wished to know. "The moment we leave the house my mother will die of horror."[14]

People had been led to think of such notification to depart as deserved punishment only for those who had committed some misdeed. Had not Rumkowski spoken of deporting the troublemakers and inmates of Czarnieckiego Prison? Given the sheer cruelty of an order of expulsion arriving at this time, in the very depths of winter, it was difficult for those receiving such orders to interpret them as anything other than a severe sentence and judgment. Yet for many, the sting of fate they delivered came unexpectedly, and seemed completely devoid of sense, not only on grounds of simple humane considerations but also because they knew themselves to have done nothing wrong, to have lived lives beyond reproach and without any offenses on their records whatsoever. They did not hesitate to remind the commission that they were innocent, that they had led blameless lives. One husband and father whose family had been instructed to report for expulsion pleaded, "I am in no way aware of the reasons why I should be subject to this order, since up until this day in my life I always have behaved uprightly and faithfully, and have no prior convictions." Moreover, suffering as he was from heart and lung ailments "so that even with the best of intentions," as he explained, "I would not be in any condition to report for travel on the assigned date," he hoped the commissioners would "grant consideration to my sad situation and that of my family and spare us from the deportation."[15]

Striking too was the mildness with which some of the supplicants pleaded for the lives of their loved ones. Writing to the commission on January 21, Szmul Ajlenberg explained that by dint of his own labor and that of his two sisters they had succeeded in adequately supporting their family of seven, among them their sixty-four-year-old father, confined to his bed. Anticipating rejection, however, he proposed most politely, "Should our request, for [whatever] varied reasons not be able to be considered, permit me to ask that only *I* be resettled and to allow the other family members to remain here until further notice."[16]

Such desperate appeals testify to the deep reluctance with which individuals reacted to the order to report for departure. Without precise knowledge of what awaited them, the prospect of abandoning even the flimsy and thoroughly inadequate shelter of the ghetto for an enforced journey, undertaken in the cold of winter, into the unknown was to be regarded as fraught with peril. That even sick infants and the elderly were also slated for deportation was perceived as cruel, and signaled a darker purpose that boded ill for the prospects of those called upon to leave. Not surprisingly, and in spite of announced penalties amounting to forfeiture of the privilege of carrying with them luggage up to 12.5 kilograms in weight and of the promised individual departure payout of ten marks, from the beginning many failed to show up for deportation as ordered. Indeed it was noted that "on the first day, scarcely half of those who had been summoned reported." As a result, "from the start of the campaign the deportees have been brought in forcibly. This has occurred most frequently at night."[17]

It was left to the Jewish Order Service to search out the missing and escort them to the assembly points on Szklana Street and at the Central Prison. Precinct search logs for the month of January indicate that when officers came looking for individuals and families, many were not at home. In an effort to discover the whereabouts of those as yet unaccounted for, policemen roamed from building to building, questioning caretakers, co-tenants, and neighbors. Frequently officers were assured that those whom they were seeking had just left for the resettlement centers on their own. Such had been the case with three large families residing at 14 Brzezińska Street, including the seven-member "family Hecht," as listed by name, "Zysla, Moszek, Sura, Symcha, Perla, Mordka, and Sara," whom the "caretaker indicated" had on "January 23, 1942, at 9:10 in the evening proceeded to the assembly point with their baggage," having "left the key to their apartment" behind in his possession. Others, found still at home, the police recorded as in the process of packing their things. For persons discovered to be physically incapable of moving on their own, most particularly those deemed severely handicapped or with their legs in casts, additional assistance in the form or stretchers or other conveyances was ordered. Instances in which persons were judged critically ill—"hemorrhaging," experiencing a "nervous shock," or "sick—in agony" and "impossible to remove"—resulted in a call for the Resettlement Commission to be notified for further action. In rare instances the police listed persons being sought as having gone into hiding, among them Ruchla Cręcińska of 34 Franciskańska Street and Szmul Cytrynban, residing at 12 Wolborska.[18]

In the days leading to the departure of the first transports, Shlomo Frank recorded the agonizing passage of those whom he called the "condemned." Seized by anxiety, some screamed, some in their desperation "run[ning] about like poisoned mice," seeking in vain anyone who might offer hope of intervention on their behalf. Some were resigned to the certainty of their approaching end: "One packs and one cries, the majority wishing to die on the spot. They feel they will not survive. The day's temperature holds at 15 degrees below zero Celsius, their hunger is indescribable." But there was anger too. From within the ranks of those departing on the Saturday, January 17, transport, anguished mothers, carrying small children, were heard shouting to others "to stay alive in order to take revenge on those who sent us away."[19]

Outwardly untouched by such tragedies, the work of the ghetto proceeded without the least interruption. Coinciding with the departure of the first trainloads of Jews from Łódź for the unknown, a new exhibition of textile products was inaugurated at the Glazer factory on Dworska Street to much fanfare. A large hall had been prepared for the ceremonies. On stage was a long table for dignitaries, including Rumkowski and his new wife;[20] Leon Rozenblat, head of the Jewish police; Aron Jakubowicz, director of the central workshops bureau; Rumkowski's secretary, Dora Fuchs; and workshop director Glazer. Behind the notables' table hung a portrait of Rumkowski and a "gigantic banner" bearing in Yiddish the ubiquitous motto "Work Is Our Only Path."[21]

Dressed warmly for the occasion in a buttoned double-breasted overcoat with velvet collar, a cane at his side, Rumkowski was led on a tour of the exhibits. Mounted "inside striking frames" were ladies' lingerie and brassieres, underclothes for men and youngsters, fine bedding, and millinery accessories. These "genuine, lovingly handled objects" were described as "articles of the utmost taste," fashioned with "artistic skill," bringing to mind wares otherwise found in the "world-renowned salons of Paris or New York."[22] Afterwards, in addressing the assembly, Rumkowski frankly acknowledged that the occasion was overshadowed by the onset of the deportations. Yet, stressing this to have been the unavoidable result of "a most uncompromising order, one I had to carry out so as to prevent others from doing it," he insisted that the ranks of the evacuees had been intentionally filled with those who, by their underhanded deeds, had brought deserved punishment upon themselves: "Now, when I am deporting all kinds of connivers and cheats, I do it fully convinced that they asked for this fate." In a severe choice of words, however, disturbingly reminiscent of Regierungspräsident Uebelhoer's own ugly characterization, Rumkowski asserted, "I have assigned for deportation that element of our ghetto which was a festering boil." Revealing a measure of sensitivity to charges of unfairness directed against those "trusted aides" of his who had constituted the Resettlement Commission, he felt compelled to insist, "This commission guarantees, basically, that it will designate people for deportation only if they deserve it." He pleaded for understanding of the pressures under which his officers were operating, insisting that they had no ill intent toward those who might have been caught up inadvertently in the operation. Seeking, too, to assuage anxieties regarding the destination of the deported, he offered this reassurance: "My expectation, based on authoritative information, is that the deportees' fate will not be as tragic as is expected in the ghetto. They will not be behind wire, and they will work on farms." Nevertheless, he conceded, "we are on the threshold of very bad times, and everyone needs to be aware of this."[23]

Contrary to whatever undisclosed "authoritative information" he may have had access to, Rumkowski's assurance to his audience was illusory. Like the Jews of the outlying provincial communities of Koło, Dąbie, Kłodowa, Bugaj, and Izbica Kujawska and the Gypsies earlier removed from the ghetto, the Jews of the Łódź ghetto were being directed toward the death camp at Chełmno, which, together with its nearby burial ground in the Rzuchowski Woods, constituted a vortex that was fast consuming an increasing influx of victims. Situated in a rural community only sixty kilometers to the northwest, near the town of Koło (Warthbrücken), the camp had begun operations on December 8, 1941, killing its victims by herding them into the cargo sections of vans specially redesigned to fill with lethal exhaust from their engines.[24] There is no evidence to indicate that Rumkowski or others in the ghetto were yet aware of what was happening in Chełmno, but on the very day he spoke, an ill-fated crew of Jewish gravediggers, drawn from the ranks of Jews from the doomed provincial ghettos, were laying into trenches "seven heavily filled vehicle loads" packed with the corpses of expellees who but a day or two before had been alive in the ghetto. The gravediggers could not help noting the deplorable condition of the new victims, their ravaged skin marked by a surfeit of "wounds and boils." These disturbing signs were manifest on strikingly light frames, severe weight loss being further evidence of malnourishment, if not outright starvation. "The dead did not weigh much," enabling a more economical distribution of their remains inside the trenches. "Instead of three truckloads, as before, the bodies of four were placed in a single layer."[25]

Late on the afternoon of that Saturday, around five o'clock, a car drove up to the site bearing orders that resulted in the execution of the sixteen men working at the burial place. They were ordered to lie down and were shot atop the day's victims piled inside one of the graves. The night before, one of their comrades, Abram Rój, had succeeded in making his escape and was still at large. His example was one that another of the men—known to us only by his first name, Szlamek, and by the name Jakub Grojnowski, an identity he adopted while on the run, fleeing for his life—was soon to emulate. Meanwhile, spared having had to work the previous Sunday, the men had hoped for respite. But instead on the next day, January 18, they were again driven to the site, arriving at the comparatively early hour of 8 AM and with "20 new shovels and [4] pickaxes" ready for distribution; soon fresh truckloads of deportees—five in the morning, four more that afternoon—came pouring in. With the killings now including Jews of the Łódź ghetto, it was apparent to the men that its scope, previously confined to the destruction of Jews from nearby outlying communities, had widened and aimed to incorporate "all the Jews of the Warthegau."[26]

On the morning of January 19, with the guards aboard positioned at the front of the vehicle and the prisoners in the rear, with the aid of his fellow prisoners Szlamek had succeeded in climbing undetected from a window of the bus as it was transporting them back to the woods for work. The rest of the day, trying as best he could to pass for a Polish workman, Szlamek made his way across the countryside. His goal was to reach the nearest existing Jewish community in the vicinity at Grabów, a town lying to the southeast of Chełmno. Along the way he dared to seek temporary shelter and directions at two Polish farmhouses. He was fed bread and coffee. Had the residents suspected his identity? Perhaps so, for as he was leaving the first home where he stopped, the farmer, he recalled, had asked "if by chance I was not a Jew?" Denying that he was, Szlamek asked him what had prompted such a question. "I heard the answer: in Chełmno they are gassing the Jews and Gypsies." In a second Polish home, reached after another hour of traveling by foot, the residents spoke of Chełmno in similar fashion, this time adding their belief that after all the Jews and Gypsies were killed, the Poles would be next. By early afternoon, having walked to within seven kilometers of Grabów, Szlamek, pretending to be "a Polish butcher" on his way to town "for work," hired a farmer with a cart to drive him the rest of the way, his new identity enhanced by the addition of "a sheepskin [coat] and fur hat." When he reached Grabów, he asked the way to the rabbi, who at first appeared taken aback by this stranger who, if not a Pole, looked rather more like an ethnic German than a Jew. "Rabbi, do not think that I am crazy or have lost my senses," Szlamek told him. "I am a Jew who comes from the world beyond. The Jews are being murdered. I myself have buried an entire Jewish community, among them my parents, my brother, and my whole family. I am all alone in the world." The rabbi asked him where these killings were taking place. "I replied: Rabbi, in Chełmno. They are gassed in the forest and all are buried in a grave." Hearing this, the rabbi's maidservant, her "eyes swollen from tears," brought him "a bowl of water" with which to wash his hands. Word of his ordeal spread through the community, and people came to listen. To them as well he related his account. "They all cried. I ate bread and butter, with which I drank tea, and said a prayer of thanks for my rescue."[27]

By early February, having first made his way, like his fellow escapee Abram Rój, to the Radom district in the Generalgouvernement, Szlamek reached the Warsaw ghetto. There he related his account to members of the underground Ringelblum archive, and from there news of what was happening in Chełmno was communicated abroad.[28] Word also spread to nearby Jewish communities of the Warthegau. In time, though circulation of the news was limited and its acceptance uncertain and at best slow in crystallizing, it reached the Łódź ghetto as well, carried by individuals re-located there when additional provincial Jewish centers were dissolved. The strong were sent to Łódź to work.[29] The weak, as before, were fun-neled to Chełmno to die.

In the meantime, the transports continued to depart from the ghetto rail-way station on their way to Chełmno, bearing 10,003 souls in January, 7,025 in February, and 24,687 in March. Within the ghetto itself the death toll mounted through the winter, the mortality curve rising with the crest-ing waves of deportation: 1,877 dead in January, 1,875 in February, and, in what the *Chronicle* termed "a shocking increase," 2,244 in March, a record number of dead for any single month to date.[30] All told, that made for 5,204 dead in the first quarter of 1942 alone. By then 2,061, or nearly 10.5 percent of the previous autumn's arrivals from the cities of the Reich, were listed among the deceased. The men proved especially vulnerable: 1,251 of them, as opposed to 810 of the women, had failed to survive the winter.[31] All this made "fertile soil for acts of desperation," noted the *Chronicle*, highlighting close to a score of suicides during the last of the three months. Several persons leaped to their deaths from the upper stories of residential buildings, among them "a 63-year-old woman . . . who had been resettled from Prague," who "on March 15" had "jumped from a fourth-story attic window of the Old People's Home to the pavement be-low. She had been exhibiting signs of nervous breakdown, caused by the most recent ordeals." So too on March 18 a very ill twenty-year-old woman suffering from typhus, whose desperate act was thought occa-sioned by her feverish state, jumped to her death "at night, when all the building's residents were asleep." Others resorted to ingesting lethal doses of sleeping agents or other dangerous substances. "On March 1, a married couple, Wiktor and Daisy Heller, resettled . . . from Prague," the husband born in 1882, the wife in 1886, residents of "the collective at 10 Jakuba Street," together consumed "an overdose of Luminol." It was reported that "the husband died before the doctor arrived, and the wife a few hours later in Hospital No. 1. They left a letter from which it appears that Heller was driven to his desperate act by illness and anguish, while his wife wished to share her husband's fate." In another especially tragic double suicide, an event described as "unparalleled in its horror," on March 24 a

Viennese widow in her fifties and her teenaged son swallowed "a strong dose of poison on the staircase of the building at 13 Limonowski Street. They lived together at 6 Miodowa Street. The son had been working in the fire department. The mother died on the spot, the son was taken to Hospital No. 1, where he died after a few hours." Others were compelled to resort to other means. On March 12 a forty-eight-year-old woman "hung herself in her apartment at 61 Brzezińska Street." A young man in his early thirties from Vienna "committed suicide by cutting the arteries of his left arm."[32]

Throughout, and in spite of such personal tragedies, the ghetto, of course, was supposed to go about its business manufacturing salable goods and thereby serving its essential military and commercial clients, some of which evidently went out of their way to convey satisfaction with the work. A Berlin model dressmaker wrote to the Ghetto Administration on February 11 to "express a thousand thanks" upon the arrival that very day of a "partial shipment" of items for his "Maxim" line, then being manufactured in the ghetto. "I am very satisfied with the work and hope that from now on work will proceed to flow between you and our firm," he wrote.[33] Similarly on March 17 a dress and blouse manufacturer in Erfurt promptly informed the Gettoverwaltung as soon as completed samples of its "Naples" dress line had arrived that "the dresses are correct in every detail."[34]

Pleasing as such encomiums must have been, Biebow found it impossible to overlook the underlying source of rising mortality in the ghetto. His concern was strictly utilitarian, entirely focused on the visibly damaging impact of the grossly inadequate quality and quantity of food rations made available to the ghetto workforce, considerably harming its ability to carry on vital production tasks. The Gestapo had formed a rather different assessment of the food situation, "suggesting that the ghetto was receiving too much food and that such allocations could not be justified."[35] Irritated at the suggestion, and apparently weary of responding to such assessments, in a memorandum dated March 4 Biebow attempted to lay out for Commissar Fuchs of the Gestapo's Jewish affairs branch the severity of the food crisis, citing the climbing rates of disease and death as a result of critical shortages. With even agreed-upon quantities of foodstuffs failing to reach the ghetto, "the state of health of the Jews is sinking by the day." What is more, complained Biebow, what the Jews did receive was, "as a rule[,] of inferior quality." In addition to an "increase in [cases] of spotted fever," he noted in the brief span from February 22 to February 26 a total of 307 deaths from tuberculosis, cardiac insufficiency, "malnourishment (better stated, starvation)," and "various cases of death which are to be derived from poor nourishment."[36] He stressed that for the preceding year even deliveries of approved quantities of meat, potatoes, vegetables, and other foodstuffs had fallen short by hundreds of thousands of kilograms. As of December 15, 1941, to give yet another example, provision of artificial honey and marmalade had been halted altogether, and in January 1942, thousands of kilograms of meat, sugar, and coffee substitute were unavailable as well. These shortages were causing serious harm to a ghetto workforce of some 53,000 persons "essentially working on behalf of the war economy." He warned Fuchs, "Everyone familiar with conditions in the ghetto knows that workers are literally collapsing from weakness at their workstations." Saying this, and surely mindful of his Gestapo correspondent, Biebow added by way of disclaimer, "The Gettoverwaltung would never distribute to the Jews more food than absolutely justifiable." Apparently alluding to complaints that the ghetto was receiving more than enough supplies, he asked the Gestapo "to put a stop to such endlessly repeated queries," suggesting that the official come and make his own inspection "to convince himself of the circumstances here on the spot."[37]

Apart from the unmistakably harmful physical effects resulting from such woefully insufficient rations, it was clear to ghetto managers that the ongoing deportations were having such a serious impact on workforce morale that productivity was suffering on this account as well. In a summary report for March 1942, the head of the department overseeing manufacturing orders in the textile sector attributed to the deportations that month's declining output, marked by "a rapid decrease in the capacity in each of the individual workshops." While indicating that even though established workers were not subject to deportation, he did find that "the general unrest and uncertainty made several work groups less efficient. On the other hand, other groups were dissolved since the workers whose relations were affected by the deportation for the most part volunteered to re-

port [for deportation] as well. At the moment," he continued, "it is un-
foreseeable whether this circumstance will soon be remedied."[38]

Indeed, the stress of continuing deportations put a terrible strain on the
nerves of the ghetto population. Uncertainty over their duration led to
grim conjecture. It was simply impossible to be sure how long the deportations might last, or to what end. At the beginning of April, ghetto
chroniclers reported that "new numbers for further resettlement are being
mentioned, and there is even talk about the ghetto's being liquidated entirely." Consequently, the community "is under the sway of uncertainty,
which is disrupting ghetto life to a significant degree, because everyone
figures that he may be deported and is acting accordingly." Uncharacteristically, Rumkowski had made himself scarce, for a time giving no
speeches. People sensed that "something is in the air, and for the time being, no one can tell what it is."[39]

Then, quite unexpectedly on April 2, "the second day of Passover," following the departure of a single morning transport, it was reported that
the deportations had come to an end. Wary of premature hope, and recalling too the bitter disappointment engendered by an all too brief and
temporary halt to the transports on March 22, people remained at first re-
strained, suspicious of an impending reversal of the apparent good news.
But by ten in the morning, Jewish policemen openly announced "the joyous news" that Rumkowski had confirmed the transports had definitely
ended, and residents of the ghetto were "happy as children" at the prospect. With the additional announcement of a new potato distribution, a
measure of renewed optimism could be detected. Expressions such as
"We've lived to see happy holidays," and "God willing, everything's taking a turn for the better!" could be heard. Having all the more reason to
celebrate were some three thousand ghetto residents who had dared to
defy deportation summonses by going into hiding and were now free
to emerge. In what was described as "a noble gesture," Rumkowski made
them once more eligible to receive ration cards and placed "no obstacles"
in the way of their retroactively claiming provisions forfeited during the
time they had been in hiding; for many this "amounted to receiving a fortune."[40] Since January forty transports had left the ghetto, bearing 44,056

citizens away to a still uncertain fate.[41] On March 1 there had been 142,079 persons residing in the ghetto, 60,829 men and 81,250 women. Exactly a month later, their ranks depleted by further deportations and rising mortality, there remained fewer still: 50,094 men and 65,008 women, in total 115,102 souls.[42]

The winter of 1942 and its deportations had delivered a terrible and unexpected shock to the ghetto, upsetting its precarious equilibrium. Hope for all rested on the promise that in laboring diligently for the Germans and remaining strong enough to withstand the worst of common stress, illness, and hunger, the ghetto and its inhabitants would survive. Now the inhabitants had to contend with the unwelcome threat of being summoned for removal and a journey into the unknown. By no means could they discern with any certainty whether this new threat, momentarily in abeyance, had passed with the season or was but a prelude to similar, indeed even harsher setbacks and perils to follow.

7

Departure, Worry, and Disappearance

On a crisp but sunny day at the end of March 1942, a month marked by transports departing from the ghetto station laden with human cargo destined for slaughter, thousands of local spectators turned out to watch long-distance runners and competitive walkers race through the heart of downtown Litzmannstadt. In a lively display of athleticism, speed, and teamwork that captured well the confident, forward-moving spirit of the times, three hundred participants—largely representing the Hitler Youth, police, Luftwaffe, SA, SS, and a local tennis association—were organized into a series of relay heats dashing from Friesenplatz northward along the entire nearly four-kilometer length of Adolf-Hitler-Straße to a crowd-packed finish line on Deutschlandplatz. A special communications link kept those waiting at the end informed of the progress of the runners. The crowds assembled at the finish to cheer competitors were but two blocks from the southern perimeter of the ghetto.[1]

Had they been able to catch a glimpse of the excitement, ghetto inhabitants would have found it cruelly at odds with the crushing reality of daily life as they knew it. For the average ghetto dweller, mere locomotion was often arduous, in its own way a kind of hard-fought defiance of the general immobility that was his or her lot. At the beginning of April, Oskar Rosenfeld watched his fellow ghetto residents struggle to make their way through the streets. "Horses almost sink into the mud," he wrote, and "passersby hug the walls of the houses." Their energies expended "all without purpose," people resembled little more than "puppets on a stage . . . and the more one observes the scene the more senseless appears the whole thing. For whom? For what? Why? For how long? None of these questions has an answer. There was no purpose in the beginning and there is no purpose at the end."[2] This was no race to any discernible goal; no crowds of spectators turned out to watch; no cheering was heard. There was no finish line. The city and the ghetto, though proximate and very much aware of each other's existence, occupied altogether distinct worlds.

Not without questions of their own, yet far more certain of the ultimate direction and purpose of recent events, the Gettoverwaltung wanted to clarify whether the deportations, though temporarily halted at the beginning of April, were likely to resume in the near future. In the meantime, eager to facilitate the processing of loot derived from ghetto-clearing operations, leading officials in the organization took the initiative in arranging for the further transport, cleaning, and temporary storage of confiscated property. In doing so, they maintained close and cooperative contact with the SS-Sonderkommando directing the killing center in Chełmno. Notes of a telephone conversation on April 4 recording particulars of a discussion between Amtsleiter Biebow and his deputy Friedrich Ribbe indicate that ghetto administrators were by then directly involved in the procurement of a facility in Pabianice, located just south of the city, that was soon to play a central role in warehousing quantities of valuables seized during killing operations later that spring. "Question: Should the things in Pabianice be processed by Jews or by Poles[?]" An additional concern of some import involved securing trucks and fuel for long-distance transport of goods to the facility. The Sonderkommando, it was noted, had not a single vehicle to spare, but had proved amenable to a "suggestion on our part to steer vehicles shipped into the districts via Pabianice." It was hoped, too, that "with the approval of the Gauleiter, if still possible, the Gettoverwaltung should buy back a large truck." Matters pertaining to fuel allocation were to be taken up with an official in the Gau capital in Posen. The summary of the conversation noted that thus far an inquiry directed to a local Gestapo official on the topic of "continuation or breaking off of the Judenaktion" had failed to yield a definite response, suggesting the need for further investigation of "this extremely precarious question."[3]

Meanwhile, trapped within the limits of their own narrow and circumscribed perspective, ghetto observers still puzzled over the fate of those sent off on the winter transports and wondered whether more would follow. Ten days after the cessation of the transports, an apparent resolution to their quandary appeared. On April 12 a man described as "a high officer of the secret police [Gestapo], who is serving as the commander of the camp where the people deported from this ghetto are now located, was briefly at Bałut Market." This was "the first definite source of information concerning the deportees," the *Chronicle* noted, indicating that the visitor had at last "confirmed" a rumor currently being discussed concerning the likely destination of those who had been deported. "It has now been irrefutably established that the camp is located in the region bordering directly on the town of Koło, now called Warthbrücken." This much was true, but accompanying details, though recorded as fact, were woefully inaccurate. Indeed, they were deliberately proffered misinformation. "The camp houses about 100,000 Jews," the *Chronicle* reported, "indicating that besides the 44,000 resettled from this ghetto, Jews from other cities have been concentrated in that camp." It was further reported that "this gigantic camp was formerly a living site for Germans from Volhynia. Apparently 30,000 people had been living there. They left the barracks in perfectly decent order, and even left their furniture for the Jews to use. The food supply at the camp is, apparently, exemplary. Those fit for work are employed on the camp grounds repairing roads and performing agricultural tasks. Workshops are to be set up in the very near future."[4]

The figure of 100,000 Jews was designed to support the deception by giving plausible substance to the notion of a work camp large enough to accommodate all the Jews so recently deported from Łódź and elsewhere. In fact, this was the very figure that Gauleiter Greiser, in correspondence with Himmler just a little over two weeks later, on May 1, would cite as constituting the number of nonessential Jews from the Warthegau targeted for killing in accordance with a writ Greiser had solicited from Himmler, quite possibly during the previous autumn. As that correspondence makes clear, Greiser's request to dispose of 100,000 Jews had been duly granted, a target figure by then nearing fulfillment.[5]

Much indeed suggests that in the coming days, decisions pertaining to an expansion of the deportations were coming to a head. At 4:45 on the afternoon of Thursday, April 16, following a meeting with Hitler at the latter's East Prussian field headquarters in Rastenburg, Himmler flew on to Posen for consultations with the top Warthegau leadership. Landing shortly after six PM, he was received by Gauleiter Greiser and the leading SS and police official Wilhelm Koppe. After a dinner that evening at the Ostland Hotel, the three men conferred, meeting together once more over breakfast the next morning. Thereupon Himmler, departing at 9:30 AM, traveled eastward across the Warthegau toward Kutno and Warsaw. Along the way he made an extended stop in Koło, or Warthbrücken, where he did in fact pay a visit to a model settlement for Volhynian German families—possibly the one to which the Gestapo visitor to Bałut Market had deceptively alluded earlier in the week—located some five kilometers outside town at Groß-Redern. It is worth noting that having reached Koło, Himmler was but a short distance from Chełmno, lying just fourteen kilometers to the south. Had he taken advantage of the opportunity to inspect the camp? No specific mention of such an excursion is listed among Himmler's calendar notations for the day, though a laconic reference to his having spent the hour from 11 AM to noon "with Koppe" is suggestive of such a possibility. As it was, on that same day a number of Jews from Sanniki were reported killed at Chełmno. Himmler drove that afternoon eastward toward Kutno and from there proceeded to Warsaw, where, upon arriving at six that evening, he paid a visit to the Warsaw ghetto.[6]

Whether or not he made a side trip to Chełmno, Himmler's pass through the Wartheland on April 17 decisively coincided with a deadly removal of populations in the province. On April 20 the Gettoverwaltung announced a "resettlement of the Jews" in the outlying ghettos, and on April 27 further noted that the resettlement was now "definite," on direct orders from Himmler. Smaller Warthegau ghettos were to be dissolved, and that portion of their population deemed fit for labor was to be routed to the central ghetto in Łódź, the remainder to be funneled into the death center at Chełmno.[7]

Whatever uncertainties lingered, the details of future deportations were now clarified in the wake of Himmler's meetings with Greiser and Koppe. The Gettoverwaltung began to act on the basis of the most recent directives. In order to create space in the Łódź ghetto to accommodate newcomers from the provinces, additional Jews—those who had arrived the previous autumn—would head the lists of those bound for Chełmno when deportations were resumed in May.

At the same time, on April 20 the Gettoverwaltung, proclaiming its authority in the matter, issued directives to provincial authorities guiding the disposition of valuables and movable property of the Jews in the soon-to-be-liquidated provincial ghettos. To facilitate the disposal and monetary conversion of goods confiscated from Jewish dwellings and properties in the wake of their owners' removal from these locations, the ghetto managers in Litzmannstadt directed that leftover household items—furniture, foodstuffs, kitchenware, and the like—be sold or auctioned locally, with cash proceeds only, less administrative and handling costs, transferred directly to the Ghetto Administration. Foreign currency, precious metals and jewelry, finished textiles and associated workable raw materials, as well as artisanal equipment, including machinery for sewing, fur manufacture, shoemaking, and carpentry, were to go directly into the possession of ghetto management. Local officials were expressly warned that "in no case is it permissible to collect from Jews prior to resettlement any sums of cash or other [financial] claims," which were "exclusively and alone the task of the Sonderkommando Lange." Any outstanding claims against Jewish owners were to be submitted to the Gettoverwaltung for consideration.[8]

Simultaneously with the issuance of these new guidelines to the provincial leadership, the Ghetto Administration ordered the ghetto unemployed to appear for medical inspection. Posted in the ghetto only a day in advance, the order called upon all unemployed persons "above the age of 10" to report, "their ID's or bread ration cards" in hand, beginning at 7:30 the following morning, April 20, for mandatory physical examinations, to be conducted at a soup kitchen located at 32 Młynarska Street. There were to be no exceptions even for the sick; the *Chronicle* reported that "the bedridden will be brought to the examination by members of the Department of Health. To expedite matters to that end, people are to report to their precinct police stations." Pointedly excluded from the requirement were persons then employed and holding valid work certificates "issued by the Bureau of Labor or by the Personnel Bureau."[9]

During these physical examinations, the very young and the elderly alike were gauged for signs of the amount of labor that might be extracted from bodies of marginal strength already ravaged by two years of deprivation and terror. "They received a stamp upon their chests like animals in an exhibit[,] . . . 10-year-old orphans with stamps upon their chests," Rosenfeld noted privately in response to the commissioners' procedure of inscribing their judgments on the flesh of even such tender bodies. As to the insensitivity of the German physicians in attendance, Rosenfeld could only register their unthinking "amazement" at the "desolate condition" of the human specimens parading before them. For anyone with eyes to see, the outward manifestations of physical ruin had long been evident in the ghetto. "Wrinkles on the face, on the throat, under the chin, around the stomach outwardly characterize the results of undernourishment and corresponding hunger," he wrote. "The swift death, the increase in stomach and intestinal illnesses, diseases of the skeletal apparatus, the constant tiredness in the extremities, is attributable to chronic lack of nutrients. The pulse slows, the blood pressure sinks. For many apathy is the beginning of death. The constant undernourishment has been a catastrophe for the metabolism."[10]

While thousands of nonworking ghetto inhabitants, both young and old, had been compelled to submit to medical examinations, the Jews who had arrived from Central Europe the previous autumn had been excluded. Untouched by this latest selection, they had reason to conclude that, at least thus far, they had perhaps benefited from a certain privilege attaching to their origin. That was not the case. For with the posting of "Proclamation Number 380" on April 29, the "Western" newcomers discovered that it was indeed they who now were targeted for collective removal.[11] The order could only have struck them as an unexpected and grievous blow. The logic of their exclusion from the recent physical inspection was now apparent: there was no need to assess their physical worth because they would be the next to go.

Although most of the newcomers from the old Reich and the Protectorate were to be deported, exemptions were made on the basis of current

employment status, record of highly honored service in the armed forces,
or, as before, favorably received petitions and complaints.[12] In a bitter reversal of its original function, however, this task, carried out in cooperation with "the chairman of the court, the director of the Department of
Population Records, and the Department of Penal Administration," now
fell to the staff of the very bureau that had overseen the newcomers' arrival
in the ghetto the previous autumn and supervised their general welfare in
the months that followed.[13] The creation of an entirely new category of
exemption contingent on presentation of proof of past distinguished military service was owing to the German leadership's cautious approach toward Jews who a generation earlier had made military sacrifices for the
imperial German and Austrian armed forces. In consequence, blanket exceptions to the general order for deportation were to be made for Jewish
combat veterans ("and a few of their family members"), as long as they
were able to certify having been granted the Iron Cross first or second
class or decorated for having been wounded during the First World War.
As for Central European Jews granted exemption from removal because
they were engaged in full-time ghetto employment, they were afforded the
additional, agonizing privilege of having to choose only "one member of
the immediate family (wife, parent, child)" to remain behind with them
in the ghetto. Special exemption was additionally arranged for a small
group of skilled translators and "their families as well."[14]

Plunging into their new tasks, the staff of the bureau responsible for
managing the affairs of the newcomers, working in close conjunction with
the Resettlement Commission, issued in all some fifteen thousand "departure warrants" to the Central European Jews.[15] In the meantime the
agency busied itself with fielding petitions from those appealing their orders to depart. A significant number, some 4,500 according to the *Chronicle,* were granted.[16] But that still left more than two thirds of those originally summoned to face expulsion. Indicative of the sizable administrative
burden this review entailed, the *Chronicle* noted that "the commission
that deals with complaints is working day and night." In the grip of overwhelming tension, people nervously awaited word of the decision that
would determine their fate:

Punctually at eight in the morning, crowds of petitioners fill the
courtyard of the building where the office is located, for it is at that

time that an official of the office reads out the names of those who
have been given exemptions and those subject to deportation or to
some postponement. The crowd listens in an atmosphere of the
most extreme anxiety; the impression is of people waiting for either a
reprieve or a death sentence. Tears of joy or of terrible despair—everyone reacts one way or the other upon hearing his name called. It
is no exaggeration to say that the morning hours in the courtyard at
8 Rybna Street are, by their nature, profoundly tragic.[17]

As veterans came forward seeking exemption from transport, many
who had served with distinction in the Great War in the German or
Austro-Hungarian armed forces were nonetheless turned away, since only
those who could incontestably document their possession of so high a
military honor were granted the privilege of remaining in the ghetto. Nor
would lesser awards for valor suffice. Even a well-placed attorney from the
first Vienna transport, who served as a block leader for the group and,
since the winter, had chaired a body of its representatives, was rejected in
his appeal for revocation of the order for deportation. His petition, presented on his own behalf as well as that of his wife and ailing mother, was
denied in spite of his insistence that he had been awarded no fewer than
four wartime decorations—including both the silver and bronze military
service medals; the silver medal for valor, second class; and the Karl-
Truppenkreuz—"each one of these," he insisted, being *fully* equivalent to
the Iron Cross."[18] Similarly, a nurse who had been decorated for her wartime service and who had, albeit in an "honorary capacity," assisted members of the Hamburg transport, generously and "free of charge" contributing medications in her possession, was rejected in her request for
exemption.[19] Widows of highly decorated Jewish veterans found their petitions rejected as well. Such had been the fate of a woman from the first
transport from Cologne who had written to state, "My husband was a
bearer of the Iron Cross. The document [testifying] to this was lost owing
to the extraordinary swiftness of the evacuation. I hereby declare under
oath, in full consciousness of the legal consequences of this declaration,
that my husband, who died as a result of the war, was a holder of the Iron
Cross, second class."[20] Another widow whose husband had received the
Iron Cross and who had herself worked for four years in a munitions factory in Metz was also turned down for exemption from transport.[21]

Among the ghetto newcomers from Germany there was a "prevailing sense . . . that the local population has been tucked away in workshops and offices to be saved from resettlement, while the Western Jews have been pushed to the fore." It was not perhaps altogether surprising that, according to the *Chronicle*, "a great many" of the Jewish veterans "intend[ed] to decline the privilege of remaining here." Specifically, they had "decided not to disclose their decorations," abandoning their only grounds for contesting their orders of expulsion, preferring instead to bring to an end their hateful sojourn in Łódź. "More than five months of hunger and cold, on bare floors, does not in the least dispose them to fight for life in the ghetto. They say that wherever they may find themselves, things will not be any worse for them, and so they are ready and willing to leave their current residence." The men were resentful over what they perceived as their second-class status, as a result of which "the majority of them have been doing manual labor in the ghetto, a great many of them working at garbage and excrement disposal."[22] Having reached the limits of their tolerance for such treatment, all of the approximately fifty decorated Jewish veterans from the third Berlin transport waived their right to an exemption in order to depart "together in the same transport," making clear that "they have had enough of this paradise!"[23]

In general, by Rosenfeld's estimation there had in fact been "hundreds of volunteers" who had reported for deportation of their own accord. That they did so in sober awareness of what awaited them at their destination appears doubtful in light of the belief, recorded in his diary, that "it cannot be any worse 'there' . . . ; perhaps even more bread and potatoes in case of farmwork."[24] For others, unwilling or unable to bear the rigors of another departure and journey into the unknown, death remained, as ever, a final option. In what was described as "a frenzy of suicides" throughout the days of the May transports, Western Europeans leaped from upper stories of ghetto buildings, downed lethal doses of sleeping potions, hanged themselves in garrets, and slit their wrists. Here too we must acknowledge that such acts, surely undertaken in a state of unfathomable despair, promised as their sole and hardly to be underestimated reward an end to suffering.[25]

The bulk of the now targeted newcomers remained particularly vulnerable to seizure. As in their coming, so in their going, the Jews from the Central European cities would travel together as a group. Nevertheless, the members of the Czech transports who had succeeded in escaping collective housing arrangements and had better integrated themselves into the ghetto economy were at a distinct advantage in evading removal at this point. Among their number, Dr. Oskar Singer remained deeply sensitive to the tragedy of the German Jews, who, until the end, seemed an alien and unwelcome presence within the larger ghetto community. It was not without a measure of sadness that he took note of the way so many of them responded to the posting of the order signaling their departure: some crestfallen, others taking the blow in stride, ready to depart in the expectation that at their next destination conditions could be no worse.[26] Oskar Rosenfeld had noted that the Jewish police, unwilling to rely solely on expectations of general compliance, had pointedly resorted to staging nighttime roundups of the "Westerners," catching them off guard by rousing them from sleep and hustling them off to the assembly points. Rosenfeld remained struck, however, by the irony of many of the Western Jews, "crowding together," a "throng of children, women, old people, and men with their sacks and knapsacks," dutifully and of their own volition showing up at the gates of their assigned enclosure. "The scene resembled a carnival or a gypsy camp. People waited and begged to be let into the prison."[27]

Beginning May 4 and extending through May 15, each morning at seven the trains departed the ghetto station. Two days prior to their scheduled departure, those summoned would have to report by noon to the initial staging points located at the Central Prison and a nearby barbed-wire enclosure on Szklana Street. Fed and held overnight, at noon the following day they would be escorted by Order Service personnel to one of two final holding areas in a "school building on Jonschera Street" and a complex of "five small buildings on Okopowa Street" in the northeastern sector of the Marysin district, close to the farthermost ghetto perimeter. There they would spend a last, abbreviated night in the ghetto. At four o'clock the next morning they boarded a tram that took them to the ghetto station. There they waited until six-thirty, at which time German security officers and police would arrive to oversee the final loading of the trains. Before entering the "third-class carriages" in which they would travel, the deportees, lined up at a distance of some "two meters from the train," were brusquely ordered to turn over their wedding rings, abandon their baggage and excess belongings, and put their hands in the air. Persons slow to act were liable to be lashed with a whip. Knapsacks were forcibly removed by a severing of their leather straps.[28]

Word that the deportees were being forced to give up their remaining possessions quickly made its way back and "cast a chill over the ghetto."[29] In a mournful sign that other ghetto residents could not fail to notice, the Jewish police, after collecting the forcibly abandoned property of the departed, "transported it all on flat, sideless, horse-drawn wagons to the Office for Resettled Persons on Rybna Street, where the ownerless items were secured in storehouses that had been cleaned out especially for that purpose. The sight of the wagons pulling up in front of the office, loaded mostly with small packages, nearly all of which contained the most essential items—bedding and blankets—caused a feeling of hopelessness among the passersby."[30]

In a mirror image of the heavy bartering that had attended the arrival of these "wealthy" visitors the previous autumn, German Jews were busy selling off to their Polish brethren the last of their personal effects in exchange for food and hard cash for the journey. Commerce was brisk at the entrances to the collectives and on ghetto squares. Among the purchasers were longtime ghetto residents untouched by this new wave of deportation. Acquisitive instincts were all too visibly at work. Likened, in accord with that same zoological imagery observers often found so apt, to "hyenas and predators," newly outfitted buyers appeared "wearing peccary-skin gloves and raincoats—blue ones, red ones, green ones, and so on—and burdened with newly-acquired clothing, suitcases, briefcases," prompting a chronicler to wonder at those taking advantage of the misery of others, loading up their wardrobes: "A change of clothes, or a change of roles as well? And for how long? No one thinks of that!"[31]

The acquired splendor of the newly attired contrasted with the almost grotesque appearance of Western Jews who, once aware that any handheld items or other baggage were being removed from deportees in advance of departure, took to bulking up with whatever they might still conceal on their persons, and had to maneuver their now "disproportionately wide bodies that bend and droop under their own weight," heavy with layers of overcoats, suits, and undergarments. But this sorry fashion trend did not endure for long. Only two days after the transports had resumed, the *Chronicle* recorded that "fewer and fewer people loaded down with sacks are to be seen, and the later transports are practically without luggage when they come to Marysin. Abandoned umbrellas and canes are strewn over the grounds of the prison." Apparently "the last and final privilege—to take a 'bag and a stick'—has been retracted from them."[32]

In stark contrast, while the ghetto endured the strain of this sorrowful and bitter separation, residents of Litzmannstadt found that the arrival of spring allowed them to take full advantage of the opportunities their newly modernizing city offered for restful outdoor enjoyment and spiritual uplift. One showpiece of metropolitan Litzmannstadt's emerging blend of well-planned urban design and environmental stewardship was already taking shape close by the ghetto's southern border. Here, under the direction of the city's garden department, a new "park-like" urban triangle, marked out to accommodate scores of carefully arranged garden allotments, was under development. Featuring a pond fed by confluent streams, a planned orchard, and walkways, the project was only the most recent addition to a more ambitiously conceived greenery belt stretching broadly from a newly reforested zone in the Stockhausen district to the east of the new garden triangle, through a nearby Christian cemetery, the Ostfriedhof, adjacent to the park, and ultimately extending westward to an area about a block south of the ghetto on the other side of Hohensteiner (Zgierska) Street at Gartenstraße. The grounds at the center of the new park promised to be a site of particular enjoyment, "especially in the springtime, when the trees are in bloom, when for the first time all the gardens will be planted," making for "a wonderful experience." It was expected that "around a thousand fruit trees will blossom here."[33]

While urban residents were being encouraged to open their senses to the enjoyment of such exquisite gifts of spring, they were at the same time sternly admonished to resist the temptation to seize and remove them. In the interest of preserving from extinction a host of endangered local flora, citizens were reminded of the provisions of a 1936 Reich ordinance protecting specific kinds of plants and animals. They were told that "even in small quantities," daphnes, columbines, arnicas, water lilies, wild orchids, and globeflowers, among many others, "were not to be plucked."[34] Such warnings were aimed at those who, proving not content merely to admire the many thousands of wind anemones and marsh marigolds lushly growing "in the wooded sections of our *Volkspark*," had taken to removing them at will.[35]

Such attention to preservation of the natural world was a manifestation of the pride the city fathers took in the urban landscape and surroundings of their newly Germanizing metropolis. The city was brimming with new life. It was this extraordinarily verdant environment that the officials of the new city wished one and all to appreciate. To read their exhortations to the public to get out and enjoy this glorious natural efflorescence, one would think the citizens of this previously neglected outpost of the expanding Reich had the privilege of inhabiting a great undiscovered garden city of the East. With life emerging all about, one had but to attune one's senses and delight in the spectacle. It was thought that Litzmannstadt had much to be thankful for.

Through the winter of 1942 the Jews had watched as thousands of their neighbors made their way in a steady, sorry stream toward the assembly points and from there to the freight station just beyond the northern perimeter of the ghetto. Initially the community had been told that it was only the troublemakers, along with those who had avoided employment, who would be selected for removal from the ghetto. In truth, those summoned to depart had come from all age groups and comprised not just individuals marked by their run-ins with ghetto justice, whether troublesome labor activists or accused petty thieves, but whole families, including distant relations, even unrelated apartment mates, all indiscriminately directed to the trains. Then in May had come the turn of the unpopular German Jews, identifiable outsiders in their midst. Yet no sooner had the last of the transports of Jews from Austria, Germany, and Bohemia been processed and departed than news came of mass deportations of Jews from the smaller suburban and provincial communities near Łódź. In these instances the weaker members of these communities were immediately dispatched to an unrevealed destination, while a few thousand deemed still fit enough for work were processed into the Łódź ghetto.

They brought with them alarming stories of their ordeal. By now the remaining inhabitants of the Łódź ghetto, some 100,000 in number, were keenly aware of the human upheaval occasioned by these massive population transfers. They increasingly and inescapably assumed the role of anxious spectators to the tragedies and sufferings of others. With the arrival of the survivors of selections taking place in outlying areas, it was now impossible to ignore the fact that elsewhere the Germans were liquidating entire communities, separating families, seizing property, manhandling and shooting innocent people, hauling them away on carts or in railway cars. Most of all, that May the provincial newcomers offered evidence of a disturbing new tactic of separation and selection. The Germans were specifically targeting for removal small children, notably those below the age of ten, and shipping them off in the company of the aged and the weak. Now the residents of the ghetto foresaw a new danger with potential consequences for their own families.

The immediate source of intensified concern were the Jews of the near-south suburban community of Pabianice, the survivors of a terrifying weekend selection and the first of the newcomers to arrive immediately after the departure of the last transport bearing away the Central European Jews. "The MOOD OF THE GHETTO has changed completely since Sunday," wrote the ghetto chronicler Bernard Ostrowski in his entry dated Wednesday, May 20, and Thursday, May 21:

> Reports of resettlements from the provinces have had a depressing effect on the entire populace. Nothing could be more shocking than to visit the site at 22 Masarska Street, where over a thousand (1,082) women from Pabianice have been quartered. In every room, in every corner, one sees mothers, sisters, grandmothers, shaken by sobs, quietly lamenting for their little children. All children up to age 10 have been sent off to parts unknown. Some have lost three, four, even six children. Their quiet despair is profoundly penetrating, so different from the loud laments we are accustomed to hearing at deaths and funerals, but all the more real and sincere for that.[36]

Policeman Shlomo Frank took note of a crushing spectacle at a corner of Bałut Market, where an emotionally broken mother from Pabianice was seen beseeching passersby, asking if anyone knew the whereabouts of her five lost children. Desperately seeking the assistance of anyone who might help in locating them, she stood, muttering a sad monologue, addressing pedestrians, addressing the Creator, addressing herself and her fate, recalling how well cared for the children had been, how properly combed their hair, and how "my neighbors always said to me, upon my children rests the beauty of the neighborhood." Imploring God and anyone who would listen, she pleaded, "Help me find my 5 dear, precious little swallows. . . . I won't bear this much longer. I sense that I will kill myself."[37]

Hearing details of what had transpired in the outlying communities, seeing the mothers of Pabianice in their quiet despair, the residents of the ghetto feared for the safety of their own youngsters. "It is no surprise that anyone with small children or old parents awaits the days to come with trepidation," Ostrowski wrote. "The greatest optimists have lost hope. Until now, people had thought that work would maintain the ghetto and the majority of its people without any breakup of families. Now it is clear that even this was an illusion."[38]

Next came the turn of the Jews of Brzeziny. In this poor Jewish community immediately to the east of Łódź, then numbering some six thousand souls, the separation of families and transfer of the working population, largely in the employ of a single textile firm, began with the order for all the Jews to place their belongings in bags outside their residences. Not a person was to carry more than the allotted eleven kilograms of weight. If anyone was discovered to have exceeded the restriction, there was "a violent reaction on the spot—such bags were thrown back into gateways or apartments, which were then at once shut and sealed."[39] As in Pabianice, there had occurred a ruthless division of the population into groups labeled "A," or *Arbeitsfähig* (able to work), and "B," including the infirm, the elderly, and children under ten. Many of the mothers, though deemed employable and placed in the "A" category, seeing that they were to be separated from their youngsters or forced to give over their infants, voluntarily left the privileged group to join those in category "B," condemning themselves to share the fate of some 1,700 persons so labeled who departed "for parts unknown." The remaining Jews of Brzeziny who passed inspection were brought south to the station in Galkówek—the weaker ones in carts, the stronger marching "on foot"—where they were "lined up" and made to wait several hours for the trains that were to take them, they were told, to Litzmannstadt. When they arrived at the ghetto on Monday, May 18, in multiple shipments at nine in the morning, at noon, and later that afternoon, they "were pained to find that their food supplies were gone, though their other things had arrived." Members of the ghetto police seem to have reverted to a malicious practice of the previous autumn, when they had victimized Jews arriving from Włocławek. "The newcomers complain that their bags were ripped open and the traces of theft were obvious," the *Chronicle* noted. "The majority accuse our police who had been in charge of receiving their baggage."[40] Once more, parents separated from their children were most distraught, among them "a local pharmacist, who left this ghetto a few months ago for a position as a pharmacist in Brzeziny," and who "returned here yesterday in a state of utter hopelessness, because his only son, a 5-year-old, was taken from him."[41] For a brief moment on the evening of the eighteenth, hopes of being reunited with the youngest children were raised when a group of two hundred children from Brzeziny arrived. Alas, "all these children were over the age of 10."[42]

The tears of the weeping mothers on Masarska Street hardly had a chance to dry before evidence of unusual activity began turning up. Resettlers from Pabianice reported that in nearby Dąbrowa "warehouses for old clothes have recently been set up on the grounds of a factory idle since the war began," said the *Chronicle*. "Thus far, five gigantic warehouses have been set up there. They contain clothing, linen, bedding, shoes, pots and pans, and so on. Each day, trucks deliver mountains of packages, knapsacks, and parcels of every sort to Dąbrowa. Everything is broken down into groups and put in its proper place in the warehouses. Each day, thirty or so Jews from the Pabianice ghetto are sent to sort the goods." In the process, the workers were coming across unmistakable clues indicating to whom the items had belonged. "Among other things, they have noticed that, among the waste papers, there were some of our *Rumkis* [internally circulating ghetto currency], which had fallen out of billfolds. The obvious conclusion is that some of the clothing belongs to people deported from this ghetto."[43] That month sizable quantities of abandoned clothing poured into three more ghetto warehouses on Brzezińska, Marynarska, and Franciskańska streets, where they were picked over and sorted by some of the men from the dissolved communities. Bundles of sheets and carpet, tied into makeshift luggage, contained undergarments and, most telling of all, papers, ghetto currency, and identification clearly pointing to people who had been deported. Some of the material came from those Jews from Włocławek who had been in the first group relocated the previous autumn and deported later in the winter.[44] Did all of this unmistakably indicate foul play? If the chroniclers who recorded these incidents thought that to be the case, they did not dare say so in their daily log. The account nevertheless suggests the possibility had entered their minds that those to whom these things once belonged had met their end, but heightened suspicion was not the same as knowing for sure. Wherever the owners of these articles now were, might they have been issued new clothing or prison uniforms? Or had they in fact been murdered? On this the chroniclers were silent, watchful, perhaps even alarmed, awaiting further evidence.

By the spring of 1942, in conformity with procedures by now firmly in place, valuables gathered in the course of clearing provincial Jewish communities and their ghettos were funneled to the Gettoverwaltung in Litzmannstadt. No quantity of currency confiscated from an individual deportee was too small to be counted and deposited at the disposal of the Ghetto Administration. Even savings books containing no more than a single Polish złoty were duly registered in the seizure.[45] Also collected were foreign currencies—U.S. dollars, including gold dollars, English pounds, gold marks, Austrian silver schillings, Argentinean pesos, gold rubles, Czech crowns, and Palestine pounds—all of which, after monetary conversion facilitated in partnership with the local Reichsbank (German Central Bank) affiliate, were credited to a specially designated Gettoverwaltung account, identified as *Sonderkonto* (special account) 12300, at the Stadtsparkaße Litzmannstadt, the Litzmannstadt City Savings Bank.[46] Located downtown at number 77 Adolf-Hitler-Straße, the Stadtsparkaße had long served as the principal financial institution through which ghetto management conducted its business affairs and controlled incoming as well as outgoing funds associated with operation of the ghetto. Swelling with the accumulated riches accruing to the Ghetto Administration as a result of the liquidation of surrounding Jewish communities, account number 12300 in turn served as the base for a fund from which the managers could draw to cover the expenses involved in collecting and transporting confiscated goods, and for the distribution of promised salary supplements for civilian personnel of the bureau involved in such tasks as sorting through the accumulating personal items and property.

Such hazard pay disbursements, known as *Gefahrenzulage*, were viewed as compensation for what was deemed especially unpleasant and even dangerous contact with the Jews and possibly infected materials once in their possession.[47] Two Ghetto Administration messengers, for example, were each accorded a supplemental monthly payment of sixty Reichsmarks, drawn on the special account, for routinely having "to sort and bundle" looted currency. Biebow argued that this "dirty and for the most part even repulsive labor," entailing as it did the "continuous danger of infection," entitled them to "the same rate" of supplemental compensation as other employees serving on-site at Bałuty Market.[48] The special account also served to pay hefty bills due civilian trucking firms contracted to haul mounds of leftover personal effects from the liquidated communities destined for outlying warehouses where the sorting for valuables and recyclable items took place under Ghetto Administration supervision. Even the smallest of sums, however, because linked to activities involving looted items, were drawn from account 12300, as when a reimbursement of two Reichsmarks was issued the man who personally transported coins from the savings bank to the Reichsbank affiliate on one occasion in late May 1942.[49]

In its dealings with as important a client as the Ghetto Administration, the City Savings Bank did its best to smooth over any technical difficulties. Minor glitches in the transfer of the new income were dealt with in a practical way. When, for instance, "heavily damaged" currency worth a total of RM4,162, which the Ghetto Administration had turned over to the City Savings Bank, was rejected by the local branch of the Reichsbank, the Stadtsparkaße informed ghetto management that it was returning the money and simultaneously levying a corresponding RM4,162 deduction against its account. At the same time, the City Savings Bank helpfully passed along the central bank affiliate's suggestion that "the Ghetto Administration may wish to ship the notes directly to the Reichshauptbank Berlin department for damaged notes."[50] The savings institution would continue to maintain an encouraging tone, informing the Ghetto Administration in a similar instance that a charge of seven marks and fifty-seven pfennigs was to be deducted from its special account owing to the Reichsbank's rejection of "damaged gold pieces," while concluding with the polite assurance that "we [are] always gladly at your service."[51] Wishing to ensure that funds relating to the "special operation" be kept separate from other assets, the Ghetto Administration went out of its way to inform provincial officials to redirect to the new special account proceeds from the liquidation of Jewish assets coming in from provincial Warthegau towns after they had mistakenly transferred funds to its standard business account instead.[52]

Facilitating the transfer of funds acquired through the disposal of Jewish property in the liquidated outlying communities were regional banking establishments in the provincial centers from which the Jews had been evacuated. In Chodecz, for example, proceeds from the sale of "Jewish furniture" were transferred that May to the Gettoverwaltung in Litzmannstadt via the Kreissparkaße (District Savings Bank) Leslau.[53] Similarly, in June the Ghetto Administration recorded sums obtained through the sale of Jewish household items in the amounts of RM2,246.66 and RM316.45 transferred to ghetto management via the Stadtsparkaßsse Alexandrowo and the Gemeindekaße Sluzewo, respectively.[54] Among the items recovered in Chodecz and duly surrendered for the benefit of the Ghetto Administration were personal articles such as razors, as well as household articles, notably silverware, including dessert forks, knives, coffee spoons, sugar tongs, a cake spatula, "silver-plated" creamers, bowls and cups, and jewelry such as silver chains and rings.[55] In August the Pabianice branch of the National Socialist Welfare Agency (NSV) transferred to account 12300 a sum of forty-six Reichsmarks through its local Sparkaße branch, proceeds from the sale of "9 old baby carriages and 1 doll carriage."[56]

In addition to making sure that proceeds from the disposal of Jewish household items were properly transferred from local financial institutions to its home bank in Łódź, ghetto management still had to take account of rival civilian corporate claims on goods which evacuated Jews had earlier bought on credit and for which payments were by contract still due. The Litzmannstadt branch of the Singer Sewing Machine Company, headquartered at 86 Adolf-Hitler-Straße, aggressively pursued its rights over sewing machines sold to Jews on installment plans whose charges remained outstanding. Learning that sewing machines were among the items confiscated from Jewish homes in Lentschutz and Poddębice, the company contacted the mayors of the two towns, stating firmly that the terms of purchase specifically indicated that the merchandise "remains the property of the company" until such time as it was fully paid for. With four Jewish customers in Lentschutz still owing a total of RM320.50 and two more with unpaid premiums of RM86.80, the company "respectfully request[ed]" that the mayors either "return the sewing machines to us or pay us the named sum." Informed on June 15 that "the sewing machines in question had been delivered" to the Ghetto Administration in Litzmannstadt, the Singer creditors were directed to take up their claim with that organization. In the end ghetto management, conforming to a developing pattern, on July 8 declared itself willing to resolve the matter by assuming the obligation, announcing that on that day the remaining amount due was being transferred.[57] A similar approach was followed in cases involving Jews who had been resettled to the ghetto yet were still being pursued by government institutions seeking to collect outstanding charges for small sums in back taxes and court fees. Such efforts involving debts owed by persons who had already been evacuated from the ghetto were at first directed to the Gestapo in Litzmannstadt. But after consultation with the Gestapo, "in order to avoid further inquiries," the Gettoverwaltung simply chose to cover the obligations without further ado.[58]

It additionally assumed payment for the considerable costs incurred in the transport of persons and goods during the course of the evacuations, entailing contractual dealings with outside firms both public and private. Typically, outside agencies supplying services directed charges to the local Gestapo in Litzmannstadt, which in turn routinely passed them along to the Ghetto Administration for payment. This was the procedure followed when, for example, a regional transport authority, the Litzmanstaedter Elektrische Zufuhrbahnen, its letterhead indicating that its bureau, located at number 77 Adolf-Hitler-Straße, shared the same address as the City Savings Bank, billed ghetto management for resettlement-related expenses. On May 19 it presented charges for RM340.10 for costs resulting from the transport on the two previous days of Jews from the nearby suburb of Pabianice to Litzmannstadt, in shipments consisting of "7 trains each with 2 trailers." Included in the bill were costs for damages amounting to sixteen marks incurred because of the destruction in transit of two panes of glass worth eight marks apiece. The same company presented an additional bill on May 25 for the three trains carrying Jews "from Osorkow to Litzmannstadt, Ghetto."[59] After forwarding via the Gestapo, charges arrived as well from the freight cashier's office at the railway station in Pabianice "for the Jewish transports to Przybylow carried out on May 17 and 18, 1942," with payment duly following through issuance of a check.[60]

On a larger scale, on May 19 the national rail authority, Deutsche Reichsbahn, similarly billed ghetto management a total of RM33,731.35 to cover the expense of twelve one-way transports, carried out daily from May 4 to May 15, hauling 10,993 Jews at a half-price charge of RM2.95 per person from Litzmannstadt to Wartbrücken (Koło), the preliminary leg of the outward journey leading from the ghetto to Chełmno. Included in the bill were supplemental charges to cover the costs of transporting guards, or "accompanying personnel," usually numbering thirteen per train, who alone required a return. It was requested that payment for these charges be made "at the booking office [at] the main railway station [in] Litzmannstadt."[61]

Above and beyond the costs of transporting people within the province and to the death center, Biebow's organization undertook responsibility for considerable sums resulting from the removal of enormous quantities of their personal belongings. These operations entailed significant dealings with fuel suppliers and private trucking firms as well. Writing on May 27 to the Economic Office in Posen regarding fuel requirements, Biebow's deputy Luchterhand indicated that the already substantial quantities of clothing seized in the course of operations to clear the provincial ghettos, now piling up at a depot at the Sonderkommando in Chełmno, were such that sixteen heavy diesel- and gasoline-powered trucks were already committed to related tasks, but that ultimately "some 900 trucks with trailers" would be required to move "370 wagonloads of clothing articles." It was estimated that to clear out the current inventory, hauling the loot to an external site for processing would "continue for some 2 months."[62]

Bills submitted by local commercial trucking companies hired to assist in these massive hauling operations indicate that related highway freight traffic was heavy in May and June 1942. One Litzmannstadt firm working for the Gettoverwaltung on *Sondereinsatz,* or special assignment, had committed vehicles to almost continual daily service from May 18 to June 15, often in excess of ten hours and in some instances even as much as fifteen or sixteen hours per day. On June 19 its charges covering drivers' and co-workers' wages, accounting for over three hundred hours of labor, amounted to RM2,381.90 after the Ghetto Administration subtracted costs for gasoline and oil.[63] Not to be overlooked were further payments to cover extras such as cigarettes for men of the Sonderkommando active in the *Judenaktion*.[64] Also paid out of special account 12300 on August 8 were costs of RM104.51 dating from July 17, due a Litzmannstadt liquor and wine dealer for seven liters of spirits and two bottles of sweet cherry liqueur.[65] A pharmacy in Posen was paid for delivery of lime chloride *(Chlorkalk)* for the wagons used to bring victims to the Chełmno death facility, with the Gettoverwaltung busy as well preparing delivery of the same chemical "for the Special Operation."[66]

In addition to assuming the cost of transporting freight and human cargo inside the Warthegau, the Ghetto Administration had to cover RM18,284.99 in charges for the "disinfection and delousing" of tens of thousands of articles processed in Pabianice under agreement with a government subcontractor, the Kindler Factory Bath and Delousing Establishment, operated by the Ethnic German Agency (Volksdeutschemittelstelle). From May 11 to June 30, 1942, for "1,093 Jews bathed and deloused" the facility processed "54,485 beds," "44,010 items of underwear and clothing," "1,259 pairs of shoes," and "439 blankets," in addition to "680 beds in the Dombrowa camp sprayed with a soap solution." Itemized charges covered costs for wages, steam, electricity, water, disinfectant, "soft soap used for delousing," "detergent for washing protective suits," and, though amounting to but twelve marks of the total, brooms, scrub brushes, and scouring cloths as well.[67]

Working hand in hand with the SS-Sonderkommando Bothmann, responsible for operations in the Chełmno death center, and with the Gestapo, under Biebow's resourceful direction the Ghetto Administration thus scrupulously attended to all matters related to the business end of the killing. Adapting seamlessly to the requirements of the emerging policy of annihilation, the Gettoverwaltung played a pivotal role in managing the collection of proceeds resulting from the operation and overseeing payment of all necessary expenses. Building on its experience in compelling the Jews to pay the costs of their own confinement in the ghetto, the administration now applied its expertise to see to it that they would be made to finance their own destruction. In doing so, it was able to count on the

Jewish onlookers silently watch as a rudimentary transport of simple possessions is transferred to the ghetto. 1940. (Photograph by Mendel Grossman. USHMM, courtesy of Moshe Zilbar.)

Mordechai Chaim Rumkowski (1887–1944). Appointed Chairman of the Jewish Council in Łódź in the autumn of 1939, he led the Jewish community from the formation of the ghetto in the winter of 1940 until its dissolution in the summer of 1944. Dated 1940–1943. (USHMM, courtesy of Ruth Eldar.)

Jews on Kościelny Square viewed through a fence looking into the ghetto from Zgierska Street (Hohensteinerstraße). The view is to the east. The low, red-brick building in the middle distance to the left lies on the corner of Łagiewnicka and Brzezińska Streets. An unidentified man crouches in the foreground. Undated, possibly July 1940. (Photograph by Walter Genewein. Jüdisches Museum Frankfurt am Main.)

(top left) A view of Adolf Hitler Straße, Litzmannstadt's central avenue, in July 1940. (Photograph by Walter Genewein. Jüdisches Museum Frankfurt am Main.)

(bottom left) Another view of Adolf Hitler Straße in Litzmannstadt. Civilians walk beneath the awnings. Facing the street, two women pause on the sidewalk. Undated. (Photograph by Walter Genewein. Jüdisches Museum Frankfurt am Main.)

Hans Biebow (1902–1947), director of the Gettoverwaltung, the administrative agency responsible for the management of the ghetto, standing beside an automobile. The sign taped to the inside of the windshield identifies the vehicle as being associated with the Gettoverwaltung. Dated 1940–1944. (Photograph by Walter Genewein. USHMM, courtesy of Robert Abrams.)

In the comfortable setting of a corner office, Hans Biebow reviews a file of documents. To his right, a bank of telephones sits at the ready. Dated 1940–1944. (Photograph by Walter Genewein. USHMM, courtesy of Robert Abrams.)

Traffic and pedestrians on Moltkestraße, downtown Litzmannstadt. Pictured at left is the headquarters of the Gettoverwaltung, with its name spelled out in large lettering above the entrance. A man can be seen peering from an open window on the second story. Estimated date: 1941–1944. (Photograph by Walter Genewein. USHMM, courtesy of Robert Abrams.)

Soup is ladled out for orphaned youngsters patiently awaiting an outdoor meal in the Marysin quarter of the ghetto. Dated 1942. (Photographer unlisted.

A small girl of the Łódź ghetto, photographed by the ghetto photographer, Mendel Grossman. Dated 1940–1944. (USHMM, courtesy of Arie Ben Menachem.)

Residents of the ghetto on a crowded cobblestone street. Aware of being photographed, some stop and look in the direction of the camera. Undated. (Photograph by Walter Genewein. Jüdisches Museum Frankfurt am Main.)

(top right) Jewish officials from the ghetto's central purchasing bureau attend to their tasks. The gentlemen, dressed in jackets and ties, write by hand; the woman on the left works on a typewriter. Dated 1940–1944. (Photographer unlisted. USHMM, courtesy of Inka Gerson Allen.)

(bottom right) An overhead view of Jews populating the sidewalks and crossing the street at Kościelny Square. Undated, possibly July 1940. (Photograph by Walter Genewein. Jüdisches Museum Frankfurt am Main.)

By night a pair of sentries stand guard outside a fence enclosing the ghetto. From an album in the possession of a member of Police Battalion 101. 1940–1944. Another guard expressed his experiences poetically, likening the nearby snow to "a burial shroud" and marveling at the "stillness, heavy as fog," as well as the "pale dome" of the heavens above. ("Verse, die am Schilderhaus gedichtet wurden. Nächtliche Gedanken eines einsamen Postens Von Paul Siegmann Pol.-Oberwachtmeister d. R.," *LZ*, 10 March 1941, p. 4.) (Photographer unknown. USHMM, courtesy of Michael O'Hara.)

Near the ghetto perimeter on a winter night, ice glistens on the branches of a tree and snow covers the ground. A striped guard house is visible in the background. From an album in the possession of a member of Reserve Police Battalion 101. The men of this unit patrolled the ghetto boundary during the late autumn and winter of 1940–1941. (Photographer unknown. USHMM, courtesy of Michael O'Hara.)

In Litzmannstadt, visiting circuses offered highly publicized popular entertainment. Featured here, decked out with banners, is the tent of the Althoff Circus, which came to town in July 1940. Undated. (Photograph by Walter Genewein. Jüdisches Museum Frankfurt am Main.)

Under a broad expanse of sky, a woman leads two small children along a sidewalk near the boundary of the ghetto. The open space and nearby rubble most likely mark an area that was cleared to provide separation between the ghetto and the city. Undated. (Photograph by Walter Genewein. Jüdisches Museum Frankfurt am Main.)

In a ghetto textile workshop, Jewish women toil at their worktables. Undated.
(Photograph by Walter Genewein. Jüdisches Museum Frankfurt am Main.)

Ghetto women braid straw used in the manufacture of winter footwear.
Undated. (Photograph by Walter Genewein. Jüdisches Museum Frankfurt am Main.)

Inside the Church of the Virgin Mary on Kościelny Square, ghetto women tend to feather bedding confiscated from resettled Jewish families. The feathers were eventually delivered to the Germans for recycling. Dated 1940–1944. (Photograph by Mendel Grossman. USHMM, courtesy of Moshe Zilbar.)

Four unidentified men and an unidentified woman together in a city park (Park Julianow) in June 1940. (Photograph by Walter Genewein. Jüdisches Museum Frankfurt am Main.)

(top right) At the home of a colleague in the Gettoverwaltung, Walter Genewein, seated on the left, participates in a quiet gathering featuring champagne. Winter 1940. (Genewein Collection. Jüdisches Museum Frankfurt am Main.)

(bottom right) In a Litzmannstadt residence, Walter Genewein, dressed in robe and slippers, reads while seated on a long sofa. October 1942. (Genewein Collection. Jüdisches Museum Frankfurt am Main.)

Unidentified men in civilian dress visit a rag warehouse in the ghetto. A soiled garment is presented for inspection. A Jewish star is visible on the white jacket of the gentleman on the right. Undated. (Photograph by Walter Genewein. Jüdisches Museum Frankfurt am Main.)

(top left) Clothing for small children on display for an internal exhibition of articles manufactured in the ghetto. On the wall display a wooden stork, its wings outspread, is pictured delivering a newborn to the world. Undated, possibly 1944. (Photograph by Walter Genewein. Jüdisches Museum Frankfurt am Main.)

(bottom left) A display of women's dresses for an internal exhibition featuring clothing manufactured in the ghetto. Undated, possibly 1944. (Photograph by Walter Genewein. Jüdisches Museum Frankfurt am Main.)

Young boys of the ghetto line up to receive a distribution of soup. Dated 1940–1944. (Photograph by Walter Genewein. USHMM, courtesy of Robert Adams.)

A kneeling woman in an apron leans close to speak to a young boy seated on the other side of a wire fence in the ghetto's central prison during a round-up of the children in September 1942. Three other young people listen in. (Photograph by Mendel Grossman, USHMM, courtesy of Moshe Zilbar.)

enthusiastic cooperation of city and provincial government institutions and commercial enterprises and their employees.

While fresh merchandise continued to flow to outlying storehouses, in the first days of June mounds of bedding arriving from the provinces were trucked into the very heart of the ghetto, deposited outside, and then piled high within the cavernous red-brick Church of the Virgin Mary dominating Kościelny Square. Feathers burst from torn fabric to swirl about, prompting Josef Zelkowicz of the Statistical Department to liken the phenomenon to snow falling in June. The snowflakes *were* only feathers, of course, but even so they were no less capable than the snows of winter of chilling the thin, undernourished blood of ghetto residents who, seeing them, knew where they came from and to whom they had once belonged.[68]

From their office located just across the street from the church, the unusual phenomenon would have been difficult for Zelkowicz and other members of the department to ignore. It certainly did not escape the attention of Mendel Grossman, a departmental staff photographer who was drawn to linger here, returning time and again, wandering with his camera through the church, photographing this strange setting amid which ghetto women, wrapped in their headscarves and dwarfed by soft mounds of bedding piled high above the altar, climbed atop the piles to stack and sort the bulging sacks of bedding. Grossman found the women outdoors in the adjacent courtyard as well, busy cleaning an ever-increasing store of feathers freed from eiderdowns, comforters, and pillows, items that until recently had warmed the Jews from the now dissolved nearby provincial communities as they slept.

A ghetto friend who survived described what had drawn Grossman to this setting:

> The picture was strange and frightening, and the darkness of the Gothic interior added to the weirdness of the scene. A small sign attached to the entrance attempted to explain what was happening inside. It read "Institute for Feather Cleaning." But the sign did not tell the whole truth. That was the place to which the bedding robbed

from Jews who were sent to death from Lodz and surrounding towns was being brought. There, in the Church of the Virgin Mary, the pillows and featherbeds were ripped open by Jewish men and women, then the feathers were cleaned, sorted, packed and shipped to Germany, to merchants who sold them in the Reich. It was hard work, and there seemed to be no end to it. Mendel spent many weeks in the church. Himself covered with feathers, he looked for varied angles which would fully explain to the future generations what was happening in that church. He created evidence of the crime, the full extent of which was not yet known to him. Only his intuition told him that this must be recorded.[69]

A ghetto is a place of many faces and many bodily forms. That the sheer human density of the heavily populated streets and workplaces afforded opportunity to gaze at and scrutinize so many of them was not lost on observant writers such as Oskar Rosenfeld and Josef Zelkowicz. Whether in compiling notes for later creative work or in composing contributions for the *Chronicle* or reportage for the Statistical Department, both proved attentive and highly skilled in reading the features of their fellow Jews for clues to the changing circumstances of the ghetto. Attentive to the physical signs pointing to the long-term effects of prolonged impoverishment on the ghetto poor, they were no less eager to record evidence of the personal care and fashionable adornments by which the better provided for sought to stave off physical decline. Women, not surprisingly, came in for particular regard, with the writers paying close attention to the condition of their hands, their legs, their feet, and scrutinizing too their waistlines, their faces, the color of their hair, the shape of their eyes, the tint of their lips. Rosenfeld, a minor novelist who in his early work had written with some passion on the subject of female attraction, left a record of those occasional flashes of beauty he glimpsed.[70] Still, given the hunger, poverty, illness, and relentless obligations to which ghetto women were subject in their daily lives, such glimpses were at best exceptional. But above and beyond the sheer physical imprint of ghetto existence on people's bodies, such observations might well have been spurred by the massive and relentless genetic stock-taking to which the Germans had been subjecting the Jews of the ghetto and the nearby provinces. That spring was marked by an especially vigorous period of population transfer and selections in which the Germans visually scrutinized and then sorted thousands of ordinary people into categories labeled "A" and "B," the useful and the useless. Even if under grave duress, the Jewish leadership, too, in compiling lists and issuing warrants for deportation, was making serious value judgments about the physical worth of one Jew over that of another. This moment included as well the brief enforced encounter in which a mass of Jews from the West had been thrust into the midst of a native population of Eastern Jews. It had unavoidably entailed for many on either side of the East-West population divide a sudden and unexpected acquaintance with a host of novel and noticeable differences in customs and appearance. But above all, in addition to the lingering impact of this restless human mixing and sorting, as spring lengthened toward summer it was becoming increasingly evident to the surviving Jews that as a people they were, if not yet marked for total destruction, slowly and in great numbers disappearing from view.

Rosenfeld, a man approaching sixty and long separated from his wife in faraway London, a woman for whom he dearly longed, remained in the midst of his loneliness an admirer, from a distance, of attractive women. Never ceasing to notice and to be saddened by the poor condition of undernourished and overworked ghetto women visible everywhere, he found all the more remarkable the unexpected sight of a woman attending to her appearance in public, of the irresistible persistence even here of an erotic dimension to existence. That June he confessed in his notebooks to having noticed women who "painted their lips, using dirty windowpanes as mirrors." He remarked, too, on a number of "young women," notable among them "blue-eyed blondes alluringly decked out, with coquettish little hats, hair curled, nails manicured, pedicured," going about in fashionable "open summer sandals" with their "painted toes" strikingly poking through. Admittedly, Rosenfeld conveyed mild disapproval of such piquant display by referring to "young girls" who, dressed in such manner in the midst of "wretched beggars" and destitute people "wrapped in tatters," had "made the rounds of the streets like prostitutes." But privately he could not help but acknowledge the appearance of such "fabulous girlish figures."[71]

With the return of warmer weather and the change to lighter garments, Jewish men were not the only ones taking notice of well-dressed ghetto women set apart from the throng as they made their way along the walkways and thoroughfares. Indeed, as an additional notation in Rosenfeld's notebooks suggests, on occasion such Jewish women unwittingly attracted the unwelcome attentions of German men who, in passing through the ghetto themselves, spotted them from afar or while advancing toward them on foot. In a brief but disturbing encounter occurring late that June, a German, "dressed in civilian clothing," noticed "in the midst of a huge crowd" outside a shop "an elegant Jewish woman" in the company of her husband. The German took the liberty of drawing her aside. Making her "stand on the sidewalk" and instructing her to "Just pose for me," the man proceeded to take "three shots with his camera," aggressively peppering her with personal questions.[72] In an atmosphere in which any encounter with a German passing through the streets of the ghetto might entail the prospect of a beating if not worse—"frequently SS men without uniform grab passersby and hit them in the face," Rosenfeld noted—he immediately recalled the menace concealed behind the German's false gallantry.[73]

Such encounters not only highlight the continued if limited contact between German and Jew even within the restricted confines of the ghetto, but also suggest the persistence of a marginal potential for a blurring of identities altogether at odds with the rigid segregationist impulse at the heart of the ghetto enterprise. The ongoing presence even now, after the removal of thousands of Jews from the West, of many Jews of fair complexion whose features did not conform in the least to German notions of what a Jew looked like spurred a new effort on the part of the Germans to reinforce the distinction. Undoubtedly motivated as well by a desire to extort from their captives additional displays of servile status, a new decree ordered ghetto residents to acknowledge by submissive gestures—a tipping of the cap or, when bareheaded, as in the case of women, by means of a nod—the passage of any and all German visitors through the ghetto whether encountered on foot or in moving vehicles. Rosenfeld thought the order "absurd." He reasoned that it was "totally impossible even for keen observers" to make out amid "the terrible dust" an onrushing German vehicle, since it was difficult enough to watch one's footing on the hazardous pavement of typical ghetto walkways, much less to distinguish in a crowd the face of a German civilian official from that of a Jew, especially "since there are thousands of blond, blue-eyed" Jewish inhabitants still in the ghetto. And because ghetto women were wearing "bright summer clothing" at this time of year, it was not at all a simple matter to distinguish from afar outsiders, who were obviously not wearing the yellow Jewish star, from those in that "wave of the human mass" who were. The prudent ghetto resident's understandable aversion to drawing attention by way of any sudden gesture argued as well against the decree's effectiveness. Children, too, he thought, would find the order especially difficult to comprehend.[74]

All the same, and perhaps not altogether unrelated to a certain sense of timeliness occasioned by the phased removal of the Jews from the local scene to "parts unknown," that spring the Gettoverwaltung embarked on an oddly conceived effort to preserve some tangible albeit highly circumscribed and controlled visual impression of the Jews of Łódź and their passage through the ghetto. The instrument of this endeavor was a most unusual in-house project whose purpose it was to meet a felt demand, coming from privileged outsiders with whom the ghetto conducted its commercial dealings, for an additional peek at the world of the ghetto and its exotic inhabitants. Biebow's notion—for indeed he appears to have been the driving force behind it—was to establish a small private exhibit in which visiting dignitaries, clients, and guests might be introduced to visual representations of Jewish productivity and culture. These were to consist of museum-quality exhibits displaying confiscated Jewish ritual objects as well as glass-enclosed dioramas portraying aspects of Jewish life, with Jews represented by miniature hand-carved and porcelain-appointed figurines. Whether or not Biebow hit on the idea of the exhibit as a way to enhance his budding credentials as a specialist in Jewish affairs, he appears to have reasoned that such a presentation of Jewish craftsmanship, even when presented solely for the private edification and amusement of a limited circle of privileged visitors, might be good for promoting future business with the ghetto.[75]

Thus it was that Biebow prompted the formation within the Gettoverwaltung of a quasi-anthropological ghetto "Research Department" whose task it would be to catalogue Jewish religious and ethnographic artifacts and prepare items suitable for exhibit, including original pieces fashioned by ghetto craftsmen and artists. The endeavor appears to have drawn inspiration from the ongoing efforts of Adolf Wendel, a German religious scholar and "professor of biblical studies at the University of Breslau" then heading "the Łódź branch" of the "Institute of the National Socialist German Workers Party for Research into the Jewish Question," operating from downtown premises at number 33 König-Heinrich-Straße. There, the *Chronicle* noted, Wendel was "at present occupied in preparing exhibits for a prospective museum, which is to be set up in the city."[76] Enlisted in assisting him in this project were "a rabbi—Prof. [Emanuel] Hirszberg," who along with "his daughter had been working, by order of the authorities in the city, as experts in the field of Judaism." With the goal of establishing "a similar museum" under his own sponsorship, Biebow had called upon Rumkowski to furnish Rabbi Hirszberg with the means to assemble a hand-picked team of skilled men and women to work on the project and to provide them with workshop space and enhanced rations in order to enable them to carry out their tasks.[77]

The German managers may have thought the idea modest enough to gain the approval of the responsible central agency charged with overseeing such matters. An official representing the Propaganda Ministry in Berlin, however, judged the plan inappropriate. Such an exhibition seemed antithetical to the very nature of a ghetto, which "aims to achieve a separation of the Jews from the national community [*Volksgemeinschaft*]" without at the same time serving to make Jewish "life in any form especially interesting to outsiders, or offer satisfaction to the curiosity of those who should be content that through the institution of the ghetto the Jew has disappeared from their area of life."[78] In reply to the these objections, and still pleading on behalf of his concept, through a deputy Biebow pointedly insisted that the proposed exhibit intended nothing of the sort. "The display is supposed to contain only a very concise overview of Jewish ritual objects in order to answer in a graphic way questions directed to me about the Jews living in the ghetto." The exhibition would comprise only "some Torah rolls, caftans, prayer books, some pictures of Jewish types as well as illustrations from the Jewish community, such as the primitive nature of excrement removal, the bad style of home furnishing, and the like. Such an exhibition should on no account and in no possible form impress the viewer as interesting, rather only as repellent."[79]

While these differences remained to be resolved, the Research Department proceeded apace toward the fulfillment of Biebow's design. By the beginning of the fourth week in June, Rabbi Hirszberg's seventeen-member team of "painters, sculptors, and their assistants" were well along in their efforts, fashioning among other objects for display a set of what were termed "remarkably artistic dolls" purporting to "represent the most diverse figures in the Jewish world. The execution of these dolls demonstrates a very high artistic level and precision, not only in the rendering of the heads and hands (which are made of porcelain) but in the garments as well." Indicative of progress to date, "the first in the series, which depicts a Jewish wedding," Biebow expected "to be finished in a matter of days."[80] His assurance that the farthest thought from his mind was to evoke empathy for the Jews appears to have been borne out by closer consideration of the work. Rosenfeld expressed cautious yet sharp criticism of the visual effects of the commissioned displays, which consisted of representations of Jewish life "mounted in glass cases" measuring "about 2 m wide, 80 cm high, 70 cm deep" and were presented by way of "figures" seemingly like those found "in a puppet theater." Highlighted "themes like 'Chassidic Wedding in Poland' and 'Candle Lighting on Shabbat,' or scenes in the synagogue" struck him as producing "a caricature effect" brought about by the disturbingly artificial, indeed, uncanny nature of the arrangement of these "figures." Perhaps oddest of all was the impression of stiffness: "The costumes—which in a normal figure are infused with life through the movements of the one wearing them, bending as the person walks, struts, sits, etc.—remain rigid in their miniature representation," as a result of which the figurines "appear doll-like, mummylike, annoying, comical, like caricatures." Indeed, "exaggerated accessories, penetrating colors, pathos of gestures—motions without words—bring unconsciously to mind puppet plays and their often maudlin and childish-dumb texts and plots."[81]

To be sure, examination of surviving photographs of the displays suggests authentic touches, no doubt respectfully rendered by the artisans. One might point to the custom-made details, the ornamentation, clothing, and furnishings for the figurines in the model wedding scene: those striped suits, the musicians' cleverly fashioned miniature horns and stringed instruments, the dresses and cloaks for the distinguished older guests, the rouging of the dolls' cheeks, the braiding of the hair, the bouquet of flowers held by a little girl, the four-post wedding canopy for the bride and groom, a little padded chair and potted palms.[82] But as Rosenfeld argued, somehow it did not add up; there was something altogether undistinguished, phony, off-putting, and disturbingly uncanny in the portrayal.

Still, and for all the exaggerated distortions of their features and the uncomfortable mingling of their persons, the dolls constituted a not altogether inaccurate reflection of the painful condition of the ghetto Jews. In this sense alone these displays were true to life: the ghetto residents, living on top of one another, crowded, rubbing shoulders, shared a similarity of circumstance to the figures that were meant to represent them. And like the rigid dolls which were now their stand-ins, many of the Jews whom the figurines depicted were by the time of their presentation just as stiff and immobile, even if, by comparison, in life their cheeks had never been quite so rosy.

In spite of all that had so recently transpired, and perhaps very much because of it, ghetto residents still hungry for civilized diversion and able to afford the price of admission continued to attend the ongoing symphony concerts. Rosenfeld, who had written a youthful novella centered on the Vienna State Opera as well as a solid body of artistic and performance criticism for prewar Viennese Jewish publications, attended as well.[83] A sophisticated observer of the ghetto theatergoing experience no less than of the capabilities, styles, and skills of the performers and the quality of their work, he would leave behind a small yet valuable body of commentary. For him the home for the ghetto symphony orchestra, the somewhat grandiloquently termed Kulturhaus, or House of Culture, located on Krawiecka Street, was passably reminiscent of "an early Greek temple at the time when the ascetic Doric style was still representative of Hellenic culture." Approaching the hall in advance of a midweek concert on an early evening in June, he spotted "mostly younger people" among the groups milling about the entrance to the theater, also including gatherings of "well-dressed" ghetto residents identifiable as native to Łódź, as well as "very young girls, and even children. At the entrance opposite the box office a handmade poster in Yiddish and German" provided a synopsis of the upcoming presentation. At intermission, members of the audience might exit into a "roomy, well-aired foyer with tall windows" giving onto a courtyard garden, where, enjoying cigarettes as they strolled and gathered, patrons could be heard discussing the performance in a variety of tongues, including "Yiddish, Polish, German or even English."[84]

The facility boasted a quite serviceable stage and a spacious auditorium, "sold out every time," capable of accommodating up to four hundred spectators arranged in rows of sixteen, supplemented by additional seating against the wall. For a Wednesday performance, the musicians could be seen taking their places "a few minutes after six o'clock," attired "in dark street suits," their demeanor "serious, silent."[85] Indeed, many of the performers had only just returned from a day's strenuous labor in the workshops. As for the composition of the orchestra, violinists, cellists, and violists constituted a decided "bow-wielding majority."[86] The conductor, Teodor Ryder, was by then some sixty years of age, an accomplished figure from the prewar Łódź musical world in which he had served "as conductor of the symphony orchestra as well as the radio symphony orchestra."[87] Ryder was a physically expansive performer whose "arms have a wide reach, not like the so-called practical conductors who hold in their feelings and presume to take control of even a gigantic orchestra with short bobbing motions." Delighting in the sight, Rosenfeld described the conductor at full tilt: "With his back slightly bent, his legs spread apart, the agile, slender, little man bounces up and down as on a swing or—maybe more precisely—like someone who is himself a spectator who follows the rhythm of the music that is just being performed."[88]

With a marked preference for "Beethoven and the Romantics (Mendelssohn, Schumann, Schubert)," Ryder's ghetto repertoire, though not lacking in works from a wider array of classic composers, suffered from a shortage of scores. Most especially works by Jewish composers, Mahler and Schoenberg as well as the lesser known, which he would have liked to perform, were of necessity overshadowed or dropped. Nonetheless, in turning to Beethoven's Fifth Symphony, Ryder succeeded in coaxing meaningful and perceptive responses from his audience.[89] Of its reception Rosenfeld remarked that the impression it made proved "naturally deeper and more powerful than before," adding that "not once in the concert halls of the major cities of Europe was such emotion to be sensed as it was here in the ghetto. Even the treatment of the fugue-like themes of the third movement," he observed, "posing as they do the highest demands in terms of musical comprehension, were met with great understanding. The liberation motif—as always in Beethoven in the concluding movements—swept mightily through the hall." Ryder himself seemed enraptured by this conclusion. "One felt, almost bodily, the vision of future salvation."[90]

Also stepping on stage to perform on July 1 was the "popular" Prague baritone Rudolf Bandler, whose resonant voice was deemed especially suitable for calling forth sounds conveying a range of moods from the "murky" to the "the grotesque and the burlesque." He was capable too of presenting "arias from Italian operas . . . in an enthralling Italian parlando, and when he sings a ballad by Loewe or a Schubert song, then even the souls born in the ghetto feel as if they were at home, remembering perhaps the poetry of Schiller and Heine," creators, Rosenfeld added, of "some of the favorite verses among the Eastern Jews until their own, Yiddish literature pushed aside these German poets."[91] And now Bandler stood before the audience to sing selections from Schubert, choosing the moving piece titled "Die Almacht," a song of "powerfully religious overtone that begins 'Great is Jehovah, the Lord, heaven and earth proclaim His might. . . .' Bandler's magnificent phrasing enabled the public to comprehend every word of the song, preparing the way for a relevant interpretation that further strengthened the salvation theme intimated in the Beethoven. The lyrical-dramatic passage 'Jehova's power, that of the eternal God,' was received with full understanding of our present fate." To no less appreciative effect, along with another work reminiscent of a folk melody, Bandler "concluded his *Lieder* program" with Schubert's hauntingly poetic "Erlkönig."[92]

This stirring piece could hardly have found an audience more receptive to its central and terrifying theme: the abduction of a child, carried away by its cunning pursuer from the sheltering closeness of a parent, lifted from the back of a galloping horse in the night. The words could not have failed to resonate with the ghetto audience assembled in the auditorium of the House of Culture that first evening in July. Beyond imagination, a dark fantasy come to life, such thefts were now common. All too real images of stolen children were fresh and present. It had happened in Pabianice, it had happened in Brzeziny, and the inconsolable parents who arrived from these parts had brought with them the news; their weeping had been heard. Many at this moment sensed it might soon happen here, not once but again and again. As Bandler's voice summoned to life Schubert's evocative rendition of Goethe's poem, his listeners might have summoned to mind another threatened child, one of like qualities yet born to and loved by Jewish parents. A Jewish father and a Jewish child ride out on horseback through the leaves on a dark and misty autumn night. It is 1815 and it is 1942 all at once. Yet now it was not a lone German voice but many that were heard calling out in the night and not just to a single child but to any and all below the age of ten. These voices did not whisper and they did not seduce, for the spirit that animated them was indifferent to the innocence of its prey. It just swept the children away, not "one, by one, by one," but batch by startled and terrified batch.[93]

8

"Give Me Your Children"

While war was being made upon the Jewish child, the German child—in the media ever an object of unceasing delight and loving regard, the beauty of its features scrutinized, its athleticism extolled, its wishes indulged, its imagination awakened—was described as if born into a world of splendid welcome, enveloping protection, and satisfaction of all wants. So it was a matter deemed worthy of note that on a day in June, climbing aboard a streetcar on Deutschland Square were young participants in that day's festival sponsored by the organization known as Strength Through Joy. Little girls with "bright dresses and beautifully tied ribbons in their hair" took their seats, while soft-spoken little boys, their hair "combed smooth atop their heads," stood in the aisle at their side. Reaching their stop outside Helenenhof, the youngsters exited the tram and quickly made for the entrance to the park. Live music, performed by local musicians, greeted their arrival. Spectators were on hand to watch as the children, dressed in sportswear, performed athletic routines under the direction of a female gymnastics instructor and later gathered for a round of singing. After speeches and servings of "delicious cakes" offered the "tiny guests" seated at tables decorated with flowers, the festival proceeded to sack and egg races and the playful beating of pots. Storytelling—featured was the "Tale of the Golden Goose"—rounded out the day's activities, culminating in a distribution of prizes by a storybook princess.[1]

Where once, it was said, children had known only dark, hardscrabble courtyards with but the tiniest sliver of sky overhead, now under the new regime German youngsters played in the open, amid greenery, under the watchful eyes of indulgent mothers whom they called to come admire their sandbox creations.[2] At last the world extended its arms to the German child, ever portrayed as the cherished delight of solicitous parents. At a swimming pool in provincial Welungen, where, it was said, experienced swimmers "rise like nymphs from splashing waters[,] . . . our small children look to the unknown 'sea' from a bit of a distance, and only dare approach the shore when mother is near."[3] Was this imagined world of Litzmannstadt and environs, its present so welcoming, its future of such promise, not indeed magical?

Precious though the German child was in this great scheme of renewal, the Jewish child, considered of no use and no value, was for now the chief target for destruction. Utilitarian considerations of the potential for labor among more physically developed Jewish youngsters meant that such targeting largely affected only those deemed too young and tender to be useful. For the purposes of categorizing who among them were to live and who to die, the Germans had drawn a line at the age of ten: those above that age, thought to possess the potential for work (fingers dexterous enough to thread a needle, coordination keen enough to guide a pair of scissors, muscles strong enough to wield a hammer) were spared; those younger, especially the infants—so hungry, so whiny, altogether useless in a workshop—were just additional mouths to feed. Along with the aged and the sick, it was the youngest children—such easy pickings in their delicate size, their defenselessness, their inexperience, so available for seizure—who were taken first. For German administrators relentlessly seeking ways to reduce the expenditures associated with production, children too young to work served no economic purpose. A drain on precious resources, they could make no contribution save through their disappearance and the attendant reduction of costs associated with their upkeep. While cost-cutting considerations lent justification to their removal, the slaughter of the Jewish young proved as well an especially satisfying way of running up the demographic score, the piling up of Jewish dead—and among them their children, their future—being the surest proof of the claim that the Jews who had once peopled the land would soon people it no more. Their disappearance reinforced the assertion of German dominance in all things and gave proof that as a people the Germans were numerically in the ascendant, and that the land was theirs just as the future was theirs, and theirs alone.[4]

Two years into the regime's efforts toward ethnically cleansing the Wartheland of its Jews, the moment of resolution was at hand. For Germans of the Warthegau all doors swung open in an expansive vision of a future of promise coming true. Many indeed were the possibilities that lay before them, and before the city, too, modernizing into the future, a city of flowers, of clean homes to live in, of pure running water available to all, of efficient transport and industry, and above all of demographic increase, its confirmation the free development of the German child.

The official portrait of the city and its people, including its children, remained, as it would until the end, one of ever-increasing beauty, health, and promise. In such a world all German children were fit—or, if unwell, soon on the mend—well dressed, and well fed, the most favored of beings in the most transformed of cities; all that was touched by German hands seemingly turned to blossom and to gold. It was largely a fantasy, of course, but each improvement was touted as offering a glimpse of a time when everything would be in place and all would be just right. The fantasy was built on another, darker one—and this was the one that actually *was* coming true—that of sweeping the city of the presence of Jews.

For the Germans it was a moment of exuberance. The death center, so close, served now as the final destination, the hidden vortex into which a population of Jews deemed superfluous to production was disappearing. Here lay the solution to the demographic problem that from the start had plagued Warthegau and Litzmannstadt officials, frustrated in their desire to expel the Jewish population and realize once and for all their vision of a land free of Jews. Now, one after another, the provincial ghettos were being closed down, their aged, their sick, and their young separated from the remainder of the population and sent to their deaths in Rzuchowski Forest. Those still considered fit were sent on to labor. Even the unwanted Western Jews the authorities had fought unsuccessfully to hold at bay were by now, thanks not only to the physical rigors of life in the ghetto but also to this new solution, reduced to a fraction of their original number.

The enormity of the crime matched the outrageousness of its method.

To the Warthegau leadership the accomplishment was satisfying indeed, but inevitably the process, so physically repugnant, demanded further review. For in truth the production of death on so grandiose a scale had left in its wake precisely the kind of mess, evoking the same disgust and the same phobia about the spread of contagious disease, whose elimination had been a principal aim of the enterprise from the start.

Unexpectedly, with the arrival of warm weather, evidence of the massive crime began to surface. In the woods of Precinct 77 the bodies were decomposing in the sun. In the heat of the clearing, the corpses became bloated and the soil over the trenches lifted and bulged; above it a "mist" or "vapor" visibly rose, a pestilential odor filling the air. Forest workers, normally toiling in the vicinity until late in the afternoon, were overwhelmed by the stench and were compelled to break off work by two o'clock.[5] The phenomenon renewed the fear of typhus. In consequence, there followed that summer a halt to killing operations, the arrival of fresh victims pending a means of better disposing of their remains. An initial effort to employ thermal explosives went awry, setting fire to and scorching a patch of woods shielding the clearing from view of the roadway. After this the installation of two outdoor cremation ovens, concrete-lined conical pits dug into the ground, proved a more effective solution. To the Jewish men of the Waldkommando fell the gruesome task of lifting the remains from the newly opened trenches and transferring them to the ovens. Bystanders witnessed the smoke rising from the vicinity.[6] The roasting of the bodies in these twin pits effectively transformed them cleanly to ash. Still, the method, effective as it was, was found to leave behind good-sized chunks of skeletal matter. These bones would have to be refined still further. For this purpose a "bone grinder" was required, and one was found. The mill worked well, reducing the parts to a fine "snow-white" powder. The purified remains were then scattered about the nearby woods and waters.[7] The laundering and cleansing had achieved perfection. Never before had so much living human substance been so systematically and so rapidly compressed to nothingness.

For the Jews of Łódź, a season of growing uncertainty and anxiety had begun. It was clear that new, destructive energies had been unleashed, directly impacting the region and the ghetto. Still, the precise outlines and extent of the damage remained indistinct. Regionally, Łódź lay at the center of events whose scope, from the perspective of the ghetto, was but dimly perceived. The Germans had succeeded in effectively sealing off the ghetto from reliable information. That tens of thousands of persons had recently disappeared without a trace was as much a tribute to the Germans' ability to control information as it was a challenge to the imagination. "Had they been taken abroad, even to the remoteness of the jungles of South America," noted one ghetto observer, "the earth could not have swallowed them as it has done so here, perhaps but several kilometers from Litzmannstadt. For it is a certainty that they have remained within the German sphere of occupation. And that extends but several hundred kilometers to the east."[8]

As the apparent lull in the deportations stretched on into the first weeks of summer, concern over the whereabouts of those previously removed combined with anxiety over the Germans' ultimate intentions, overshadowing life in the ghetto. Worry over the fate of Jewish children was especially grave. It was clear that they had been especially targeted for selection in the provincial ghettos, a matter that understandably raised fears for the lives of the community's own Jewish youngsters in the event of future operations. Unconfirmed reports about the fate of previously deported youngsters circulated with increased frequency. Amid the swirl of plausible rumor, one altogether untrue and misleading conjecture surfaced. On July 9 Shlomo Frank recorded that a report had been picked up from the underground Polish radio station, "Swit,"[9] referring to the destruction of provincial Jewish communities, alleging that a number of Jewish children were being kept alive in labor camps, where their blood was supposedly drawn as a source of "transfusions for wounded German soldiers."[10] Even a tale as ominous as this may have offered some limited hope that the rumored destruction of the children had been less than total. Later in the month, amid menacing pronouncements in the German media about the ghetto's liquidation and the impending total annihilation of the Jews, came the welcome if seemingly contradictory news of a new order for the production of fifty thousand children's beds, necessitating an increase in the labor force in the ghetto carpentry works, a sign of the ghetto's continued usefulness and a reason for its survival. Masking the authorities' true intentions while serving to allay mounting anxieties within the ghetto, a Gestapo agent reportedly explained "that the little beds will be made for Jewish children who are in a special, large camp not far from Lublin."[11]

That reference to the supposed camp sounds similar to another report, recorded in the *Chronicle* on July 26, indicating that people who had disappeared during the spring selections were in fact "alive and well in various camps in the vicinity of Poznań. Exact addresses and some people's serial numbers were even mentioned."[12] Very much in people's thoughts, the deported children were rumored to have been "placed in Poznań itself, in the so-called Judenkinderlager [Camp for Jewish Children] at 5 Rudolfstrasse." But in truth there was "no street in Poznań" by that name. Whether or not the ghetto chroniclers were aware of that salient fact is unknown. Though conceding the "understandable interest" in the rumors, and even the "great calming effect" they were having on the ghetto population, the chroniclers remained deeply skeptical, concluding, "It may be supposed that these rumors, like so many others, are without any foundation whatsoever."[13]

One might have seen in all this the clever machinations of the German security apparatus, eager to spread disinformation. For if the Jews inside the ghetto were carefully watching the Germans, piecing together fragmentary reports about the nature and extent of the harm they intended, the Germans were also observing them. The Criminal Police and the Gestapo were on heightened alert for any signs that their now stepped-up program of extermination had aroused the suspicions of the living. Had the ghetto population gotten wind of the regime's locally escalating murderous deeds? It would have been a logical question to ask. By their own assessment, this much struck the Criminal Police as clear: most of the Jews in the ghetto now realized that ultimately they would not survive. That said, it was imperative to control even more effectively the flow of information to the ghetto from the outside world, and internally to identify and destroy any who might try to exploit the increasing state of deprivation and desperation to make trouble for the authorities. The Kripo were particularly at pains to cut off all contact between the ghetto and those outside. For months there had been a ban on mail. Letters addressed to the inhabitants of the ghetto were without exception destroyed. Arriving aid packages—and they were still being sent—were confiscated and rerouted to military hospitals. Apart from that, the Kripo suggested, in the interest of creating the illusion that no harm had come to the deported, that it might prove useful to pass along to the Jews letters indicating that all was in fact well with their absent brethren.[14]

The Kripo understood the workings of the world, both as it once had been and as it existed now. They had reason to believe that in spite of mounting evidence pointing to their destruction by some recognizable means (by starvation, or even by execution), the Jews could be persuaded that Germany had not crossed some unknown line, implementing a far more outlandish, unimaginable campaign of mechanized killing as efficient as it was thoroughgoing. Fully aware that such a line had indeed been crossed, the German security establishment saw to it that the regime's wider intentions remained hidden, banking on the victims' inability to piece together the truth. In this way the Jews might yet be fooled into believing that although they had been singled out for exceptional punishment, their oppressors were guided by fundamentally rational considerations. All could see that the ghetto was organized for work. It was self-evident: production suited Germany's needs. Insufferable as the conditions were under which they labored, the enterprise they were compelled to serve promoted an understandable purpose. The Germans would exploit this thinking to full advantage, counting on the logic of production to reassure their victims that Germany's plan was consistent with established norms.[15] The Jews might faint at their workstations, they might fall ill and die in the course of their labor, but the Germans did not slaughter them on the floor of the workshops. Rzuchowski Forest did not come to the ghetto. The gas vans did not appear all of a sudden in its streets, rumbling down Łagiewnicka, Franciskańska, or Marysinska, choking the life out of the Jews where they lived. Instead, everything within the ghetto proceeded according to long-established routine. The Gettoverwaltung successfully pursued orders from military and commercial clients, and its highly organized and extensive network of workshops diligently satisfied the demands of its parent organization. All could see that ghetto wares were a necessity and that the Germans had organized the ghetto for their manufacture. That alone was a matter of satisfaction to the Gettoverwaltung, the Gau leadership, and the Security Service, each deeply engaged in the concealed project of murder. In this way the Jews would have reason to discount unconfirmed reports of the worst, still believing that, however cruelly applied, the way of the Germans was the way of work.

It was Rumkowski's way as well. And throughout that terrible season in the aftermath of the year's deportations, he would cling to it more than ever. Early on the evening of May 31, following an extended absence from the rostrum, Rumkowski rose to address a ghetto audience of five thousand listeners assembled in the courtyard of the fire department on Lutomierska Street. "Loudspeakers and a podium had been set up." In addition, "the crowd was calm and orderly, [and] the weather was lovely—sunny and warm." Once again "face to face" with his "brothers and sisters in the ghetto," Rumkowski spoke frankly of recent losses, recalling the 55,000 who had been deported during the previous months. His anger was evident, though it was directed at those who were illicitly dealing in their own rations, in the process "trad[ing] in their own blood and in the blood of their own children," most recently taking advantage of the desperation of German Jews to acquire their possessions on the eve of their departure. On a more positive note, with the ghetto population now consisting of approximately 100,000 souls, he was pleased to state that 70,000 of them were integrated into the labor force, though there was still room for more. "The problem of work ran like a red thread through the Chairman's entire speech," according to the *Chronicle,* "creating the impression that although the question of resettlement has been averted for the time being, it could crop up again if the labor reserves are not entirely exhausted in the ghetto's workshops." Most important, "he spoke of the creation of new workshops, of easy work for children and old people, for he would then be able to place those who have registered but have not been assigned, or have not been assigned to suitable positions." Children still too young for work were a particular concern. They were going to have to be kept off the streets and looked after more carefully. Either they would be assigned to day care centers while their parents were out at work, or else the parents would have to work alternate shifts so as to take turns looking after them. Above all, this was not a time to credit irresponsible rumors but a time to keep one's head down and "sit quietly at work," following Rumkowski's own example. "We must work in order to be able to exist. . . . Do your work fully in peace, do not daydream. I stand watch over our common interests," he assured his people, the source of the "only happiness in my life."[16]

The school department, taking the lead in establishing apprentice positions in the workshops for school-age children, was stepping up the pace of its placements. By the third week in July some thirteen thousand youngsters were serving in the shops, their apprenticeships supplemented by a model program devoted to the rapid training of the young in tailoring and other trades. In response to the sense of urgency—one observer spoke of the "lightning, American speed" of the undertaking—a program that, in ordinary times, was designed to last for years was compressed into only two months of intense instruction. On the premises of the tailoring works at 29 Franciskańska Street, three hundred apprentices at a time, organized into twelve sections, participated in classes from eight in the morning until four in the afternoon, learning all aspects of the trade, from hand and machine stitching and sewing to cutting and the creation of "technical drawings," as well as knowledge of tailoring machinery, with supplementary training in trade-specific "accounting and mathematics" and a weekly hour of instruction in "occupational hygiene." It was further noted that "for the convenience of the students there is a dining area on the premises where they consume the meals normally provided to working people in the ghetto. The establishment of these educational courses must be acknowledged as an event of far-reaching importance for the future of the children who reside in the ghetto."[17]

Ghetto orphans too were increasingly being integrated into the labor force. By the end of June 1942, out of a total of 589 boarders at institutions, 155 were employed in the workshops, a figure more than double the 75 who had been working at the end of March. And many of the newly employed orphans were noticeably younger, for whereas in March the majority of those employed had been sixteen and older, by this later date nearly all were between the ages of eleven and fifteen.[18] Similarly, by July 31, half of the 1,569 youngsters in ghetto children's colonies, or 784 (454 boys and 330 girls), had taken positions in a variety of workshops. By far the greatest number, 348 (274 of them boys), were occupied in shoemaking, while 139 of the girls specialized in needlework; lesser numbers were employed in "tailoring workshops," "wood wool factories," "corset and brassiere manufacture," and "sorting and recycling departments."[19]

In a society where survival, as all by now surely understood, depended on proving one's usefulness, the elderly were most especially at risk, even more endangered than the very young, who, embodying the future, might count on the community's solicitousness and protection. Their sense of peril found quiet expression. Woefully, on July 12, 1942, in a desperate effort to demonstrate that they too were able to contribute material value to the community, thereby justifying the sums spent on their upkeep and survival, the residents of Old Age Home Number 2 on Gnesenerstraße

presented Rumkowski with the gift of "a handmade carpet," asking that
he accept their offering "as proof of their devotion and thanks" and a token of their "productive will and capacity," a reminder that "most of the
residents are able to carry out craft labor of various and similar type, such
as: knitting, darning, stuffing [cushions], sewing, and the like." Their
fondest wish was "to demonstrate, through *work,* our right to exist in the
ghetto. We appeal to your generosity . . . and ask: Give us the chance of
delivering, by way of deed, *the proof* of our ability to work. We are fully
conscious of the fact that only *work*—as your motto proclaims as well—
can afford the possibility of *alleviating* the food situation for us."[20]

By the end of August, surveying the expanding list of provincial Jewish
communities suffering violent uprooting and dissolution, yet having little
to go on save the experience of survivors, ghetto observers remained
baffled as to the fate of those who had vanished into the unknown. "Jews
have arrived here from Pabianice, Bełchatów, Ozorków, Zelów, Wieluń,
Stryków, Sieradz, Łask, and, recently, from Zduńska Wola, and the process continues," the *Chronicle* recorded on August 28:

> At the same time, bedding from those small towns has no longer
> been arriving by truck but by tram dump cars, and this new phe-
> nomenon has come to dominate everyone's thoughts. The newcom-
> ers tell all sorts of stories about their recent experiences, but the same
> note of pain and despair runs through all their accounts. Not every-
> one has arrived here—families have been separated and it is difficult
> even to determine why some were sent to this ghetto while others
> had to take another, more dolorous journey. It is difficult to discover
> any guidelines in all of this, which is precisely what grieves everyone
> most. Once again a cloud of uncertainty has seized the ghetto; peo-
> ple are shaken by the tales the newcomers tell and by the great un-
> known, which is worse than the worst reality.[21]

All the same, people had heard enough to know that terrible things were
happening to the children out in the provinces. On August 27 Oskar
Rosenfeld took note of the murdered children, or "yeladim," of Zduńska

Wola, who were "separated from old people and parents," and "ordered to lower" their "head[s]—then shot with [a] revolver."[22]

As best they could, parents kept vigil, watching over their children while they slept. Irena Hauser, a survivor of a transport from Vienna, hard pressed by deplorable material circumstance and fast approaching the limits of her strength, devoted the last of her declining energies to the care of her young son. Lying awake beside him, she watched helplessly as flies circled about her sleeping child's mouth, anxious lest he awake. For what would she do then? Twenty-four hours had passed since either had eaten, and still she had nothing with which to satisfy the child's hunger.[23] Suicidal thoughts invaded her consciousness, and she confided to her diary a wish to throw herself from the window and be done with her anguish, a temptation she abandoned, she wrote, solely out of consideration for her responsibility to her child. She awakened to recall "an interesting dream," its content perhaps reflecting a resurfacing of persistent suicidal thoughts. In the dream she observes "a long train" standing "ready to leave." She is about to climb aboard, sensing that the train will not leave without her. The conductor is watching and "waiting for" her "to give the signal to depart."[24]

Sleep was precious, a ready escape for ghetto inhabitants who found within it temporary relief from unbearable worry. Yet the pressures of daily life and the attendant concern for survival meant that for many, burdened with physical pain and mental suffering, sleep remained an elusive blessing. On a night in late August, while elsewhere in the household his wife and "three grown daughters" slept, a husband and father remained awake, tending with difficulty to a small boy, an orphan he and his family had taken into their care. Hoping gently to ease the child's own journey toward sleep, the man sang to him a variety of familiar songs, to no avail; restless, the boy remained stubbornly awake, crying, screaming, altogether inconsolable. No melody succeeded in calming the child until, at last, the man sang a particular lullaby—a very sad one that told of the death of a king and, in turn, of his unhappy queen, and of the abandonment of the king's vineyard, within which, nesting on the branch of a small tree, had rested a little bird. Upon the death of the king and queen, rousing itself the bird departed, taking flight "like an arrow shot from a bow." Somehow, to this song alone the child proved receptive, even joining in humming the lullaby's refrain, "slumber, slumber, slumber, little child of mine," so that finally, "closing his little eyes," the boy nodded off to sleep. Alone at last, "like a tireless night watchman," the man "lay awake" through the night, pondering the significance of the odd lullaby that, after long hours of restlessness, had brought the child a measure of peace. The key, he concluded, lay in the song's reference to the death of the king, who, as he imagined the child to have recognized, had failed utterly to fulfill his duty to serve as provider and protector to those who needed him most: the children. This was nothing less than a betrayal of trust, resulting in a wound that, until eased by the death of the failed sovereign, offered the child no peace. To this father there could be little doubt that the king to whom the tale alluded was none other than Rumkowski, on whom he heaped his scorn, attributing to the restless child all the anger and bitterness he felt over the failings of a leader who, though looked to as a "protector," had proved nothing of the sort, a sovereign utterly incapable of saving the innocent in his domain from suffering and destruction.[25]

Soon enough the unsettling anxieties of that dreadful summer were to culminate in the terrible realization that the sick, the elderly, and above all the children of the Łódź ghetto were indeed targeted for removal. What had occurred in the Jewish communities in the outlying provinces was to happen here as well. In spite of the growing sense of threat, the blow, when it came, was experienced as a shock of unimagined magnitude, leaving those who survived it forever scarred. All that Rumkowski had staked in attempting to secure his people's survival by diligently serving the Germans, accommodating their perceived economic goals and obediently executing even the most unwelcome of their demands, was to be tested as never before.

At seven o'clock on the morning of Tuesday, September 1, three years to the day since the invasion of Poland and a day similarly beautiful and bright, pedestrians walking past the ghetto hospitals on Łagiewnicka, Drewnowska, and Wesoła streets noticed what struck them as the curious if at first unalarming appearance of what were described as military trucks just then driving up to the buildings.[26] Of late, rumors had circulated to the effect that in order to clear space for the creation of additional workshops, the hospitals were soon to be closed, their patients and medical facilities transferred to barracks currently under construction on Krawiecka and Tokarzewski streets.[27] But this work was nowhere near completion, and even more unsettling, it would have been highly unusual for the Germans to send military transports to the ghetto to accomplish the task. Apprehension mounted as observers took note of the unusually heavy presence of Jewish policemen in the vicinity of the hospitals, keeping the growing crowds, increasingly drawn by the strange goings-on, from approaching. That same apprehension quickly turned to panic when they saw the Germans roughly forcing patients out of the buildings, even pushing some children from the windows, and piling them onto the vehicles. Stunned, bystanders soon realized that they were witnessing not just the closure of the hospitals but the beginning of the wholesale deportation of the patients.[28]

Biebow was on the scene, a fact he would acknowledge at his postwar trial in 1947 even while denying in the face of eyewitness testimony that he had approved or participated in such acts of brutality.[29] One of those Jewish eyewitnesses, hiding in a linen closet of the Łagiewnicka Street hospital to avoid being seen, first spied Biebow passing along the corridor in the company of two unidentified "high-ranking" men in uniform. Biebow was speaking of the need to speed the operation. Shortly thereafter, patients at the nearby medical facility on Mickiewicza Street, by now alerted to the threat, began climbing from the windows and taking flight. Biebow rushed to the scene. Rounding the corner at Łagiewnicka Street, quickly assessing the fast-moving events unfolding before his eyes, he reportedly struck a woman and, seizing a man by the hair, dragged him back to the building before hustling down to the corner and shouting for uniformed assistance.[30] Szyja Teitelbaum, who had been passing through the vicinity, remembered noticing Biebow shouting at three young people; he ordered them into a garden and made them turn to face a tree. When Gestapo officers Fuchs and Stromberg arrived, the men "all drew their revolvers and fired. Biebow was standing in the middle. I got a good look," Teitelbaum insisted, "because I was standing at a distance of 6–7 meters from the incident."[31] Hersz Janowski, a ghetto cart driver, also spotted Biebow in the company of these same agents participating in the murder of three youths, aged in his estimation around sixteen to seventeen years old. "Each of the three Germans shot one of the boys from behind," he said, and Biebow was heard crudely joking about it.[32]

Meanwhile, Rumkowski, "in the hospital on Drewnowska Street since early morning," appears to have been attempting, with unspecified success, to intervene, presumably in order to exempt certain individuals from the *Aktion,* as did the director of the Order Service's Special Department, Dawid Gertler, who, taking up position in the main hospital on Łagiewnicka Street, was "surrounded by petitioners of every sort."[33] The Germans were not in the least inclined to let any escapees off the hook. The Jewish Order Service was consequently charged with hunting them down and delivering them for removal with the rest. The Germans demanded a quota of two hundred persons, instructing that should some of the fugitive patients prove unrecoverable, their relatives were to be seized in their stead; also declared eligible for seizure was anyone "who had applied for admittance to the hospital," regardless of whether he or she had been a patient on the morning of September 1. The Order Service complied as instructed.[34]

The following Friday, September 4, was intensely sunny and hot. At two in the afternoon posters went up announcing an assembly set for 3:30 in the fire department square, where at last Rumkowski and other leaders were going to address the ghetto. In advance of the assembly rumors had it that perhaps the children were to be spared after all, or that the *Aktion* was to be put off for another three months. But these were only conjectures. In tears, mothers were already nervously crowding around officials to appeal on behalf of their children. On the main pedestrian bridge over Zgierska Street there was unusually heavy traffic. Rumkowski's carriage had been seen passing at high speed. The atmosphere was feverish. It looked, said one observer, as if "all hell has broken loose." On top of everything else, with the shops and workplaces now to be closed the following day, people were worried about the shortfall in the day's rations. Amid the restlessness of the moment, however, there were pockets of apparent calm. On the grounds of the Church of the Virgin Mary, in the blazing heat the women who stacked and cleaned the featherbedding could be seen lounging atop piles of "eiderdowns and pillows," enjoying their soup. Elsewhere policemen mingled with crowds of anxious ghetto residents, offering reassurances. The routine sound of children hawking sweets could still be heard. But the general mood of the ghetto was tense, if not desperate. Another rumor had it that Polish workers, operating under German supervision, were digging graves on Wolborska Street. Everyone anxiously awaited the promised words of the chairman.[35]

Even in advance of definite news, parents were half crazed over the prospect of losing their children. "Mothers race about in the streets, one shoe on and the other off, half of their hair combed and the rest unkempt," wrote Josef Zelkowicz, "kerchiefs half draped over their shoulders and half dragging on the ground." As yet, however, the worst had not happened. "They still have their children. They can still clutch them fiercely to their shriveled bosoms. They can still kiss their clear eyes. But what will happen afterwards, in another hour, tomorrow? Rumor has it that the children will be removed from their parents today and sent away on Monday. Sent away—where?"[36] But at least "for now, for the moment, every child is still with his mother." In consequence, mothers would lavish small luxuries upon their children: their "last loaf of bread" and, if available at all, some margarine to go with it, even a bit of sugar.[37] "Today, the ghetto has cast aside all thoughts of the future. It is living for the moment, and for the moment every mother is clutching her child." Attended with such unexpected solicitousness, the children could not help but wonder: "Am I ill?" Yet logic led them to ask: "If I am ill, why am I walking about the streets? Why don't they make me stay in bed? Why don't they take me to a doctor?" Zelkowicz knew the truth: "But they are very ill, these wretched Jewish children. They are like baby birds, and like sick birds they are doomed to die."[38] Facing imminent deportation, an elderly person of sixty-five or older might in the end give up, resigned to an unalterable fate, reasoning that "one can't live forever anyway, and what does it matter anymore—to die a few days, a few weeks, even a few years earlier than otherwise?" Again likening the endangered ghetto youngsters to little birds, Zelkowicz could not countenance the same resignation with respect to "the children, who have just poked through their eggshells, whose first glimpse of God's world was through the prism of the ghetto, for whom a cow or a chicken are creatures from the land of fantasy, who have never sensed the fragrance of a flower, the shape of an orange, or the flavor of an apple or pear—is their fate sealed? Must they experience the terror of death at this early juncture[?]"[39]

Time's relentless passage never seemed more acute. No one cheated time. Whether old or young, with each passing day, everyone was one day closer to death. But the inhabitants of the ghetto also knew that for every man, woman, and child there existed in the accounts of the ghetto population registry a second, representational self in which, for administrative purposes, his or her official age was listed. Although time could not be fooled, records were alterable: if only on paper, an elderly person might miraculously be made to appear suddenly more youthful, a little boy or girl instantly more mature. A clean erasure, perhaps, or a precise mark, and at a stroke what was a 3 could be reborn a 13. But the Department of Population Records, under the pressure of the hour, was made off limits. On the night of September 3–4, its bureau was "sealed" to public access.[40]

Meanwhile, at 4 Kościelny Street the Evacuation Committee (the Resettlement Commission referred to in the *Chronicle*) had set up headquarters on a separate floor of the same building as the population registry, where employees were busily compiling lists of candidates for removal from the ghetto.[41] Yet, given the widespread uncertainty over the precise age categories involved, the evacuation bureau was quickly thrown into a state of "chaos, commotion and confusion." Apparently at the start even the chief members of the committee, "Mr. Jakobson, Mr. Blemer, Mr. Rosenblatt, Mr. Neftalin, and Mr. Greenberg," were in the dark with regard to where they were to draw the lines defining the targeted population, and this uncertainty resulted in contending interpretations of the edict. If, as the decree asserted, "the stipulated age was from one to ten," did that not mean that infants under twelve months were excluded and to be left untouched? Or was the measure actually to be "applied to children from the age of one minute up to nine years and three hundred and sixty-five days"? So too there were "similar disagreements about the elderly: did it include those aged sixty-five, or did it begin only after the completion of one's sixty-fifth year?"[42] Nor was it at all clear whether possession of papers might serve to exempt an individual from eligibility for removal.[43] Ghetto inhabitants were only too aware that, however the regulation was interpreted, even those who were healthy, employed, and neither too young nor too old were hardly out of the woods. And should they be spared, they still had to worry about the fate of their children and elderly parents. For word got out, and this time it was true, that together the young children and the elderly, even when all had been seized, would constitute only about thirteen thousand persons, while the demanded quota amounted to some twenty thousand. If so, this meant that others outside the targeted categories would be taken as well. And given the reports that exemptions were to be made for the families of ghetto police and firemen, and workshop managers and other officials as well—a rumor that would also turn out to be true—it was clear that the circle of potential victims would have to widen even further to make up "the difference." As always, those who lacked rank and connections would be the most exposed. Such awareness only spurred the desperation and panic in the streets.[44] Scenes at the remaining food centers still open that day were especially tense. "The shoving and congestion were so terrible that even people who pushed their way through to the distribution yard received their potatoes helter-skelter amid an orgy of fury and madness. Most of the mob, however, after a full day of queuing, went away just as they had come—with empty sacks."[45]

On the afternoon of the fourth, in anticipation of Rumkowski's arrival a crowd estimated at 1,500, among them a large number of concerned parents with children at their side, and many elderly men and women, gathered outside the firehouse at 13 Lutomierska Street to await further news of their fate. In spite of the bright sun and the intense heat of the lengthening afternoon, a cluster of spectators, shunning the patch of shade off to the side, claimed positions close to the speaker's platform. Determined to keep the public at a more comfortable remove so as to control the crowd, the ghetto fire chief, Henryk Kaufman, officiously directed those in front to step aside. Given the evident anxiety gripping those present, Kaufman's brusque demeanor seemed strikingly inconsiderate, and was likely, Zelkowicz thought, a reflection of a lack of concern born of the knowledge that whatever the scope of the impending tragedy, he and his own family would remain unaffected.[46]

Belatedly, at 4:45 Rumkowski appeared, making his way to the podium accompanied by two advisers, Dawid Warszawski, "senior manager of the needleworkers' workshop," and Stanisław-Szaja Jakobson, head judge of the ghetto court and experienced co-coordinator of the year's prior deportations.[47] It was clear at a glance that Rumkowski himself was weak, unsteady; his movements were slow and painful, and he seemed to shuffle forward like "a frail old man who can barely put one foot in front of the other." Rumkowski's crown of "white hair" now appeared noticeably unattended, displaying "unkempt tufts" atop a head that was no longer held erect but was uncharacteristically "stooped, as if he [could] hardly hold it atop his shoulders." As for his mouth, "the tsk-tsk motions of his lips" left no doubt that from them would issue "not even one word of consolation."[48]

Reticent, holding back, Rumkowski came forward only to announce that Warszawski would be the first to address the assembly. Warszawski immediately laid out the details of the decree, forthrightly acknowledging its terrible dimensions while arguing that the ghetto must bow to its demands in full and at all costs. To be sure, he offered a word on Rumkowski's behalf, noting the irony that of all people, this man whose life had been dedicated to the education of children should now be compelled to take upon himself the anguish of directing the forcible removal of young children from the ghetto. Sad as this surely was, Warszawski insisted that for the community there was "no choice" but to submit. "The sentence has been handed down. It is irrevocable. They are demanding sacrifices and sacrifices must be made." By way of justification he invoked the specter of events known to be occurring in Warsaw, where that very summer, in operations still under way, the ghetto was being ruthlessly cleared of nearly its entire population: "There was a decree such as this in Warsaw, too. We all know—it is no secret—how it was carried out." Although his name was not mentioned, in what may have been a veiled allusion to the passive defiance of Adam Czerniaków, head of the Warsaw Jewish Council, who, faced in July with an order to assist in assembling children and others for deportation, had taken his own life, Warszawski, speaking for the Jewish leadership in Łódz, declared that failure to cooperate with the decree would only compel the Germans to use their own forces to do the job. "But we have decided to do it ourselves," he explained, "because we do not want and are unable to transform it into a horrific, terrible disaster." In order to avoid a repetition in their streets of what was happening in Warsaw, there could be no other choice but to cooperate and carry out the evacuation by their own hands, and in this way alone at least ameliorate the effect. "Can I give you any solace? Any comfort?" he said to the crowd. "I can tell you only one thing. It may calm and console you a little: It seems, according to all indications, that we will be able to stay on here uneventfully after the decree."[49] He would be right about that point, but it is doubtful that any who heard it could have followed the weak logic of a final, supposedly consoling thought:

Warszawski asked them to consider that, in the conceivable event that
Litzmannstadt might be subject to air assault, and inhabitants of the
ghetto forced quickly to seek shelter, it would be better if adults were not
encumbered by the elderly and the very young. Coming at the end of an
otherwise forthright presentation, the idea, to say the least, sounded un-
convincing.[50]

Judge Jakobson, next to mount the dais, could only underscore
Warszawski's sad revelations, though adding that, of the figure of twenty
thousand which his predecessor had noted would constitute the ultimate
number of deportees the Germans were demanding, the projected daily
quota would be three thousand.[51] More significantly, Jakobson revealed
that "to prevent disasters" during the course of the operation the entire
ghetto would be subject to a curfew.[52] It was clear, however, in whose interests it was to confine the population to their residences for the duration
of the roundup. "Everyone knows that the Evacuation Committee wanted
it this way to make its work easier," wrote Zelkowicz. "How simple it is to
make everyone wait at home and be ready to be hauled away, obviating
the need for a search."[53] All the same, both Warszawski and Jakobson had
at least been forthcoming in regard to "the truth about the number of deportees, the types of people to be sent away, and the curfew," an improvement, Zelkowicz thought, over proffering "half-truths, rumors and random conjectures." But the assembled had yet to hear from Rumkowski. It
was now his turn to speak.[54]

This time there would be none of his typical bombast, none of his
famed self-puffery; today there would be no haughty declarations, no
scolding, no admonitions, no threats. The man was obviously troubled,
his vaunted ego visibly injured. "The President cries like a little boy,"
Zelkowicz recorded. "One can see how the agony of the masses has buffeted him, how grievously the decree has hurt him though it applies to
him neither directly nor indirectly. These are not crocodile tears. They are
Jewish tears, emanating from a Jewish heart."[55] Rumkowski would not
dwell on the matter, but in what may have been an effort to evoke from
listeners at least a small measure of empathy, even if it was only an expression of self-pity rising to the surface of his awareness, he spoke sorrowfully
of his own childlessness, compensated by the many years he had dedicated
to the care of children. It was for him a matter of personal anguish to have
to bend to a demand that he surrender the young. "I lived and breathed

together with the children," he told the crowd. "I never imagined that my own hand would have to bring the sacrifice to the altar."[56] Yet he was careful to concede the greater suffering of parents whose impending loss was immeasurable and crushing. "I understand you, mothers. I see your tears. I also sense the throbbing of your hearts, fathers, who will have to go to work the day after they have taken away your children, when only yesterday you amused yourselves with your beloved offspring. I know and feel all of this."[57] He would not be so presumptuous as to think he could lessen their hardship. "I bear no tidings of consolation today. Neither have I come to calm you today, but rather to expose all of your pain and sorrow. I have come like a thief to deprive you of that which is dearest to your hearts."[58]

Yet he was not going to abandon hope of winning understanding for his position. So unexpected had been the emptying of the hospitals that even he had been unable to prevent harm to his own in-laws. Of course, for some time he had been doing his best to reduce the exposure of young people in the ghetto to new threats. He had endeavored to put more and more of them to work. Touching on the decisive order of the moment affecting the elderly and the young, he indicated that he had not received it until the afternoon of the previous day. He had succeeded, he claimed, in reducing the initial demand from 24,000 victims to 20,000. Though his fervent appeal to exclude nine-year-old children from the general order of deportation had categorically been denied, those aged ten and older had in the end been granted an exemption. Inadequate as this was, he asked the ghetto to take some solace in this small concession. In any case, he wished it known that he had done all that he possibly could; he had even dropped down on his "knees and begged" the Germans to reconsider, "but it was useless."[59] Be that as it may, like his lieutenants, Rumkowski saw no choice but to submit to the edict in exchange for permission to conduct the removal of the young, the elderly, and the ill with the community's own forces. In this way alone might the ghetto avoid the brutality and violence sure to follow should the Germans send in their own troops to carry out the order.[60]

From the start, Rumkowski told his audience, confronted by the edict, he and his trusted associates had been "guided not by the thought 'How many will perish' but 'How many can be saved.'"[61] He reminded them of the fate of the population of the provincial communities, with which they were familiar. "Hardly a thousand Jews reached the ghetto from small towns where seven to eight thousand Jews used to live." The choice facing the Jews of Łódz was as stark as this. "So what's better? What do you want? To leave eighty to ninety thousand people [alive] or to destroy them all, Heaven forfend?" With that, his listeners might have sensed the man finding toward the end of his oration a measure of his familiar dominant bearing. In any event, knowing that in carrying out the order he was a criminal in their eyes, he embraced once more the comparison he knew suited him at this moment only too well. "It takes the heart of a thief to demand what I am demanding of you. But put yourselves in my place, think logically, and draw the conclusion yourselves. I cannot behave otherwise, since those who may be saved far outnumber those whom we are ordered to hand over."[62]

The logic of the argument, cruel as it surely was, was compelling. But given the exhaustion of a last desperate appeal to the Germans to modify their demand, was there truly no alternative to submission and compliance? It is worth noting that Rumkowski remained, as ever, publicly silent about the fate of the deportees. He offered no hope that they were merely being shifted to a new location. His reference to the altar and to sacrifice left little room for conjecture that even the children would survive the journey, though as Zelkowicz and the *Chronicle* attest, speculation to that effect still circulated. But the likelihood of their death—by what means still remained beyond confirmation and beyond imagining—left parents in tears. The members of Rumkowski's audience that afternoon of September 4 were not entirely passive in their grief. At the very moment when he relayed to them the Germans' promise that "if you hand over the sacrifices by yourself, it will be quiet"—that is, compliance would "prevent further sacrifices" and the community would be left in peace— people were heard to shout: "'We'll all go'; 'Mr. President, don't take only children; take one child from families that have other children!'" Rumkowski responded that he would not accept such "hollow clichés," adding, "I haven't the strength to argue with you."[63]

Apart from the question of substituting youngsters from larger families for those who were their parents' only children—yet another grievous choice implied by the already insane terms of the edict—what if Rumkowski had accepted the logic of those who shouted "We'll all go" and on that Friday afternoon had announced that, at the potential cost of the dissolution of the ghetto, he would not lend his own hand to the destruction of the elderly, the sick, and most especially the young? It would have been a courageous act, and Rumkowski and the ghetto he administered would have been honored for it on that day and on all days of remembrance thereafter. Nevertheless, as Rumkowski knew, it took little imagination to comprehend that such defiance would constitute a direct challenge to a German security establishment whose cruelties both the leaders and the inhabitants of the ghetto had long endured. In all likelihood such an act would have brought the Łódź ghetto to a swift and bloody end. Well before reaching this terrible juncture, Rumkowski knew what to expect from any overt act of defiance. Any Jewish leader who resisted such a decree would have to reckon not just with death but with torture as well. Rumkowski would not have forgotten the fate of the first Beirat and the treatment that preceded their deaths in autumn 1939. And they had done nothing to provoke their torment. But what of a symbolic refusal, one that cheated the Gestapo of the satisfaction of vengeance against a defiant Jewish underling? In his speech Rumkowski had alluded briefly to his own death, if only in the context of wondering if he would live long even after compliantly executing the impending decree. He would have known about Czerniaków's suicide, undertaken in the face of similar pressures, only weeks before in late July. But if the idea of following a similar course crossed his mind now, he dismissed it, whether out of understandable reluctance to take his own life or because Czerniaków's gesture, honorable as it was, had done nothing to prevent the mass deportation that followed. In Warsaw, others had been found to carry out the order.[64] The world would not read of Rumkowski's suicide, or of a courageous ghetto whose people chose, by his word or by his example, to be led away to their deaths rather than offer up with their own hands their aged, their sick, and above all their defenseless young; nor would we hear of those who might have rushed the wooden fence posts and the wires, to die there under fire or, if successful in fleeing the precincts of the ghetto, hunted down and shot in the countryside beyond or, more likely, in the streets of the nearby city.[65]

The words of Warszawski and Jakobson indicate that in advance of addressing the public, internal discussion of how to respond had been going on among a small circle of leaders close to Rumkowski. Others were consulted as well, or at least informed in advance. Speaking of this moment long afterwards Arnold Mostowicz would recall:

> When Rumkowski learned that the Germans had decided to remove all the sick, the elderly, and the children, he called a meeting of doctors. . . . I took part in that meeting. In the course of it ninety percent of the doctors agreed that it had to be done, that the decision must be observed. At the same time they were fully aware that to those deported it meant death. Naturally you can ask me—and it would be a fair question—how did I react? Well, I reacted in the most cowardly way imaginable: I said nothing. I cannot tell you what made me act that way, except one thing which I am sure of now. . . . Personally, I was under no threat; that was one of the reasons for my silence, but it would be too easy to say that it was the only reason. I guess I kept quiet because I was ashamed to say that we should do as the Germans told us, since there was no escape from their decision, but at the same time to admit that it was an utter disgrace.[66]

The speeches ended and evening approached, marking the conclusion of a crushing day. "The sun dips to the west. Dusk has come. As the sun sets, everyone feels the encroachment of impending events," Zelkowicz wrote, groping to express the unrelieved terror of that moment. "No one believes in miracles anymore. All three speakers made it clear that the decree is irreversible—twenty thousand Jews must be deported from the ghetto. Sent away for good. Never to be seen again." Surely "there has never been a sunset like today's." On other days, sunset had brought to the residents of the ghetto the promise of rest. It was the time

> when you returned to your wife after a day at work. After a whole day apart, parents and children gathered for a pitiable dinner. In the courtyard they met with neighbors who declaimed their woes and they breathed musty air into their lungs—musty but, nevertheless, better than the air inside the cramped apartments. Every day, people yearned for sunset. Today, however—how many years of people's

lives would they forfeit to keep the sun from setting, to make this day last interminably, to avert the bleak, grotesque morrow forever?[67]

"Once night falls, everyone trembles at the sight of his lengthening shadow." The courtyards are abandoned as people return to their homes to wait out the darkness, or to wait out time's passing:

So the ghetto residents sit in their apartments. Many of them do not even turn on a light. Why bother? For what purpose should people see their own agony and tears in other faces? In other rooms, however, the lights are on. Mostly, these are rooms inhabited by children to whom the hideous decree applies. The best beds have been prepared for these children. Mothers and fathers stand at these beds, not to safeguard the children's slumber or to drive away the ghetto flies, but to contemplate them in their last remaining hours. They can still be together; the parents can still engrave their children's faces into their memory.[68]

A sentence of death hovered over the elderly too. Who, Zelkowicz asked, will watch over them on this night? For them hope is all but extinguished. The old are so obviously useless to the Germans. While death likely also awaited the young, there was at least the sliver of a chance that, under parental protection, children might yet be spared the worst.[69] But as for the elderly, though once their lives had been filled with family, many now were all alone. Zelkowicz thought of them; surely they must "amble along the walls of their rooms, like shadows of stray dogs on a moonlit night in some Godforsaken place." Their fate was grim, their future all but annulled. If any could be sure that this ghetto night was their last on earth, it was they. Their smallest sensory perceptions, momentarily experienced in the vanishing here and now, would be among their last. "So the elderly totter along the walls of the narrow rooms that they now love and cherish so. Even the spider webs and the stains of fleas on the walls have become dear to their hearts." Among them, "who knows what the morrow, and the day after, will look like? Will they have a room at all, or will they share a pit with two hundred, with a thousand people, men, women, children all together—those who have been 'discarded'?" For the last time they enjoyed the comfort of a mattress, a pillow, some sheets, a coverlet:

this "bug-infested bedding," uncomfortable as it was, had "suddenly become agreeable" and, in a sense, "their live-in doctor. It allows them to refresh themselves and to relax for a few hours. In their dreams, it reflects the faces of their dear children and grandchildren. How dear this bedding is to an old man in his final hours!" Thus drawn "to that place, to that side of life, to the land of dreams," for one final time an old man might find himself in the company of those who had given a declining life its meaning.[70]

From the outset the ghetto had endured an unsettled relationship with time; ultimately the Jews of Łódź staked all hope on waiting out the Germans until their fortunes failed and the war came to an end. There was always the possibility that through perseverance, through merely holding out, the great remnant might be saved and, once freed, reenter the world. The ghetto would not endure forever. Just as, with all certainty, they knew that at this very moment there existed a world beyond the ghetto, they knew as well that there would be a time to come after it. Whether they might live to experience that future was another matter. Possibly they would. In this hope they could only wish that the intervening time would pass as quickly as possible, that the day of liberation might be near. It was only when a sentence of death drew nearer still that they wanted nothing so much as for time to slow, for the present to be never-ending. But time for them did pass, as time does. Who but a Joshua had the power to delay it?[71] And so the sun set on this day, as on all days before and after, just as surely as it would rise up again and again with each new dawn.

Worry undermined slumber. "Here and there a broken heart issues a groan that emanates from an open window like the sound of an overused violin string, a bleat from a strangled throat like the sound of a slaughtered calf. A child occasionally screams in his restless sleep like the last flickering of a dying candle." But the people knew that nearby existed a kind of peace, the enjoyment of which fed off the misery of the ghetto. It pierced the night with sounds from farther afield. "From that side of life, from the other side of the barbed-wire fence, the ghetto sometimes hears the clatter of a passing streetcar or the screech of a hoarse phonograph record, like the mocking of a drunk nomad who has been placed in charge of the pointless lives of a hundred thousand leprous dogs, that tomorrow or the next day will get their just deserts. 'Cling-clang—one in five to be torn away. Clank-clank—one Jew in five.'"[72]

Night vanished. A new day began. By seven o'clock on the morning of Saturday, September 5, the streets were filled. In anticipation of the curfew, people headed out in the hope of stocking up on any available foodstuffs. "It is utterly impossible to stay at home. Everyone runs out. They literally run—rushing, hustling, as if propelled by someone wielding a whip."[73] For all the commotion there was also an uncharacteristic atmosphere of quiet: "No one converses, it's as if people have left or forgotten their tongues at home. Acquaintances do not offer greetings, as if ashamed of each other. They freeze as they walk. They freeze as they stand in lengthy queues at the distribution points and the vegetable yards. An eerie silence has overtaken the ghetto."[74] Such anxious motion brought to mind a picture of "sinners' souls circulating in the netherworld. This is exactly how they would look: lips buttoned in stubborn silence, eyes filled with a great terror." For Zelkowicz, hellish visions evoked further images of a grotesque metamorphosis: "The three bridges in the ghetto swarm with hundred-headed snakes, an encampment of snakes that moves continually back and forth, hither and yon. The creatures racing about, scurrying in the thick air, are people."[75]

The Jewish police made ready to comply with the tasks ahead, prepared, as on prior occasions, to see to it that orders were carried out. This time they would be assisted by ghetto firefighters, whose cooperation had also been sealed by the promise of safety for their own children and relations and extra servings of bread and sausage to fill their bellies and provide needed energy for the work. Ghetto porters and teamsters, among them men of considerable strength, making up what came to be known unofficially as the White Guard (taking their name from the powdering of "flour, sugar, and rice" that stuck to their garments), were needed as well. These strong men were said to have undertaken preparations to defend their young by mounting guard at the thresholds of their residences "with axes in [their] hands." The display of force proved unnecessary; their cooperation was purchased like that of the police. Their children protected, the transport workers went to work assisting in the operation.[76] Their young children and those of the Jewish police, firemen, and workplace managers—recipients of passes exempting them from resettlement—were brought to a shelter on Łagiewnicka Street, protected for the duration of the *Aktion*. Removing their small sons and daughters to the shelter when it opened on Sunday, even many of these privileged fathers were anxious, unsure at first that the pledge they had been given would hold.[77]

Even in advance of the curfew, set to begin at 5 PM, the Jewish police started collecting the first of those marked for capture. They began by emptying the old age homes, a relatively effortless undertaking, for the victims were physically weak, isolated from others, certain to be on the premises and there for the taking. In such a place the police could be sure of getting off to a successful start; there they could practice their technique, developing a feel for the *Aktion* while encountering as little difficulty as possible. "There, as they say, the table's been set. Everything can be taken as is," wrote Zelkowicz. "No need to be selective. Everything is old and fit to be 'thrown on the garbage heap.'"[78] So too "in the old-age homes, the policemen can work in a calm and businesslike way. No one disturbs or annoys them; there are no mistakes. . . . They load the old men and women onto the wagons like pieces of scrap metal."[79]

That would prove the standard procedure, soon to be extended to the ghetto as a whole: those to be removed would climb up onto horse-drawn wagons, guarded by Jewish police and driven by ghetto teamsters to designated assembly points or holding areas established inside the newly cleared hospitals and on the grounds of the ghetto's Czarnieckiego Street prison. From there, in successive transports, they would be loaded onto German trucks that exited the ghetto bound for Chełmno. On that initial weekend morning as well, the first of the carts filled with children were spotted being loaded on Rybna Street. Zelkowicz would record that in stark contrast to grieving parents and other adults nearby, the youngest of the children, apparently oblivious to their fate, were beside themselves with excitement, if also a bit confused. "These children see no reason to cry," he wrote:

> They are quite content: they have been placed on a wagon and they are going for a ride! Since when have children in the ghetto had such an opportunity? If it were not for all those wailing people, if their mothers and fathers had not screamed so as they placed them in the cart, they would have danced to the cart. After all, they are going for a wagon ride. But all that shouting, noise and crying upset them and

disrupted their joy. They jostle in the elongated wagon bed with its high barriers, as if lost, and their bulging eyes ask: What's going on? What do these people want from us? Why don't they let us take a little ride?[80]

Oskar Singer, however, noted that there were also older children, more experienced in ghetto life and its misfortunes, who appeared soberly resigned in the face of what was happening to them.[81] Afterwards—apparently on the evening of September 5—the men of the Jewish Order Service saw to the roundup of the children in the Marysin homes. While some of the estimated 850 youngsters who had been staying there had left in advance of the *Aktion,* Rumkowski, arriving to oversee the removal, made sure that none evaded capture or were left behind.[82]

Confined to their residences, people confronted the knowledge that their own parents, husbands, wives, daughters, sons, sisters, and brothers were potentially targeted for removal, if not already taken, perhaps never to be seen again. The tension and grief, difficult enough to endure by day, became immeasurably worse with the onset of darkness. From the perspective of the following day, Zelkowicz reviewed the distinctive mood prevailing during the nighttime hours of the fifth, wondering: "Who could sleep tonight? Mothers whose children had been taken from them? Men whose wives, their helpmeets, had been taken? People whose ailing loved ones were removed from their beds? . . . The ghetto tosses on its bed and knows no sleep. The aching, enfeebled bones cannot lie still. The ghetto's brain is incurably feverish. All those screams and roars, sighs and groans that split the silence of the night through the open windows and doors have landed on its heart." Sounds of anguish traversed the darkness. For the bereaved, night brought not the least diminution of their suffering: "Hours have passed since these woes, these agonies, were inflicted on those wretched people, but the situation has not calmed down one bit. Mothers have not yet tired of shrieking, fathers' wellsprings of tears have not yet been sealed, and the silence of the night amplifies the reverberations of the screaming and sobbing."[83]

On that same Saturday, September 5, the day that followed Friday's dreadful pronouncement of the irrevocable order for the ghetto to yield up the aged, the sick, and the children of most tender years, an additional camera team from the Ufa studios, recently arrived to continue documenting the city's reconstruction, set up their equipment on location, first at the Telefunken works, and then once more at the site of the newly opened municipal beach and water park in Erzhausen.[84] The filmmakers recorded a charming setting. As the camera rolled, people in bathing suits could be seen diving off a bridge into the water. Panning downstream, the camera found three people seated in a rowboat, another boat overtaking them, passing by. Panning toward the shore, it highlighted two shirtless young-sters seated on a grassy bank. In a sequence lasting only seconds, one of the them, a fair-haired boy, was seen to raise an arm, casually propping it on his knee.[85] In brief, yet another ideal image of a city without Jews, qui-etly indulging in the pleasures of a lazy, late-summer afternoon. This was but one aspect of the newly emerging city the filmmakers would docu-ment as they traveled to numerous sites over the course of what would prove, for the ghetto though decidedly not for the city, a week of unprece-dented horror.

But even these images of a relaxed citizenry at play beside gentle waters were but one contrasting facet of the new Litzmannstadt, whose changes were hailed as stunning and whose fast-paced tempo was admired for be-ing precisely what one would expect from a major urban center in the making. Indeed, according to the local press, downtown was jumping, its streets and crossings increasingly crowded, an observation said to have been noted by citizens returning from holidays in the country, as well as by the mayor of Posen, who on a recent visit to the city had commented on the phenomenon as well. To offer a more precise view of just how heavily trafficked the streets were, on September 5 the *Litzmannstädter Zeitung* publicized an informal survey gauging the number of people and vehicles traveling a busy city block, a stretch along Adolf-Hitler-Straße be-tween Meisterhausstraße and Straße des 8. Armee—a distance of some five hundred meters in length—between six and seven o'clock in the eve-ning. The results, published in the paper's Saturday edition, were said to be altogether "startling": during that single evening hour, and along just this one stretch of avenue, had passed no fewer than 3,288 pedestrians, 69 automobiles, 178 streetcars—each loaded with an estimated 100 riders, hence ferrying some 17,800 persons in all at an average rate of three cars per minute—along with 14 trucks, 18 motorcycles, 2 freight trams, 27 horse-drawn cabs, 117 bicycles, and 6 handcarts. The point one was to draw from all this was twofold: Litzmannstadt was indeed a big city, fast-paced and energetic. That said, such a rush of crowds and cars was "synonymous with life and development. In Litzmannstadt life pulses mightily, work is being done, people bestir themselves, they have things to do. Already they are creating today the foundations for the Litzmannstadt of the future."[86]

By dark that evening Litzmannstadt readied for entertainment. As ever, audiences in search of lighter fare that Saturday were invited to stop by the Tabarin cabaret, whose new September lineup included solo dancer Maria Reill, entertainer Jack Barlott imitating a chimpanzee, a team of "comical jugglers" by the name of Waldero and Pifo, the Carinis performing their "Liliput-Trio," as well as the dances of the La-Czarina Ballet, the music of the Kapelle Bojanowsky, and the Trio Nino singing "well-known hits."[87] For audiences in search of more serious entertainment, the Theater an der Moltkestraße was opening its 1942–43 season with a performance of *Kabale und Liebe* by Schiller. Recalling the recent words of Oberbürgermeister Ventzki in stressing the significance of theater to Litzmannstadt, "the easternmost large city of the great German Reich," a correspondent jubilantly proclaimed: "Curtain up! Let the show begin!"[88]

By the following morning, Sunday, September 6, not satisfied that the Jewish police alone could do the job, the Gestapo intervened, sending German forces into the ghetto to oversee the roundup. Far from being relieved of their duties, the men of the Jewish Order Service acted as auxiliaries. As Isaiah Trunk, briefly summarizing the tactics now in force, would note: "Gestapo and SS-men, accompanied by their Jewish helpers, went from house to house, and a very few minutes after hearing the signal (generally a reckless revolver shot), all tenants had to present themselves for the selection. Here everything went at a lightning fast tempo. Fates were determined in a matter of seconds: a glance or a gesture with the hand (left or right)."[89]

Shlomo Frank, himself a Jewish policemen, would recall that in the hours before the Gestapo's arrival, the Jewish police prepared for an escalation in violence. The matter was discussed after midnight, during the course of a conference at Jewish Order Service headquarters on Lutomierska Street. By seven the next morning the word went out to the Order Service rank and file. A Jewish police commander informed his men that the number of people who were going to die in the coming hours was incalculable, but they were ordered to show "no mercy": there could be no disturbances; the ghetto population had to submit.[90] Heading toward Bałuty Market at 7:30 AM, Jewish police encountered a team of Gestapo men, "no more than sixteen" in all, entering the ghetto "on the march" and "with automatic rifles on their shoulders," announcing their presence with an extended volley of gunfire that lasted a good ten minutes. Typically, with a cordon laid down in a targeted sector of neighboring streets, the Gestapo swept in, forcing occupants to assemble in residential courtyards. Children clung to their mothers, begging not to be separated: "Wherever they send you, take me. Together, let's go together."[91] Loaded onto the carts, they cried out for help: "Mama, Mama, save us, do not let us be killed." Some dared to leap from the wagons, attempting to make a break, only to be shot, their blood pooling in the streets. Amid the slaughter, the killers taunted the others, already "frightened to death," cynically asking "if they wanted to jump off the wagons as well."[92] These men were onto the ways of their prey, easily discovering the usual places where parents had hidden children. Other families, attempting to stay one step ahead of the selections, dashed into the streets. But to no avail. They were easily cut down by gunners stationed on rooftops, firing down on fleeing parents and children below.[93] The killers made a sport of the chase; they joked with one another, they teased and taunted their victims, delighting in catching them unawares, shooting them at close range as well as from afar. After pumping a bullet into one victim, a Gestapo official asked, "Taste good?" His colleague was said to have a penchant for tapping Jewish women on the shoulder, telling them to turn around, then shooting them from behind; if his victims were still breathing as they lay in a pool of their own blood, he would stand on top of them until they died.[94] Another "ran about like a wild ox, his nostrils sniffing out places where children were hiding." When he found them, rather than letting them emerge, he opened fire on them where they hid, then ordered neighbors to come and "drag out the filth."[95] On Łagiewnicka Street one of the killers was said to have forced four ten-year-old boys to their knees, ordering them to open their mouths, into which, one by one, he fired. Incredulous, the children were said to have thought he was merely "joking with them."[96]

By mid-morning on that same Sunday, Zelkowicz had succeeded in gathering some initial accounts. They were impossible to bear, though they recorded only the first of many wounds that would be inflicted that week on families throughout the ghetto. Among the very first to suffer such agonies would be a young poet, married, father to a pair of daughters, one no older than eight years of age, another born less than two days before. On Saturday—it was "in the late afternoon"—the first of these daughters, a beautiful child with "golden curls, blue eyes and gleaming white teeth," was taken by the Jewish police; then on Sunday morning the Germans arrived and seized his wife, "ill" and "feverish," still bedridden from having just giving birth. The newborn daughter resting by her side, "a tiny infant with two miniature round fists" and "quiet, motionless eyes," as yet nameless, too weak even to suckle a bit of milk, was taken too. "What miserable, shocking and utterly illogical felicitations come in from the street," wrote Zelkowicz. "The mind does not accept them; the intellect cannot grasp them. Nevertheless they are the absolute truth!"[97] In a courtyard on Zytnia Street, neighbors who had been assembled there witnessed another unfolding crime when a mother, quietly defiant though smiling, remained steely in defying a German ordering her to let go of her four-year-old daughter's hand. Uncharacteristically, the mother was given a few moments to reconsider. "Neighbors standing in the lengthy ranks sneaked a tearful look at the two of them, standing alone and smiling at each other—the girl in contentment for remaining with her mother who clutched her hand, and the mother in contentment for having her daughter next to her and within her." She was told, "'Face the wall. . . !' Holding even tighter that small hand, she and her child were shot to death from behind."[98]

Residents of another building were witnesses to the fate of another little girl, the only child of a dignified, well-attired German Jewish woman from Danzig whose daily absence from home unleashed in the child fits of sobbing and screaming. Ceaselessly crying for her mother, she "spent whole days mired in tears, unconsolable by anyone but her mother," an odd child, "her head pointed, her face round as a ball, her legs thick and stiff, and her eyes large, black, and almost motionless. She looked more like a clown than a living girl." Early on Saturday her mother, thinking at first the *Aktion* was not yet imminent, had gone to work, only to race back to the residence upon getting word of the impending roundup, retreating to her apartment with the child. Shortly before six that evening, the Jewish Order Service came and took the girl, who, suddenly dignified

and silent, a small version of her mother, "walked next to the tall, stiff policeman" while "dressed in a tiny coat and hat, a small girlish pocketbook
under her arm," her "round black, expressionless eyes" looking straight
ahead. In contrast, her mother's composure was shattered. At the sight of
her daughter being led away, she "issued an inhuman scream that reso-
nated throughout the courtyard and on the stairs. . . . She continued to
circulate tearfully in the courtyard for hours on end, until late in the evening." Eventually "the neighbors, after strenuous efforts, managed to
bring her inside. All that night she lurched from corner to corner in her
room," shouting her daughter's name.[99] The sound of screaming filled the
air. The despair of parents who had lost their children was immense. One
woman "lay on the ground and pounded her head against the pavement."
A man ran about, "an ax in his hands," shouting for the return of his
child, threatening death to those who would bring it harm.[100]

Meanwhile, only too aware of the perils of displaying outward signs of
age, older adults did their best to appear a little younger. Perhaps, they
reasoned, it might be possible to fool their would-be captors, given to instant judgment of their features for signs of vitality, of youth, of health,
separating the fit from the potential castoffs—the moribund, the decrepit,
the sick, the useless—who were their targets. What, after all, did the elderly have to lose by looking well clothed, younger and healthier, fresher,
even more attractive in anticipation of that second or two when, at a
glance, the captor's eye would glance their way. Hair that was not white,
lips and cheeks of a reddened as opposed to a pale or washed-out hue,
meant life. One had but an instant to make the right impression. "No one
knows what to wear when he or she descends to the courtyard for inspection," wrote Zelkowicz. "If people go as is, without a hat and coat, it may
create the impression of disrespect." Or perhaps not. "If you came to the
courtyard in ordinary clothes, it showed that you took the matter lightly;
if you put on a hat and coat, it meant you were ready for a trip, so why
not join the transport?"[101] A man might don a hat or coat, but women
could do more. They could "doll up," as Zelkowicz put it. If a woman's
lips were pale and she had no lipstick, she had only to bite her lips, forcing
the blood to rush to the surface. The same with her cheeks; in the absence
of rouge, she had only to pinch them or rub them with a bit of red paper
to produce instantly a spot of color. At the very least, gray hair could be
tucked away beneath a scarf.[102] Men hoping to achieve a temporarily
younger look took to dyeing their hair with coffee.[103]

Others tried more direct means of resisting capture. A fifteen-year-old girl, caught up in a selection and desperate to escape being carted away with the others, repeatedly battled tooth and nail against a Jewish policeman who was determined to foil her efforts to break free and save her life. Ordered onto a wagon full of captives, she begged him to look the other way so she might make a run for safety. Her plea was greeted with brute force. She later recalled the man seizing her arm and pushing her against the already packed vehicle, forcing her aboard. "As I made an attempt to jump down[,] . . . the same Jewish policeman caught me by the hair and pulled me back." When she reached for the side of the transport to make contact with an acquaintance she had spotted on the street below, "the same Jewish policeman caught me, slapped me across the face, and threw me to the floor." On arrival at the collection point on the fenced-in grounds of the hospital on Drewnowska Street, making a break from the others to find a hiding place, she scuffled with yet another Jewish policeman who "screamed as he came running." He took hold of her, tearing her dress, as she "kicked, scratched and struggled" for dear life.[104]

Some children hid in furniture and bedding, others in basements, in heaps of garbage and laundry, or in woodpiles.[105] Parents did whatever they could, concealing their children "in barrels in the attics, in ditches in the field, covered with leaves and branches."[106] One child sought refuge in a tree but was shot dead when discovered.[107] Another, thanks to his father's efforts to fashion an unusual hideout, rode out the danger concealed in a chimney on the roof.[108] Though isolated and abandoned by the time they had been assembled in the collection area, child captives fought and scratched at the walls in a last-ditch effort to resist removal.[109] But these and many other desperate grabs for survival, courageous as they were, were undertaken individually, in an unorganized way, without help from the Jewish authorities, who dared go no further than securing approval to spare the children and elderly relations of the ghetto police, firemen, teamsters, and well-connected officials. The rest, whether children or adults, were on their own and, as far as Rumkowski and the ghetto leadership were concerned, regrettably but necessarily fated to be sacrificed to save the others. Having acquiesced to the Germans' demand, he wanted them to be taken away quickly and with their removal the dirty business finished and put behind him.

One week after commencement of the *Aktion,* on September 12, by "posted" announcement the Gettoverwaltung informed the residents of the ghetto that the curfew was lifted; the terrible roundup came to an end. In the course of these seven days the operation had resulted in the deportation of an estimated 15,859 persons, with "a minimum of 600 shot to death on the spot." Labor, Biebow informed them, was to resume at the beginning of the workweek the following Monday, September 14. "Every manager, worker, and employee is obligated to occupy his workplace punctually if he is concerned to protect himself from the greatest unpleasantness imaginable," he warned, calling upon them "to fulfill their tasks with the greatest diligence and take pains to make up as quickly as possible for the arrears caused by" what he referred to bizarrely as their "rest break."[110]

In the aftermath of the operation, building caretakers and ghetto police inventoried and secured the personal effects left behind in apartments abandoned by the deported. In some of the residences along Marysińska and Marynarska streets, for example, they found jackets, coats, shirts, sweaters, trousers, underpants, skirts, gloves, umbrellas, scarves and handkerchiefs, pillows and pillowcases, blankets, sheets, suitcases, tablecloths, dishware, cutlery, clocks, candlesticks, skullcaps and prayer shawls, rags, and unwashed laundry held in containers or merely lying in a heap.[111]

It was always thought best to have the Jews handle these goods, but the operation being what it was, the Gettoverwaltung had its own tasks of cleanup to perform as well. Appealing to the city Health Department, on September 21 Biebow's deputy, Friedrich Ribbe, requested approval for the provision of additional soap for "around 60 members" of his staff whose tasks brought them "continually in contact with Jews and such things of Jewish origin." It almost went without saying that they were being exposed "to great danger of infection,"so it was "perfectly understandable that these people are compelled to wash their hands more often than normal." Approval was granted within seventy-two hours.[112]

Sunday, September 13, would be the final day of shooting for the Ufa film crew; some two hundred meters of footage would be shot that day. After an abbreviated trip to the stadium, they proceeded to the municipal zoo, an institution celebrated for its contribution to the recreational potential of the new city. Litzmannstadt was depicted as a family-oriented, child-friendly city in a filmed sequence that highlighted visitors arriving at the zoo and delighting in its attractions. A small child is seen walking toward the entrance between two men in uniform. Its hands are raised to be held in theirs. A woman, accompanied by a female acquaintance, is pushing a baby carriage. A group proceeds down an outdoor staircase leading onto a wide tree-lined path. A couple—a man in a raincoat and a woman dressed in a lightweight coat, their pace a bit quicker—walk on ahead of the others. The day is bright. The camera pans to take in the image of a gentle stream, a gazebo in the distance, trees reflected on the glassy surface of the still waters. Caged animals come into view: a camel, a tiger, a chimpanzee, a lion cub, a bear.[113]

Summer was coming to an end. One reliable sign of the season had been the daily 7:45 AM departure of the familiar "special" transport from Deutschlandplatz, a regional tram carrying children bound for a government-run day camp in Erzhausen. With the end of the camp's last session approaching, the children would have been boarding for their final trips to the city's much-admired recreational district. Based in a home run by the National Socialist Welfare Agency (NSV), the camp, appropriately situated on Sleeping Beauty Street (Dornröschenstraße), lay in a park with lovely wooded surroundings. All told, some four hundred youngsters, divided into month-long rotating sessions accommodating a hundred campers at a time, got to enjoy the out-of-doors—a published photograph depicts girls in summer dresses joining hands to form a ring—their bodies attended to, cleansed in saltwater baths, and nourished by an ample, healthful diet. Many children had completed their stays "several kilos heavier" than when they arrived. On the third weekend in September a festive farewell Saturday program marked the season's end.[114]

Oblivious to the cruelties to which the elderly and the young had recently been subjected inside the ghetto, writers who served as the public voice of the regime, even in highlighting efforts to promote the welfare of German mothers, proved unable to resist an opportunity to curse the Jews. Evidence of the harm they were alleged to have caused seemed even now, and in spite of their long absence from the city, to keep cropping up, complicating the great tasks of renovation and renewal. That autumn a villa, formerly a Jewish old age home, was being remodeled to accommodate a city training facility for German mothers. A tour of the facilities, beginning with promising impressions of the building's sunny, park-like grounds, from which were heard the delightful sounds of voices singing to "the accompaniment of a flute," occasioned in the mind of a local news-paper correspondent only the brightest of thoughts. Those initial impres-sions proved altogether at odds with what were described as the horrifying conditions reportedly confronting those whose task it had been to prepare the property for its new occupants. "Even the Polish workmen," thought to be "in this respect used to all sorts of things, were shocked when they discovered the swarm of bugs behind the wallpaper. The filth in this Jew-ish home was indescribably if authentically Jewish." That past unpleasant-ness happily overcome, the home was successfully completing conversion, providing facilities for some 225 German mothers at a time to receive in-struction in family health, infant care, cooking, sewing, handicrafts, and household decoration. Attractive rooms, including a winter garden, added pleasant touches, and overnight facilities, equipped with showers and baths, were at the disposal of "out-of-town participants" in the courses as well as staff. In brief, the facility was an expression of the party's striving "to enrich the family, and particularly to help make easier the tasks of our women and mothers."[115]

In further material confirmation of the Germans' claim to the land, two weeks after the conclusion of the terrifying roundup inside the ghetto, on the morning of September 26 the city's prehistory museum, located on Deutschlandplatz, was at last ready for the public. An advance tour of its rooms revealed a prominent selection of local archaeological finds: in ad-dition to the usual assortment of iron lances and buckles of gold, silver, and bronze, worthy of special note were relics supposed to offer insight into the practices and belief systems of Nordic settlers dating from as long ago as 1200–500 BC. As an aid to picturing the awesome dimensions of some of the burial sites common to the region, a mockup depicted an im-pressively long grave, measuring some 130 meters in length. Original arti-facts bespeaking practices associated with early Germanic settlement high-lighted changing funerary customs, advancing from burial to the burning of the dead. Displayed too were a selection of ash-bearing urns, some with bell-shaped lids and carvings of faces, some bearing the inspiring design of a winged swastika, of local significance because the pattern had been in-corporated into the Litzmannstadt city flag. Readers following this ac-count of the exhibition were reminded of previously highlighted finds re-covered from a recent excavation in the Erzhausen district. At last citizens would have opportunity to admire in person a selection of these rare finds, among them "a small, twinned vessel" and, perhaps most poignantly, a child's rattle fashioned out of clay that had been discovered inside one of the graves.[116]

At the same time that the archaeological presentation on Deutschlandplatz made available a glimpse into the remote Germanic past, "the first German color film," the Ufa production *Women Make Better Diplomats,* a musical starring Marika Rökk and Willy Fritsch, was playing at the newly renovated Casino cinema. Deemed a historic technical advance comparable to the introduction of sound, the achievement promised to revolutionize the medium, eventually eclipsing black and white. The novelty had been so great as to require an initial period of adjustment for the viewer. The technical reproduction of color, while said to have been, at least in part, astonishingly true, seems to have had a way to go before all colors could be reproduced convincingly. All the same, a feature film of this nature, full of song and dance, was considered ideally suited for showcasing the medium's new potential. Adding a local touch to the premiere, the city's police orchestra was on hand to perform a selection of popular cinematic show tunes.[117]

Walther Genewein, Gettoverwaltung accountant, amateur photographer, and unofficial visual documentarian of the ghetto's administration, might well have taken an interest. For he too had been working in the new medium of color photography, and had by now accumulated a significant and growing collection of images recording the activities of the Biebow administration and ghetto labor.[118] Taking the opportunity to record as well a moment of his own private relaxation and contemplation, in an image dated October 1942 Genewein photographed himself at bedtime, seated at the end of a long, green-cushioned sofa. He wears a red-striped bathrobe and brown slippers, his legs crossed, his head slightly lowered over an open book in his lap: the accountant at leisure, absorbed in his reading, his shadow a dark silhouette cast on the bare wall behind him. A brown or tan throw pillow lies nearby. An oriental carpet fills the space of the floor. On a table to his left, toward which he inclines, sits a substantial wooden box radio, a pair of decorative figurines, and a shaded table lamp with a shiny gold base. Behind them the tiles of what appears to be a tall ceramic oven help create the impression of a cozy niche.[119]

The first days of autumn promised ample opportunity for citizens of the new Reich city to develop their cultural sensibilities. While the opening of the new Museum of Prehistory served to document the Germanic origins of the region and the culture of its past, modern artists attended to the representations of the moment. Currently on display at the Volks-bildungsstätte was the work of a sculptor, Marta Kronig, a hometown art-ist since moved to Munich, again in town for an exhibition of her work. In an interview with a local reporter, she spoke of giving artistic shape to the depiction of human emotion, and of the sensibilities most appropriate to creative receptivity in both artist and viewer. As a contemporary artist, Kronig attended to the present, declaring: "In my works I want to give shape to the people of today. . . . Not those of yesterday nor those of to-morrow." On the topic of suffering, a theme of some prominence in her work, she remarked, "When I depict suffering . . . I do not give form to suffering that cries out, but to that suffering which is already beyond the scream, accepting of its fate. And in the face of suffering one must have reverence." As for future projects, "what she would most like to create are little fountains. Little in the sense that they are not meant to be mag-nificent, but fountains situated in peaceful park locales seldom visited by anyone and where all is cozy and still, where the splashing of the fountain waters speak to quiet visitors of fairy tales." To this she added, "Most of all I would like to create such fairy tale fountains for children's play-grounds."[120]

Rounding out the season's new offerings on the evening of November 5, 1942, the Städtische Bühnen, expanding into a new realm of performance, launched its first full season of opera under its own management, selecting for the occasion a performance of Engelbert Humperdinck's 1890's musi-cal rendition of the fairy tale classic, *Hansel and Gretel*. Defying not just the shortage of available musicians and singers but above all the "primi-tive" nature of the "technical apparatus," said to have been a legacy of the abstractly derided "Jewish-Polish want of culture" long dominant on the local arts scene, the performance had brought forth a masterly rendition. A critic praised the production for so richly evoking what he termed "a genuine fairy-tale mood, born of the joy in assuming a childlike perspec-tive on the world."[121]

On the night of that autumn premiere the audience had been privi-leged to enjoy one of the most enduring of tales. Its theme of lost children ultimately rescued from peril had been well selected to appeal to the sensi-bilities of Litzmannstadt operagoers, and appeal it did. Following the performance, the stage manager, orchestra leader, and cast stepped in front of the curtain to receive both a warm ovation and the presentation of a gift of flowers. The municipal orchestra had cleverly arranged key elements of the score. The lighting, so essential to the addition of scenic color, had been magnificent. Actors and actresses, assisted by a boys' chorus, had succeeded admirably in evoking the atmosphere and drama of this long-popular tale. It remained an appealing fable even now, and on that November evening in the city, nightmare had given way to deliverance. In the final scene the children, held captive on the grounds of the witch's hideout, were seen to rise miraculously from the gingerbread in which they had been imprisoned. Lurking evil had been defeated. Life had been granted them anew. Parents and children, long separated, were united once again.[122]

For the deported children of the ghetto and the parents they left behind, there was no solace. To the parents, details concerning the destination and fate of their young sons and daughters remained shrouded in darkness. This much alone was evident: wherever the Germans had taken the children, there would be no sandman to sprinkle sleep-dust in their eyes, no angels to watch over them as they slumbered in the forest by night, no dewman to awaken them in the morning, no rescue, no release, no reunion with mothers and fathers who, inconsolable, looked into their eyes no more.[123]

9

Who Shall Live and Who Shall Die?

The terrible year 1942 had left its imprint. Nothing could erase the awareness that the community had suffered grievously and that its numbers were in unmistakable decline. Even more, it seemed that the surrounding land had been all but totally cleared of Jews; never had the Jews of Łódź been so isolated, so alone. As a people, they were dying out. What had been done to the children in September weighed most heavily. Their dreadful fate signaled the diminishing prospects for the future of the community as a whole. Rumkowski had failed to shield them from harm; an abject leader, his powerlessness exposed, he had assented to the removal even of the orphans. Nothing would change this even though, anticipating their endangerment, in the months prior to the crisis he had undertaken to integrate the young into the workshops, hoping in this way to protect those whom he could, ultimately abandoning to a bitter fate those whom he could not. It had been the same with the sick, the aged, the weak, the defenseless. The population of the ghetto, repeatedly assaulted, had diminished and was shrinking still. The year to come promised to be another marked by irresistible demographic erosion and decline. And yet there would be no change in course. As before, Rumkowski's strategy for survival was to hold on and wait. Losses had been cut, but only a remnant remained, even as, within the ghetto and the countryside all around, the

Jewish presence was becoming ever fainter. The community was poised on the brink of extinction. Signs of vitality and hope for the future—courtship, marriage, birth—had not altogether vanished, but as observers would note, these took on the distorted appearance of a weakened life force increasingly restricted to the shadows.

By January 1943 slightly more than half their original number remained.[1] Of the departed there was no news, for they did not communicate; of the vanished fathers and mothers and youngsters, the elderly from the old age homes, the little children from the orphanage, one heard not a word. Where were they? The trains that had borne them away had come back empty. Apart from those younger men sent off to do grueling road work in the province, and who sometimes returned, their numbers depleted, no one sent off was known to have disembarked at the ghetto station and walked home to reappear at the gate, the courtyard, the workshop. The ghetto was less crowded now: there were fewer couples, fewer elderly and sick—and certainly fewer of the very young. Oskar Rosenfeld thought that he detected a change even in the general appearance of the population. As he surveyed the crowd in the streets, readily identifiable Jewish faces and features seemed to him far less in evidence. Of course those all about him were decidedly Jews, people of the ghetto, but a certain unmistakably Jewish look was less apparent now; a more "Slavic" element characterized the faces of people he saw in the ghetto.[2] His assessment was subjective, but observers were hard-pressed to conclude otherwise: the Jews were witnessing their own decline, their disappearance from the city and from the world.

Life was, as the ghetto saying had it, narrow indeed, and the grip of circumstance squeezed even tighter than before. Rumkowski's hold on power, never fully to be relinquished, had suffered several blows. Biebow was less supportive now, granting the favor of expanded authority, particularly in the area of provisioning, to Rumkowski's internal rivals in the Jewish Sonderkommando.[3] All the same, no one emerged to challenge Rumkowski's basic approach as the Germans, who held the Jews within the vise, turned the screws ever tighter. Would 1943 be any different? At best it would be a year of relative respite, of watching and waiting out the oppressor. In the meantime, the Jews staked everything on the prospect of saving the remnant. So they held on, feeding their hungry bellies and, where possible, clutching at life.

To be sure, 1943 would bring home to the Germans unmistakable evidence of their own fallibility and setbacks. The defeat at Stalingrad early that winter could not be denied, and a note of doubt began to darken the prospect of victory and a glorious German future. But whatever the cost, the regime took satisfaction in the disappearance of the Jews, and however indirect and circumspect official references to their actual fate might be, knowledge that the Jews were now so reduced in number gave the leaders' ever-lengthening endeavor to achieve victory a second wind. The disappearance of the Jews served as a way of keeping score, tangible confirmation of the power of the regime and its ideology and the righteousness of its cause. At the same time, the growing numbers of the Germans, visible in the continued repeopling of the Wartheland, were a matter of deep satisfaction and pride.[4] Sixty thousand ethnic German families were reported as having been settled in the Warthegau in 1942. Overall, with new settlers continually adding to existing numbers, an estimated 850,000 Germans now populated the province.[5] Such figures were closely monitored, for they were a confirmation of increase and life, proof that a substantial increase in the number of Germans populating this corner of the earth was matched by a diminution of the Jews, a mere remnant soon to disappear for all time.[6]

So for the Germans too, 1943 would be a time of taking stock, a time marked not solely by anxiety over the war's progress but by satisfaction as well in knowing that the promised vision of a Jew-free land was coming true, evident for all to see. Once more the prophetic voice of doom, loudly asserting the impending destruction of the Jews, reached Litzmannstadt from afar. At the end of February, addressing the party faithful gathered in Munich, Hitler proclaimed that the war would end not in Jewish triumph over the Aryan peoples but in the elimination of the Jews.[7] Inside the ghetto, both Rosenfeld and Dawid Sierakowiak took note, the latter having learned of the threat from the local paper, where it was featured on page one. Late the previous autumn, Sierakowiak had heard too of Hitler's sadistic pronouncement alluding to a time of diminishing Jewish laughter.[8]

After a year of deportation, anxiety, fear, and crushing loss, the ghetto had entered its age of maturity. Perpetrators and victims alike had had time to gain a certain wary familiarity with each other. The surviving population, long experienced in the ways of the ghetto and schooled in the methods of their oppressors, also understood the ways of a Jewish leadership that reflexively offered its compliance in the face of German demands. Disease and hunger and death were a constant backdrop to daily life and continued to define the nature of ghetto existence. That said, the weakest of the weak by now were gone. The deportations of the prior year had taken them away and left only the fit. Yet among the surviving remnant, those whose sole purpose was to toil and produce, mortality had not ceased to rise. Complicit in the killing yet as committed as ever to driving production, Biebow sounded a note of alarm, pleading with Gau authorities for an increase in the delivery of provisions to the working population. Little was done. And yet people somehow were still on their feet; they walked the streets of the ghetto, arduously mounting the steps of wooden bridges, proceeding daily to work. In the offices, pens were still being put to paper, in the workshops needles were still run through fabric, bales of cloth were still transformed into uniforms, dresses, caps, and cloaks. Out of recycled containers or rolls of fresh paper the most remarkable creations were shaped. Half in jest, half in great earnest, Jews spoke with pride of their skills of invention, proving time and again their ability to make something virtually "out of nothing."[9]

Scarred by the tragic events of 1942, their *annus terribilis,* the surviving Jews of the ghetto sensed no alternative but to work even harder in order to demonstrate their usefulness to their captors more convincingly than ever. Only through their continued, reliable productivity and the outstanding quality of the products of their labor could they hope to earn the right to exist and inhabit this German world. By quantity alone the output of Jewish industriousness had proved powerfully impressive. In the month of December 1942, at a time when ninety-four ghetto enterprises were active, the tailoring works had turned out just over 70,000 individual articles, 41,790, or well over half of these items for the German military, and a still sizable production run of 28,492 items for the civilian branch of the economy. That same month, other workshops succeeded in producing nearly 200,000 pairs of shoes, some 100,000 boot legs, 70,000 hats, nearly 24,000 caps, over 160,000 earmuffs, about 5,800 pairs of gloves, more than 1,800 pillows, 7,200 mattresses, more than 34,000 brassieres and corsets, over 56,000 pieces of furniture, 700,000 metal articles, and in excess of 1.8 million paper products as well.[10]

Not by quantity alone did they seek to impress but by the acknowledged quality of their creations. Inside a multistory building on Żydowska Street the paper goods workshop, long one of the ghetto's most prolific enterprises, continued to turn out a steady supply of salable products, among them paperweights, albums, pen and pencil holders, wastebaskets, paper signs, decorative containers and boxes, and once again, in amazing quantity, children's toys.[11] By winter 1943, 286 youngsters were employed there; they worked in teams, often alongside adults. Among the young, one visitor praised the sharp eyes, the swift-moving hands, the inventive artistry indicative of outstanding talents. One boy had the "hands of a born pianist" and worked the material diligently, displaying exceptional coordination, concentration, and purpose. In constructing a paper bag, the boy knew with expert assurance precisely how to cut the material, apply the glue, place a ribbon, and fold the corners just so; a sure-handed perfectionist, he was aware that, because fashioned for city clients, each and every sack had to be built just right—neither "too tight" nor "too loose"—so that when it was filled, the contents would not rupture the walls of their containers and spill out.[12]

On an upper story of the workshop, dollhouses were being lovingly built. Here the children's versatile, small hands and inventive fantasies were put to especially productive use. Outfitted with electric lights, these constructions were tiny worlds unto themselves, complete with furnishings, including miniature beds and chairs, vanities, carpets and curtains, even pictures on the walls. Here too remarkable talents were at work, the standout being a girl who specialized in filling those little pictures with imaginative drawings. On their own—though it was against the rules—some of the youngsters appropriated paper scraps so that, allowing their particular fantasies to take flight, they might make little items for their own amusement, fashioning "fabulous winged ponies, ships with smokestacks, boats with full sails."[13]

Young eyes, nimble fingers, and energetic minds were still of some use to the Germans. The little interiors of the dollhouses these children helped design suggested a recollection of the world they had once enjoyed. That elsewhere German children were having fun was hard to overlook. At Christmastime bags of coffee were brought in for recycling, including packaging from a Bremen coffee company decorated for the holidays. Beneath the firm's logo—an eagle with wings spread wide—was an image of Saint Nicholas, his cornucopia filled with toys. Also among the inventory of recyclables were bags of cocoa displaying ships at sea and the image of a smiling Dutch girl welcoming them and their wares safely to port. A container for tea likewise featured an attractive Japanese woman in a kimono presenting "a little tray with a small teapot and cups."[14] But neither the coffee sack eagle and its wings, Saint Nicholas and his bag of toys, the Dutch girl and her smile, nor the Japanese maiden with her tray was there to serve the Jews. Imaginary representatives of a world of welcome, ambassadors of commercial bounty, the icons existed to flatter, entice, and appeal to a clientele other than the impoverished Jews through whose hands they passed. For the ghetto workers they were but a fleeting reminder of the existence of a world of goodwill and comfort from which they had been exiled long ago and yet to which, God willing, they hoped one day to return.

For the present, the bounties of this earth were not for them; as they had done from the beginning, the Jews toiled in order to serve the wants of others. Mainstays of a ghetto workforce dedicated as well to the production of ladies' apparel, Jewish women applied themselves and their talents with all necessary diligence to the unwelcome task of catering to the requirements of German fashion. Ghetto photographs reveal some of these Jewish women modeling for the camera a selection of articles of ghetto manufacture, among them robes, suits, dresses, and coats. Standing atop a stool placed in a hallway or a table in the corner of a room—in one series of photographs a closed doorway is visible behind them—young ladies display these creations with a suggestion of big-city sophistication. Rarely smiling, they assume elegant, mannequin-like poses, simulating the mannerisms of models in a magazine—arms at their sides or resting on their hips, or with hands extended slightly, fingers delicately open. A dark-haired little girl, alternately attired in a folk costume with matching vest and blouse and various dresses, shows slightly more animation, photographed in the midst of performing a little skip, her knee raised a bit, delicately fanning the hem of a short skirt. A few ghetto gentlemen with stern expressions are also pictured, modeling articles of men's outerwear. One man, though, photographed in profile and wearing an overcoat, breaking ever so slightly with the neutral decorum, seems unable to resist a theatrical gesture, posing with his index finger raised as if on the point of revealing a thought or declaiming some meaningful truth.[15]

Rumkowski's strategy remained one of waiting out the Germans and then, when no other way seemed possible, yielding to the oppressor's demands, absorbing whatever human losses he had to in order to spare the rest. So long as his constituents proved useful and productive, the ghetto, he surmised, would survive. With luck, time might turn to the community's advantage: the war would end and the ghetto population go free.[16] Still, even if the Germans refrained, as it appeared for the moment they had, from further massive deportations, privation remained a constant of daily existence. With every passing season more would die, raising anew the question at the heart of bitter ghetto life: given the scarcity of resources available to the community, who among them would have sufficient access to supplies vital to basic survival and who would be deprived? Outwardly communitarian in the sharing of goods and the exposure to risks, in truth the ghetto remained as internally divided as ever, with favoritism, corruption, and privilege setting the few apart from all the rest.

Though instituted in a spirit of fairness, in practice the system of rationing proved in many respects inequitable and incompetently supervised, if not altogether rigged for the benefit of administrative staff and the well connected. "Provisioning! I must lay down my pen," wrote Yisroel Tabaksblat, commenting bitterly on the whole organization:

> It is really difficult to write. Does there exist an expression, a description for what has taken place in that muck, which was at first called the Provisioning, later Grocery and Bread Department? Laziness, clumsiness, mixed with meanness, predatory management, arbitrariness—this altogether still does not give the least concept about what went on in that department. When all were starving, not plain "hungry," but simply flooding the cemetery with corpses, swollen from hunger, they buried millions of kilos of potatoes and vegetables in the fields on account of laziness.

Even Rumkowski's efforts to regulate official corruption through the institution of a general regulatory authority, the Supreme Control Chamber, proved a sham.[17] When it came to his attention that one member of the commission had begun to investigate food supply practices, Rumkowski immediately put a halt to the effort. Mismanagement and corruption within the provisioning bureaucracy were allowed to flourish unchecked. Given free rein to set aside scarce commodities for their private use, "sharing out right and left products in the thousands of kilos for their own kin and acquaintances," many of those same officials, far from dedicating themselves to alleviating the ongoing misery, only contributed to the privations of a population already suffering from inadequate quantity and poor quality of consumable products which the Germans grudgingly provided the community as a whole.[18]

Adding to the inequities of a system that tolerated such misconduct, valuable supplemental distributions of food were granted exclusively to selected members of the Ghetto Administration. As Isaiah Trunk noted:

> In time, a provisioning pyramid formed in the ghetto. . . . At the pinnacle of the supply pyramid stood all those who had the right to benefit from the so-called *"Beirat"* allocations (ration cards with the letter B). To this category belonged members of the *Beirat,* high officials of the ghetto administration, like the directors of departments and factories, master craftsmen, and technical instructors, and the members of the physicians' and pharmacists' cooperatives. Beyond the normal rations, they would also receive a supplement of various articles, mainly meat, flour, and sugar, at the four special shops or in the so-called cooperatives. This most privileged group was not large. In the first half of May 1942, these privileged people numbered nearly 1,500 persons.

By 1942, with the program somewhat expanded,

> *Beirat* supplements in various lower gradations—BI, BII, BII, C.P. (Polish: *ciężko pracujący,* hardworkers)—also included certain other categories of workers. These included, for example, those working in hazardous sanitary conditions: excrement transporters *(fekalistn),* pressers, tanners, and highly qualified skilled workers, as well as so-called hardworkers and overtime laborers. . . .

> On the second rung of the provisioning ladder stood the general officials, workers in the ghetto factories, building watchmen, those employed in public works, Jewish police personnel, firefighters, and chimneysweeps. Aside from the normal allocations for all, they would . . . get supplements . . . including foods that were rarely distributed in the ghetto, like meat, sausage, and potatoes. . . . These

supplements would be issued on so-called "extra-coupons" from time
to time, or (from March 1942) on systematically introduced supplemental ration cards, number 1 for laborers (with a better ration) and
number 2 (for office workers) with a weaker ration. . . .

Workers in the factories would each also get one or two soups
daily (not on their ration cards) for a price of 25 to 30 pfennigs at the
workplace.[19]

Unfortunately for the average ghetto dweller, materially bereft and cruelly excluded from these offerings, no supplemental allotments awaited to
satisfy their no less demanding appetites. They were left instead to their
own meager devices to gather what little of the ghetto's insufficient rations
they could. And for many even this paltry quota, officially their due, was
inaccessible because it was routinely appropriated by others who were
stronger or better connected than they. The weak and mild-mannered
who obeyed the rules and waited patiently in line were likely to be mus-
cled aside by others—stronger and lacking respect for fairness and order—or swindled out of their portion by those who, taking advantage of
lax bookkeeping, obtained multiple ration cards, or made use of connections with personnel at the distribution centers to obtain more than their
allotted quantity. Honest clients knew what the cheaters were up to, but
woe to them if they dared speak out. Anyone who complained would
"hear the stereotypical excuse: 'We didn't eat up the products: As much
as arrived to us we have distributed. Moreover, why are you yelling? . . .
What kind of gripe do you have against us? Go and complain to Rumkowski, about why he sends so little and it doesn't suffice for everyone!'"[20]

A typical resident, lacking the resources to get additional commodities
on the prohibitive black market, was compelled to make do with a meager
ration of bread and other staples which was usually exhausted long before
the next date of distribution. At best the average daily diet (eventually
amounting, for a non-employed resident of the ghetto, to some 1,600 calories a day, and for workers in the range of 2,000 calories per day) fell well
short of the nutrition needed to ensure basic survival.[21] These wretched
allotments lacked not only the calories but also the vitamins necessary to
support the immune system and prevent the onset of disease. Ghetto physicians knew only too well that ailments such as bronchitis and pleurisy

were on the rise, as well as "renewed frequent occurrence of what is called bone softening, that is, loss of calcium in the bones." To sustain itself, the body demands fresh infusions of the essential vitamins B, C, D, and E, so difficult to acquire under these conditions. One might absorb vitamin D from sun lamps or from sunshine, but the confined population had little access to either. Sauerkraut, best eaten raw to preserve vitamins otherwise lost in cooking, as well as beets, red cabbage, and turnips, proved the best available sources of vitamins. Vigantol, a popular supplement, was in great demand, but available supplies were hopelessly inadequate, and whenever they appeared were quickly snapped up by the privileged few. The doctors were at best engaged in a hopeless rearguard action against the inevitable effects of malnutrition. Acutely aware of the symptoms of his own worsening ailments and physical decline, feeling within his own body both a "terrible pain in the ribs and hollow of knees" and that same "softening of the bones due to a lack of calcium (fat, butter, fresh vegetables, cod liver oil)" which the ghetto physicians had reported, Rosenfeld watched as others, having reached the final crisis, gave way under the burden of their ailments. "Have you ever seen a human being shortly before dying of hunger? His legs hardly support him, stomach caved in, sunken temples right and left, yellowish white coloring. Dizziness: collapses on the stairs, despite cane. He's quickly administered some ressort soup. Another ten hours! Too late. Dies, slowly fading away . . . with a sigh on his lips. Every day a dozen."[22]

Rumkowski was still banking on the prospect that whatever threat lay ahead, a remnant would survive. Among them surely would be many from the ranks of the Jewish police—guardians, as he saw it, of a precarious stability. Rumkowski found no reason to proceed in any way other than that with which he had begun. From the start he had set his course by the light of a single star; peace, order, and work remained for him the watchwords of survival, and the indispensable instrument of that policy was the Jewish Order Service, his loyal police force. At the end of February, on the anniversary of its founding in 1940, he spoke, praising the men for a difficult job well done. Cautiously giving expression to the thought of surviving the war, he foresaw how the world would perceive them. They would, God willing, live on to see a world after the ghetto; and lest anyone question their deeds, they need only reach for the certificate he pledged each would carry. It would attest that they had, in so trying a time, served the Jewish people with honor. Their task had been difficult, but at great cost to themselves and to their ranks, they had accomplished much. They had every reason to feel proud. The world could not but acknowledge their sacrifice and their contribution. In a revealing image bespeaking wellsprings of intracommunity rancor and personal bitterness, he thanked them most especially because, as he stated, without their actions, "the people of the ghetto would have torn themselves to pieces" long since like wild beasts. Rumkowski closed with well-wishes and with his thanks for discharging additional responsibilities that lay ahead. With that the leader concluded his remarks. His shoulders still draped with the coat his aide had thoughtfully placed over them as protection against the damp and cold, he proceeded to the precinct headquarters, where hot tea and other refreshments awaited indoors. That evening Jewish Order Service commander Rozenblat, traveling by carriage, would halt briefly at each of the precincts, where meals had been prepared for the celebration.[23]

In conceiving of the policemen as self-sacrificing and honorable defenders of the community, no doubt Rumkowski was engaging in pro forma flattery. This was, after all, their day, and an occasion for strengthening his bond with these men. They were on the same side. They shared his basic assumptions about the right way to carry on; each had acted upon those assumptions and knew himself to be open to an accounting. But the point could not have been lost on his listeners: if any were likely to survive to see the liberation and begin a new life, it would be they. They would have earned that privilege, and their leader was here to reinforce them in that belief. There could be no greater reward than to make it out of the ghetto alive. In the meantime, these men were in a position to make the best of a bad situation, and a share in whatever there was to be had in this place of anxiety, scarcity, and confinement was just compensation for fulfilling such a challenging assignment. As a further token of recognition for services rendered, Rumkowski granted senior policemen additional ration premiums, and to all 519 members of the corps the promise of a newly manufactured suit and coat.[24]

Many in positions of authority proved only too ready to make the most of their stay in the ghetto. When on occasion the veil that concealed their privileges was lifted, the ghetto elite could be seen enjoying themselves in unseemly display, openly consuming food and liquor otherwise unavailable to the others. On the eve of the New Year, private parties had afforded occasion for dressing up and going out. A large gathering was held at the residence of Rumkowski's secretary Dora Fuchs, and "women coiffed and in elegant evening toilette" could be seen heading off to similar engagements.[25] Among privileged men, it was no secret that the benefits of relative wealth and status included enhanced prospects for dalliance and romance. Some of the men, well placed to gain access to food and private quarters suitable for entertaining, took full advantage of their opportunities for attracting desirable if often desperate women. "So-called dignitaries are now seen quite publicly with their lovers in the street, left trembling their wives and now strut with their cats," Rosenfeld would comment in late February, adding that this was "done quite shamelessly and publicly, especially [by] young policemen."[26] Not surprisingly, many viewed such displays with contempt. "It's being said in the ghetto: They are carrying on too much. Every Kierownik [manager] has a girlfriend— officially. The young girls are being protected." On at least one occasion when a man yielded to the temptation to cast common decency aside, his behavior was so outrageous that Rumkowski felt compelled to step in and reestablish an appearance of propriety. When it came to his attention that, rather than "waiting to hear of [his deported] wife's fate," the man had seen fit to take a new bride, Rumkowski had him incarcerated. In Rosenfeld's view, the example had not the least impact on the continuing spectacle. "That didn't solve the problem. Pretty girls are generally well dressed, good stockings and shoes, next to them thousands of wretched beggars."[27]

Given what appears to have been a penchant for exploiting his authority in the ghetto to his own sexual advantage, Rumkowski would seem to have been ill-placed to set an example of private decorum. A few women who survived the ghetto recalled having been the object of the chairman's awkward, off-putting advances. Captivated by her singing at a stage performance in a program he attended at one of the tailoring workshops, Genia Bryl remembered, Rumkowski arrived one evening at the rest home where she was staying as a guest and invited her on a walk, which ended at his Marysin residence. Once inside, he made an unwelcome advance. In the face of her efforts to resist, he spoke of wanting only "to play for a while—to forget myself," seeking through physical intimacy relief from his burdened existence. Appalled, she fled for her safety and her honor.[28] No further harm came to her, though she feared Rumkowski's wrath, and not without reason, for, in the words of another woman likewise distraught in the wake of a similar unwelcome advance, "he was a vindictive man."[29] Rosenfeld would recall that from the window of his residence at the hospital building on Łagiewnicka Street, Rumkowski had been wont to call down to women in the street below, motioning for them to come up and visit. (The diarist's cryptic reference in this context to "orgies" suggests the proposed sexual aim of these unwelcome invitations.) On one such occasion a married woman, the wife of a physician, turned him down. The Jewish Order Service investigated and, finding out her address, entered the couple's residence and exacted punishment by trashing the furniture and leaving the "floor planks ripped up."[30] These incidents speak poorly of the chairman and raise anew unsettling questions about his personal conduct. He appears to have displayed rather more empathy for the predatory instincts of powerful men than for the women who might fall victim to their approaches. After the jailing of a thirty-nine-year-old ghetto policeman found guilty by a ghetto court of having taken indecent liberties with an underage girl entrusted to the officer's care, Rumkowski intervened, putting forward his wife, the young attorney Regina Weinberger Rumkowski, to handle the appeal. When even that failed to sway the court toward greater leniency, during a general amnesty later in the year Rumkowski released the man, allegedly on the grounds that the girl had by her own behavior "provoked" her guardian's attentions.[31]

Lacking status and resources, impoverished, unattached men were compelled to fend for themselves in attending to their physical and emotional needs. One can only guess at the unspoken longings and desires to which such men fell prey, as well as the frustrations engendered by the amorous successes, real or imagined, of other men who, taking full advantage of their access to a greater share of material resources, succeeded in attracting a mate to relieve their loneliness. Although as a member of the Statistics Department Rosenfeld was among the better situated, as a man whose wife was absent he knew only too well the prosaic details of the ghetto bachelor's lonely life: carrying home one's solitary ration, crossing the threshold of an empty room, breaking apart chips of wood and coal with which to light the stove, cooking one's soup and consuming it alone, then stretching out on a pallet of straw, laying one's lonely head upon one's pillow or outstretched arm, and drifting off to sleep. Such were the details he evoked to set the scene for the fictional bachelor of "My Two Neighbors," a story composed in 1943 and later discovered among his abandoned notebooks. In a tale that blends elements of the realistic, the surreal, and the absurd, a ghetto bachelor, long made aware by the thinness of an adjoining wall of the routine comings and goings of another lonesome stranger next door, one day suspects that his neighbor is no longer alone but rather living with a woman. Returning from a textile workshop where he is a supervisor, he overhears the neighbor addressing her as one would a lover, presenting her with a gift of sugar, passionately extolling her delightful appearance: "Your dress was designed by the greatest of all artists. Noble in cut, elegant in color . . . ash gray I love best, especially a black dice-patterned waistline and back. . . . Not to forget the yellowish brown of the skirt. . . . Really a harmonious combination. . . . Topped off with little black ankle boots, shoes to show off, or, what one now calls—pumps."[32] But quickly the affectionate words turn to words of anger and rebuke, followed by the menacing sounds of impending confrontation. The neighbor seems agitated, "running about the room, knocking against the wall." Fascinated, though increasingly concerned and of a mind "to knock on the wall and call out" to interrupt the encounter, the listener is at the same time hesitant, seemingly powerless to intervene when he hears "a soft scratching of the feet, a rustling of the upholstery, [then] a choking scream," followed by the neighbor's "heavy breathing" and a torrent of curses: "Now you have enough, beast, contemptible, faithless . . . why aren't you screaming when I strangle you, when I squash your legs . . . despicable tramp . . . Go to the devil!"[33] Compelled to investigate, he waits for his neighbor to depart before stealing into the next-door apartment. In search of evidence of the woman, he tears away the covers of the bed, a miserable pallet of straw, but neither here, nor beneath a nearby pile of clothes, nor anywhere else he sets eyes on does he find her. Then at the window he finds a decorative plate; it is rimmed "with white flour and sugar," and inside the bowl rests a large fly, its ashen color and long legs recalling the words with which his neighbor had described his unfortunate companion. "The fly was dead. Murdered, strangled. Waistline and back in a black dice pattern, belly and legs yellowish brown, the balls of the toes black," victim of his neighbor's bizarre outburst of frustration and rage.[34]

Though love of a sort still flourished and found sanctification in marriage, births were minimal, far from sufficient in number to make up for the dead. Hitler's prophecy was coming true: "Death is flourishing. There are practically no births. The ghetto is liquidating itself."[35] Dawid Sierakowiak, only too aware of the inequalities and the corruption that had carried off his beloved, soft-spoken, long-suffering mother the previous September, now himself in rapid physical decline, was desperate to be accepted into the ranks of the Jewish Sonderkommando. He knew that there alone lay his hope for survival, and said so in one of the last diary entries before his death, only months away.[36] For Sierakowiak, it was too late.

Were the Jews dying out? Certainly. But only in the Germans' own good time. For now the Germans judged operations to have arrived at a satisfactory plateau. The number of Jews had been stabilized at what they considered an efficient and cost-effective level. The time had come for a halt to the systematized, high-density killing operations centered in the remote village of Chełmno. Those operations, since the winter of 1942 under the command of SS-Hauptsturmführer Hans Bothmann, had fulfilled well the assignment of emptying the provincial ghettos, annihilating the weak, the aged, and the infirm and secretly disposing of their remains. The physically useful inhabitants of the lesser regional ghettos had been transferred to Litzmannstadt, the central ghetto, or Gau Ghetto as German official correspondence sometimes termed it. For the time being, it alone was left standing, its population systematically cleansed in similar fashion of those who were deemed unfit. In this leaner form it was left to linger, solely in order to serve the requirements of wartime production.

In the first days of spring the Chełmno death center was on the brink of planned dissolution. Late in March, Gauleiter Greiser wrote to Himmler of his great satisfaction with the accomplishments and bearing of Bothmann and his men. In acknowledgment of their contribution to the Reich, as well as in reward for their difficult service, Gauleiter Greiser honored the men with his presence at a feast in a restaurant in nearby Koło.[37] Writing to Himmler, Greiser spoke warmly of their generosity, noting that together the eighty-five men of the Sonderkommando had collected a sum of more than RM15,000, which he wished in turn to place at the Reichsführer's discretion, suggesting that the money be donated to the orphaned children of ethnic Germans, a proposal to which Himmler gladly assented. To reward the men for their service, Greiser requested Himmler's permission to invite them for a stay on the Gauleiter's own private estate so that they might enjoy a relaxing leave. Himmler also responded positively to the men's request, conveyed to him by the Gauleiter, that they remain collectively under the command of Bothmann and attached to the Waffen-SS Prinz Eugen division, in this capacity assisting German occupation forces who were battling partisans in occupied Yugoslavia.[38] Soon after, in the first days of April the men of the remaining work crew at Chełmno, fully aware that their own deaths were imminent, in a final effort to alert the world to the crime and exhort due vengeance, drafted and hid brief notes testifying to the truth that here the Jews of the province and of the Łódź ghetto had been horribly murdered.[39] On April 7 explosives were detonated inside the manor house from whence, packed with victims, the killing vans had departed for the nearby forest. The building was turned into a ruin. Although the killing would resume in 1944, for now the work at Chełmno was done.[40]

Springtime settled once more upon the land. The city and the countryside teemed with signs of life, increase, and renewal. In town, storks were spotted once again returning to their nests, and with the onset of warmer weather in the Hitler-Jugend-Park, come evening, swarms of bats could be seen swooping over a pond, in a frenzy, snatching with their talons at butterflies and other unsuspecting airborne prey.[41] Indeed, amid earnest expressions of pride in German stewardship of local wildlife, much attention was lavished in the local press on the eternal spectacle of the hunter and the hunted. An experienced bird conservationist, pleased to discover a variety of avian species populating a nearby marsh, delighted in observing the self-protective instincts of new hatchlings threatened with harm. They would stretch skyward their "long, vertically striped, slim, feathered necks" in a desperate effort to fend off attack by blending into the reeds. All the same, one could not help noticing that with their eyes darting uncontrollably in the direction of the oncoming threat, the helpless creatures involuntarily revealed their underlying fright.[42] The city zoo opened once more, its stock of animals enhanced by recent additions. Even in captivity life flourished. Already there had been many successful live births, and it was delightful to observe the steady growth of newborn lion cubs. It was no less amusing to gaze at bears which, "routinely" doused with spray, could be found "agreeably dry[ing] off in the sun" or taking a slide along the slippery floor of their enclosure. Elsewhere a young chimp, in need of solace after being slapped by an older male, was seen racing back to the loving arms of its mother, while others comfortably "snuggled" between both parents, forming the very picture of a loving "family idyll." For the entertainment of young visitors, a new petting zoo, slated for installation that year, would include a donkey, a pony, some goats, and in recognition of its place in the "world of fairy tales," a wolf.[43] Elsewhere cherry trees blossomed, and flowers bloomed in great variety.[44] Just south of the ghetto, vegetable gardens and fruit trees were cultivated in ever greater quantity in Helenenhof Park. But here as well the spectacle of growth in nature evoked the struggle for existence. One correspondent, observing a gardener pulling weeds and then throwing these dangerous pests onto a compost heap, found himself looking into the distance and thinking of the ghetto. The Jews, he thought, were like those weeds, at last safely removed, just like a pile of garden waste. The safety of all rested on keeping such enemies soundly locked away and under vigilant watch.[45]

Setting a personal example, in the city German officers tended conscientiously to the maintenance of their own health and fitness as well as that of the citizenry. Litzmannstadt prided itself on its athleticism. By official claim, in "the prior year around 300,000 Germans had visited the city swimming pool," 120,000 its athletic grounds, and 40,000 its winter sports facilities; indoor municipal gymnasiums too were impressively filled. During spring and summer, on days when the weather was warm and sunny typically as many as 10,000 people flocked to the new beach at Erzhausen. The mayor and his deputy, as well as members of party and city government of all ranks, from high officials to policemen and postal workers, reportedly included athletic workouts in their daily routines. Even members of the city orchestra and theater company were said to enjoy regular athletic exercise and swimming in their spare time.[46] For those who were ill, there were new places for rest and care. A newspaper article featured a convalescent home for German settlers that had been opened in a former home for Jewish weekend vacationers in the attractive surroundings of the nearby Tuschin Forest. The Jews, long absent, were of course blamed for any evidence of hygienic neglect, but under German administration the home was reported to be remarkably suitable now.[47] A visit to the Siegfried-Staemmler-Hospital in the city similarly revealed clean, well-regulated, ultramodern facilities, in contrast to the overcrowded and unsanitary conditions allegedly prevailing under Jewish and Polish administration. Heart patients benefited from the introduction of the latest electrical technology, while those suffering from contagious illness and undergoing lengthy treatment could enjoy being cared for in an attractive setting.[48]

Solicitous as the regime proved for patients deemed worthy of healing and care, the young, the altogether healthy, the fit, and the strong were accorded highest regard. On a Sunday in mid-May, Mother's Day, sporting men and women and youngsters gathered along with thousands of visitors at Erzhausen Beach to inaugurate the outdoor bathing season. Facilities included ample changing rooms and sunbathing areas. Athletic organizations were on hand, and Oberbürgermeister Ventzki opened the festivities, delivering an address and christening the new recreational watercraft. There followed a demonstration of lifesaving techniques, while athletic groups staged a series of exhibitions and competitions. Hitler Youth clambered into boats and paddled across the water, women tossed athletic balls and clubs, male and female gymnasts performed on parallel bars, soccer teams battled, and boxers paired off in competition. Folk dancing rounded out the occasion's entertainment.[49]

A week after the opening of the new beach season by the lake in Erzhausen, Reich Health Leader (Reichsgesundheitsführer) Dr. Leonardo Conti arrived in the city by train and, accompanied by an entourage of dignitaries, strode down the steps of the main railway station. Following a tour of a maternity clinic for ethnic German resettlers and of the medical facilities in the downtown "Haus der Gesundheit" on Anweilerweg, he spoke before an audience of physicians, nurses, pharmacists, and related medical personnel in the Sporthalle. Conti underscored that in the National Socialist conception public health was a matter not merely of curing disease—a limited goal only nations less enlightened than Germany would think sufficiently all-encompassing—but of promoting the purity and unity of the racial community, defined by its unique lineage of common blood. In this the Warthegau was deserving of praise, he noted, expressing satisfaction that both maternal and infant mortality revealed a favorable decline. Most positively, and undoubtedly a matter of local pride, he took note as well that the Warthegau evidenced the highest birthrate in the entire Reich. Far more than a reflection of enhanced funding, fecundity, the minister declared, constituted nothing less than a courageous and life-affirming "expression of vital energies."[50]

Providing a dignified institutional setting for just such an affirmation was the majestic matrimonial hall housed on the premises of the city registry office, featured in the pages of the *Litzmannstädter Zeitung* two days after the health minister's address. From an attractive antechamber, couples wishing to take their marital vows were ushered into a richly, indeed majestically appointed, softly lit hall. Amid thick woodwork, candelabras, ivory-toned walls with complementary red-upholstered furnishings, and flowers, their bond would be sealed. A heavy wooden table on which rested a registry book and a ceremonial pen, the centerpiece of the ceremony, was placed beneath the watchful embodiment of the state, a massive wooden eagle affixed to the wall above.[51] In a venue befitting the strict decorum appropriate to official sanction of the union of man and woman, expression of their sensual bond was understandably left to the province of art. In June the *Litzmannstädter Zeitung* published a photograph of a work by the sculptor Joseph Thorak, presenting the image of a sensually reclining couple, naked, peering into each other's eyes, reaching out to each other in commencement of a rapturous embrace while floating on a cloud.[52]

In September the Sporthalle played host to a traveling public health exhibition, featuring, in an apt expression of its title, "The Miracle of Life," a remarkably formed, translucent, internally illuminated model of a human being. A creation of the sponsoring German Hygiene Museum in Dresden, the "Glass Man," as he was known, stood tall, his arms raised high, a three-dimensional, state-of-the-art representation of the species, transparently a picture of health. To facilitate popular understanding as well as to instill a sense of "wonder" at the otherwise hidden workings of the human organism, the Glass Man's internal organs were visible, and when lit, displayed in most dramatic fashion both their specific location and "method of operation." Accompanying the exhibit was a series of displays and posters, one of which, reproduced in the local press, highlighted in comically illustrated form the mechanisms of the human digestive cycle from ingestion to excretion. At the top of the display, three men in black uniforms direct an obliviously smiling, anthropomorphized globule of food to proceed onward; in the next section it is chopped into little pieces by a second team of uniformed men, one of whom wields a pick, another a shovel, a third a hose, then stuffed into the funnel of a long industrial-looking tube—the esophagus. Down below, at the level of the stomach, attendants gather about the rim of a large tub, some pouring in fluids from watering cans, others stirring the contents with long poles. Beyond the stomach lies a narrow curving chute, the small intestine, where the re-sulting liquids are processed. Hand pumps are positioned along its rim, and at the base of the sluice, a tap catches the excess; along the sides, the crew is at work carrying off small bowls, passing along their contents. Far-ther down, other men ladle off the contents of the thick-walled lower in-testine while a trough siphons away a portion of the soupy matter. At the very bottom of the intestinal sluice, an earnest dark-uniformed man, his hand on a long lever, works the gate-like sphincter leading from the colon. A grotesque touch is added: a thin, dark, two-legged figure—a trailing bit of excrement—its arms raised high in the air and its face expressive of pain, is suddenly halted in mid-stride while running for its life and all but free. Its trailing foot, excruciatingly caught in the barrier, remains stuck, immovably rooting it to the spot, its escape foiled by the gatekeeper's timely reflexes. On the occasion of the exhibition's ceremonial opening, acting Oberbürgermeister Dr. Otto Bradfisch welcomed the assembled dignitaries, praising the exhibition as an example of German achieve-ments in a city that had come so far in regard to public health in compari-son to the altogether shameful mismanagement under its predecessor re-gime and the harmful influence of its Jewish population.[53] Adding his own gloss, in a commentary accompanying that same grotesque sketch of the workings of the digestive cycle, a newspaper reporter commented on the remarkable and mysterious nature of humankind. "Were one to capture the history of earth on a film of a hundred hours in length," he mused, humanity's presence would occupy but three minutes of that time. "On this planet we are so young, and yet surely we have impressed our stamp upon it. There must certainly be something wondrous in this work of precision we call man. But it only works when all its parts are in accord, when body and spirit are most perfectly in harmony."[54]

That in the ghetto this miraculous "work of precision" that was the human body had been unimaginably damaged was only too clear, not only to the physically weakened population but also to the German administrators responsible for the ghetto's oversight and maintenance. Only at the peril of its productionist goals could the Gettoverwaltung have been able to overlook the exigencies of supply and the limitations of the human body. However they denied the equal human standing of the captive Jewish community, as a practical matter the managers were forced to attend to the requirements of weakened Jewish bodies. In the lengthening history of the ghetto, this had been for Biebow a matter of ongoing concern. Even now, and in spite of his own long participation in the process of annihilation, desirous of preserving the ghetto and with it the security he and his top employees enjoyed—for the "essential" nature of their positions freed them from military call-up—Biebow remained a determined proponent of the productionist assumptions he had championed from the start.[55] In April, in conversation and correspondence with Oberbürgermeister Ventzki, he again expressed grave concern that, months after the last wave of deportation, and in spite of the consequent streamlining of the workforce, weakened Jewish laborers continued to collapse "at their workstations," and mortality in the ghetto remained high. More immediately, rations were dangerously limited; deliveries of necessary fats were completely insufficient. The soups dished out in the workshops were of little nutritional value. It had been a long time since whole milk had arrived, and remaining stores of potatoes were being stretched. A deputy to the Gauleiter, responding though Ventzki to the Ghetto Administration's complaint, could only reply that in the face of the greater necessity of providing for the general population, such a request was unlikely to receive a positive hearing.[56] An officer of the city Health Department did offer some support, reluctantly conceding in a message to Ventzki that, to an objective observer, it was evident that Jewish workers lacked sufficient food simply to keep going, and recommended boosting their rations to match those of their Polish counterparts.[57]

Rumkowski had a plan. He would find a way to enhance the diet of undernourished working men and women. The stress, as ever, was on ensuring the productive capacity of the workforce. While there was so clearly a need to help one and all, he bowed to the logic that in the face of scarcity, he first had to help those deemed most essential to the ghetto's collective survival. With that in mind, that spring Rumkowski came forth with a new supplementary food regime based on creating kitchens exclusively for favored employees of the workshops and administrative bureaus. These "special nutrition kitchens," or *Kräftigungsküchen*[58]—the first one opened at the end of May, a second at the end of June—were designed to strengthen the physical resources of essential workers by providing them with the extra rations they required to remain healthy and productive while minimizing the possibility that they would attempt to share a portion of their food with less useful members of their families. Workshops would select "contingents" of workers, each entitled to partake, over the course of fourteen consecutive days, of substantial, well-cooked meals. In advance of opening the first dining hall, Rumkowski attended to various details, now in the kitchen inspecting preparation of the food, now looking over the wait staff. When he was satisfied that all was in order, the customers were admitted. Order Service men directed them to tables where bowls and silverware were set before each seat. No sooner had the diners been seated than waitresses bearing trays arrived to present the first course, servings of soup thick with potatoes, and to collect from each diner the requisite tokens. A second course followed, featuring "mashed potatoes and gravy, meat-filled dumplings and mustard, cabbage, [and] red vegetables." Pudding and cake were later added to the menu. Mouthwatering and rich, the meals were clearly intended to offer salaried staff and laborers not only a hearty supplement to their inadequate diet but a pleasant experience as well, as much akin to a remembered visit to a prewar vacation resort as conditions might permit. Conscientiously attending to essential details of food preparation and presentation, Rumkowski personally took charge of ensuring both the orderliness of the occasion and the quality of the dining experience, routinely spending an hour or two on the scene and even, like a popular restaurant owner circulating among his customers, taking time "almost daily" to stop and "linger" with the clientele.[59]

The kitchens were intended to serve the staff of offices and workshops, excluding everyone else, most pointedly their spouses, children, and other relatives. The ghetto production army marched on its stomach. Rumkowski knew his people; surely there would be those who would attempt to evade his orders. And in fact, some workers entitled to eat at the kitchen did try to switch places with a spouse, typically taking turns by arriving at the kitchen on alternate days; others were caught smuggling delicacies from the hall. Sharp-eyed controllers invariably discovered the odd meat dumpling elaborately wrapped and concealed inside the pocket of an exiting diner. On the first day as well there were four no-shows. The wives of two of these men arrived to explain to Rumkowski that their husbands were ill and asked if they might take their meals home to them. Concerned that granting a single exception would lead to others, thereby undermining the scheme, Rumkowski rejected their requests out of hand. Two youngsters showed up on a similar mission, children of the other missing workers; they appealed to Rumkowski in their own special way. According to Oskar Singer, Rumkowski thought hard about this. His gestures betrayed his unease. "His mouth twitch[ed]" and "he lift[ed] his glasses." It was clear that he was conflicted. He did not like to turn down the pleas of the young. He considered their case. But in the end the answer again was no, though it pained him to turn away empty-handed children who had offered the sincerest of entreaties.[60]

Like the rest homes for officials, adult workers, and working youth, the *Kräftigungsküchen* were quintessentially Rumkowskian creations, inventive minor achievements, practical and undoubtedly welcome in principle, yet in the end serving largely the needs of a select minority while neglecting the rest. Viewed in their most flattering light, however, the new dining establishments were further proof that as an organizer and provider, Rumkowksi had not lost his special touch. Even now he could deliver the goods. For Rumkowski was, at least in his own eyes, a good man, and further proof of his goodness lay in the blessing of those mashed potatoes smothered in gravy and in those altogether delectable meatballs, rare vegetables, and babkas for dessert. Rumkowski had orchestrated the entire scene: the spacious setting, the "new tables and seating," the kitchenware, the specially commissioned bowls, the spoons thoughtfully placed in the soup and the attractively attired young waitresses who served it.[61] The efficient and clean service bespoke the fulfillment of the chairman's promise to the guests: enter, though solely with my permission, and for the next fortnight, come what may, in this world where little else is certain, you can count on a place set just for you, and a stool that is, for the course of the meal, yours alone. This was Rumkowski's creation, and each and every customer rising satisfied from that table was to know just whom to thank for his or her good fortune.

On May 23 a new rest home was opened in Marysin for young workers, aged ten to seventeen. It was located by the cemetery on Kaufmannstraße and near Rumkowski's own residence as well. Rumkowski became a frequent visitor to the institution, which offered further occasion for him to socialize among the young, whose company he so enjoyed. The home—accommodating more than a hundred boys and girls at a time—was an extension of an adult rest home network, first established for the benefit of select administrators and staff in mid-1941, that had expanded to include additional homes for workers the following summer. It was a throwback to the colonies for children that had been so dear to Rumkowski's ambitions from the start. Here too a special class of fortunate, hardworking teens and preteens, blessed with a week of relaxation and freedom, were afforded neat apparel and bright surroundings, as well as plentiful servings of delicious bread, cheese, and meat. Another object of pride for Rumkowski, and a source of the ineffable pleasure he took in the spontaneity and fawning regard of the young, the home was described, in Singer's obsequious publicity, as a creative accomplishment of the first order: by Rumkowski's "hand" there had been brought forth a "Garden of Eden from out of the ruins,"[62] a place to admire, the very "antithesis of the ghetto" and "a monument for all times," offering the lucky children a "dreamlike" experience, however briefly enjoyed, beyond the daily realm. "These are my friends!" Singer quoted Rumkowski as saying. "And what wouldn't one do for true friends!"[63]

This official presentation by Singer—who was in other reports quite critical of the systemic cruelties of ghetto life—would prove uncomfortably flattering in its praise of Rumkowski's most recent success. But no accomplishment on behalf of the young could ever expunge Rumkowski's responsibility for arranging the removal of the children at the time of their seizure and deportation in September 1942. Increasingly less forgiving of the chairman, in his private notes Rosenfeld recalled hearing someone thinking back on how Rumkowski had turned up in Marysin to direct in person the removal of the children from orphanages. Thwarting the efforts of staff members seeking to hide some of the youngsters, he had demanded that all be brought out for removal.[64] This same man still thought of himself as the "savior of the children," and woe to anyone who dared challenge that role. A modern-day Noah, he would preserve the remnant in the face of the storm and the rising waters. Indulging in fantasies of glory, Rosenfeld noted, Rumkowski "wants to play a historical role for the future. Talks about leading the people and marching in front of them. Has already created some kind of organization that will carry out the necessary preparations."[65]

That spring ghetto departments and workshops entertained select audiences with the staging of a series of anniversary theatrical revues, none more impressive than those mounted by the main branch of the Order Service and its Special Department. In a competitive atmosphere, each department sought to outdo the others in the originality and quality of their productions. Not to be eclipsed, the Order Service, though including in its ranks a number of accomplished professionals from the world of Jewish music and theater, set out to "borrow" talent wherever it might be found, and succeeded in mounting one of the most impressive performances. Tickets to the shows, staged in mid-June in the House of Culture, proved difficult to come by, so as a result the audience remained strictly limited to a narrow elite. The Order Service made a point of keeping outsiders away from the hall altogether, posting guards at the entrances even during rehearsals and barring the general public. The success of its production owed much to the skills of leading theatrical lights, most prominent among them Beda Saxl, a professional theatrical performer from Prague who served as both actor and director. Order Service men contributed not only to the music, performed by a Jewish Police orchestra led by officer Jakub Szpilman, but to the scenery and lighting as well. The show featured a series of theatrical sketches, among them "Dzialki," set in the ghetto agricultural gardens (with texts set to *Lieder* by an Order Service man named Fogelbaum); a duet, "Amor in the Park," sung by Mrs. Szpilman and Order Service man M. Braun; "Minister Parade"; and "Longing for Havay," a choreographed song and dance number *(Bild mit Gesang)* for five women and three men. In addition, a "serious" piece bearing the intriguing title "The Mummy of Princess Nefretis," written by Daniel Engliszer, featured Dienstleiter Saxl as Professor Svante, officer Karabanow as "Fabian, his assistant," officer Kanczuk as "Representative of the Museum," Mrs. Szpilman again as Princess Nefretis, and, also making a second appearance, the singing Order Service man Braun, now in the role of the mysteriously named Prince Chu-Fu-Ra. A lighter sketch, titled "How to Make a Hit" ("Wie entsteht ein Schlager?"), attributed to and also starring Saxl, appearing again alongside officer Braun, brought to the stage a composer and his friend as well as a toreador, a man named Góral, and a woman, Columbine.[66]

That spring, too, marriages were celebrated in the House of Culture, and in Marysin, in a residential courtyard (resulting in the ghetto's first outdoor ceremony), as well as inside a rest home. Rumkowski officiated.[67] Such hopeful harbingers of springtime and new life notwithstanding, heading into the warmer season the ghetto remained a place dominated by the diseased and the dying. People were very sick. Subsisting in circumstances of general malnutrition and crowding, by April some ten thousand persons were suffering from tuberculosis, and approximately as many again were "predisposed" to contracting it. It had assumed the status of the ghetto's leading communicable illness; by July it was the cause of over two thirds of recorded deaths. Hospitals for infectious disease—of which there were only two—were sometimes so overtaxed that only a small number of the ill could find a hospital bed, while the overwhelming remainder were left to suffer at home.[68]

Come June, the welcome arrival of shipments of potatoes, "the most precious food that can be wished for in the ghetto," promised a long-awaited measure of salvation. "The streets would come alive, whips cracked, draymen whistled, and boys ran after the wagons to grab the few potatoes that might tumble off." But such good fortune was not to be sustained. By the latter part of the month the potatoes were gone, "replaced by vegetables—spinach, red beets, carrots, radishes—too little to fill empty stomachs."[69] With the weather alternately cool and damp, then hot and parched, the available produce seemed unlikely to improve. Even the better off took on a misshapen, unhealthy look. Bellies swollen by the watery diet were a common enough sight, detracting, in Rosenfeld's eyes, from the "undeniable grace" of those "pretty young girls, their hair styled and waved, their nails manicured, their bodies soft, round, and good-looking," whom he would notice while surveying the mass of the downtrodden who filled the streets after the workshops let out in the late afternoon. "Even twelve-year-old girls often look like pregnant women."[70]

To the misery of malnourishment was added the discomfort of one's dwelling. In high summer, that time of "bathing in one's own sweat," residents desperate for relief fled their stifling, vermin-infested apartments. Many took to congregating in their residential courtyards and camping out at night. But the crowding was extreme, and the more spacious, desirable spots were quickly claimed. In time, little ground remained where one might comfortably sit, let alone find rest for weary legs. Latecomers were forced to stand, forming awkward "little clumps that seem to be leaning on one another," ready at any time "to collapse like a dilapidated building." They conversed with neighbors, and this helped to pass the time. At last, after heading back indoors to retrieve from darkened residences "a pillow, or a blanket, or a sheet," the lucky ones located a place to bed down on the hard ground for the night. "Ah-ah-ah, wonderful! Rest for the tired and exhausted body." But such satisfaction was short-lived. "The hours drag on through the ghetto night. The stones of the yard press themselves ever deeper into the shriveled bodies. Every side is sore from lying down"; some, awkwardly positioned, discovered that "their bodies have been bent crookedly," while others, the heat of the day long since dissipated, felt as if "their skin is shivering from the cold."[71]

The very walls of their apartments "repulsive" with damp and vermin and mold, ordinary ghetto dwellers had no decent shelter whatever the time of year, and certainly not in the extremes of winter or summer.[72] Walls, meant to protect, were now, like some decayed outer garment, yet an additional source of harm. They served only as a cruel complement to the agonizing torments of the starving, sickly bodies they enclosed. To the unhealthy residents of the ghetto, pain was impossible to ignore, for the body was insistent: gums and nasal passages abscessing, tongues blistering, lungs filling, bones softening, bellies swelling, extremities aching.[73] Their ailments and their pains staked an increasing claim to their consciousness and their very being.[74]

September was to be, once more, a month burdened with grim memories. Jakub Poznański, remarking on the date in the privacy of his diary, thought back—as surely, he surmised, must everyone who had been there at the time—to the appearance four years before of aircraft in the skies above the city, when, self-righteously claiming to be striking back against unwarranted aggression, the Germans had invaded in force.[75] Three years

later, on September 1, 1942, the clearing of the ghetto hospitals had initiated the terrifying, unforgettable period of the *Allgemeine Gehsperre,* the
general curfew that had facilitated the carrying away of so many of the
ghetto's children. Long afterward, reflecting the kind of persistent psychic
injury suffered by so many, Rosenfeld would be prompted to revisit the
catastrophe, time and again jotting down a remembered occurrence or episode relating to the trauma of what his colleague Josef Zelkowicz would
term "those terrible days."[76]

Outwardly, though, it was as if nothing had changed. Well into the autumn of 1943, and in spite of the slow, ongoing decline, the ghetto endured. No one knew from one day to the next what new shock might
befall the population. With one exception—there had been a limited resettlement in March—the year 1943 had passed without more of the mass
deportations that had characterized the appalling year 1942. Still, the
forces responsible remained powerfully intact, and the routines by which
they ruled and by which the population lived persisted in a form that had
changed remarkably little since the first year of the ghetto's operation.

As ever, the logistical center and focal point of this enclosed, captive
world remained Bałuty Market, the locus of the ghetto's central institutions
of administration, commerce, and security. Safe behind a guarded wire
perimeter, off limits to both the general ghetto population and the outside
world, it dominated the life of the ghetto and determined every aspect of
its fate. Seeking a closer look, early one morning an unknown ghetto observer took up a position in the window of a nearby building overlooking
the square with the goal of recording whatever his eyes might discover.[77]

In the near-darkness of six AM, peering from a window in the offices of
the ghetto Health Department at 27 Łagiewnicka Street, the writer surveyed the scene. Here stood an array of wooden barracks housing the field
offices of the Gettoverwaltung and the Merchandise Receiving Division
(Warenannahme). Directly opposite the latter were the main institutions
of the Jewish administration, among them Rumkowski's own office and
Central Secretariat, and the all-important Workshops Division. Just beyond the square stood the two-story building housing the German sixth
police precinct and the Gestapo. By 6:30, "little by little," people began to
materialize, signaling the commencement of a new day. The square was
coming to life. First to appear were ghetto teamsters and the ghetto police,
who at this hour had already taken up their posts. Next came the work-

shop division directors, a number of them bearing "heavily-filled" brief-cases. Several female office workers just then approached. Young and attractively attired, stepping briskly, they headed off to their desks. "Punc-tually at ten minutes after seven," men of the Sonderkommando were on duty. Shortly after 7:30, anticipating the arrival of the first delivery vehi-cles from the city and desperate for any evidence that they might be bringing improved rations, a crowd had gathered along the perimeter of the square. Just then the first shipments of the day, loaded onto carts steered by Polish drivers, began pulling up onto the square. Taking over the reins, ghetto teamsters climbed aboard, ready to deliver the wares to their destinations inside the ghetto. Visibly excited, people began pepper-ing them with questions. They moved in to get a closer look. One team-ster, playfully gesturing, smiled and, affording the crowd a glimpse, drew back a section of the tarp covering his load. Alas, his shipment contained only workshop supplies. But it was to be a good day after all, for just then a cart drove in filled with potatoes. Transfixed, the crowd followed it with their eyes as it headed down the street. Thereafter, pulling in at intervals of one every several minutes, one cartload of potatoes followed another. More vehicles arrived, some, like a truck labeled Deutsche Reichsbahn, bearing fresh shipments of vegetables—parsley and carrots.[78]

While the transports rolled in, leading ghetto dignitaries and bosses ap-proached the square, a "long procession" of bureau heads, some traveling in carriages, others on foot. So too, members of the Gettoverwaltung ar-rived, riding to work in automobiles and carriages. "Punctually at fifteen minutes before nine" there appeared a most impressive sight: a "freshly lacquered" coach, a white horse in front, guided by a driver "impeccably dressed in white livery." Rumkowski had arrived. On this day the man ap-peared at his sartorial best, dressed in a "good-looking bright blue sport coat, gray trousers, and black boots." He was in buoyant spirits, too, with a smile on his face, and fairly sprang from his carriage as it came to a halt on the square. Word of Rumkowski's good-humored entrance and the welcome news of renewed potato shipments traveled fast. Now the square, so quiet and deserted in the first light of dawn, came busily to life. More carts rolled by, some bearing raw materials—hides and denim headed for the workshops, valuable staples such as parsley and milk bound for the storehouse—others bearing finished goods for export, such as linens from ghetto textile works and children's furniture from the carpentry shops. In the midst of the hubbub, one could make out the comings and goings of the ghetto bosses: German personnel still coursing about in their carriages and labor chieftain Aron Jakubowicz in his; Baruch Praszkier, administrator of long standing, was on the scene too, and on the move. One could still make out the figure of Rumkowski, rather less imposing now than when seated in the stanhope behind his fancily outfitted driver, but looking a bit more his true self, his "stooped" posture betraying his weariness and his age. All around the square was a picture of movement and energy. Busy fulfilling their errands, office messengers sped past on their bicycles. A new day had begun.[79]

The measured rhythms of the ghetto provided an illusion of certitude that day would follow upon day and the normal patterns and rhythms would be maintained. The reassurance of such routines, reinforced by moments of promise and grace, may have sufficed to sustain the sense that time would indeed rest lightly on the shoulders of the ghetto leadership and dependent members of the community alike.

That year Yom Kippur, the Day of Atonement, fell on an unseasonably warm and sunny Saturday, the ninth of October. While otherwise marked by prayer and remembrance of the dead, it proved for many a day of exceptional blessings. In all the sorrowful days of the ghetto's existence, thought Rosenfeld, few had been so peaceful. For once on this High Holy Day the workshops were closed, enabling many to enjoy the freedom to relax in the company of their families. Also marking an exception, on a subsequent evening workers entitled to access to the exclusive kitchens were permitted to take food home to share with their spouses and children.[80] If there was a single image that symbolized the special character of the holiday, it was the sight of families promenading "silently through the streets in their Sunday best." On this day boys, otherwise accustomed to going about barefoot or in clogs, had donned better footwear and appeared neatly dressed in "ironed shirts," while "the girls wore ironed dresses. And the adults too made a point of presenting a well-groomed appearance. . . . Once again families could get together, as they had not been able to do in a long time. Parents took their children by the hand and went strolling" beneath a sun that, exceptionally for this time of year, "burned with summerlike intensity."[81]

The Germans provided just enough evidence to support the hope that maybe, after all, if they were cooperative and productive, the Jews of the ghetto might be allowed to survive. But the goal of annihilation had not dissolved. Repeated expressions of hatred signaled both a wish and a certainty; the fantasy of annihilating the Jews, the ever-repeated refrain, was an accompaniment to the daily stream of words that defined the political culture which the regime had impressed on the city and the land. Such expressions gave voice to a persistent and mean-spirited joy in the disappearance of the Jews from their midst.

Publicly, the city had not forgotten its Jews, frequently invoked, though invariably in celebration of their irrevocable passing. In the pages of the *Litzmannstädter Zeitung* they were mentioned only in order to focus public attention on their alleged past misdeeds and harmful influence, each reminder reinforcing the perception that, thankfully, today the Jews were a presence no more. Cited with approval were historical precedents underscoring the long-standing popular hatred of Jews. In Welun, for instance, in 1566 the citizenry had appealed successfully to the Polish king to banish them from the city. Although the Jews subsequently returned, they were now gone, this time "forever."[82] In Grotensee, formerly Grotniki, a lovely watering place popular with day trippers from Litzmannstadt and nearby locales, the Jews had long been made to feel unwelcome by residents who had affixed a banner to the town's picturesque railway station warning Jews not to stop there. That would appear to be no longer necessary, as they were now safely absent from a setting "more free of Jews than even before." They were gone and never again to be encountered seated in rowboats (charmingly reminiscent of gondolas) floating by on the waters of the nearby river Linda, never to share a dance floor, or dine in the town's outdoor cafés, or stroll along its new promenade, just then under development.[83] In September the anniversary of the birth of the German writer Wilhelm Raabe provided an occasion to cite from one of his works that set forth an unsavory portrait of Jews. It proclaimed that since the destruction of the temple in Jerusalem, everywhere Jews had made themselves at home among unwary hosts, and that in times of national ruin it was they who, like the survivors of a shipwreck, knew how to strap on their lifebelts and float to safety.[84] Tales were rehashed of the Jewish underworld, of notorious Jewish thieves and pickpockets who supposedly terrorized the Bałut in an earlier age.[85] Time had long since passed when their kind was able to live among the good residents of the city and the region. In images such as these the regime bid farewell to a people so unwanted that their disappearance was welcomed as an ages-old wish come true.[86]

Time and again, in public statements delivered from afar, Hitler had, with barely suppressed malicious satisfaction, intimated that the Jews would not survive the war, and time and again the subject of the Jews' disappearance found reinforcing expression in the pages of the newspapers. Everything was being stated—and yet not quite. Broadly expressed, repeatedly issued indications abounded, but specifics were few, and outright revelation was intentionally suppressed in favor of discretion and secrecy. On October 4, in the Gau capital of Posen, Himmler, addressing a select audience of men thoroughly experienced in and knowledgeable about the killing, commented favorably on the self-imposed code of silence surrounding their deeds: "It was with us, thank God, an inborn gift of tactfulness, that we have never conversed about this matter, never spoken about it. Every one of us was horrified, and yet every one of us knew that we would do it again if it were ordered and if it were necessary. I am referring to the evacuation of the Jews, to the extermination of the Jewish people."[87]

The passing of the Jews remained a central preoccupation of the city fathers, and the hometown paper embodied their outlook and aspirations. The verbiage of hate ceaselessly cascaded through the local press. Tracing its origins to the German-language publication the *Freie Presse,* to which it was a successor, in November 1943 the *Litzmannstädter Zeitung* marked the twenty-fifth anniversary of its founding. The date provided an occasion for a reporter to offer readers a glimpse behind the scenes at the workings of a great metropolitan daily. And so they would learn: a newspaper never sleeps. Appropriately, the tour of the facilities commenced at the onset of darkness, a time when the offices of the *Litzmannstädter Zeitung,* far from shutting down until the next day, readied for work. Even as lights were being switched off elsewhere in the building, the night shift busily set about its tasks. Ceaselessly reports came in over the wire, transcribed by a secretary into shorthand; the teletype clattered, pouring out reams of text. The morning edition was under way: headlines were selected, lead molds poured, galleys prepared, the presses set to spinning. Advanced machinery capable of turning out the day's edition—by 1943 reaching a circulation exceeding 100,000—ran all night. Toward dawn the completed edition was stacked, bundled, and tied for loading onto delivery vans. Snow had fallen overnight. Wary of icy conditions and the slow going ahead, the drivers anxiously inspecting their vehicles wiped headlights and windshields clear, checked fuel levels, mounted chains, and loaded shovels. In the early morning hours the trucks set out for their destinations, drop-off points for local distributors; along the way bundles would have to reach outlying railway stations on time in order to be loaded aboard early morning trains. Moving on, negotiating rural highways, deep into the remotest corners of the Warthegau the deliverymen drove. In small towns and villages the people lent their assistance. Approaching the end of the line, a remote village in Kreis Turek, a delivery was passed to a boy riding a bicycle; behind the bike a German shepherd faithfully trailed. On command—the boy's outstretched finger pointing the way—the dog, clasping the newspapers in its jaws, set off at a run. Dodging and weaving a complex path through the underbrush, yet instinctively conscious of its goal, the determined beast made for its destination, the banks of the river Warta, where it surrendered its package into the hands of a waiting boatman. As the dog ran back, the boatman, his cargo safely aboard, set off, ferrying across the river to a farmstead on the opposite shore. The journey begun in that faraway newsroom in Litzmannstadt was now all but complete as the day's edition made its way to the farthest corner of the province.[88]

Words mattered. Sweetly contextualized, reassuring evocations of a world at last without Jews, broadly disseminated, spread a message central to the regime's purposes and worthy of contemplation by the public at large. To the Jews, officially excluded from the readership (though clandestine copies of the local press did circulate), the words and the images they conjured were an incessant accompaniment to the misery of their days, a reminder of the seal affixed to the proclamation of their destruction. In the ghetto too, the theme of the dying of the Jews made its way into the common idiom. For all the improbable efflorescence of talent and energy born of the desperation to survive, the underlying experience of daily life in the ghetto remained the constant presence of death. At once one of the dying and a detached chronicler of death's hovering presence within the community, Rosenfeld thought each inventive reference to death a precious artifact of this place and this time. The ghetto was linguistically resourceful. He had hoped that those of a later time who might seek to understand the reality of the ghetto would take note.[89]

Cold returned and autumnal darkness descended. November was always for Rosenfeld a time of year saturated with memory, and no date was to him more poignant than November 28, the anniversary of his 1937 marriage to his beloved wife, now safely far away in London. His thoughts drifted back to the day of their wedding, a Sunday, when they had walked together through narrow streets, making their way to a café. Such reminiscence was saturated with longing, bittersweet. He retained at least a measure of hope for his survival, but he was unflinchingly aware that all such memories were traces of an irretrievable past, and that, sad as it was to acknowledge, his loved ones were quite possibly lost to him forever. "When will we see each other again, embrace? A dream? An illusion? . . . I feel her breath, her hands, her love and care, as if she departed yesterday."[90]

"Heavy snow," he noted, fell on December 27.[91] Chanukah arrived to grace the year's final days. The fortunate found a measure of light and warmth in quiet celebration among family and friends. Passing through the streets Rosenfeld came upon a candle seller, bundled like "some mummified creature" against the elements, hawking his wares: *"Lecht! Lecht!"* Lights, lights for the holiday. Households set out their menorahs—ritual articles many had borne with them into exile in the ghetto—and lit the first candles. Daughters sang the prayers. Invited guests arrived bearing small gifts: "some toy, a piece of babka, a hair ribbon, a few empty colorful cigarette boxes, a flowery plate, a pair of stockings, a warm bonnet." Then, the evening's modest festivities at an end, the candles extinguished, "with pressing of the hands," visitors said their good-byes and made their way down shadowy corridors and stairways into the open air and the dark of the winter night.[92]

10

Numbered Are the Days

From his field headquarters in East Prussia, Hitler delivered his 1944 New Year's address to the nation. Germany, he declared, was in the fight of its life; its very existence hung in the balance. By the tens of thousands, German women and children were being targeted by the enemy; gladly would that enemy raise the number of victims a hundredfold.[1] Yet difficult as circumstances surely were, the public was to rest assured, knowing that "in this world every war has finally come to an end, and so this war too shall not last forever." That said, he could state with all confidence that the Jews would pay for the war with their lives. He used a biblical phrase to sum up Germany's determination to inflict due punishment upon the Jews for their role in unleashing such a deadly assault: "An eye for an eye and a tooth for a tooth! That the Jewish goal, the destruction of Europe, will in the end bring about the certain extermination of European Jewry is therefore beyond all doubt."[2]

Indeed, one day the war *would* come to an end, though surely, as one local commentator noted, no one was likely to emerge from it quite the same as before.[3] Nor would the city. Even as Litzmannstadt prepared for yet another year of struggle, the city fathers were shown to be devoting their attentions to a more peaceful tomorrow. On January 7, accompanying municipal division directors, acting Oberbürgermeister Bradfisch and

Bürgermeister Marder toured the grounds of Litzmannstadt's principal German cemetery, then afterwards reviewed plans for its expansion and development. Just south of the ghetto a new main entrance would open onto the redeveloped grounds, the centerpiece of which was to be a crematorium, and whose beauty would be enhanced by fresh landscaping, the laying of a path with stone steps, and the planting of trees amid the burial markers. "The gravestones are to be arrayed in such a way that one will hardly experience the impression of being in a cemetery," noted the *Litzmannstädter Zeitung*. Indeed, the effect was to create an altogether "park-like setting," attractive and welcoming to the public. "Life triumphs over death! That will be the motto invisibly wafting above the new cemetery." In this way the remodeled space would contribute to the creation of that long-awaited belt of greenery which was to extend for miles along the northern edge of downtown Litzmannstadt, incorporating open terrain resulting from urban clearance south of the ghetto. Anchored by Deutschland Square and stretching from Helenenhof Park in the east to the Volkspark in the west, the new parkway was to be a signal achievement of enlightened city planning.[4]

On that same day, Bradfisch put in an appearance at Bałut Market. He had come in order to insist on renewed compliance with the 1942 order mandating that Jews deferentially acknowledge German personnel whenever in their presence. "Apparently the mayor had ascertained that people were not saluting cars that drive through the ghetto, as regulation prescribes," the *Chronicle* reported. The Jews would have to demonstrate respect, as Rumkowski was compelled to remind them, stating by proclamation: "I again emphatically point out that all ghetto inhabitants (male and female) must unconditionally and unprompted salute all uniformed personnel and all German officials (civilians) in the street as well as in the workshops and factories. . . . At inspections of departments, workshops, and factories, [by Germans both from outside] and from the Ghetto Administration, everyone must rise from his seat at the command, 'Achtung!' [Attention!]."[5]

Behind Bradfisch's insistence undoubtedly lay an increasing concern that high-ranking visitors should see nothing less than a picture of discipline and efficiency. Just then the ghetto and its administrative leadership were increasingly becoming the subject of external scrutiny. For more than half a year the SS, eager to incorporate the ghetto into its own economic and administrative domain, had been mounting an internal campaign to wrest control of the ghetto from local authorities. As early as June 1943, Heinrich Himmler had given the go-ahead to effect the ghetto's transfer to SS jurisdiction. He had two potential administrative arrangements in mind. One was linked to Odilo Globocnik, Higher SS and Police Leader in Lublin, who proposed dismantling the ghetto and transporting its remaining viable workforce, along with any necessary equipment, to "the Lublin region," where some 45,000 Jews confined to labor camps under his authority were still working for war industries. As an alternative, the SS considered the possibility of assuming outright control over the ghetto and transforming it "into a concentration camp." Such plans, however, posed a challenge to the productive interests of the German military, which was heavily dependent on the ghetto's reliable uniform-making capacity, as well as the prerogatives, material interests, and jurisdictional authority of Gauleiter Arthur Greiser of the Wartheland. From these quarters the SS would encounter forceful opposition to the implementation of its plans.[6]

From summer 1943 through the winter of 1944 there would be numerous inspections as representatives of competing agencies undertook fact-finding missions to gather evidence with which to argue their case. In one of the skirmishes in this administrative tug-of-war, in November 1943 a military intervention had successfully headed off the SS in its effort to transform the ghetto into a concentration camp. Yet by December the SS was pressing ahead once more. Adolf Eichmann, accompanied by Otto Horn, director of Ostindustrie, a subsidiary of Oswald Pohl's concentration camps directorate, the Economic Administration Main Office (Wirtschaftsverwaltungshauptamt), arrived in Litzmannstadt to undertake a fresh assessment. Horn returned to conduct a follow-up inspection in January 1944, and not unexpectedly, his report cast doubt on the ghetto's viability and recommended its definitive transformation into a concentration camp under SS management. In February, Pohl's representatives met with the Gau leadership in Posen. As talks turned to the sizable sum of money the Gauleiter demanded in compensation for yielding control over the ghetto, Himmler intervened, postponing the proposed incorporation of the ghetto into the SS domain. Greiser informed Pohl that he and Himmler had achieved an understanding that the ghetto would remain in place. It was to be regarded as the "central ghetto" of the

Gau Wartheland. Nevertheless, in strict accordance with the principle that "only as many Jews would remain as were unconditionally needed for . . . war production," its population was to "be reduced to a minimum." To see to it that this was carried out, Himmler agreed to reactivate the Sonderkommando in Chełmno, promising to recall "Bothmann, and his unit . . . and again place them at Greiser's disposition." For the foreseeable future the ghetto would remain under immediate Gau and Litzmannstadt city administration. The understanding further specified both that "the use and sale of the ghetto's moveable property was in Greiser's domain" and that "after deportation of the Jews and dissolution," still the undisputed final goal, "the entire ghetto terrain would revert to the city."[7]

For the moment, then, the ghetto would continue under existing management. Nonetheless, Biebow could hardly remain indifferent to the effect a successful effort to transfer control over the ghetto to so powerful an outside organization as the SS would have on his own authority and that of his organization. Long plagued by the loss of valued personnel to military call-up, Biebow had worked diligently to ensure that at least he and his leading deputies and divisional directors, as well as staff members directly attending to the processing of Jewish property acquired during the course of the killing operations, were exempted from military service. No less essentially, in the face of the SS challenge to wrest control over the ghetto, Biebow had turned to allies in the armaments establishment for institutional backing. Still dependent on the ghetto as a reliable manufacturer, it was too eager to maintain the status quo.[8] Fully aware that the ghetto would one day be dissolved, he and his associates were not eager to hasten its disappearance. Biebow's unflagging determination to drive production by squeezing out even the smallest inefficiencies in the system received impetus from the growing concern that others might seize on perceived inadequacies to undermine his position or that of his organization as a whole.

Knowing that the ghetto's future was once again an object of increased internal discussion, Biebow was determined to see it present as efficient and orderly an appearance as possible. Already on December 7, 1943, at a moment when the SS was pressing its bid to transform the ghetto into a concentration camp under its own authority, he had mounted the stage at the House of Culture to address an audience of four hundred ghetto workshop directors and administrative leaders. During the course of a

meandering ninety-minute address attended by three leading Gettoverwaltung officers and an agent of the Criminal Police as well, Biebow went
out of his way to criticize behavior he found detrimental to the ghetto's
image. While conceding that he and his staff did not place undue importance on such formalities as snapping to attention when visitors arrived,
such demonstrations of formal respect were nonetheless essential to creating the necessary "good impression." So too was it vital to eliminate any
sign of disorder in public settings, such as children roaming the streets
and numerous persons on bicycles. Both constituted a real hazard, endangering themselves and others. As for the Jewish teamsters, Biebow warned
them against striking the horses entrusted to their care. Wagon drivers
were also going to have to improve their basic skills; too many carts were
going about in an "undisciplined" manner, veering "one minute left, then
right." Ghetto pedestrians might also do more to help keep traffic moving. Why did they not volunteer to assist when a cart ran into difficulties?
The Jews would do well to follow the German example. Germans knew
how to pitch in and lend a hand. In another critical area too, the Jews
might do well to think about the wider impact of their failings. He reminded workshop directors of their responsibility to ensure that their
workers washed thoroughly, and not merely for their own well-being but
out of consideration for others, since "lice and vermin" had been discovered infesting articles emerging from the workshops. This alone should
give them pause. In working among them, he and his staff, parents with
children of their own, were being continually exposed to the risk of contamination.[9]

The Gettoverwaltung and its administrative allies continued to gather
evidence supporting their case that the ghetto must endure. In a report
delivered to the Oberbürgermeister on April 1, chief city inspector Quay
presented a structural overview depicting the ghetto as altogether praiseworthy in its well-run institutional arrangements and its vital contributions to the military and the war economy. His conclusions presented a
sober picture of the ghetto as a soundly organized, smoothly functioning,
financially solid, mature enterprise strongly deserving to be maintained
for the duration of the war. Quay did all he could to bolster the argument.
The ghetto was now self-sustaining. Through 1943 the ghetto population,
numbering some eighty thousand, had proved itself capable of paying its
own way at no additional cost to the city. The ghetto's goods utiliza-

tion division, where confiscated or voluntarily redeemed cash, jewelry, and valuable textiles were processed, continued to provide an important stream of income. The supplementary services of the City Savings Bank, the Reichsbank, and local jewel assessors and retailers were duly noted as assisting in facilitating the successful conversion of Jewish property to help pay for running the ghetto. He noted that ghetto production, which had begun modestly at the level of artisan labor, had gradually developed a series of enterprises increasingly enhanced through the introduction of appropriate machinery. Key branches of ghetto industry had proved altogether successful in fulfilling orders for the military, the ghetto's chief contractor, as well as a number of "respectable" firms operating in the private sector. The report sought to stress the extraordinary effectiveness of ghetto enterprises in utilizing every available resource, carefully recycling strips of fur, paper products, used clothing, bedding feathers, and bits of wood to create not merely utilitarian but highly desirable commercial products of ultramodern design, fit, and finish. Indeed, the ghetto had only recently geared up for production of a line of commercially developed prefabricated housing units. An initial three hundred units were expected in April 1944, with production quickly ramping up to double that figure, on the way toward an eventual goal of a thousand units per month. The ghetto textile works, organized by product line, employing some "19,500 workers of both genders," including four thousand youngsters, and operating with an inventory of 5,100 sewing machines to turn out no fewer than five thousand uniform parts per week, was itself a prime generator of high-quality articles derived from clever use of recycled materials. As an additional service to the Wehrmacht, the ghetto laundry undertook the cleaning and repair of "dirty and damaged" articles, such as "uniforms, fatigues, and underclothing," amounting by weight to some thousand kilos per month. All in all, the Jews had proved enormously useful, constituting a form of such valuable "exploitable capital" that, in the inspector's opinion, barring a "peremptory" change of course driven by "superior political considerations," one would "be ill-advised to recommend the ghetto's dissolution during wartime."[10]

Yet as committed as it remained to defending the ghetto's hard-won reputation as a source of production, the Gettoverwaltung proved as cooperative and forthcoming as before in providing material assistance to the killing center where those deemed superfluous to the effort were systematically destroyed. In fulfilling the wintertime agreement to further reduce the ghetto population, by the month of April, Sonderkommando Bothmann was gearing up to receive from the ghetto additional victims deemed incapable of work and hence worthy of disposal. Returning to the killing field they had left behind in April 1943, Bothmann's team, newly reassembled, spent spring 1944 readying the camp to receive a new wave of victims from Łódź, in the process setting up barracks and constructing new crematoriums. To be freshly dug into the ground in the clearing of Forest Precinct 77, the new ovens would require bricks, cement, ductwork, and rails. Materially assisting the effort, the Gettoverwaltung met these needs, supplying, in addition to furniture for the Kommando, requisite building materials, including shipments of cement, sheet metal, and iron.[11]

From the ghetto came workmen who were essential to performing the tasks of heavy construction. Rounded up, they were transported to the killing center to fulfill their odious assignments. Szymon Srebrnik, a teenager employed in a ghetto metal shop, was one of the first to be dispatched. Abruptly seized off a ghetto streetcar, he was taken to Bałut Market to join a transport of some fifty others, who were loaded aboard vehicles and driven to Chełmno. There the men were divided into two teams. About forty of the more robust were assigned to labor in the forest assembling the furnaces, while the other group, to which at first Srebrnik was assigned, would work on the grounds of the former manor house. Srebrnik would later recall that the men were shackled, which "prevented us from walking in a normal way. We had to take very short steps. The shackles on our ankles were also chained to our waists. We slept in the granary on a cement floor. It was very cold." Routinely the men at work in the forest were badly beaten, and many were killed; not infrequently barely half their number returned alive from their day's work. The survivors told the others that two furnaces were under construction. To the men their purpose was at first unclear; initially, the ovens were thought to serve the manufacture of charcoal. In the meantime, while work went on in the forest, new crew members were being delivered from the ghetto. Srebrnik counted "eight transports" of thirty men each. So great was the mortality of the workmen that only eighteen in all were left in the entire camp by the time wholesale transportation of victims from the ghetto began. The bodies remained temporarily concealed under "a pile of sand. After the furnaces became operational, the bodies were burnt."[12]

That spring the city played host to interested visitors and, with the arrival of a new wave of ethnic German families fleeing southern Russia, to incoming settlers alike. In mid-April a delegation from Hamburg, Litzmannstadt's famed urban partner and sister city, arrived on a ceremonial three-day visit. The distinguished guests were treated to a tour of local highlights, including a drive through the city and a trip to the ghetto. Any discomforting impressions of this "horrible" *(abschreckend)* attraction were said to have been mitigated by a contrasting visit to a model housing development.[13] For their evening's entertainment, the members of the Hamburg delegation were treated to a performance of a lighthearted stage production, *The Secret of Madame Kegel,* being performed at the Theater an der Moltkestraße.[14]

Never missing an opportunity to delight in the doings of Litzmannstadt's youngest citizens at play, on the same mid-April Sunday when the Hamburg delegation was busy gathering dubious impressions of the ghetto, spectators had assembled in the downtown Volkspark to watch a citywide gathering of young *Pimpfe,* ten-to-fourteen-year-olds enrolled in the Jungvolk organization, participating in a game of capture the flag. The defenders, having skillfully prepared for their final stand by coating their wooden flagpole in coal tar, carried the day. All in all, it was thought a highly useful exercise that, in addition to helping hone the youngsters' physical skills, offered an opportunity for developing mental "cunning" as well.[15]

With the warmer weather, once again the city's main boulevard was temporarily cleared to make way for athletic competitions. On a Sunday in May, runners dashed northward along Adolf-Hitler-Straße toward the finish line on Deutschlandplatz. A crowd estimated in the "tens of thousands" was on hand. Adding a note of festivity, a band performed. On this occasion a team from Romania and the Black Sea region had entered the race. Averaging thirty-two years of age, the men, members of a police company, were somewhat older than the other competitors and failed to come away with a win. All the same, at this time of unceasing official attention lavished on integrating newcomers of ethnic Germanic stock, they were thought deserving of praise for taking part and demonstrating their fitness.[16]

Once more a circus came to town, pitching its camp on Blücherplatz to prepare for its opening performance on May 2. Billed as a must-see "sensation," it would feature, in addition to artistic feats, a host of amusing animal acrobatics: a skillful horse pushing a roller, elephants dancing with improbable grace, fearsome panthers heeding the commands of a trainer, and a remarkably talented creature named Bongo whose antics prompted the question, "Man or Monkey?" Especially entertaining were a quartet of clowns, "Theodor, Nici, Toto, and Cicero," whose performance of an outrageous bathing routine, described as too hilarious for words, awakened the "roaring enthusiasm" of spectators "young and old."[17] It must have been fun. Sadly, one six-year-old girl was turned away. To her grave misfortune, as the ghetto *Chronicle* would note on May 16, the police "detained" her on the point of seeking admittance. Discovered to be a Jew, she was remanded to the ghetto. Piecing together her story, the *Chronicle* noted that at the time of the deportation of the Jews from Łask—in August 1942—"she had allegedly fled to Litzmannstadt with her parents," where she "had been in hiding with a Polish family." Her uncle, a dentist residing in the ghetto, was informed of her arrival, and arrangements were promptly undertaken to facilitate her adoption.[18]

Residents of the ghetto were now only too aware that, come what may, their survival remained very much in doubt. On May 3 Rosenfeld wrote, "The question gains ever greater urgency: Are we going to be here during the hour of the final showdown? Still be alive?"[19] As ever, people were left to their own devices to keep mind and body together. Most could do little but plead. Some, fully aware of the zero-sum nature of survival, were willing to do everything in their power to acquire scarce resources. They exploited whatever advantage came their way. A ghetto troubadour popularly known as Yankel openly admitted—though not without humorous intent—that "not *all* can survive the war. That's why the *one* who endures will be the one who takes from *the others*. Those who stay alive do so at the expense of others. And I want to stay alive."[20] Writing at the end of May, an anonymous ghetto observer noted that people, sensing their vulnerability, were decidedly on edge, physically sensitive, jumpy, reacting to

the least noise, "indifferent to everything."[21] Rosenfeld described an atmosphere of caution and worry marked by general concern over future resettlements. He reported on the appearance of a postcard from Częstochowa
"from brother to brother. 'Come if you can; it's better here than elsewhere. No easier place to survive the war.'" But, Rosenfeld cautioned,
"fear is so deeply etched in, nobody wants to believe it."[22]

On the final weekend in May the weather proved fair. The festival of
Shavuot arrived, prompting ghetto residents to head outdoors. "Thousands of people in the *djalkas* [garden plots], the sun is burning, a few
tanned faces can even be seen," Rosenfeld noted. "But it is precisely the
bright light and the sated green that throws the soul into even greater despair."[23] Unbidden, visions of his relations came to him while he slept. "I
was dreaming of Henuschi. Arm in arm with her, she was guiding me,
protecting me, keeping me warm. I regained my strength; then I was
dreaming of Father and Mother as so often [happens] lately."[24] Days later,
listening to a friend singing, he was made aware not only of the existence
of a wider world beyond the ghetto but also of its loss to him, perhaps forever, his notations slipping at this point from his native German into the
sometimes unsteady English he liked, on occasion, to exercise: "I felt the
deep meaning of the ether; that we are not alone on this earth, *that there
abroad, a world exists with human sense and spirit."* A moment of "rapture"
is invoked: *"I heard . . . heard tones . . . music . . . a slowfox,"* only to be followed by the stark realization that *"now I know what we have lost. . . .
There are moments where you can answer only by tears."*[25]

The Gettoverwaltung and Gau leadership had made their case well, successfully mounting a rearguard action against SS efforts to gain control
over their domain. But with the approach of summer, productionist efforts to postpone the ghetto's dissolution, buffeted on the one hand by
powerful countervailing ideological and administrative pressures and on
the other by deteriorating prospects for delaying the advance of Soviet
forces, came to an end. Casting aside objections, in early June Himmler
ordered the ghetto to be shut down. This time Greiser, long a proponent
of postponing the day, knew that there could be no turning back. In firm
alignment now with Himmler's directive, Greiser seized the initiative to
undercut a last-minute maneuver by armaments minister Albert Speer to

halt the dismantling of the ghetto, and with it the loss of its valued productive capacity. When he learned that Speer had assigned a representative of the weapons inspectorate to assemble fresh numerical data on the size and productivity of the ghetto workforce, Greiser immediately reported the matter to Himmler. Grateful for the advance warning, Himmler directed Greiser to proceed immediately with the evacuation of the ghetto.[26]

By the middle of June the ghetto was on alert for further signs of trouble. Acclimatized to the shifting political winds, the population had developed its own highly sensitive "barometer" for gauging the "atmosphere" of events.[27] People took apprehensive note when, late on the morning of June 15, acting Oberbürgermeister and local Gestapo chief Otto Bradfisch arrived at Bałut Market, accompanied by a commission including local officials and an unnamed "high-ranking officer." Bradfisch met briefly with Rumkowski; in turn, Gestapo officers Fuchs and Stromberg arrived to confer with Rumkowski's secretary Dora Fuchs, and with ghetto police commandant Rozenblat. "Shortly after these visits," the *Chronicle* reported, "the ghetto was full of the wildest rumors. But all of them ran in one direction: resettlement!" As best the ghetto chroniclers could piece together from available "second-hand" accounts, Bradfisch had informed Rumkowski of the necessity of shipping specified contingents of workers to German cities to clear debris in the wake of Allied bombardment. An initial contingent of five hundred was to be ready by June 21, rising to three thousand per week thereafter, with no clarification as to how long such transports were to continue. There was indeed justification for concern that the ghetto was facing outright "liquidation." Some residents proved extremely anxious, though it was reported that many were "apathetic," being "already so worn out" from lack of food that they took the attitude that things "can hardly get any worse."[28]

There is no mention of Biebow appearing in the company of Bradfisch and the commission; his authority, it appears, had been bypassed, the order carried out over his objections. In a rage, Biebow entered Rumkowski's department, first ordering Jewish staff to leave the premises at once and lock the door behind them. Then, stepping into Rumkowski's private office, he lashed out at the old man, severely beating him about the face. Such was Biebow's fury that two of his aides were forced to restrain him, though not before Rumkowski's cheekbone had been badly injured, prompting his hospitalization, and not before Biebow had damaged his own hand, apparently after smashing it against a window, shattering the glass.[29] Noting the unprecedented nature of the outburst, and in the face of Rumkowski's subsequent silence on what had prompted the incident, the chroniclers suspected that Biebow, having already argued that no more ghetto workers could be spared for resettlement, was furious that in acceding to Bradfisch's demand, Rumkowski had contributed to undermining Biebow's authority.[30] That this signaled a serious defeat for Biebow's ongoing rearguard action to preserve the institution of the ghetto appears to have played an important role in raising his anger to the boiling point. His tightly wound temperament, usually kept carefully under control, had snapped. When, a day or so later, Biebow was spotted en route to the same ghetto hospital where Rumkowski still lay recovering from the assault, people speculated that he was paying a visit to effect a reconciliation with the chairman. That turned out not to be the case. Biebow's sole intention was to obtain treatment for the wound he had inflicted on his own hand.[31]

The fighting was coming closer. Late in the morning on June 21 alarms sounded, signaling an impending air attack. At Bałut Market, Gettoverwaltung staffers quickly headed for cover in a newly constructed shelter, located on-site for their exclusive protection. Having no choice but to ride out any possible assault, residents of the ghetto reportedly kept "absolutely calm," remaining "in apartments, workshops, offices, building entrances, and some, in so-called slit trenches. . . . From somewhere in the vicinity, a few shots fired by anti-aircraft guns could be heard. A large air squadron, perhaps 300 planes, was observed flying east at an altitude of about 2,000 meters. No bombs were dropped. The all-clear signal came at 12:40."[32] Two days later, on the morning of June 23, deportations commenced. The initial transport took away 562 people. Such things had happened before, though a voyage into the unknown seemed particularly frightening at this time. The German authorities, aware of the true purpose and destination of the transports, did everything in their deceptive power to maintain the illusion that the deportees would be decently treated. Gestapo officer Günter Fuchs appeared at the station early in the morning to reassure the deportees that "they would be working in the Reich and that decent food would be provided. . . . [T]hey would initially be loaded onto freight cars but be transferred to passenger cars en route. No one had anything to fear." In a token of apparent regard for their well-being, luggage from the first transport was placed on carts, driven to the Radogoszcz station, and "stowed on separate freight cars. Everything was properly numbered. People were treated correctly."[33] As a further indication that they were indeed headed off to work in Germany, Biebow had arranged for half a million Reichsmarks, authentic currency, to be made available to the ghetto for distribution to deportees. Each would receive ten marks for the journey. Supplemental hard currency "up to a maximum of fifty marks" was available in exchange for personal property delivered to the Central Purchasing Agency, which was also authorized to pay deportees for household items. As a service to those summoned for departure, its agents were made available to visit residences for the purpose of assessing the value of items and taking them away.[34] Meanwhile, outside the offices of Central Purchasing in the courtyard at number 4 Kościelny Street, piles of red-colored bedding caused one observer to liken the scene to "a coral reef pounded by the surf of a dreary mass of anonymous resettlees."[35]

The trains were closely guarded. The authorities spoke of a journey to the Reich, but that information proved difficult to reconcile with the fact that the very same trains that had so recently departed were arriving back again at the station after only a brief interval. A note was rumored to have been left behind in one of the returning cars saying that the trains were traveling "only as far as Kutno," fifty-three kilometers away, "where the travelers were transferred to passenger cars," presumably for the next leg of their journey. All the same, the rapid turnaround made people highly anxious, such logistics being only too reminiscent of the pattern characteristic of prior deportations.[36] A week later, on July 2, observers were still at a loss to identify the transports' ultimate destination. People simply had "no idea," even though the trains, still returning quickly "for the next dispatch," were surely just "shuttling" passengers and were "no doubt going only as far as Kutno." On arrival there, passengers "are reportedly screened. Rumor is that healthy, able-bodied persons are then placed at the disposal of farmers. Naturally, no confirmation of this rumor is available."[37] The rumors were actually more lurid than the chroniclers noted. Yakov Hiller, an employee in a ghetto bakery, had heard—similarly without the least confirmation—that the camp resembled some kind of human market, and "landowners or farmers" were encouraged "to come there and buy Jewish workers like slaves."[38]

The weather had turned oppressively hot. On July 4 the sun rose brightly and only grew more intense as the day progressed. People avoided going out, leaving the streets of the ghetto all but deserted. The heat affected everyone; even the reasonably fit struggled with it. Those few who were out and about were visibly straining to make progress, their pace closer to creeping than to walking. Heat and hunger, twin scourges, would prove an especially burdensome challenge to the constitutions of even the young, who now predominated among the surviving population, though outwardly many were hardly recognizable as such, with a sunken appearance that made them look prematurely aged. Like Zelkowicz before him, Hiller, observing all these weakened and haggard people, thought that they resembled residents of an old-age home rather than the young men and women they were.[39]

About the only ones seemingly enjoying the heat were some of the ghetto's remaining children, those three- to eight-year-olds sheltered from earlier waves of deportation, now enrolled in the many day care centers, or *świetlicas,* attached to the *resorts.* Hiller glimpsed them playing in the courtyards in the shade of one of the ghetto's few trees, or clustered about an outdoor pump, fetching water. Their overseers, young women who, in Hiller's opinion, showed more interest in the soup they received for their efforts than in the youngsters under their care, were decidedly less enthusiastic. While the children—"little swallows," he would affectionately call them—frolicked, their caretakers, as overwhelmed by the heat as everyone else, lay on a nearby bench, still exposed to the sun.[40]

And yet come early evening, with the exit of the day shift from the workshops, the streets again filled with people, in spite of the still powerful heat of the day. They shed their outerwear and went about in light summer clothing. Women appeared in attractive thin dresses, while men could be seen in fairly decent-looking, if "refurbished," suits. It seemed to Hiller as if many had put on their finest clothes in order to take advantage of a last opportunity to enjoy wearing something nice. Some of these garments looked to him as if they had been stored away from the beginning and only now, five years into their life in the ghetto, brought out and worn.[41]

Whatever the truth of the rumors concerning the destination of those sent out in the latest wave of transports, people were determined to remain behind in the ghetto rather than venture into the unknown. They did not wish to go, not now, not after all these years; most wanted desperately to stick it out a bit longer. It was better to stay put, to sleep in one's own bed at night rather than in some unfamiliar location. Even so, fearful of nighttime raids, many avoided sleeping in their own residences. Adapting to the tactic, the Jewish Police waited to capture deportees "during the day," when they emerged to "go to work."[42] As in the past, the ghetto leadership made it as difficult as possible to evade compliance with the unwelcome summons. The order to report was followed by withdrawal of one's right to draw rations. To hide meant losing access to food. One would have to have saved something up at least, or to have established a hiding place in advance. But the denial of rations and relentless pursuit by the Jewish police proved effective, and in most instances sufficient to thwart these efforts and compel compliance. The result was that in those late June days ghetto residents made their way when called to the collection point, hauling as best they could their heavy belongings en route to the Central Prison, the way station to the trains.[43]

There was little pretense of fairness in the selection. When had there been, after all? The pattern was well entrenched. Always it was the least protected who were the first to be surrendered. Only by now the Germans were reaching deep into the ranks of useful workers. This deportation was affecting the workshops. Power of selection was placed in the hands of their directors, who drew up lists of their own workers, indicating who was to go. This gave them enormous discretion, with ample room for favoritism as well as the settling of scores. "Shady deals that involve human lives are negotiated behind the scenes, among the workshop managers," reported the *Chronicle*. "By the time the Inter-workshop Committee completes the clearing procedure, the managers have come to terms. You cross out my Jew and I'll cross out yours; if you list my Jew, then I'll list yours. Personal intrigues and vendettas are rampant."[44] Desperate to gain a hearing, employees crowded the corridors of their workplaces in an effort "to submit their petitions for exemption to the managers. There is a petition for every name on the list. Similar scenes are enacted in physicians' offices."[45] Others, however, whether through exhaustion of their resources, "recklessness," or what they took to be a rational assessment of their chances, proved agreeable to climbing aboard the transports in place of another—for a price. The going rate was "three loaves of bread, a half-kilogram of margarine, [and] one pound of sugar," along with "shoes and other items of clothing" sometimes thrown into the bargain. The chance to "eat one's fill," a satisfaction in its own right, proved an enticement too immediate and mouthwatering to pass up. A willing "substitute" could expect to be "deluged with offers."[46]

As in each preceding wave of deportation, those who lacked connections, the weak, the poor, the lonely, were most exposed, and their fate struck sensitive observers as the most tragic of all. As the destitute made their way toward Central Prison, an elderly gray-haired woman struggled under the weight of her last possessions. Wearing, incongruously, "instead of a dress, a tattered fur vest to which a girl's short skirt of coarse linen is attached," her "feet so swollen that they can barely squeeze into the almost heelless shoes; bundles large and small in her hands," and with eating utensils "dangling around her thighs," she caught Rosenfeld's eye. The poor creature was having a difficult time making her way to the prison. "The old woman's back is so bent that her weathered face and toothless mouth become visible only when she supports herself against a building wall. She stumbles more than walks. The ghetto pavement doesn't permit an even stride." She was, he ascertained, the remaining survivor of a family that had been extinguished; one more sad ghetto story, hers included the loss of "her husband, children, and close relatives."[47] There was for her no one left in the world.

Aware that many workers were trying to evade seizure by moving to hideouts overnight, the Jewish Order Service took to sweeping up passersby in dragnet operations. Those captured "were marched to the precinct houses and screened." In an altogether new variation on this tactic, on July 13 they swarmed down on a group of ghetto pedestrians, "herding [them] together" into a courtyard where many more had gathered to claim their soup ration. The police closed a gate, locking everyone in, before proceeding to an inspection. "'What's wrong? Let us out! We have to carry our soup home!' screamed the women in disorderly chorus. They received no answer." The police succeeded mainly in terrorizing the population. "Everyone was scared to death. . . . The ghetto was paralyzed. Limbs went slack; throats were tight with relentless panic. The ghetto had never experienced a raid like that in the four years it had been in existence." Even then, the day's assault had been for the police a distinct disappointment. "The catch was meager." In their own fashion, though, the Jewish Order Service were proving themselves students of their German namesakes. "'We have learned something from our guards after all,' said a ghetto philosopher: 'How to hunt human beings.'"[48]

Although it was difficult to imagine them engaging in behavior more worthy of opprobrium than this, according to Hiller a distraught young woman came to him with word that Jewish policemen at Czarnieckiego Prison were approaching some of the women assembled there in advance of deportation with promises to free them in exchange for sex. She spoke of a "special room" to which these desperate souls were taken. Bursting into tears, the young woman asked if this was any way for Jewish men to treat their "sisters," and whether even Germans acted this way toward their own. Hiller had no answer for her then, though what she told him sounded like the kind of trading of sexual favors for food he knew to have occurred in the ghetto.[49]

On Friday, July 14, a tenth transport departed the ghetto with a cargo of 700 Jews; that made for 7,196 deported in the three weeks since the operation had commenced on June 23.[50] At midday on Saturday, July 15, however, Rumkowski received word from the German authorities that the transports were to be halted. Following a telephone call to inform the card ration bureau, he climbed aboard his carriage and raced "from workshop to workshop and to Central Prison" personally spreading the word. The welcome news unleashed a wave of joyous emotion. "People embraced in the streets, kissed in the workshops and departments," and rejoiced: "The resettlement's over!" Most relieved of all were those who were now released from detention. Rescued from their fate, they made their way back through the streets to their former ghetto apartments, "just four bare walls, for all belongings [had been] sold off as fast as possible. No beds, no chairs, no cabinets. They'll have to sleep on the floor, but once again, they'll manage. The ghetto dweller is like a cat, he always lands on his feet. . . . The Main Purchasing Agency will probably return everything. The Chairman will undoubtedly see to it that those returning from Central Prison and the staging areas receive assistance." The only ones likely to have felt a letdown were those who profited from the desperate comings and goings at the detention center. "After all, they were living it up, eating their fill on the misfortunes of others. But the ghetto ignores the disappointment of these few persons. All in all, a day of joy such as the ghetto has never known."[51]

But the ghetto was still on edge, watching closely for any sign of a further shift in the winds of fate. A day later, news that Biebow, stressing that he was acting at the behest of the Gestapo, had requested from Henryk Neftalin a statistical survey of the ghetto population was taken as a matter for concern. Especially worrying was the news that the survey was to account for all ghetto residents deemed unfit for work.[52] On July 18 people sensed further reason to remain on guard. Biebow had driven up quite early in the morning to a package distribution center in order to speak with Special Department director Marek Kligier. "People talk of lists that are being compiled; and no sooner do they hear the word 'list' than they jump to the conclusion that workshops must submit new lists." The chroniclers attempted to sort fact from supposition, stating, "There is not a word of truth in any of this."[53] Wednesday, July 19, brought the deadline for submission of the demanded "statistical survey," while "talk of registrations and lists" went on. "The agitation increased around noon," after Dora Fuchs was spotted on her way to 4 Kościelny Square "to fetch Neftalin—and in Biebow's car. What was going on?" people wondered. In the end, it appeared that this was merely a matter of expediency. Biebow "was about to drive to the city on urgent business, but first he demanded a change in the statistical report that had already been handed in, a change pertaining to the number of people unfit for labor, estimated at 7,000. Since a droshky would not have been fast enough, Biebow sent Miss Fuchs on the errand by car." As for Neftalin, he "proceeded to Bałut Market, took care of the matter, and that was all." Still, there was one point sure to raise alarm: among the last-minute changes, "Biebow ordered Neftalin to present the figures on children nine years of age and under according to year of birth rather than in one category."[54]

However unsettling these developments were, the Germans, anticipating the necessity of lulling the ghetto population into a state of quiescence and ignorance of their fate, had prepared a further deception. Before being shipped to their deaths at Chełmno, some had been compelled to compose reassuring notes, written on postcards, thirty-one of which arrived, stamped to indicate they had been mailed just days before, and claiming that conditions at their destination were good—indeed, far superior to those in the ghetto. Deportees were housed "in comfortable barracks" and well fed. "One card addressed to a kitchen manager says in plain Yiddish: 'Mir lakhn fun ayre zupn!' [We laugh at your soups!]." People took heart. "The ghetto is elated and hopes that similar reports will soon be arriving from all the other resettled workers. It appears to be confirmed that labor brigades are truly required in the Old Reich."[55]

Another observer knew better. He may have served in the Jewish Police or Special Department, for he wrote in his diary that on June 16, in the wake of the beating Biebow had inflicted, he had personally escorted Rumkowski to the hospital. Of the diarist's personal circumstances we know little other than that he was living with a younger sister. The diary was scribbled in the conveniently wide margins of a French-language text that had come into his hands. He wrote in Polish, in Yiddish, in Hebrew, and in English, sometimes repeating in one language what he had stated in another, perhaps hoping to improve the chances that, if discovered, his words would find their way to a reader.[56] A talented witness, he composed his anguished thoughts, hurried, anxious, yet clear-eyed, with a heart deeply embittered by an awareness of cruelties inflicted and endured.[57]

The young man had reason to be clear-eyed about what awaited those soon to be deported. On June 20, he notes, he had spent "several hours" in discussion with unidentified colleagues talking at length about Chełmno, citing the name quite openly. The very existence of such a place struck them as a sign of the utter debasement of European civilization, and it left them sickened. In the face of more immediate worries, it was difficult to measure "the depths of the tragedy." But those privy to the discussion were left badly shaken.[58] It was little wonder that he knew immediately how to interpret the significance of a letter found in a railway car being cleaned which stated that the recent transports had passed near Koło, "the place of the [']abbatoir.'"[59]

The diarist, whose father had died "of starvation" and whose mother's fate is unclear, was looking after his sister, a child of twelve. She too, he learned, had been keeping a kind of ghetto diary. Unable to resist, he peeked inside, only to be overcome in discovering there her halting attempt to find solace by looking back on her earlier years. "Many a time in the past," she wrote, "I began to write my memoirs, but by unforseen [sic] circumstances I was prevented from putting this mind-easing and soul-comforting practice into reality—to begin of those days when cares and sufferings were unknown for me." He quotes from her verse the following passage:

> Childhood's dear days
> Alas so few they were!
> That dimly only I remember
> t[h]em.
> It is only in my dream that I'm
> allowed to imagine days bygone
> Short indeed is human happiness
> in this world of ours.

"So write children," he commented, "whose only school was Teutonic life in A.D. 1944."[60] It was enough to make one wish for nothing less than an end to the entire project of creation. "If a G[h]ettonian should get power over the universe," he opined, "he would understandably not hesitate a moment and would have destroyed it and indeed! he would have done the only right thing."[61]

As July wound down, only this remained: an awareness that the end was near. But what did the end mean for the survivors of four years in which disease, starvation, and deportation had carried off the rest? Repeatedly the air raid sirens sounded in the city. German reports filtered back into the ghetto. The German high command spoke of fighting on the outskirts of Warsaw. If Warsaw were to gain its liberation, that of Litzmannstadt must surely follow. The hour was full of promise. There was undeniably a feeling in the air that all might indeed end well. Meanwhile, those still in a downcast mood were being urged by more optimistic souls to lighten up; could they not acknowledge that the long-awaited deliverance was at last at hand?[62]

The ghetto stood poised at the crossroads. Whatever the final outcome, there could be little doubt that the residents did not have long to wait for its arrival. Exhausted German troops were seen making their way along Zgierska Street and near Marysin.[63] "We are facing either apocalypse or redemption," Rosenfeld wrote in his last diary entry. "The chest dares breathe more freely already. People look at each other as if to say: 'We understand each other, right!'" Yet Rumkowski continued to caution restraint. He "knows that such looks are dangerous and he issues an order not to let the feelings of joy bubble over but to retain the same posture as before. It is still too soon. The eye of the sentry is still awake. A laugh can betray us, a cheerful face can endanger the ghetto. Therefore, quiet. Conceal it all."[64]

While there was no shortage of optimists, the pessimists still had reason to hold back; experience cautioned against giving in to wishful expectations. Rosenfeld acknowledged the wisdom of their innate reserve, saying: "The heart is marred with scars, the brain encrusted with dashed hopes. And if, at long last, the day of 'redemption' should be at the doorstep, it is better to let oneself be surprised than to experience yet another disappointment. That's human nature, this is the human mentality of Ghetto Litzmannstadt at the end of July 1944."[65] Hoping for the best, the unidentified young diarist expected the worst. He knew that the Germans were fully capable of killing his sister, killing him, killing them all, even now, even at the very end. In that case, though this was a matter of deep regret, the Germans should have done them all a favor and killed them at the beginning of this ordeal, sparing them five years of unmitigated suffering. His final words are filled with foreboding, an awareness that those who remained were marked like all the others. They had been spared for a time that was useful for their masters but now they were fit only for slaughter.[66]

On August 1, accompanied by Kligier and Jakubowicz, Rumkowski was summoned to a meeting with the local German police commander and informed that the ghetto was at last to be cleared.[67] Commencing on August 3, a total of five thousand persons were to be evacuated per day. As word of the planned operation spread, anxiety mounted. The "news hit like a bolt of lightning," wrote Jakub Poznański. "The factories emptied instantly. People ran about in a frenzy." It was clear what the Germans had in mind. Still, it was open to question whether they yet possessed the resources necessary to effect the removal of tens of thousands of ghetto workers at a time when, as Poznański and other well-informed observers knew, the front was nearby and the Red Army approaching. Under the circumstances, he thought "it would be impossible to evacuate such a large city in a few days."⁶⁸ Amid growing concern, there was at last some basis for hope. "In their hysteria, the crowds veered toward the other extreme: laughing and making jokes about evacuating 'quick as lightning,' alluding to the Nazis' notorious Blitzkrieg."⁶⁹ By early evening, speaking to his workshop managers, Rumkowski too presented a less ominous picture. "When he told them the nature of his conversations with the German authorities, they all understood that a final decision has not been made, that the date of the evacuation has not been set, that we are in the war zone (apparently 120 kilometers from the front!), and that unforeseen events might yet occur, including liberation." That, coupled with emerging word early that evening "about a possible postponement of the evacuation for 20 days" and a seemingly reliable revelation "that only machinery and goods are to be sent out, and that the people are to remain in the ghetto," Poznański felt reassured. "In my view," he wrote, "this whole affair will end up, as the proverb has it, 'light rain from a huge cloud.' Mass evacuation under present circumstances is not feasible." Even if the Jews were in the familiar position of awaiting the outcome of circumstances beyond their control, for once it seemed that the Germans too were perhaps no longer masters of their own fate. Any such evacuation, he reasoned, "will depend not on the Germans, or the Jews. The last word in this matter will come from the Red Army."⁷⁰

Indeed the Gettoverwaltung and the Gestapo seem to have been anxious about their ability to conduct another mass deportation with the same ease as in the past. Up until now coercion, deception, and, most important, division (promising continued survival of the remnant population in exchange for the surrender of the rest) had succeeded in compelling the Jews to assist in their own removal. But now, with a wholesale evacuation their announced goal, such policies had little chance of being effective. They knew that it was only a matter of time before their hold on the city would be imperiled. And so in the immediate wake of the announcement, both Biebow and Bradfisch took the extraordinary step of visiting selected workshops to address the employees in person, offering words of assurance that they wished only to make sure that the Jews survived and carried on their work on behalf of the Reich.

Early on the afternoon of Wednesday, August 2, however, "managers of the metal and tailor shops were called to Hans Biebow's office" and informed that their workers and equipment would be the first to be evacuated, beginning with the tailoring shops on Thursday, August 3, and extending through the weekend in shipments of five thousand per day, with the metal workers to follow soon after.[71] In advance of that, also on August 2, "at a public meeting in the metal shop, Biebow made a fervent request for everyone to listen to him, and leave for the Reich. His voice was especially sweet" when he referred to them as "Meine Juden" (my Jews). "He stressed that the evacuation was for the good of the ghetto population, because the front was moving toward us and the Russians would be cruel to all those who had worked for the German army." Quite possibly in response to a perceived weakening of the German position, "his entire speech was devoid of harshness and was rather a kind of pleading. For the first time in a very, very long while, the Jews could feel some sense of triumph."[72] The German charm offensive resumed during a noon meeting on Thursday, August 3, the day of the scheduled departure of the first of the tailoring shops. On this occasion, during which Rumkowski was heard "advising people to heed the German authorities," Bradfisch, speaking "in a lyrical voice, advised the Jews to leave voluntarily." Continuing to carry the seeming message of goodwill, "Biebow spoke in a few shops, growing sentimental over the fate of people whose stubbornness would keep them in the war zone. He assured everyone that the authorities were motivated by their honest desire to save the Jews from 'certain annihilation.'"[73]

The "sweet" and thoughtful words seemed to have little immediate effect. The tailors were holding back. "On Thursday morning, fewer than 100 people appeared at the Radogoszcz [Radegast] Station, but even they couldn't leave, since there were no trains."[74] The Germans appeared to be in a logistical bind. A day earlier, Poznański, offering his own "rough estimate," calculated "that 100 railway cars would be needed within a few days, just to transport people, not to mention machinery and goods. Where will they get this many cars in the present situation, on the eve of defeat?"[75] An angry response in the form of a proclamation bearing the signature of the Oberbürgermeister swiftly followed on August 4. Taking note specifically of the failure of the workers in tailoring *ressorts* numbers 1 and 2 to report for the transports, it decreed an "immediate" cutoff of rations for their family members. Food would be issued solely to those at the station. Most ominously, the notice gave unambiguous warning that the punishment for anyone found harboring their relatives was death.[76]

It was a sign of things to come. Bradfisch and Biebow, their feigned concern for the well-being of the ghetto population and assurances for their safety having fallen on deaf ears, understood that force alone remained their surest option. And so the dreary process of rounding up the population commenced. German police, reinforced by armed German firefighters, entered the ghetto to conduct the evacuation. Their chief tactic involved dividing the ghetto into sectors, throwing a blockade over several streets at a time, and forcing residents from their apartments and hiding places, bringing them downstairs, and sending them on to the transports, which had finally arrived. Once more they worked closely with the Jewish police, who, reinforced by willing auxiliaries, were sent in to conduct the preliminary sweep. On the morning of August 10 a cordon was imposed around a quadrant bordered by portions of Żydowska, Franciskańska, Brzezińska, and Kościelny streets. From his hiding place in a building on Żydowska Street, Poznański observed as events unfolded all around him. "It's 10 AM," he wrote in his diary on that day:

> We can hear rifle shots nearby. One, two, three, four, then more frequently. A new round-up has started, this time in the area where the paper shop is located. I'm watching its entire progress from our third-floor window. . . .
>
> The action takes place as follows: the German police or firemen scare people by firing a few shots. Then come the Jewish police, assisted by the ghetto firemen and chimney sweeps. This group calls the occupants of the various buildings to come down, and after a few minutes a search of apartments ensues. Often the fate of an entire family depends on the whim of a fireman or policeman; influence and the jingle of money play a big part.
>
> After the occupants are searched and sent to the assembly area, the apartments are searched again by the German authorities. All of it is accompanied by terrible crying and screaming. A veritable manhunt.

The search went on for hours. "About 2 PM, the area was finally 'cleaned out' and the operation was transferred to the other side of the bridge, where it lasted till late in the evening."[77]

Word spread that the entire western sector of the ghetto was subject to evacuation. "People who knew about it were moving *en masse* to our side," Poznański noted. "At 5 AM I went outside. There was great activity and an incredible tumult. People were running in every direction, while at the same time residents from the other side were moving into our streets in great panic. In a word: indescribable chaos. The ghetto is like a huge insane asylum."[78] On August 13 the entire area west of the bridge was placed under order of wholesale closure effective the following day, forcing everyone remaining there to abandon that part of the ghetto district. Communicating to the frightened residents via posted announcement, Rumkowski notified them that "TODAY THE WESTERN PART OF THE GHETTO MUST BE ENTIRELY CLEANED OUT. Tomorrow, Monday the 14th of August 1944, the western part will be totally closed off, so that no traffic in and out of this part will be possible."[79]

Even in the end, inhabitants of the ghetto hoping to evade transport were left to their own devices. Some, like Poznański, found refuge in hiding places, but given the threat of death in the event of discovery, the relentless search of abandoned buildings, and the withering effect of dwindling stocks of food and water, for most the effort to remain behind proved altogether too daunting. Whatever doubts the Jews may have had about the ultimate destination of the transports, the Germans appeared to be keeping their promise of providing bread and sugar to those getting on the trains. Some people, among those not yet affected by the order, were said to have headed to Marysin "just to see if the deportees were getting their promised food," and discovering that to be the case, had decided to join them then and there, without even bothering to go back home.[80]

At Radogoszcz station the trains were waiting. The Germans had promised that the ghetto residents were being relocated for work. While the extra rations seemed to offer some reassurance of this, there was disturbing evidence of a more sinister purpose. Yisroel Tabaksblat found the thousands of pieces of baggage heaped and strewn about in disorderly piles, many visibly ripped open, their contents exposed, an ominous sight. It was clear, he would later recall, that articles handled so recklessly were never intended to be returned to their owners.[81] The crowds were overwhelming. "A sea of heads and bodies. In front of us are freight cars standing wide open," Irena Liebman remembered.[82] Long planks were laid as narrow wooden gangways leading from the ground to the open doorways at the sides of the boxcars; the Jews, their weight sufficient to cause the boards beneath their feet to buckle and bow, mounted them single file and walked into the cars.[83] Family members not yet on board when a particular boxcar was declared to be filled endured the anxiety of separation. Inside the cars were oppressively crowded, "up to eighty to a hundred persons to a wagon" crammed in "like herring in a barrel." Worse, the August heat proved intense, and many found it difficult to catch their breath. Somewhat more fortunate were those whose transports journeyed not in the heat of the day but "by night."[84]

Even as Rumkowski officially urged the population to report for the trains, he apparently did not bar the issuance of rations to those who failed to do so.[85] Yakov Nirenberg recalled that Rumkowski was even willing to go a bit further, proposing to appease the Germans through a deliberate policy of partial, as opposed to full-scale, compliance. His suggestion: to buy time by deliberately restricting to "a minimum of 700–800 persons" the number deported "each day." Though short of the demanded quota, it remained a sizable number, and one, Rumkowski reasoned, likely to demonstrate to the Germans that he remained capable of ensuring that the residents would appear for the transports. Once more Rumkowski insisted that without the credible appearance of cooperation, the Germans would resort to bringing in their own men to carry out the job, an outcome he wished above all else to avoid. By Nirenberg's account, he and other ghetto representatives of the prewar Jewish Bund, a socialist faction, took a hard oppositional line, rejecting Rumkowski's proposal outright and insisting that everything in their power be done to urge the population to evade the transports.[86]

But the ghetto, bearing to the end the impress of Rumkowski's "miracle" strategy for survival, its remaining population ground down by four years of deprivation, was ill equipped to mount anything like a coordinated act of armed resistance. The fact was that Rumkowski's approach had succeeded to the extent that in the ghetto as late as the end of July, 68,561 persons were still alive. It was evident that the German army was in retreat and that the battlefront was nearing. Even without taking the risk of a direct challenge to the German police and the Gestapo, the ghetto might be overtaken by advancing Soviet forces, its people suddenly freed.[87] Or so it seemed. The detectable waves of optimism of late July suggested that Hitler and his murderous regime were not long for this world. There was plausible reason to believe that now, more than ever, staying the course might well result in survival; steadiness and above all just a bit more patience held a greater prospect of rescue than staging a last-minute rebellion. The valor of the Warsaw ghetto fighters was broadly known, but the Warsaw ghetto, as SS General Jürgen Stroop had proclaimed, was "no more."[88] Now, over a year later, the Litzmannstadt ghetto, albeit reduced in number and badly traumatized, still stood. Yet even to think about an uprising assumes that the groundwork for such an enterprise, entailing armed resistance, had been prepared, and this was decidedly not the case. Although isolated weapons had occasionally turned up in the ghetto early in its existence (and when discovered were dutifully handed over to the Germans by the Jewish police), there were no arms to be had now.[89] A small, resistance-minded independent circle associated with Daniel Weisskopf, a highly regarded and courageous doctor, "and his assistant, the teacher, Sabina Witenberg," did emerge. Their group, said to have been active in "spreading radio reports" and "carrying out acts of sabotage (fires) in several factories in February and March 1944," apparently "attempted to make contact (through a letter smuggled out with the help of Biebow's bribed chauffeur) with the Polish underground movement in the city and asked it to send weapons into the ghetto. No answer was received, and the swift liquidation action of August 1944 put an end to all daring plans."[90]

Those who did dare to evade the deportation order were on their own. Many were understandably conflicted, and there is evidence that people actively discussed the choice. Families were divided on the issue; husbands and wives, parents and children engaged in anguished arguments that spilled out of ghetto residences into the streets. "Everyone knew by now that this was liquidation," Arnold Mostowicz would recall. "It was an evening in August, nine or ten o'clock, I was in Jakuba Street—not far from my flat. There was a crowd of people who did not know what to do. They were debating, shouting, trying to persuade one another." Mostowicz caught sight of an acquaintance, an accountant, in an impassioned struggle with his spouse. Defying her wishes, he had decided to settle the matter once and for all. "With his two children he was pushing through the crowd to get to the tram. His wife was tugging at him and trying to drag the children away from him. He believed the proclamations, she didn't.

This was in the midst of the crowd which went on debating in almost total darkness—with stars as the only light." This was a moment that
Mostowicz, who was himself to be deported, could never forget, "as it is
connected to another image—that of the same man in Auschwitz, when
he already knew the meaning of the smoke billowing from the crematorium where his wife and his children had been burned."[91]

Whatever their decision, parents attended as best they could to their
children, orphaned sisters and brothers cared for younger siblings, solitary
children with no one else in the world looked to one another. Some residents took their chances in hiding; most others, at the limits of their physical endurance, hungering for bread, fearful of discovery and execution, in
the end followed the summons to report and made their way to the trains.
Everywhere in these final days people gathered clothing and possessions
and remaining bits of food for the journey. "We take along some bread,
sugar, soap, a few photographs, writing paper, and a fountain pen," Irena
Liebman would relate. Her sister, a nurse with access to potentially lethal
sleeping compounds, had "luminal and veronal in her bag, enough for the
two of us."[92] Some found occasion to bid others a final good-bye. Genia
Bryl, the educator who had long attended to the children working at the
Glazer undergarment and dress factory, met with the director one last
time. Glazer spoke of his decision to leave the ghetto with his family, Bryl
of her determination to remain behind with her young brother and her
sister. "There's in my room so many apples, so many apples. I would like
to give them to you," he unexpectedly told her.

> So I went with him to his room to get the apples. Glazer's room was
> above my Kancelarja [office]. He had his own private room there. I
> had never entered that room before. I know that he didn't have any
> other intentions other than to give me the apples. All of a sudden he
> took me into his arms, and there I was in his arms . . . it was so safe
> there. We had forgetfulness and I didn't fight him. We made love
> and we spent a few hours together. I believe that in my heart there
> was a feeling of tenderness for those horrible hours when we both
> stood in front of destruction and death.[93]

Many who had succeeded in holding off until the end of the month
were compelled to face an ultimatum. On the afternoon of Monday, August 28, there appeared a final order to report no later than six in the

evening to one of the assembly centers on Krawiecka or Czarnieckiego streets. Anyone found illegally residing in the ghetto after that would be subject to penalty of death. It was a threat to be taken with absolute seriousness. For many, the certain risks entailed in going into hiding seemed too great. In consequence, there followed a final rush to join the exodus. Jakub Poznański, one of those who, along with his wife and daughter, nevertheless chose to remain in hiding, discovered that others who had initially made the same choice had been "frightened by the notice" and in consequence had "decided to report for relocation." "Early in the morning" Poznański watched friends of his "getting ready for the trip"; they were "visibly upset, and the least sound rattled them."[94] By the time he ventured "outside in the evening" of August 28, he observed "intense activity. People are hurrying to get ready for tomorrow's transport. Everyone wants to be first. No one wants to get on the train last."[95]

In the beginning as in the end, parting and separation remained at the emotionally devastating core of private life in the ghetto. Removal from home, from the city, and from the wider world had been but a prelude to the fatal deportation of loved ones. Death, a constant, was the last unbridgeable divide. In this final hour no one wished to be alone or abandoned. Dressed in his ample raincoat and with the simple briefcase in which he carried his camera, Mendel Grossman remained faithful to his task to the end, never ceasing to document in photographs the ragged columns of Jews marching through Marysin on their way to the trains.[96] Long aware of the need to preserve his unique visual record, he had made a point of distributing prints among his circle of friends. In advance of his own departure later that autumn—Grossman would be assigned to a labor force that would stay in the ghetto until October—he prepared the remaining images from his collection for safekeeping, placing them in jars and burying them inside the walls of a hiding place in the hope that they might be recovered at war's end. On these precious strips of film were preserved both the streets and buildings of the ghetto and the faces of those who inhabited that unfortunate domain.[97]

With the end approaching, Rumkowski had cast aside all doubts. He knew that his critics, if granted the opportunity, would excoriate him for his actions, yet to the end he remained headstrong, even defiant. He feared neither the Germans, even though his life might soon be lost at their hand, nor the Jews, who, if given the chance, would surely subject him to the harshest of judgments. He was prepared to face any tribunal. He had lived a full life and, in his own eyes, had acquitted himself well and to the best of his abilities. He took pride in having devoted his energies to the task of rescuing lives, and while fully conscious of the terrible human losses the ghetto had endured throughout his tenure, he took saitisfaction in pointing to the presence even now of so sizable a remnant. Such had been the gist of Rumkowski's own musings during the course of a private, informal talk he had with the director of his tobacco department, Solmon Uberbaum, one Sunday during the summer of 1944, some "two months before the liquidation of the Ghetto." Speaking openly and in confidence, he admitted, by Uberbaum's account, to outbursts of temper in which he physically lashed out at people. "Because I'm irritable. . . . I can't control myself," he confided. Rumkowski contrasted his decision to remain in charge with that of Adam Czerniaków, who until his suicide in July 1942 had directed the Judenrat in Warsaw. He praised the man's courage but pointedly argued that his act had had no practical consequences. "But what happened afterwards[?]" Uberbaum recalled Rumkowski as saying:

> They liquidated the Warsaw ghetto. I am sitting here today (July or August 1944). There are 78,000 Jews in the Ghetto. And the Russians are advancing! They have already reached Lublin. They're approaching Warsaw. If I save 78,000 Jews. 60,000. 50,000. I'm not afraid of anything. What will they do to me? I'm an old Jew. Sick. I have no children. . . . So what will be? I think I will save some of the Jews. All my work here is to save as many as possible. Afterwards . . . if I survive, let them try me. Let them! I don't care.[98]

Rumkowski had remained in the ghetto until the final days. But his turn had finally come. Unable to secure Biebow's permission to free his own relations from the transports, Rumkowski agreed to join them. And so, in the end, Rumkowski too boarded the train.[99] Biebow had finished with him. There would be no further meetings between the two at Bałut Market, and for Rumkowski no more demands to which he must accede. The population over which he had presided had gradually vanished from the ghetto; since January 1942 they had set out, one human mass following another, wave upon wave upon wave, and now he too was carried off with the last. For the Germans, the ghetto had served its purpose; its time had passed, and with it the need for such a leader. To them he was a Jew as worthy of disposal as any other. Already of an advanced age at the start, he was an even older man now who bore like a heavy cloak the accumulated weight of nearly five years of leading his community through its darkest time. At last the burdens of office were lifted from his shoulders; yet his decisions, his deeds and misdeeds both personal and public, were irrevocable, their consequences never to be undone. As the train bearing him and his small extended family glided out along the rails through the northern outskirts of Litzmannstadt, Rumkowski went the way of all the rest. He had chosen to remain at his post and, yes, to stay alive a few years longer, and he had accomplished all that was possible under impossible circumstances, even at great cost to his fragile reputation and honor. He knew that the Germans had humiliated him and his people, and on one unforgettable occasion he had been physically bloodied and battered. For all that, he was a man of many years; he had tasted life's offerings and enjoyed his portion. He would not be forgotten. In a verbal exchange with an unknown challenger he is said to have exclaimed: *What are you telling me about Jewish history? I am myself a piece of Jewish history.*[100] He at least would find his place there. To the very end he held on, he cooperated. We shall never know whether, in stepping aboard the railway car, he dared acknowledge that now his life was forfeit. But of this we can be certain: like all the transports before it, the train left the Radogoszcz ghetto station, passing again through the outer reaches of the city, this time bearing Rumkowski—a self-made man, and in his own peculiar way one assuredly possessing a real knack for creating something out of nothing—into the the void.[101]

In the final days of August, even before the departure of the last transport, city agencies set about the task of clearing the ghetto and reclaiming salvageable property and infrastructure. The initial task demanded the creation of a commission to assess the viability of ghetto buildings and identify those deemed structurally sound and—after thorough cleaning, including clearance of usable furnishings and household articles and disinfection—suitable for new occupancy. Structures deemed defective and a loss were to be demolished. For this purpose the city Building Department, with its urban planning division in the lead, and working closely with the Gettoverwaltung and the city's health, finance, and property departments, directed an inspection of individual buildings within the emptied zone.[102] Operating sector by designated sector, inspectors conducted an on-site selection: buildings to be saved were marked with a "large red circle," those to be destroyed with a "large red cross."[103] By mutual agreement, for the purpose of supplying needed household items to ethnic German settlers, the Volksdeutsche Mittelstelle(Vomi), the welfare agency that tended to their needs, was accorded first choice of household articles and furnishings left behind in ghetto residences; "fabric, raw materials, and finished goods," however, were to remain in the possession of the Building Department in advance of sale to "third parties."[104]

The work of clearing ghetto buildings, courtyards, and toilets, described in the administrative correspondence as being of a thoroughly "disgusting nature" *(ekelerregender Art),* would necessitate supplying non-Jewish workers with supplemental rations, including butter, prepared foodstuffs, sugar, and, once again to counteract nausea, milk. Provision of these staples, it was hoped, would contribute to making the workers healthier and therefore more resistant to a range of illnesses, including tuberculosis and typhus, to which close contact with such an unsanitary environment would expose them. Citing the precedent of like distributions to those who handled the dead, a weekly ration of a half liter of alcohol was strongly recommended as a means of overcoming the sheer odiousness of their labors.[105] When it came to excrement removal—the very worst of these tasks—there was no question that Jews alone were to be engaged. Undoubtedly, Marder indicated, new toilets would have to be installed, but this could only be done after the emptying of abundant waste from existing outhouses and cesspits. For that job city workers quite simply could not be spared, nor should they be. The distasteful undertaking, he stressed, would be left for Jews to complete. Conceding the labor-intensive nature of the task, the Gettoverwaltung estimated that "at least 250" workers would have to be assembled to handle the job.[106]

Even the task of clearing out abandoned ghetto residences proved an overwhelming assignment, as Bendet Hershkovitsch, delegated to one of the cleanup operations, later recalled: "We shuddered when we entered the apartments and found everything just as the people had left it, but in place of the owners there were mice and flies. There were cases when corpses were found in the beds. These were such as had hidden out during the deportation and later died from thirst or illness. In one such place, an entirely bitten up body was found."[107] Two camps were established within the ghetto to house the necessary contingent of Jewish workers. Five hundred persons, men as well as women, including "30 children," were bivouacked at 36 Łagiewnicka Street. Most of the team had been handpicked by longtime ghetto workshops bureau chieftain Aron Jakubowicz, whose request to avoid deportation Biebow had honored.[108] "Officially, the 500 people were all needed for production. In fact," noted Hershkovitsch, "there were 100 real workers and the rest were people whom Jakubowicz wanted to do a favor; the majority were managers with their families."[109] Jakubowicz and his people were to assist in sorting through recovered belongings and service a prefabricated housing operation to be disassembled and shipped to a new location in Germany.[110] An additional work crew, numbering between five hundred and "nearly 1,000," was installed at a second location, 16 Jakuba Street.[111]

The city Medical Department, on guard as ever against all potential sources of contagion emanating from the Jewish district, identified the tasks that demanded immediate attention. Salvageable bedding and clothing could not, as a general rule, be chemically disinfected in any effective way on-site. Sealing apartments in preparation for localized chemical disinfection was impossible where windows failed to close and door panels had been "knocked out." Consequently, before textiles could be safely distributed to new owners, they would have to be loaded into vehicles and driven to a municipal sanitary installation in order to undergo steam treatment. Moreover, prior to releasing former ghetto apartments for later occupancy, vermin would have to be dealt with. In fact, apartments were found to be so badly infested with what were described as veritable bee-like "swarms" of flies that the insects would have to be combated by any and all means.[112] Above and beyond employment of available insecticides, the Health Department hit upon a simple and promising remedy: a homemade concoction consisting of a mixture of formalin (a solution of formaldehyde and water) and beer would be applied with brushes and sticks to surfaces or pooled in dishes strategically placed about the rooms.[113]

Elsewhere, with an eye toward resupplying the depleted inventory of municipal hospitals, city medical officers took a special interest in acquiring from the ghetto's own hospitals abandoned medical hardware, linens, and clothing. Among items "secured" from ghetto stocks in late September and early October were microscopes, surgical instruments, gynecological exam tables, operating tables, wheeled instrument tables, instrument cabinets, operating lamps, sunlamps, sterilization units, lidded bowls, scales, wastebaskets, dental forceps, dentists' chairs, a foot-activated dental drill, a dental x-ray unit, a wheeled stretcher, a maternity bed, and a box of eyeglasses.[114] Cleaned and ready, in one five-day period between September 21 and September 25 alone, great quantities of serviceable textiles were delivered to Bałut Market from the ghetto hospital on Mickiewicza Street, among them nurses' caps, doctors' coats, operating gowns, bed sheets, pillowslips, covers, hand towels, shirts, undergarments, trousers, sweaters, scarves, nightgowns, and pajamas. Specifically for children, there were sheets, flannel blankets, bibs, diapers, blouses, trousers, underwear, bathing trunks, pajamas, and—together accounting for more than 2,200 separate articles—little dresses, little jackets, little shirts, and little caps, each of these diminutively categorized *Kleidchen, Jäckchen, Hemdchen,* and *Mützchen* painstakingly counted and added to the list.[115]

Meanwhile, assisting in overseeing the systematic clearance and dismantling of the ghetto over which he had ruled so long, Hans Biebow veered ever further in the direction of unrestraint and violence. His pummeling of Rumkowski in June 1944 was but the latest outburst of a man increasingly exercising physical as well as administrative force. Now, as the end approached, Biebow's personal behavior became cruel, not to say outlandish. Sacrificing whatever remained of his personal dignity, he had taken to entering the Jewish women's quarters on Jakuba Street and ordering the young women to lie down on their beds and strip off their clothing while he watched.[116] In a further outrage, behind the locked door of an office at 36 Łagiewnicka Street he assaulted the teenaged daughter of a ghetto physician, Dr. Simha Mandels. Interrupted in the act (to get him to stop, witnesses pelted the door and rang the office phone), Biebow fired a gun and fled the scene. The young woman was removed naked and badly wounded. Summoned to her assistance, Dr. Michał Eliasberg discovered her face "covered in clotted blood," the result of a bullet that had entered "the back of [her] neck" and exited her left eye socket. "She was conscious," Dr. Eliasberg would testify in 1947. "In response to my question, what had happened to her, she replied: 'I was shot,' and did not want to say more. Biebow shot her, but all circumstances indicated that she had been raped."[117]

Only days later Dr. Mandels, along with "his wife, and three children," were put aboard a vehicle carrying six ghetto tailors and driven to Chełmno.[118] Upon their arrival at the camp, the tailors, each carrying a sewing machine, were ordered out and sent to work; the Mandelses were pointedly ordered to remain put. The vehicle proceeded to the forest. Two hours later the family's belongings were shipped back to the worksite; the men, barely initiated into the workings of the camp, were "stunned" by the realization that the family had been killed.[119] A similar fate befell longtime director of the ghetto health department Dr. Wigdor Miller and his family as well. Singling out Dr. Miller, Biebow had him shipped off to Chełmno. A day later he came to get Miller's wife and the couple's eight-year-old son. Sensing the threat, the boy became wild with fear (jak opętany). One witness to his terror recalled, "I can never forget how, at that moment, the boy ran away and screamed, 'Save me, I want to live.'"[120]

Although the process of killing had since shifted to Auschwitz, in Chełmno there was still work to be done. Bags of ground-up, powdered bones had to be hauled away, lifted onto shoulders, and poured from a bridge into the fast-rushing current of a nearby river. Henryk Kruszczynski, a young bookkeeper working on a nearby property, was an eyewitness to these peculiar errands. Through the experience of his own senses (he would testify to the characteristic greasy smell of burning corpses and the unmistakable "pillar of smoke [słup dymu]" rising over the forest) he had long been aware of what was happening in Chełmno.[121] One night—he thought it was sometime during the summer of 1944—with word circulating that human remains were being disposed of nearby, he went to have a look. At around eleven o'clock at night he saw a vehicle drive up onto the bridge spanning the river Warta. A group of men in uniform got out and lifted sacks onto their shoulders. With flashlights to guide them in the dark, they appeared intent on seeking out a spot below where the current ran the swiftest before emptying the contents of those sacks into the water. The men went about their task "silently," afterwards sweeping the bridge clean with a broom. In the early hours of the following morning, men could be seen digging out human debris from the crevices of the bridge, apparently in a follow-up effort to clear the site of any overlooked traces.[122] Some evidence must have remained, however, for Franciszek Kazmierski, owner of a nearby mill who, like Kruszczynski, had been a witness on more than one occasion to these same late-night visits to the bridge, recalled that the crew once left behind a paper sack. Daring to approach, he looked inside the bag, finding there "tiny, shattered pieces of bone."[123]

Through the summer and autumn Sonderkommando Bothmann continued to oversee the extensive task of processing goods forcibly abandoned by the victims. Valuables, including suitcases full of watches and chains, were separated out and sent on to the Gettoverwaltung.[124] Meanwhile, Jewish workmen assigned to the Hauskommando on the former estate grounds at Chełmno (close by the granary that served as their nightly prison) were given the task of sorting, repairing, sanitizing, and recycling salvageable textiles. Earlier, while the transports were still under way, the work had gone on in two barracks situated in an adjoining park.[125] Sometime afterward, however, lending to the operation a "carnival"-like dimension,[126] "the central part of the palace courtyard" was occupied by "a circus tent," described as "about 80 m long, 15 m wide, and about 8 m high," where "the victims' clothes were sorted and searched." Unusable items "were shredded into fibers" by means of a steam-powered device supplied by the ghetto. The team assigned to this task, no fewer than forty Jewish workers, many of them young men ranging in age from seventeen to twenty, prepared the clothing in advance of distribution to needy ethnic German and Polish laborers.[127] The mayor of the nearby town of Dąbie visited the camp to collect articles for distribution to German residents.[128] Jewish tailors were also put to work fashioning various articles "for the Sonderkommando and various German dignitaries," among them Bothmann, Greiser, and Biebow. Items considered unsalvageable or of no value—"old clothes, papers, photographs"—were committed to the flames, "burnt in a ground hole at the edge of the park, next to three apple trees. . . . The fire was burning there day and night."[129]

In the interests of removing the final traces of the crime, in Rzuchowski Forest the two cone-shaped underground ovens used to incinerate the human remains were systematically dismantled, the first of the two "by August, 1944, because transports were coming to a halt," noted Walter Piller, Bothmann's deputy, the second "in January 1945."[130] Here too nothing recyclable was to go to waste. In the autumn of 1944 the SS carried away a shipment of bricks that had been removed in the course of dismantling the crematoriums to be used at a local estate.[131]

The city too was compelled to attend to the mounting necessities of the hour. On the last day of August it was reported that the Musikschule on Danzigerstraße had just completed the very last of its locally famed open-air "Little Evening Music" summer performances in the conservatory garden. Conducting the city orchestra one last time, Adolf Bautze had selected for the occasion works by Grieg and Haydn. After the dying of the slow final movement of the latter's "Emperor Quartet," the evening concluded with the playing of "four variations on the melody of the *Deutschlandlied*," its beloved sounds "the last . . . with which the orchestra and its deserving conductor took leave of their loyal listeners."[132]

There had been an unavoidable note of wistful finality to the performance. Bowing to the exigencies of wartime, the city's cultural institutions, embodiment and symbol of Litzmannstadt's revived Germanic identity, were compelled to abandon their audiences. Appreciatively, one reviewer looked back on the musical events of the past years. Who could forget the opening performance of the city opera, where, only two years earlier, on November 5, 1942, *Hansel and Gretel* had premiered? Though encountering difficulties from the start, the opera had in the end proved a success, as had the staging of ballet.[133] And now, after a season in which more than 300,000 visitors had attended 572 performances of theater, operetta, opera, and dance, the time had come for city theaters to fall silent and shut their doors.[134] Apart from those facing imminent military call-up, actors and actresses, singers and dancers, and musicians were compelled to join the remaining theatrical personnel in contributing their labor to the war effort. In September, stage artists were photographed setting out en masse for a local factory where, upon completing labor registration and receiving cards entitling them to food and work uniforms, they would take up their new assignments. One reporter still looked forward to the day when they might return to exercising their original craft,

at such future time when the theaters would once again entertain, as they
had done so effectively throughout these past seasons of Litzmannstadt's
cultural revival.[135] Until then, providing popular diversion was left to the
city's many movie houses. To the very end, the Ufa-Casino, the Capitol,
the Europa, the Ufa-Rialto, the Palast, the Adler, the Corso, the Gloria,
the Mai, the Mimosa, the Muse, the Palladium, and the Roma advertised
popular cinematic entertainments.[136]

In a report on the occasion of the fifth anniversary of the city's incorporation into the Reich, the Gauleiter stressed the year's major accomplishment, namely, the arrival of some 250,000 resettlers from the region of the
Black Sea. In addition, local residents could once again take pride in the
Gau's record birthrate of 27.6 per thousand, well in excess of the 16.1 per
thousand that marked the norm for the Reich as a whole.[137] In the end as
in the beginning, the regime's goal was to reclaim the land as the precondition for peopling it with those of German stock, and to create the conditions suitable for German life and reproduction. Without regard to the
losses this entailed for others, in the interests of creating a healthful environment Litzmannstadt was to be a city cleansed of Jews. A city free of
Jews was by definition a city free of disease. This was the central tenet of
the new German city, and though of little substance beyond the tissue
of myths and lies that enveloped its core beliefs, these assumptions, proclaimed and acted upon by the leadership, propagated day after day, year
upon year by the intellectual elite that served the regime's journalistic and
cultural institutions, continued to find expression, even as the great project neared collapse. Hans-Jürgen Seraphim, director of the Osteuropa
Institut in Breslau, interviewed on the occasion of the publication of a
new issue of its journal, *Ostraum-Berichte,* asserted unequivocally that in
spite of the "temporary" loss of "influence" over the territories of the German East, "now more than ever" it was necessary to proceed with scientific investigation of the East and its future. The research was essential,
and the institute would carry out this work, which it deemed not merely
of significance to Germany but a task of "pan-European" importance, indeed "of service to all humanity!"[138]

Still opening wide its arms to beleaguered Germanic brethren, the leadership wished to be known as open-hearted toward those most in need. In December, with Gauleiter Greiser presiding, a conference on the economic integration of ethnic German refugees from Russian lands was held in the main auditorium of the Reich University in Posen. Before an audience of representatives of the German refugee community, officials reviewed with pride the successful reception of some 40,000 families, numbering an estimated 200,000 souls; already, it was reported, "2,000 families had been settled onto farmsteads [*Höfe*] ranging in size from ten to forty hectares." Impressively, over 5 million Reichsmarks had been expended on food for the newcomers; to them had been distributed some 2 million assorted articles, 1.3 million of them new and 700,000 used; they had been issued "around 277,000 pairs of shoes." Conveying to them Himmler's telegraphed regards, the Gauleiter spoke of his own warm feelings for the settlers and expressed his appreciation that their families comprised so many children, who were sure to be of "great assistance in the fulfillment" of the "great task" of promoting the "Germanization of this Gau and its soil."[139]

The most precious thing of all was the German child. Throughout the summer and the autumn, thoughts were directed to the needs of children. On successive July mornings a visiting Berlin radio celebrity, Adele Proesler, had read "fairy tales and ballads" to Litzmannstadt schoolchildren. In an atmosphere of "breathless stillness," reciting a maudlin tale, she evoked the voice of an old man who, though long dead, called from his grave to youngsters passing through a churchyard, offering to each the gift of a succulent pear.[140] As a special treat to the very young, in early September it was announced that children "up to ten years of age" were eligible to be registered for a 250-kilogram distribution of honey.[141] As in seasons past, time and effort were devoted to creating toys for deserving youngsters. The war still continued, but as the Nazi Party motto, visible in official displays, proclaimed: "Even so we celebrate Christmas!" With an eye to helping the less fortunate, and in recognition of the special needs of the children of the Warthegau's newest wave of arrivals, Hitler Youth busily constructed toys for young German settlers from the Black Sea.[142] Similarly, women of the NS Frauenschaft organized popular evening courses to teach the basics of toy making; grandmothers were said to be among the eager trainees.[143] At Post Office number 1, visitors crowded before a glass barrier to admire a display of stuffed and wooden animals, party games, dollhouses and buggies, jumping jacks, toy soldiers, and tanks.[144]

The hour was late. Litzmannstadt, city of high aspirations, the fruit of noble conquest, now stood in the path of a powerful enemy poised to advance in its direction. On this city, its people, and their future the regime had staked much, investing it with the promise of their vision of a new German metropolis, clean and modern, its citizenry well housed, healthy, culturally sophisticated, ethnically proud and pure. Because of the leadership's efforts to record its accomplishments on film, highlights had been preserved for all the world to see. If nothing else, at least this much would remain. But the film had yet to be completed, though the task was as vital as ever. During the first week in July a copy was packed away for safekeeping "in the cold-storage cellar of the Staemmler Hospital."[145] On August 23, from the Ufa studios in Berlin came word that, although the negatives were to be preserved, "for reasons of security" the remaining film positives were going to have to be destroyed. The studio was therefore anxious to learn whether the city would approve of the film in its present form.[146] Released from storage, the film was delivered to a downtown theater for presentation to an audience of municipal officers on October 5 and 6.[147] Writing to the studio, a city official, who remained upbeat in his assessment, conveyed the audience's considerable approval of the latest version. Still, he underscored, there was work to be done. There was dissonance in the synchronizing of images and sound, and the film's tempo was still too slow. To "enliven" it *(um in den Film ein lebhafteres Tempo hineinzubringen)*, he suggested inserting elements of photomontage. Well into the autumn the film work occupied the attention of the municipal leadership. The studio was informed that Bürgermeister Marder would arrange to meet with representatives in Berlin to go over these matters in person.[148]

But time was running short. On December 10 it was announced that acting Oberbürgermeister Bradfisch, summoned to expanded duties as commander of the security police, was stepping down from his post. On this occasion as well it was reported that Marder had recently been called to military service, creating a second significant vacancy at the top of the municipal administration. In their stead, combining in one office the duties of both Bradfisch and Marder, a Dr. Trautwein, formerly

Bürgermeister and city councilman in the Gau capital, Posen, was stepping in as Oberbürgermeister of Litzmannstadt.[149] At police headquarters
too there had been a change of leadership. In November it was announced that Police President Karl Wilhelm Albert, in office since suc-
ceeding Johannes Schäffer in the spring of 1940, had accepted a new post
as Regierungspräsident in the Warthegau town of Hohensalza. Danzig
Police President SS-Oberführer Stein was to be his replacement. With "his
personal drive and his special liveliness," reported the *Litzmannstädter
Zeitung,* Albert was going to be missed.[150]

In the face of the deteriorating military situation, efforts were under way
to prepare for the city's defense, including attempts to procure gas masks
for air raid shelters. In addition, workers were being assigned to dig forti-
fications. City officials hesitated only in going ahead with plans for digging mass graves—a potential necessity in the event of the worst—out of
consideration for the alarm this might arouse among the public.[151] Yet in
spite of outward signs of readiness, in the end the city and the provincial
authorities proved slow to react to the peril of the Soviet advance, which
was launched westward from the line of the river Vistula on January 12.
By later official admission, they had utterly failed to organize a timely and
orderly evacuation. Most of the city's German population stayed put. The
Food and Economy Office, working from rationing records, estimated
that of approximately 140,000 Germans in the city early in the previous
year, some 100,000 were still in residence. The new mayor, however,
thought that the actual number was far greater, for living in the homes of
the residents were relatives and others who had come to stay with them in
the hope of escaping the bombardment of their cities deeper inside the
Reich. In addition, by mid-January many residents who had left the city
were now drifting back.[152]

As late as Monday, January 15, with Soviet forces on the move, life in
Litzmannstadt continued to function largely as normal. There were few
evident signs of people readying for departure; even financial institutions
were experiencing no noticeable pressure from withdrawals. Not until five
o'clock in the afternoon on January 16 was an initial evacuation ordered.
With that, the situation quickly deteriorated. Adding to the rapidly developing anxiety and confusion, early that evening, for the first time the city

was subject to an hour-long bombardment. By the time the first evacuation train departed, it was one o'clock the following afternoon, January 17, fully twenty hours later, and the city was under renewed attack. People swarmed the main railway station, with the result that the approaches became indescribably crowded. By late in the afternoon the mounting panic was intense, and remained palpable into the night as people streamed toward "the main roads leading west from the city."[153] Long spared the immediate experience of combat, yet now under fire at the very moment of disorganized flight, the citizens were terrified.[154] To be sure, many longtime German inhabitants, including a contingent of local fire department personnel, chose to remain, but all others, desperate to get out, were now left to their own devices. In advance of the potential evacuation, the authorities had promised that sufficient vehicles would be at the ready to speed the population's departure. The reassurance proved false. Apart from transport arranged for select city officials, such means failed to materialize. Untold numbers would succeed in climbing aboard military transports—for by now fleeing German units were streaming through the city—thereby effecting a quicker exit, but the rest had no other option than to set out on foot on an arduous, poorly guided "trek" in disorganized columns along "snow- and ice-covered paths." The terror of fleeing the city by night was intensified by artillery attack—rounds were reported striking "in the vicinity of the zoo"—and the chance of encountering Soviet tanks in the distance or Soviet aircraft overhead.[155]

There were few to lead the exodus. City hall employees, anxious to get themselves and their families to safety, left their posts to arrange their own transport to towns beyond the immediate line of fire. Shortly past midnight on January 18, top city officials rode out of town in an evacuation coordinated with the regional leadership. Apart from the destruction of unspecified sensitive municipal documents, many records had to be left behind. Employees of the City Savings Bank, however, managed to remove essential financial records, spiriting them away and securing them in another location behind the lines. But that was all. In practical terms, the city administration had abandoned Litzmannstadt and its remaining citizenry to their fate.[156]

For the killers and their helpers as well, it was high time to end it all and depart. With the Red Army bearing down on the region, in Chełmno too the murderers had to close down operations and flee. Late on the night of January 17–18 the men came for the remaining Jewish work crews, housed in their cold quarters in the granary on the grounds of the former manor house, to lead them away to execution. Living unbearably with the knowledge of what the Germans had done to their neighbors and families, they were aware that the ghetto had been in large measure emptied into this godforsaken place. In advance of what they knew to be their own impending death, several of the men had succeeded in committing to paper an anguished account of their final journey to Chełmno. They related the murders of family members which they themselves had witnessed. They poured out their grief, their bitterness, and their fury at the Germans.

One of the most eloquent, Israel Zygelman, looked back on the death of both of his children in the ghetto, one an infant who had died of starvation, the other, his "most precious treasure," carried off during the evacuation of September 1942. Recalling the day in mid-July 1944 when he too was at last sent off to what he had thought would be "a labor camp," his wife had expressed yet a measure of hope, "uttering these words: 'Maybe you will come across a camp for children and see our dear child,'" he would write, "as if she felt I was going to follow in our child's footsteps." He would not find that child, but he knew with certainty that this was the place where it had been taken and murdered.[157] Deeply frustrated at their inability to strike out at their killers, the men exhorted the world to show no mercy in punishing the unspeakable crimes which they had been the last to witness. "If you happen to find any trace of the Germans, rub it off from the face of the earth, just as they have done to us," Zygelman would write in his final message, composed on January 9. "On behalf of 47 comrades, I ask you who remain alive, to avenge our and your wives, children and all those innocent people killed in the most bestial manner. Kill and burn their wives and children, just as they killed and burnt ours. I beg you once more: fulfill our request, because this is our last request before death."[158]

On the night of the execution the men of the SS-Sonderkommando in Chełmno came for the remaining forty-seven Jewish men, driving up to their prison-like quarters in the locked granary on the grounds of the ruined manor house. With the site illuminated by the glare of headlights, the men were ordered to come out, five at a time, and lie on the ground, face down, and then each was shot. One of their number,

Szymon Srebrnik, the teenager transferred to Chełmno from the Litzmannstadt ghetto in the spring of 1944, took a bullet in the neck. The
round entered his mouth and pierced his cheek and nostril, but to his unexpected good fortune did not prove fatal. Immediately after the initial
batches of victims had been led out, Mordka Żurawski, pulling a knife,
succeeded in rushing the exit, slashing at his captors, and in spite of being
struck by a bullet in the leg, successfully fled the scene. Two of the Germans upon entering the granary were unexpectedly attacked by the remaining prisoners and killed, one hanged, the other "shot . . . with his
own weapon." In the midst of the chaos, the Germans set the structure
ablaze, trapping the remaining prisoners in the flames and firing on any
who tried to flee. Żurawski and Srebrnik would be the only two still alive
when, on January 19, a Soviet unit arrived in the village, putting an end to
the horror.[159]

In the ghetto a similar gruesome fate was to have been in store for the
members of the remaining Jewish workforce. Inside the Jewish cemetery
"nine large ditches"—mass graves, each one thought sufficient to accommodate a hundred dead—had already been dug "the week before." But
alerted to the approach of the Russians—not only had the ghetto workers
got hold of a radio, but also the powerful sight and sound of Soviet bombardment was evident even from their enclosure—and hearing on the evening of the seventeenth that the Germans would call them to assemble
as a group the next day, most of the Jewish laborers went into hiding. By
the time a convoy of vehicles pulled up at the remaining ghetto work
quarters to take them to the cemetery, all but a small number had fled,
many into hidden bunkers and shelters. In consequence, and in the face
of the impending arrival of the Soviet troops, the plan to execute the last
of the Jews of the ghetto was foiled. Jakub Poznański, along with his wife
and daughter, ducked into a deep cellar at 10 Żydowki Street, where they
were joined by dozens of others determined to wait out the final hours of
the drama.[160] On January 19 the Russians entered the city. Poznański
would recall the sound of a voice high overhead, shouting down to them.
Was this "a provocation" designed to lure them to their death or a genuine announcement of their liberation? But then the voice called to them
by name. Poznański and some of the other men took their chances and
emerged to find that word of their rescue was true. Spurred on by the
sound of additional voices, they raced toward the bottom of Franciskańska

Street. The gate was open. Just beyond, on Smugowa Street, a Soviet tank was surrounded by well-wishers. A small contingent of Soviet vehicles and soldiers on foot and mounted on horseback soon arrived as well. An officer, seated in a vehicle, reported that a new government had been installed.[161] The ghetto was no more.

Epilogue

The ghetto had died, and along with it the vital and populous Jewish community of Łódź, among the largest in Europe, one of many centers of Jewish life that the Nazis wiped from the face of the earth. A loss so devastating brought shock and sadness but also, understandably, not a small measure of recrimination as well.

Less than two decades after the end of the war, the role of the Jewish leadership in the ghettos became a topic of explosive controversy. Spurred by Hannah Arendt's accusation that by their cooperation with German demands the Jewish Councils worsened the human costs to European Jewry under Nazi occupation, historians familiar with a broader range of sources decisively challenged and modified the single-mindedness of that view. To Isaiah Trunk in particular, a pioneering researcher of that time, we owe a fuller picture of Jewish leadership responses to oppression in the ghettos of Eastern Europe. Without discounting a predominant pattern of coerced submission on the part of Jewish leaders and the ghetto police, his investigation, and that of others to follow, revealed overlooked instances in which courageous Jewish leaders refused to submit to German demands, and even offered clandestine support for nascent Jewish resistance efforts.[1]

Rumkowski was not alone among Jewish leaders in assiduously clinging to a policy of amelioration of hardships, "rescue through labor," and delay.[2] He and other leaders wagered everything on the remaining hope that by working hard and demonstrating the ghetto's usefulness to the German war effort, they might stave off indefinitely the day when the ghetto would be dissolved and its inhabitants sent the way of all the other Jews. According to this strategy, no matter how crushing the force deployed against them, the Jews could take solace in the expectation that with the defeat of German arms, German power over them would cease. Should the ghetto still be standing at war's end, those who remained would go free. By working diligently to satisfy the very real economic interests of their overlords, it was hoped that the number surviving to see that long-awaited day would be substantial indeed. It was a desperate calculus, but the cost of acting on the alternatives—sabotaging production in the workshops, preparing hiding places in the event of future roundups, or, most especially, refusing outright to comply with German orders to assemble quotas of residents for deportation—was all but certain to be the ruthless suppression and deportation of the remaining population. Each day the working Jews of the ghetto returned safely to their beds seemed a small victory, each day completed and crossed off the calendar a day that brought the community closer to the moment of its hoped-for salvation.

Ultimately, in Łódź both the leaders and the led were in an untenable position. Their masters were nothing if not cunning, and what they had prepared for the Jews of the ghetto and their leaders was genuinely "a trap."[3] The trap was both material and psychological. For the Jews possessed neither the freedom nor the means to earn their livelihoods and care for their dependent brethren, as they had in times of peace and freedom. In the ghetto they were captives subject to an overwhelming force, the exercise of which they had had ample occasion to observe and to fear. Up to a point, Rumkowski and the Jewish leadership could and did successfully pursue a tried and true strategy of "intercession" and reluctant cooperation with their oppressors. Strange and unforeseen as it surely was for the Jews to be thrust in the midst of the twentieth century back into the restricted enclosure of a ghetto, as an institution the ghetto was still one they could approach with a degree of familiarity. Even enslavement, serving one's oppressor through work, was not without precedent. What is more, the work the Jews were now required to perform was recognizably purposeful: the dresses and coats, hats and shoes, and the host of accesso-

ries they produced were purchased and worn by Germans; German soldiers could and would use all the belts, trousers, shirts, caps, and boots the
Jews stitched for them. The ghetto's overseers signed contracts with suppliers, raw materials flowed in, the work was done, and real income was
generated, all to the benefit of the productionist-minded administrators
who governed life in the ghetto. From this labor the ghetto received little—indeed in material terms far less than required to maintain itself
without having to endure inordinate suffering and death. But at least outwardly the system within which the ghetto functioned was "rational." It
made sense. The Jews were being exploited. That was unfair, hurtful, and
cruel. Innocent people, among them the very young, were dying. And yet
to all appearances the ghetto functioned according to comprehensible
principles that conformed to the way one understood the world to function in times of adversity.[4]

Then, almost imperceptibly at first, yet decisively and fatally, the context of this relationship changed. In 1941, the widening campaign of annihilation against the Jews in Soviet-occupied eastern Poland, the Baltic
states, and Russia, followed by the establishment at Chełmno of the first
of the death camps, signified a radicalization of the destruction.[5] Never
before in their long history of persecution had the Jews experienced an assault of such magnitude and design.

An unforeseen chasm had opened up before the victims, and the Germans, who alone knew the way, led them blindfolded toward the preci-
pice. Over its edge the Jews fell to their intended wholesale destruction.
As has often been remarked, what the Germans did exceeded the limits of
common perception. A place like Chełmno, to speak again only of this
one example of the unfolding network of destruction, had never existed
before. It was new to the planners, a bold invention surprising even to
them, and they were astonished and delighted that, initial technical difficulties aside, their novel conception worked so well. Alone in seeing the
wider picture, knowing for certain both the functional details and the full
scope of the killing operations, the Nazis easily got the jump on their victims. It is understandable that there would be a lag in understanding after
the first information began leaking out and, even then, much skepticism
about the veracity of the reports. People were being herded into the back
of a truck, asphyxiated within minutes, their bodies immediately buried
or burned in a remote forest setting. Who had heard of such a thing? The

difficulty in understanding not just this but the overall plan of destruction presented a challenge to the world as a whole, and to the leaders and residents of the ghettos in particular.[6]

It remains difficult to pinpoint exactly when and with what precision Rumkowski fully comprehended that those whom his police delivered to the trains were journeying to a certain death. There seems little doubt, however, that by the time when, on that terribly hot Friday afternoon of September 4, 1942, he rose unsteadily to address the grieving parents of the ghetto, imploring them voluntarily to surrender their children to him, he understood, as did they, that in all likelihood this was tantamount to delivering them to their destruction.[7] This is not to discount the fact that, in the absence of verifiable proof, there was a strong urge to reject the unthinkable. Even in the wake of the brutal seizure of the children a measure of uncertainty about their fate remained, as unsubstantiated rumors surfaced suggesting that somewhere they were still alive.[8] But even before then, the spring and summer of 1942 were marked by foreboding, filled with firsthand reports of shootings and the forced separation of families in the smaller ghettos in the provinces. The Germans, in the interests of efficiency of operations, sought to allay troubling concerns, preferring to keep their victims off guard by way of deception, reassuring them that they meant them no real harm, and that if they cooperated, all would be well. Rosenfeld offers an occasional glimpse, during this time, of Rumkowski complaining of sleeplessness: if you knew what I knew, he hinted, you would not be able to sleep either. After the war it would be reported that, sometime in the spring of 1942, a ghetto member of the Jewish Bund, on receipt of an account of the killings in Chełmno from the rabbi in a nearby town, was dispatched to inform Rumkowski of the news. According to the account, Rumkowski told the messenger that he already knew. But although the arrival of that information about the death camp can be credited, the details surrounding the supposed meeting between the Bundist delegate and Rumkowski are difficult to confirm.[9] A more intriguing incident is recounted in a 1954 memoir composed by a German who claimed to have had occasion to enter the ghetto and meet privately with Rumkowski as well as Leon Rozenblat, the chief of the Jewish police. Rozenblat is recalled agonizing over the torments he suffered time and again in having to assemble people for deportation, knowing that they were going to be destroyed by gas.[10] If Rozenblat, who was as close to Rumkowski as anyone in the administrative hierarchy of the ghetto, was aware that these unfortunates were being shipped to their deaths, it is difficult to imagine that Rumkowski did not know as well. Yet even then, Rumkowski, and most others who learned of such reports, were hearing something previously unknown to their prior experience and understanding. Nor have we reason to assume that he grasped in all certainty that the killing of the Jews of Litzmannstadt and the Warthegau, horrible as it was, was not a local phenomenon and limited in scope. It was indeed difficult to comprehend that even if the Jews of the ghetto were being destroyed in some new and diabolical way, this was part of wider project of unprecedented scope whose goal was the destruction of every Jew on the continent.[11]

If Rumkowski did know the whole truth, what possible purpose could continued labor have served except as a means of delay? Taking advantage of countervailing pressures to exploit ghetto labor for the war effort, Rumkowski staked all he had on "forestalling" the dissolution of the ghetto and the deportation of the remaining population. If he could just keep everything up and running, the clock might run out on the Germans, who finally would be gone, while the Jews would still be there, tending the machinery of production to the very end. This was Rumkowski's gambit. But it failed. Until the end, the Germans remained the unassailable arbiters of the Jewish fate. The ghetto was built to their specifications. From start to finish they controlled the setting and dictated the parameters of daily life and the pace of destruction, for in their hands alone rested all power over time.[12]

But by the summer of 1942, with the prospect of renewed deportations into the unknown indisputably in store, the system of work—the "only way," as Rumkowski's oft-repeated watchword had it—the sole guarantor of peace and survival, had to serve a more desperate purpose. Until then it had existed solely to preserve the ghetto as a going concern and a refuge, however flimsy, within which to ride out the privations of captivity. Now it had to stave off the day when, God forbid, the Germans might shut the enterprise down and kill them all. The extreme rationality of German production demands increasingly made clear that the unproductive must be jettisoned, but those who could work would remain. Now, for the Jewish leadership and the remaining members of the community, work was literally their only path to staying alive. Rumkowski understood the calculus this way. The long hiatus following the terrible resettlements of 1942 suggested that, given sufficient time to wait out the Germans, who, once defeated, would vanish, the gates of the ghetto would swing open, and like "a miracle," a modern exodus, a remnant ten, twenty, even sixty thousand strong would walk through those gates back into the city and freedom. Rumkowski is said to have pondered such a possibility, imagining himself "leading the people out of the ghetto and marching in front."[13] That was how he hoped the nightmare might end.

Indeed, with the ghetto still standing in the summer of 1944, that day seemed tantalizingly close. The Allies had by then successfully landed in France, and Soviet troops were advancing on Warsaw. On July 20 Hitler was nearly killed in a failed attempt to assassinate him and bring down the regime. If a German defeat had been more swift in coming, or if a new government had come to power and brought an immediate end to the killings in Auschwitz, the camp to which nearly all of the 68,500 remaining Jews of the Łódź ghetto would be sent in the coming weeks, this substantial remnant might conceivably have been spared.[14] This can only be conjecture. The Soviet offensive stalled, the plot against Hitler went awry, and the regime, more vengeful than ever, relentlessly pursued its campaign of annihilation against the Jews to the final hour. Nowhere did the Nazis willingly surrender captive Jews to the advancing enemy. Even if the killing installations at Auschwitz had ceased to function and to receive fresh waves of victims, as they still were doing at the time the ghetto was emptied, the Germans would have remained fully capable of either killing them "on the spot" or marching them on a murderous journey toward camps deeper in the interior of the Reich.[15]

Might escape nonetheless have been possible, even at the final hour? The ghetto was hardly a fortress. Though guarded by sentries quick to employ deadly force, the perimeter of the zone was largely composed of wood, as were many buildings inside the ghetto as well. It would have been possible to set the quarter ablaze, creating chaos and offering the prospect of effecting a break. Such a tactic was indeed attempted in some of the smaller ghettos farther to the east at a moment when it appeared to residents, and in some instances to the Jewish leadership as well, that their imminent deportation signaled certain death. Many were shot to death in the effort; some succeeded in fleeing; still others, after making their way to the countryside, were later hunted down and killed.[16]

By location and topography, the situation of the Łódź ghetto was decidedly unfavorable to the prospects of organizing resistance and flight. Łódź was increasingly a German city, incorporated into the Reich, a bastion of German colonization. Łódź had become Litzmannstadt, a city under German administration in a province heavily ruled by German ideology and force. Undermined by German countermeasures, Polish resistance in the vicinity remained weak. Independent efforts on the part of a few politically active individuals in the ghetto to make contact with Polish sympathizers proved sporadic and ineffective. The woods close by the city were useful only for recreation; the dense forests that provided shelter to the partisans and fleeing Jews of the ghettos of eastern Poland, Lithuania, and Belorussia were far away. In short, Litzmannstadt was too German a city and nearby wilderness too sparse to offer refuge for a population on the run.[17]

Rumkowski and his strategy succeeded in saving a small number. And some among the fortunate attributed their survival largely to his efforts.[18] He was not a likable man, was egotistical to be sure, and as one survivor termed him "a boor."[19] One can imagine others more honorable. No doubt had he chosen defiance, we would honor him today, and memorial candles would be lit in his memory. His efforts led to failure. But compliance under circumstances of extreme coercion is not the same as collaboration. Rumkowski did not hasten to do the Germans' bidding, nor did he act out of a desire to reap material advantage for himself; neither did he share their convictions, nor, most assuredly, did he seek the destruction of the people over whom he held restricted sway.[20] No judgment should overlook for a moment the fact that, ultimately, it was the Nazi leadership that sought that destruction, developed the means to bring it about, and exercised the overwhelming instruments of deception and coercion at their disposal to bring about its accomplishment.[21]

By war's end, many of the perpetrators, having at long last dispatched the Jews to their fate, had departed the scene. Hans Biebow, for one, returned to Germany, hoping to find refuge in the familiar setting of his native city of Bremen. To his misfortune, it was there that he was found, taken into

U.S. custody, and remanded back to Łódź. In April 1947, in a brief trial lasting only days, confronted by written evidence and the testimony of surviving witnesses to his crimes, he was sentenced to death by a Polish court for his role in presiding over the ghetto, deporting the Jews of Łódź and of the outlying provincial communities to their deaths in Chełmno, and for participating in the assaults on and killing of individual Jews.[22] Biebow would be among the few who would be compelled to answer for their crimes. In all, of the nearly two hundred members of the Ghetto Administration staff, from department heads to employees, secretaries, and workers, only four men other than Biebow were brought to justice and sentenced, each condemned to death by Polish courts, though one of them would see his sentence commuted to a ten-year term of imprisonment. Cheating justice, after being taken into custody by the British, Friedrich Ribbe, Biebow's prewar business associate and second in command within the Ghetto Administration, succeeded in taking his own life. Among the most prominent of the regional and municipal officers of the regime—Regierungspräsident Friedrich Uebelhoer, Oberbürgermeister Werner Ventzki, Bürgermeister Karl Marder, and Police President Karl Wilhelm Albert—none were compelled to stand trial and answer for their actions.[23] The head of the Litzmannstadt Kriminalpolizei, Walter Zirpins, escaped justice as well. Otto Bradfisch, director of the Litzmannstadt Gestapo and successor to Ventzki as Oberbürgermeister, however, was brought before a West German court in 1963. Joining him on trial was Günther Fuchs, head of Jewish affairs in the Litzmannstadt Gestapo. Both Bradfisch and Fuchs were found guilty for their role in the murder of the Jews of the ghetto, though each was spared the penalty of death. Unrepentant, at trial Fuchs did not refrain from heaping scorn upon the Jews for their alleged brutality to one another and prevailing disregard for cleanliness.[24]

The city that was Litzmannstadt has vanished. Its existence as cornerstone of a new Nazi vision for the East had proved in the end short-lived. Seemingly in the blink of an eye, by the winter of 1945 all that the new rulers had worked to achieve was gone, their dreams left unfulfilled. All the same, so grandiose a project, product of the energies and aspirations of so many, could not fail to leave behind evidence of its creation. Whereas the film the city leadership had sought to document the regime's vision for Litzmannstadt was never completed, the visual fragments of that work

are to be found in a Berlin archive, testimony to the local regime's determination to fashion a city modern in design and demographically pure.[25]
Before the war ended, one of the writers associated with that film would
publish a novel set in the new city of Litzmannstadt, drawing upon the
themes and sensibilities animating this cinematic work in progress. Titled
Stadt im Sommerwind, or "City in the Summer Wind," it too found inspiration in the Nazi project of destruction and renewal. In its pages young
Germans, newly arrived from the Reich and from German communities
abroad, meet in the city's cafés, taverns, and nightclubs, mock the Jews
while riding in a streetcar passing by the ghetto, swim, and hike through
city parks. In a private apartment once owned by Jews, by candlelight a
young couple consume cherries, chocolates, and wine, and kiss before
rushing off to meet an early morning train.[26] In contrast to the former city
of Łódź with all its evident shortcomings, Litzmannstadt's great future is
constantly before their eyes. One night, while walking home from an en-
chanting summer concert in the courtyard of the Musikschule, a young
man meets an acquaintance, an architect, who invites him on a virtual
tour of the city as it once was and as it was soon to be. Inside a darkened
villa, flashlight in hand, the guide leads his visitor through unlit rooms.
Arrayed in the darkness, amid the drawing boards, architectural implements cast eerie shadows. When a beam of light is directed upon the
walls, a series of maps come into view. One, identified as a product of the
city's abject past, reveals the former city of Łódź to have been marked by
geographical isolation, thoughtless planning, and disorder. A picture of
urban impoverishment and human misery takes hold of the visitor's imagination. He envisages the face of a "grinning" Jew hovering with satisfaction above it all. By contrast, on newer maps the visitor discovers depic-
tions of the future city, a sleek metropolis linked by autobahns, canals,
and railways to the wider networks of communication and commerce of
the German East. Farther on, a tabletop mockup portrays in "toy-like
scale" a three-dimensional view of the future city. Attractive buildings
present pleasing façades adorned by many windows, alcoves, and balco-
nies, and charming white rooftops dotted with chimneys. New parks,
filled with trees, attractively complement the urban spaces. An avenue
leads to the new town center, where a great domed assembly hall towers
over a ceremonial square. Visible on the heights beyond stands magnificent new housing for German residents. The visitor, at one instant

imagining himself looking down on it all from the sky above, next pictures himself on the ground, walking along downtown streets and entering the spacious town square, his footsteps resounding on the pavement as the colonnaded entrance to the great hall rises up before him. In speaking of the future the architect draws his visitor's attention to the "happy people" of the city relaxing on a "sunny beach" beside a lake of blue waters.[27]

Overtaken by impending defeat, lesser participants in the creation of the Nazi city and the annihilation of its Jews quietly slipped away. In time they would find new lives and careers, making their peace with the political realities of the postwar era and living out the remainder of their lives as private citizens free from all judgment. They too would not have failed to remember their sojourn in Litzmannstadt. At least one of them, as the world was to learn, retained in his possession an unusual memento of the city and its ghetto. In 1987, after his death in Salzburg, the name of Walter Genewein, director of the Gettoverwaltung's financial division, unexpectedly emerged. For decades he had preserved a collection of hundreds of color slides of the Litzmannstadt ghetto. But upon inspection it became clear that the collection, the product of Genewein's own photographic efforts, was above all intended as a visual record giving witness to the quiet success of the ghetto as a model of German organization and efficiency. In this unusual compilation it is not the Jews but the German managers who stand front and center in the narrative of these years, their diligence and sobriety highlighted in pictures portraying them seated responsibly at their desks, attending to their files, counting out confiscated valuables and cash, and going over the administration's accounts. The images are a testimony to the fashioning of an illusory, narrow vision in which the ghetto could be regarded not as the instrument of destruction that it was but as an enterprise in many respects like any other, and they its agents, dutifully fulfilling their necessary daily tasks. Revealing another side to their professional lives, the slides provide a reminder that as diligent representatives of the new order, the men and women of the Gettoverwaltung had been entrusted with a vital task: seeing to it that the Jews were safely and productively at a permanent remove, making possible the citizenry's enjoyment of the promise of a Jew-free and Germanically pure city of the East. In addition to those pictures of German managers at work in their offices, Genewein's camera recorded private moments, warm intimacies, as friends and colleagues relax after hours. Modest comforts surround them as they gather close on soft sofas, smoke cigars or cigarettes, share at table a bottle of champagne, embrace, leaf through magazines, or, dressed in bathrobe and slippers, read before bed by lamplight. The pictures clearly meant much to their creator, for at war's end Genewein chose to spirit them away, carefully preserved, taking them along as he journeyed homeward to Austria. In his possession they remained, a private treasure he would hold secure until his death.[28] In what for Genewein and his colleagues must have signified a unique record of professional accomplishment as well as a vivid memento of a past chapter in their lives, we find an unsettling confirmation that it was once possible to construct, on the scale of a modern city, a world at once a place of welcome and of annihilation.

But where were the Jews? In his visual catalog Genewein did not neglect them altogether: they are pictured, unsmiling, seated at their workstations, stitching fabric, weaving straw, tending machines, sorting old clothes, hauling carts, and bearing their dead toward burial in the ghetto cemetery. Photographed surreptitiously through the slats of the perimeter fence, they cross Kościelny Square, their yellow stars revealed as flecks of bright color against the dry background of dusty cobblestones and gray buildings.[29] True to the narrative that guided the Nazi revitalization of Litzmannstadt, the Jews were not to be entirely forgotten; indeed, they had been central to defining and giving impetus to the grand project of renewal. They had, in this view, marred everything, and brought to the city exploitation, ugliness, pestilence. If the city was to be reborn, they would have to be removed. This had been the unquestioned assumption of the new city fathers from the beginning. In order for the city to grow and prosper and for its citizenry to live well, one way or another the Jews had to go. And this was accomplished, soberly, methodically. At the beginning, seeking the most effective means toward that end, the regime felt its way. The ghetto had been but an expedient. By means of the same rationality and planning by which city engineers and architects had refashioned the look of the city, the managers who supervised the ghetto went about their task of eliminating the Jews from its daily life, and, when called upon to do so, assisted in sending them to their deaths.

Years later, digging at the site of their destruction at Chełmno, researchers would unearth bits and pieces of discarded personal possessions of the victims, among them medicine vials, jewelry, cosmetics, work utensils, and small toys. The objects bespeak benevolence: medications to alleviate pain, earrings to lend adornment to a young girl's ear, cufflinks to decorate a man's sleeve, a hand mirror to examine a face and makeup to adorn it, tools to assist an artisan, a portable alarm clock to wake a traveler, a brass top to spin for the amusement of a child.[30] Like the clothing, the bedding, the warm footwear and hats and furnishings the Jews of the ghetto had fashioned to placate their German masters and serve the wants of their people, these lost possessions were tokens of a world that for the Jews of the ghetto had long since ceased to exist. They were of another time, prior to the arrival of the Nazis and the creation of the ghetto, when the Jews too had reason to imagine that the world welcomed their presence, saw to their needs as it did those of humanity as a whole, and wished them joy and comfort and long life.[31]

The regime that engineered the destruction of the Jews understood such sentiments, pointedly reserving all prospect for their realization for themselves alone. In doing so the Nazis had achieved the unparalleled; but neither then nor afterward was the familiar world far removed. The murder ended, the floodtide of transgression receded, as it had to. All too soon for them, the time came to leave Litzmannstadt. They would have wished to enjoy well into the future their realized vision of a city and a world reborn. Much had been left on the drawing boards, awaiting completion during the anticipated era of victory and a German peace. But one thing had been accomplished, and in astonishingly little time: the Jews of Łódź, a community of more than 200,000 souls, were gone. Held captive in the ghetto and wanting only to survive, to linger one more day, and then another, they had toiled hard for their masters. To no avail. Their time was up. At a safe remove, far downstream of the same waters where Germans rowed their boats and sunbathed close by fairy-tale lanes, the river Ner, merging into the river Warta, flowed past a different shore. Here, agents of the regime had neatly disposed of the last remains of the citizenry's former Jewish neighbors. Reduced to powder, pure and clean at last—just as the Germans wished—what was left of them was given to the river to wash away. Unknowing, the current flowed on, the waters dissolving all earthly substance, sweeping away all living trace.[32]

NOTES

ACKNOWLEDGMENTS

INDEX

Notes

Abbreviations

AmL	Akta miasta Łodzi (Records of the City of Łódź)
APL	Archiwum Państwowe w Łodźi (Łódź State Archive)
GKBZpNP-IPN	Główna Komisja Badania Zbrodni przeciwko Narodowi Polskiemu—Instytut Pamięci Narodowej (Main Commission for the Investigation of Crimes against the Polish Nation—Institute of National Memory, Warsaw)
GV	Gettoverwaltung (Ghetto Administration)
LZ	*Litzmannstädter Zeitung*
PSZ	Przełożony Starszeństwa Żydów w Getcie Łódźkim (Records of the Jewish Eldest, Łódź Ghetto)
SV	Stadtverwaltung (Records of the City Administration, Litzmannstadt)
USHMM	United States Holocaust Memorial Museum
YIVO	YIVO Institute for Jewish Research, New York
ŻIH	Archiwum Żydowskiego Intstitutu Historycznego (Archive of the Jewish Historical Institute, Warsaw)

Prologue

1. APL Aml GV 28677, p. 214: filming log for 2 September 1941.
2. APL Aml GV 28677, pp. 211, 214: press clipping, "Mit Kameramännern

unterwegs: In Litzmannstadt wird weiter am Kulturfilm gearbeitet," *Ostdeutscher Beobachter* 5 (September 1941), and filming log for 2 September 1942.

3. Erwin Thiem, *Plan von Litzmannstadt* (Litzmannstadt: Buchhandlung S. Seibelt, 1942).

4. APL Aml GV 28677, pp. 214–226: filming log, 2–26 September 1941, indicating departure date of 27 September.

5. Wiesław Puś, "The Development of the City of Łódź (1820–1939)," *Polin* 6 (1991): 5–8. Julian K. Janczak, "The National Structure of the Population in Łódź in the Years 1820–1939," *Polin* 6 (1991): 25–26. Janczak indicates that on the eve of the Second World War the city's population had climbed to 665,000. According to another frequently cited statistic, by 1939 there were 233,000 Jews in Łódź. Julian Baranowski, *The Łódź Ghetto, 1940–1944/Łódźkie Getto 1940–1944* (Łódź: Archiwum Państwowe w Łódźi & Bilbo, 1999), p. 8.

6. A. Volf Yasni, *Di geshikte fun yidn in Lodz in di jorn fun der daytscher yidnojsrotung* (Tel Aviv: I. L. Peretz Library, 1960), pp. 44–49, 52. Barbara Wachowska, "The Jewish Electorate of Interwar Łódź in the Light of the Local Government Elections (1919–1938)," *Polin* 6 (1991): 165–166. Janusz Wróbel, "Between Co-existence and Hostility: A Contribution to the Problem of National Antagonisms in Łódź in the Inter-war Period," *Polin* 6 (1991): 204–206.

7. Jerzy Maleńczyk, *A Guide to Jewish Lodz* (Warsaw: Our Roots, Jewish Information and Tourist Bureau, 1994), p. 42.

8. Isaak Kersz, "Jewish Community in Łódź and the Jewish Cemetery: A Brief Historical Account," trans. Małgorzata Wojciechowska and Zofia Snawadzka, in Kersz, *Szkice z dziejów Żydowskiej oraz cmentarza w Łodzi* (Łódź: Oficyna Bibliofilów, 1999), p. 137. Maleńczyk, *Guide to Jewish Lodz,* p. 26.

9. Kersz, "Jewish Community in Łódź," pp. 129, 138. Arnold Mostowicz, *Łódź, moja zakazana miłość* (Łódź: Oficyna Bibliofilów, 1999), p. 20. Paweł Spodenkiewicz, *Zaginiona dzielnica: Łódź żydowska—ludzie i miejsca* (Łódź: Lódzka Księgarnia Niezależna, 1999), p. 96. *The Chronicle of the Łódź Ghetto, 1940–1944,* ed. Lucjan Dobroszycki, trans. Richard Lourie, Joachim Neugroschel et al. (New Haven: Yale University Press, 1984), pp. 57–58, n. 67. Pinchas Schar, "Mendel Grossman: Photographic Bard of Ghetto Lodz," in *Holocaust Chronicles: Individualizing the Holocaust through Diaries and Other Contemporaneous Personal Accounts,* ed. Robert Moses Shapiro (Hoboken, N.J.: KTAV Publishing House, 1999), pp. 125, 132–133.

10. Joseph Roth, *Werke: Das journalistische Werk, 1924–1928,* ed. Klaus Westermann, vol. 2 (Cologne: Kiepenhauer & Witsch, 1990), p. 952. Also cited in Spodenkiewicz, *Zaginiona dzielnica,* p. 64.

11. Alfred Döblin, *Reise in Polen* (Freiburg im Breisgau: Walter-Verlag, 1968), pp. 317–319.

12. Recollections of Don Goren and Sara Zyskind, quoted in Spodenkiewicz, *Zaginiona dzielnica,* pp. 25, 32–33.

13. *Les cahiers d'Abram Cytryn: Récits du ghetto du Łódź,* trans. Véronique Patte (Paris: Albin Michel, 1995), p. 23.

14. USHMM RG-12.146: Genia Bryl/Jean Beller, "If My Heart Didn't Break Then," ed. Sheila Beller, unpublished diary, pp. 18–19. Arnold Mostowicz, *Łódź moja zakazana miłosc* (Łódź: Oficyna Bibliofilów, 1999), p. 20. "Souvenirs de Lucie Cytryn-Bialer," in *Les cahiers d'Abram Cytryn,* p. 171. Sara Selver-Urbach, *Through the Window of My Home: Memories from the Lodz Ghetto* (Jerusalem: Yad Vashem, 1986), pp. 24–26.

15. Bryl, "If My Heart," pp. 14, 51, 54; ŻIH 302/222: Pamiętnik, Irina Libman, p. 20.

16. YIVO: "People of a Thousand Towns," On-line Photographic Catalog, PO, catalog numbers 393.09/1829.01/1834/1834.08/F1835/1838.02/1864.01/1874/ 1892/6746 and PO/Forward, http://yivo1000towns.cjh.org, accessed 19 September 2007.

17. Bryl, "If My Heart," pp. 13, 45, 46.

18. Elie Wiesel, *Night,* trans. Marion Wiesel (New York: Hill and Wang, 2006). Raul Hilberg, *The Destruction of the European Jews,* rev. ed. (New York: Holmes and Meier, 1985). Claude Lanzmann, *Shoah: An Oral History of the Holocaust: The Complete Text of the Film* (New York: Pantheon Books, 1985). *Shoah,* dir. Lanzmann, Paramount Home Video, 1986. Thomas Keneally, *Schindler's List* (New York: Simon and Schuster, 1982). *Schindler's List,* dir. Steven Spielberg, Universal Home Video, 1994.

19. USHMM RG-05.008M Reel 1, File 31, pp. 134–135, 142, 147: Drehbuch zu dem Kulturfilm *Aus Lodz wird Litzmannstadt,* Buch: Hans F. Wilhelm, Mitarbeit: Wilm v. Elbward, Dr. Heinz Heesemann, 31 March 1942.

1. Autumn 1939

1. Tania Fuks, *A vanderung iber okupirte gebitn* (Buenos Aires: Tsentral-Farband fun Poylishe Yiden in Argentine, 1947), pp. 11, 15. Of the weather, Fuks refers to the "bright, pure blue sky without a cloud" marking September 1, and the "golden sun" of September 2, and in general the exceptional "clarity" of the "cloudless" skies marking all the days of the invasion.

2. Ibid. p. 17.

3. Ibid., pp. 9–12.

4. Ibid., pp. 20–21. Alan Adelson, ed., *The Diary of Dawid Sierakowiak: Five Notebooks from the Łódź Ghetto,* trans. Kamil Turowski (New York: Oxford University Press, 1996), entry for 6 September 1939, pp. 34–35.

5. Fuks, *A vanderung,* pp. 23–25.

6. Ibid., pp. 26–27.

7. Ibid., p. 28.

8. Adelson, *Diary of Dawid Sierakowiak,* entry for 8 September 1939, p. 36.
Tgr., "Die Deutschen marschieren ein!" *Freie Presse,* 10 September 1939, p. 2.

9. W. B. (Sonderberichterstatter), "Der Führer fuhr durch Lodz!" *Freie Presse,*
14 September 1939, p. 1. Je, "Ich habe den Führer gesehen!" *Freie Presse,* 14 September 1939, p. 3.

10. Reproduced in *The Chronicle of the Łódź Ghetto, 1941–1944,* ed. Lucjan
Dobroszycki, trans. Richard Lourie, Joachim Neugroschel et al. (New Haven:
Yale University Press, 1984), in unnumbered photographic section following
p. 103.

11. Reproduced in Alan Adelson and Robert Lapides, eds., *Łódź Ghetto: Inside
a Community under Siege* (New York: Penguin Books, 1989), p. 6.

12. Fuks, *A vanderung,* p. 29. Adelson, *Diary of Dawid Sierakowiak,* entry for
12 September 1939, pp. 37–38.

13. "The History of the Litzmannstadt Ghetto," pt. 1, "From the City to the
Ghetto," excerpted in Adelson and Lapides, *Łódź Ghetto,* p. 22.

14. Fuks, *A vanderung,* p. 34.

15. "History of the Litzmannstadt Ghetto," pp. 21–22.

16. Edward Reicher, *Une vie de juif,* trans. Jacques Greif and Élisabeth
Bizouard-Reicher (Paris: Lieu Commun, 1990), p. 36.

17. "History of the Litzmannstadt Ghetto," p. 23.

18. Julian Baranowski, *The Łódź Ghetto, 1940–1944/Łódzkie Getto 1940–1944*
(Łódź: Archiwum Państwowe w Łodzi & Bilbo, 1999), p. 18. Reicher, *Une vie,*
pp. 26–27.

19. Fuks, *A vanderung,* p. 31. Holocaust Testimony of Sally Abrams (transcript
of audiotaped interview), 13 October 1981, Josey Fisher interviewer (Holocaust
Oral History Archive, Gratz College, 1996), p. 1–2–9.

20. Reicher, *Une vie,* p. 39; also quoted in Baranowski, *Łódź Ghetto/Łódzkie
Getto,* pp. 18–19.

21. Holocaust Testimony of Sally Abrams, pp. 1–2–10, 1–2–11.

22. Adelson, *Diary of Dawid Sierakowiak,* entries for 28 and 31 October 1939,
pp. 54–56; Reicher, *Une vie,* pp. 25–26, 34. Holocaust Testimony of Sally
Abrams, p. 1–2–9.

23. Baranowski, *Łódź Ghetto/Łódzkie Getto,* pp. 21–22. Joanna Podolska, *Traces
of the Litzmannstadt-Getto: A Guide to the Past* (Łódź: Piątek Trzynastego, 2004),
p. 8.

24. Baranowski, *Łódź Ghetto/Łódzkie Getto,* pp. 18–25.

25. A. Volf Yasni, *Di geshikhte fun yidn in lodzh in di jorn fun der daytscher jidn-
oysrotung* (Tel Aviv: I. L. Peretz Library, 1960), p. 97. Shmuel Huppert, "King of

the Ghetto: Mordechai Ḥaim Rumkowski, the Elder of Lodz Ghetto," *Yad Vashem Studies* 15 (1983): 131.

26. On the matter of his forwardness as a speaker, see Leonard Tushnet, *The Pavement of Hell* (New York: St. Martin's Press, 1972), p. 8. Huppert, "King of the Ghetto," p. 129. Yasni, *Di geshikte,* pp. 64–65.

27. Raul Hilberg, *The Destruction of the European Jews,* vol. 1 (New York: Holmes & Meier, 1985), pp. 191–192.

28. Cited in Huppert, "King of the Ghetto," p. 132. Huppert refers to Rumkowski as "the Elder." The Germans conferred on Rumkowski the title "der Älteste der Juden," otherwise translated as "the Eldest of the Jews," or "the Eldest."

29. Sarah Zyskind and Isaac Rus, cited ibid., p. 129.

30. Cited ibid., p. 132. Tushnet, *Pavement of Hell,* pp. 10–11.

31. Michal Unger, *Reassessment of the Image of Mordechai Chaim Rumkowski,* Search and Research Lectures and Papers 6 (Jerusalem: Yad Vashem, 2004), pp. 14–16.

32. For elements of such a characterization, see ŻIH, 302/11–13, diary of Leon Hurwicz, pp. 4, 17–18, 22–24. Rafael F. Scharf, *Poland, What Have I to Do with Thee: Essays without Prejudice (Co mnie i tobie polsko . . . Eseje bez uprzedzeń)* (Cracow: Fundacja Judaica, 1996), p. 285. Reicher, *Une vie,* pp. 44–49. Tushnet, *Pavement of Hell,* pp. 4–9. Philip Friedman, *Roads to Extinction: Essays on the Holocaust,* ed. Ada June Friedman (New York: Jewish Publication Society of America and Conference on Jewish Social Studies, 1980), pp. 335–336.

33. Yasni, *Di geshikte,* pp. 100–101. On Rumkowski, see also introduction to *Chronicle,* pp. xlv–xlvi. Arnold Mostowicz, *With a Yellow Star and a Red Cross: A Doctor in the Łódz Ghetto,* trans. Henia Reinharz and Nochem Reinharz (London: Valentine Mitchell, 2005), p. 116.

34. "'Sotsial-gezelschaftlikher shpigel,' II. Vi azoy iz entstanen der internat in 'Helenuvek'?" *Der Yosem* 1, no. 1 (June 1926): pp. 18–19.

35. Karol Jurczak, "Wrażenie z Helenówka," *"Helenówek": Kwartalnik wydany przez Internat i Ferme dla Dzieci żydowskich w Helenówke* 1 (March 1931): 13.

36. Ibid.

37. Ibid.

38. Dr. David Rozenzweig, "Der yosem un zeyn soyne," *Der Yosem* 1, no. 1 (June 1926): 9–10.

39. M. H. Rumkowski, "Rikht-linien," *Der Yosem* 1, no. 1 (June 1926): 5.

40. See Yasni, *Di geshikte,* pp. 64–65. Huppert, "King of the Ghetto," pp. 130–131. Tushnet, *Pavement of Hell,* p. 8. Reicher, *Une vie,* pp. 44–46. Friedman, *Roads to Extinction,* pp. 335, 349, n. 4. Lucille Eichengreen, *Rumkowski and the Orphans of Lodz* (San Francisco: Mercury House, 2000).

41. Reicher, *Une vie,* p. 44.

42. Ibid., pp. 44–46.

43. USHMM RG-15.083 M, Reel 2, File 6: Rumkowksi to Bäckerei Lajzerowicz, 13 November 1939 (p. 241); Rumkowski to Bäckerei M. Leizerowicz, 11 December 1939 (p. 42); Rumkowski to Bäckerei Kalman Cwilich, 4 December 1939 (p. 90); Rumkowski to Szymon Rogozinski, 19 November 1939 (p. 188); Rumkowski to Herr Schwazschulze, Gut Małozow, Kreis Brzeziny, December 1939 [day of month illegible] (p. 66); Rumkowski to Firma M. Fogel u. Co., 12 December 1939 (p. 29); Rumkowski to Bäckerei Zimmerman, 14 December 1939 (p. 24); Rumkowski to Kommissar der Stadt Lodsch, 11 [30] December 1939 (p. 48); Rumkowski to Szyman Rogozinski, 10 November 1939 (p. 188); Rumkowski to Fräulein Advokat Regina Pływacka, 10 December 1939 (p. 30); Rumkowski to Wydziłu Aprowizacji, 18 October 1939 (p. 439); Rumkowski to Inhaber des Hauses Ziegelstr. 17, 1 December 1939 (p. 101); Rumkowski to Herrn Kommissar der Stadt Lodz, 16 Oktober [1939] (p. 447). Examples of charges for care of youngsters during fall 1939 and bills directed from the city to Rumkowski may be found in USHMM RG-15.083, Reel 4, File 16, pp. 237, 238, 241, 242: Fürsorgeamt to Aeltesten der Juden in Litzmannstadt, dated 12 June 1940.

44. *The Goebbels Diaries, 1939–1941,* trans. and ed. Fred Taylor (New York: G. P. Putnam's Sons, 1983), entry for 2 November 1939, p. 36.

45. Ibid., p. 37.

46. Ibid., entry for 3 November 1939, p. 38.

47. Yasni, *Di geshikte,* pp. 119–121.

48. Ibid., pp. 128–129. Isaiah Trunk, *Łódź Ghetto: A History,* trans. and ed. Robert Moses Shapiro (Bloomington: Indiana University Press, 2006), p. 34. Podolska, *Traces of the Litzmannstadt-Getto,* pp. 11–12.

49. Reicher, *Une vie,* pp. 49–51.

50. Götz Aly, *"Final Solution": Nazi Population Policy and the Murder of the European Jews,* trans. Belinda Cooper and Allison Brown (London: Arnold, 1999), p. 77. Christopher R. Browning, with contributions by Jürgen Matthäus, *The Origins of the Final Solution: The Evolution of Nazi Jewish Policy* (Lincoln and Jerusalem: University of Nebraska Press and Yad Vashem, 2004), p. 49.

51. Aly, *"Final Solution,"* p. 77. Browning, *Origins,* p. 49.

52. Browning, *Origins,* pp. 50–51.

53. Yakov Nirenberg, "Di geshikhte fun Lodzher geto," in *In di yorn fun yidishn khurbn* (New York: Farlag Unser Tsait, 1948), pp. 216–217.

54. Ibid., p. 217.

55. Ibid.

56. Ibid., pp. 216–217.

57. APL GV 29189, pp. 215–219: Der Regierunspräsident zu Kalisch [Uebelhoer], "Bildung eines Ghettos in der Stadt Lodsch," 10 December 1939.

58. Ibid., pp. 215–218 [1–4].

59. Ibid.

60. Ibid., pp. 215–216, 219 [1, 2, 5].

61. Ibid., pp. 217, 219 [3, 5].

2. A City without Jews

1. Of interest in this regard is Martha Nussbaum, *Upheavals of Thought: The Intelligence of Emotions* (Cambridge: Cambridge University Press, 2001), pp. 316–320, 334–335.

2. "20405 Rückgeführte: Bisher 30 Züge Galizien- und Wolhyniendeutsche bei uns," *Lodscher Zeitung*, 2 January 1940. Artur Utta, "Auf dem Weg in die neue Heimat: Die 'L. Z.' bei den Heimkehrern in einem Lager der Volksdeutschen Mittelstelle," *Lodscher Zeitung*, 1 January 1940, p. 3.

3. Artur Utta, "Auf dem Weg in die neue Heimat," *Lodscher Zeitung*, 1 January 1940.

4. "Neue Straßentafeln: Die neuen Straßenschilder werden angebracht," *Lodscher Zeitung*, 18 January 1940, p. 5. Adolf Kargel, "Von der Buschlinie bis zur Spinnlinie: Die deutsche Stadt Lodsch hat deutsche Straßennamen erhalten," *Lodscher Zeitung*, 21 January 1940, p. 7.

5. W. J., "Ein festliches Haus empfängt seine Besucher . . . : Rundgang durch das neugestaltete Gebäude des Theaters der Stadt Lodsch in der Ziegelstraße," *Lodscher Zeitung*, 14 January 1940, p. 4.

6. Adolf Kargel, "Unsere Wünsche am Neujahrsmorgen: Was wir vom Jahr 1940 für die Stadt Lodsch erhoffen—Einer neuen Zukunft entgegen!" *Lodscher Zeitung*, 1 January 1940, p. 2.

7. Wilhelm Hallbauer, "Bauliche Aufgaben im deutschen Lodsch," pt. 1, *Lodscher Zeitung*, 28 January 1940, p. 5.

8. Ibid., pt. 2, *Lodscher Zeitung*, 4 February 1940, p. 12.

9. Ibid., pt. 1, 28 January 1940, p. 5, and pt. 3, 18 February 1940. "Das neue Lodsch wird geformt: 'L.Z.'-Gespräch mit dem Oberbürgermeister von Lodsch, Pg. Schiffer," *Lodscher Zeitung*, 14 January 1940, p. 5.

10. Hallbauer, "Bauliche Aufgaben," pt. 2.

11. APL SV 31866b, pp. 37–38: Denkschrift über die Notwendigkeit der Einrichtung eines Ghettos in Lodsch, 1 February 1940. "Der Wohngebiete der Juden und Polen," *Lodscher Zeitung*, 11–12 February, 1940. "Zeitplan zur polizeilichen Verordnung vom 8. Februar 1940 betr. Wohn- und Aufenthatltsrechte der Juden," *Lodscher Zeitung*, 18 February 1940.

12. APL SV 31866b, p. 37: "Denkschrift."

13. Ibid.

14. Ibid., p. 38.

15. Ibid., pp. 38–39.

16. Ibid., pp. 39–40.

17. Ibid., pp. 40–41.

18. Ibid., p. 41.

19. "Ein Verbrechen an die Volksgesundheit: Lodsch—eine Brutstättte der Tuberkulose—Jetzt wird es endlich anders werden!" *Lodscher Zeitung,* 11–12 February 1940, p. 10.

20. USHMM RG-05.05.008M, Reel 6, File 73, pp. 16, 19–22: Stadtgesundheitsamt Lodsch, Auszug aus dem Verhandlungsprotokoll, 5 January 1940; Gesundheitsamt der Stadt Lodsch, Protokoll, 5 January 1940; Aktenvermerk betr. Einrichtung des jüdishcen Krankenhauses, 10 January 1940; Aktemvermerk betr. Einrichtung des jüdishen Krankenhauses, 11 January 1940.

21. USHMM RG-05.008M, Reel 6, File 73: Aktenvermerk über die Sitzung betr. Einrichtung und Festlegung der Schutzzonen in nördl. Stadtteil, 13 January 1940, p. 26. USHMM Rg-05.008M, Reel 6, File 73: Gesundheitsamt, Aktenvermerk über die Sitzung, 18 January 1940, pp. 31–32.

22. USHMM RG-05.008M, Reel 6, File 73: Aktenvermerk über die Sitzung betr. Einrichtung und Festlegung der Schutzzonen in nördl. Stadtteil, 13 January 1940, p. 26.

23. APL PSZ 1093, p. 237: "Historia Geta Litzmannstadt," pt. 1.

24. Ibid., p. 238.

25. Ibid.

26. Ibid.

27. Ibid., pp. 239, 240.

28. Ibid., pp. 245–246.

29. Ibid., pp. 241–242: "Historia Geta Litzmannstadt," pt. 1.

30. Ibid., pp. 239, 241.

31. W. J., "Nationalsozialistische Gesundheitsführung in Lodsch: Die verantwortungsvollen Aufgaben des Städtischen Gesundheitsamtes, *Lodscher Zeitung,* 4 February 1940, p. 5.

32. APL GV 29189, pp. 294–296: Lodscher Zeitung: Amtliche Bekanntmachungen. Polizeiverordnung über die Wohn-und aufenthaltsrechte der Juden Auf Grund des Polizeiverwaltungsgesteztes vom 1. Juni 1931, dated 8 February 1940.

33. APL GV 29189, pp. 294–305: Lodscher Zeitung: Amtliche Bekanntmachungen. Polizeiverordnung über die Wohn-und aufenthaltsrechte der Juden Auf Grund des Polizeiverwaltungsgesteztes vom 1. Juni 1931,

Polizeipräsident SS Brigadeführer Schäfer, dated 8 February 1940; Ausführungsbestimmungen zur Polizeiverordnung vom 8. February 1940, signed Schäfer, 8 February 1940. APL PSZ 18, pp. 38–40: Zeitplan zur Polizeiverordnung vom 8. Februar 1940. The new residential area for Poles was to be established well south of the city center. *Lodscher Zeitung*, 11–12 February 1940, p. 5.

34. APL PSZ 1095, p. 102.

35. Ibid., p. 103.

36. Shlomo Frank, *Togbukh fun Lodzsher geto* (Buenos Aires: Tsentral-farband fun Poylishe Yidn in Argentine, 1958), entry for 8 February 1940, pp. 34–35. Josef Zelkowicz, *In Those Terrible Days: Notes from the Łodz Ghetto,* ed. Michal Unger (Jerusalem: Yad Vashem, 2002), pp. 380–381. See too Arnold Mostowicz, *With a Yellow Star and a Red Cross: A Doctor in the Łódź Ghetto,* trans. Henia Reinharz and Nochem Reinharz (London: Valentine Mitchell, 2003), pp. 1–12; and Ben Edelbaum, *Growing up in the Holocaust* (Kansas City: by the author, 1980), pp. 46–48.

37. APL PSZ 1095: "Referat Mieszkaniowy," p. 42.

38. Artur Eisenbach, expert testimony at the trial of Hans Biebow, 27 April 1947, reproduced in Jerzy Lewiński, *Proces Hansa Biebowa* (Warsaw: PRS, 1999), p. 154. The figure of two hundred dead during the March action is also noted in Jan Waszyński, "Z problematyki odpowiedzialności karnej za zbrodnie popełnione na Żydach w Łodzi (1939–1945)," in *Dzieje żydów w Łodzi 1820–1944: Wybrane problemy,* ed. Wiesław Puś and Stanisława Liszewski (Łódź: Wydawnictwo Uniwersytetu Łódzkiego, 1991), p. 366.

39. APL PSZ 1095, p. 108.

40. ŻIH 302/11–13: Leon Hurwicz, diary, pp. 3–4.

41. YIVO RG 241/No. 1050: Album des Erziehungswerk in Marysin, Litzmannstadt Getto 1940–1941.

42. YIVO RG 241/No. 873: untitled and unsigned report, 18 September 1942, p. 9.

43. "Goethes 'Faust': Gute Leistungen erfreuten ein vollbesetztes Haus," *Lodscher Zeitung,* 24–25 March 1940, p. 6.

44. Ibid. "Das Theater der Stadt Lodsch steht jetzt vor neuen Aufgaben," *Lodscher Zeitung,* 17 March 1940, p. 11.

45. "Besuch im 'Casanova,'" *Lodscher Zeitung,* 10 March 1940, p. 4.

46. "Ein Ding, das gefingert wird: Die Hohensteiner Puppenspieler gaben ein Gastspiel in Lodsch," *Lodscher Zeitung,* 10 March 1940, p. 4.

47. "Lodsch heißt jetzt Litzmannstadt," *Litzmannstädter Zeitung* (hereafter *LZ*), 12 April 1940, p. 1.

48. A. K., "Tondichter benennen Lodscher Straßen; Händel, Haydn, und

Mozart im Denkmal des Straßennamens," *Lodscher Zeitung,* 7 March 1940, p. 4. "Schubert, Schumann, Strauß, Wagner: Hervorragende deutsche Tondichter benannten Lodscher Straßen," *Lodscher Zeitung,* 6 April 1940, p. 5.

49. "Ein Mann, eine Straße und Großdeutschland: Ein paar Gedanken über das Gesicht der Adolf-Hitler-Straße, der Lodscher Handelsstraße," *Lodscher Zeitung,* 24–25 March 1940.

50. "Abschied: Kinder gehören nicht auf der Straße," *LZ,* 25 April 1940, p. 5.

51. "Droschken ohne 'Romantik' und Wanzen: Sauberkeit und neue Tarife der Personenbeförderung in unserem neuen Lodsch," *Lodscher Zeitung,* 5 April 1940, p. 4.

52. "Aus der Gauhauptstadt: Davidsterne füllen die Metalsammlung," *Lodscher Zeitung,* 9 April 1940, p. 5.

53. Dr. Rtg., "Mit unserem Gauleiter unterwegs: Der Reichsstatthalter in Wolhynienlagern und Siedlungen und in den Dörfern bei Litzmannstadt," *LZ,* 13 April 1940, p. 4.

54. USHMM RG-15.007M, Reel 3, File 14, pp. 1, 6–8: Der Reichsminister für die kirchlichen Angelegenheiten to Reichskommissar für die Festigung des deutschen Volkstums, Berlin, 2 April 1940; Der Führer des SD-Abschnitts Litzmannstadt to Reichsicherheitshauptamt, Amt II, Berlin, 24 May 1940.

55. USHMM RG 05.008M, Reel 1, File 32, pp. 104–109: W. Hallbauer, Stadtoberbaudirektor to Oberbürgermeister, 29 April 1940; Merkblatt für alle Volksdeutschen in dem durch die Verordnung des Herrn Polizeipräsidenten angeordneten Wohngebiete der Juden in Litzmannstadt, 29 April 1940.

56. APL PSZ 1093, p. 282: Historia Geta Litzmannstadt, pt. 1.

57. USHMM RG-05.008M Reel 1, File 36, pp. 36–37: Rumkowski to Oberbürgermeister der Stadt Lodsch, 6 April 1940.

58. APL PSZ 1093, p. 283: Historia Geta Litzmannstadt, pt. 1.

59. APL PSZ 24, p. 224: Der Polizeipräsident in Litzmannstadt, SS-Brigadeführer Schäfer to Aeltesten der Juden, 16 April 1940, Abschrift.

60. USHMM RG.05.008M Reel 1, File 36, pp. 34–35: Rumkowski to Oberbürgermeister der Stadt Lodsch, 5 April 1940.

61. USHMM RG 05.008M, Reel 1, File 36, pp. 25–28: Günther Schwarz Kommanditgesellschaft, "Anregungen zum Wiederaufbau der Bekleidungsindustrie im Wartheland," 18 April 1940.

62. APL PSZ 1093, pp. 283–284: Historia Geta Litzmsannstadt, pt. 1.

63. Yisroel [Israel] Tabaksblat, *Khurbn-Lodzh: 6 yor natsi-gehenem* (Buenos Aires: Tsentral-farband fun Poylishe Yidn in Argentine, 1946), p. 43.

64. APL PSZ 1093, p. 285: Historia Geta Litzmannstadt, pt. 1.

65. YIVO RG 241/No. 873: untitled and unsigned report on care for the orphans of the ghetto, 18 September 1942.

66. "Walpurgisnacht: Die Hexen werden ausgetrieben," *LZ,* 30 April 1940.

3. The Enclosure

1. Of the estimated 163,777 persons restricted to the ghetto, 62,379, or 38 percent, were found to have been residents of the Bałut; 94,927, or 58 percent, resettled from elsewhere in the city; and 6,471, accounting for the remaining 4 percent of the initial ghetto population, came from outlying areas. The estimate of an initial ghetto population of 163,777 emerged from a review of statistics resulting from a formal census of the ghetto population undertaken on 16 June 1940. By that date it was believed that the population had fallen to 160,423, amounting to a density of 40,105 persons per square kilometer, or nearly four times the prewar density of the city as a whole (10,248 persons per square kilometer), as measured according to a citywide census in 1931. See YIVO RG 231/ No. 800: Department of Statistics (Łódź), "Statistical Tables of the Ghetto for the Period May 1940 to June 1942," pp. 3, 6.

2. Indeed, such an option had its advocates. See Christopher R. Browning, *The Path to Genocide: Essays on Launching the Final Solution* (New York: Cambridge University Press, 1992), pp. 3–56.

3. APL GV 29234, pp. 390–391: Vermerk über die Besprechung vom 27.5.[19]40 über Ghetto-Fragen, 27 May 1940.

4. Ibid., pp. 390–392.

5. Julian Baranowski, "Administracja niemiecka i tzw. samorząd w getcie łódzkim 1940–1944," in *Dzieje żydów w Łodzi 1820–1944,* ed. Wiesław Puś and Stanisław Liszewski (Łódź: Wydawnictwo Uniwersytetu Łódzkiego, 1991), pp. 311–312. On Biebow's background and his appointment, see A. Eisenbach, ed., *Dokumenty i materiały do dziejów okupacji niemieckiej w Polsce,* vol. 3, *Ghetto Lodzkie,* pt. 1 (Warsaw: Centralna żydowska Komisja Historyczna, 1946), pp. 252–256. APL GV 31298, p. 88: Vollmacht, 4 May 1940. On the figure of fifty-eight employees in May, see APL GV 29234, p. 267: Bericht über die Tätigkeit der Ernährungs- und Wirtschaftsstelle Getto vom 1. bis 31. Juli 1940, dated 31 July 1940. The ghetto department was officially referred to as the Ernährungs- und Wirtschaftsstelle Getto.

6. APL, GV 29215, p. 292 [792]: Ernährungs- und Wirtschaftsamt Hauptstelle, Rundverfügung I (Allgemein) No. 16, signed Dr. Moldenhauer, 4 June 1940.

7. APL GV 29215, pp. 273–274 [773–774]: Ernährungs- und Wirtschaftsamt Hauptstelle, Rundverfügung I (Allgemein), No. 18, 19 June 1940, signed Dr. Moldenhauer.

8. APL GV 29215, pp. 280, 281 [770, 771]: Urschriftlich gegen Rückgabe der Abteilung 0231 zur Kenntnis, 18 June 1940 (including added initialing by Pa[lfinger], 19 June [19]40); Ernährungs- und Wirtschafatsstelle Getto, Umlauf, 19 June 1940, initialed Pa[lfinger].

9. APL GV 29215, p. 125 [625]: Rundschreiben, signed Andersch, 8 February 1941.

10. APL GV 29215, p. 242 [772] and reverse page: Augusiak, Anneliese, et al., to Leiter der Ernährungs- und Wirtschaftsstelle Getto, Herrn Hans Biebow, Betrifft: Arbeitsschürzen für die in der Abteilung beschäftigten Damen, 15 August 1940; Hans Biebow, signed response, 19 August 1940.

11. APL GV 29215, pp. 289 [789], 207 [707]: Ernährungs- und Wirtschaftsstelle Getto, Umlauf, 3 June 1940, signed Palfinger; Ernährungs- und Wirtschaftsstelle Getto, Umlauf, 25 September 1940.

12. APL GV 29215, p. 272 [772]: Umlauf, 21 June 1940.

13. APL PSZ 727: Graphische Darstellung des Organisationsplanes der Getto-Verwaltung. USHMM RG-15.083M, Reel 161, File 727.

14. APL PSZ 727: Graphische Darstellung des Organisationsplanes der Getto-Verwaltung. USHMM RG-15.083M, Reel 161, File 727.

15. APL PSZ 727: Graphische Darstellung des Organisationsplanes der Getto-Verwaltung. USHMM RG-15.083M, Reel 161, File 727.

16. Julian Baranowski, *The Łódź Ghetto, 1940–1944/Łódzkie Getto 1940–1944* (Łódź: Archiwum Państwowe w Łodzi & Bilbo, 1999), pp. 38–40.

17. Der Polizeipräsident, Sonderanweisung für den Verkehr mit dem Ghetto, 10 May 1940, signed Schäfer; Kommando der Schutzpolizei, S 1a (Ghetto). Sonderbefehl für den Schusswaffengebrauch bei der Bewachung des Ghettos Litzmannstadt, 11 April 1941, signed Keuck, in Eisenbach, *Dokumenty i Materiały*, vol. 3, pt. 1, pp. 83–84, 86–87.

18. Baranowski, *Łódź Ghetto/Łódzkie Getto,* pp. 38–41.

19. Bracken, Krim. Inspektor, Betrifft: Sonderkommando der Kriminalpolizei im Ghetto, 19 May 1940, in Eisenbach, *Dokumenty i materiały,* vol. 3, pt. 1, pp. 92–94.

20. Kriminalinspektor Bracken, Betrifft: Einrichtung einer Kriminalpolizeiliche Zweigstelle im Getto, 21 May 1940, in Eisenbach, *Dokumenty i materiały,* vol. 3, pt. 1, pp. 94–96.

21. Baranowski, *Łódź Ghetto/Łódzkie Getto,* pp. 38–39. Ben Edelbaum, *Growing Up in the Holocaust* (Kansas City: by the author, 1980), pp. 79–87.

22. USHMM RG-15.083M, Reel 161, Files 729, 730: Graphische Darstellung der Organisation des Ältesten der Juden in Litzmannstadt, diagrams dated 15 February and 12 May 1941.

23. Ibid. Baranowski, *Łódź Ghetto/Łódzkie Getto,* pp. 54–55. APL GV 29234, p. 214: Ernährungs- u. Wirtschaftsstelle Getto, Aktennotiz, 2 September 1940.

24. USHMM RG-15.083M, Reel 161, PSZ File 729: Graphische Darstellung der Organisation der Juden in Litzmannstadt, diagram dated 15 February 1941.

25. Ibid. A. Volf Yasni, *Die geshikte fun yidn in Lodzh in di yorn fun der*

daytscher yidn-oysrotung (Tel Aviv: I. L. Peretz Library, 1960, pp. 268–270. Isaiah Trunk, *Łódź Ghetto: A History*, trans. and ed. Robert Moses Shapiro (Bloomington: Indiana University Press, 2006), pp. 54–55.

26. Also known as the Ordnungsdienst-Sonderkommando and the Sonderpolizei.

27. Baranowski, *Łódź Ghetto/Łódzkie Getto*, pp. 62–63, 66–67. See also Trunk, *Łódź Ghetto*, pp. 40–45.

28. USHMM RG 15.083M, Reel 161, Files 729, 730: Graphische Darstellung der Organisation des Ältesten der Juden in Litzmannstadt, 15 February and 12 May 1941. Baranowski, *Łódź Ghetto/Łódzkie Getto*, pp. 42–46. Trunk, *Łódź Ghetto*, p. 39.

29. APL PSZ 1109: images numbered 71–2353–2, 71–2353–4, 71–2353–5, 71–2353–6, 71–2353–8, 71–2353–10, 71–2364–4, 71–2367–3, 71–2367–4, 71–2367–5; APL PSZ 1112: images numbered 23–706–5, 23–706–6; APL PSZ 1116: images 42–1444–5, 42–1444–6, 42–1445–4, 43–1480–3, 43–1480–4, 43–1480–5, 43–1480–8, 6–150–7, 6–150–9; APL PSZ 1126: images 6–150–1, 6–150–2. Also see Baranowski, *Łódź Ghetto/Łódzkie Getto*, p. 42.

30. APL PSZ 1126: images 42–1457–1, 42–1457–2, 41–1457–3, 42–1457–4, 42–1457–5. Baranowski, *Łódź Ghetto/Łódzkie Getto*, p. 45.

31. ŻIH, photographic collection, Łódź, Inv. 773.

32. USHMM RG-05.008M, Reel 27, File 128: "Güterbahnhof im Getto," *LZ*, 12 May 1940; "Judenbahnhof in Litzmannstadt," *Magdeburger Gen. Anzeiger*, 18 May [19]40; *Brandenburger-Anzeiger*, 19 May [19]40; *Mülhäuser Anzeiger*, 20 May [19]40.

33. APL GV 29234, pp. 384–386: Bericht über die Tätigkeit der Ernährungs- und Wirtschaftsstelle Getto vom 1.–31. Mai, dated 31 May 1940. Sonderanweisung für den Verkehr mit dem Ghetto, Polizeipräsident Schäfer, 14 May 1940, in Eisenbach, *Dokumenty i materiały*, vol. 3, pt. 1, pp. 83–84.

34. APL GV 29234, pp. 384–386: Bericht über die Tätigkeit der Ernährungs- und Wirtschaftsstelle Getto vom 1.–31. Mai, dated 31 May 1940.

35. A. Volf Yasni, *Di geshikte fun yidn in Łódź in di jorn fun der daytscher yidn-oysrotung* (Tel Aviv: I. L. Peretz Library, 1960), pp. 259–262.

36. APL GV 29234, p. 385: Bericht über die Tätigkeit der Ernährungs- und Wirtschaftsstelle Getto vom 1.–31. Mai, dated 31 May 1940.

37. APL GV 29234, Aktennotiz, Betr. Schneiderarbeiten im Gettto.-Besprechung, 28 May 1940. Initialed B[iebow].

38. Ibid.

39. Yasni, *Di geshikte*, p. 261.

40. APL GV 29234, p. 385: Bericht über die Tätigkeit der Ernährungs- und Wirtschaftsstelle Getto vom 1.–31. Mai, dated 31 May 1940.

41. Yasni, *Di geshikte,* pp. 262–263.

42. APL PSZ 1093, pp. 289–291: "Bericht ueber die Stimmung der Bevoelkerung im Ghetto," 12 June 1940, signed Rumkowski, reproduced in *Historia Geta Litzmannstadt,* pt. 1.

43. APL PSZ 1093, pp. 289–291: "Bericht ueber die Stimmung der Bevoelkerung im Ghetto," 12 June 1940, signed Rumkowski, reproduced in *Historia Getta Litzmannstadt,* pt. 1.

44. YIVO RG 241/No. 800, pp. 25, 60: Department of Statistics (Łódź), "Statistical Tables of the Ghetto for the Period May 1940 to June 1942"; Todesfälle nach Todesursachen im Jahre 1940; Gemeldete Ansteckende Krankheiten, May 1940–June 1942.

45. APL SV 31866b, p. 75: Todesfälle vom 1. Mai bis zum 30. Juni 1940, statistical summary dated 7 July 1940.

46. APL SV 38166b, pp. 61–62: Protokoll aus der Filter und Fäkaliengrubenkontrolle in den Häusern Hohensteinerstrasse und Alexanderhofstrasse am 13. Juni 1940, dated 14 June 1940.

47. APL GV 29234, pp. 278–281: Protokoll, Betr.: Verhandlungen über Seuchenbekämpfung im Getto auf dem Baluter Ring am 21. Juni 1940, 16 Uhr, dated 22 June 1940. See too APL GV 29234, pp. 372–373: Vermerk über die Besprechung vom 25. Juni 1940 über Gettofragen, signed Biebow.

48. APL GV 29234, p. 266: Bericht über die Tätigkeit der Ernährungs- und Wirtschaftsstelle Getto vom 1. bis 31. Juli 1940. On Richter, see also Jan Waszcyński, introductory essay in Jerzy Lewiński, *Proces Hansa Biebowa* (Warsaw: PRS, 1999), p. 20, n. 31.

49. APL SV 31866b, p. 135: Ernährungs- u. Wirtschaftstelle Getto, Aktennotiz! Betr.: Das Überwachen der Leerung von Fäkaliengruben im Getto, 19 July 1940.

50. Ibid., pp. 136–137.

51. Ibid., pp. 137–138.

52. APL SV 31866b: Bericht über einen Zwischenfall bei der Fäkaleinabfuhr am Montag, den 22. Juli 1940.

53. Yasni, *Di geshikte,* pp. 268–270. USHMM RG-15.008 M, Reel 168, File 867, pp. 1. 16, 18, and charts labeled "Die zusätzliche Ernährung in den Schulen" for "Schuljahr 1939/40" and "Bekleidungsaktion in den Schulen."

54. USHMM RG-15.008 M, Reel 168, File 867, pp. 50–58. Yasni, *Die geshikte,* p. 275.

55. APL GV 29361, p. 123: Rumkowski to Gheime Staatspolizei, 11 July 1940, Abschrift. As late as the spring of 1941, in addition to three Reich citizens, there remained as many as sixty-four Poles of Christian faith still living inside the ghetto. Some were likely Jews who had converted to Christianity, such conver-

sions having failed to spare them from being sent to the ghetto, or else Poles with family ties to Jews, including non-Jewish spouses, as well as housekeepers who, at least for a time, had chosen to remain with Jewish households they had served before the war. YIVO RG 241/No. 800, p. 891 [34]: table, "Nichtjuden im Getto." APL PSZ 1093, "Das Getto Litzmannstadt," pp. 332–333 [32–33]. See also "History of the Ghetto," in *Łódź Ghetto: Inside a Community under Siege,* ed. Alan Adelson and Robert Lapides (New York: Penguin Books, 1989), pp. 59–60.

56. APL GV 29361, p. 124: Ernährungs- u. Wirtschaftsstelle Getto 02331/B/A Bürgermeister, 12 July 1940, initialed B[iebow].

57. APL SV 31866b: Dr. Wigdor Miller to Aeltesten der Juden in Litzmannstadt, 1 August 1940.

58. APL GV 29234: Rumkowski to Geheime Staatspolizei Litzmannstadt, 1 August 1940.

59. APL SV 31866b, p. 81: Rumkowski to Städtische Gesundheitsamt z. Hd. des Herrn Obermedizinalrat Dr. Merkert, 10 July 1940, in which Rumkowski makes reference to a previous communication on 10 June concerning this single instance of suspected rabies, subsequently ruled out.

60. APL PSZ 1072, pp. 13–14: Aufforderung No. 75, 2 July 1940; Bekanntmachung No. 76, 2 July 1940; USHMM RG-05.008M, Reel 6, File 65, pp. 77–80: Aufstellung betr. Hunde-Anmeldung; additional lists in APL PSZ 24, pp. 165, 171.

61. APL PS 1072, p. 26: Bekanntmachung No. 88, 20 July 1940. APL PSZ 24, pp. 164–165, 171: Der Polizeipräsident [in Vertretung: signed Hauke] to Ältesten der Juden in Litzmannstadt-Getto, Betrifft: Die Haltung von Hunden im Getto, 18 July 1940.

62. APL PSZ 1072, p. 46: Bekanntmachung No. 112, 27 August 1940.

63. USHMM Rg 05.008M Reel 27, File 128: "Hundehaltung im Getto verboten!" *LZ,* 21 August 1940.

64. "Reichsleiter Bouhler in Litzmannstadt: Zweitägiger Aufenthalt auf der Rückreise aus dem Generalgouvernement," *LZ,* 1 June 1940.

65. Dr. Rtg., "Mit Reichsleiter Bouhler im D-Zug: 'Deutscher Osten— blühendes Land'—Eindrücke in Litzmannstadt," *LZ,* 2 June 1940, p. 5.

66. H. W——k., "Handöh! Handöh! Er glaubt noch in 'Lodz' zu sein," *LZ,* 27 June 1940, p. 5.

67. "Unbefugter Grenzübertritt: Das Schnellgericht sprach Recht," *LZ,* 19 June 1940, p. 6; "Gauner, Gangster und Gesindel," *LZ,* 6 July 1940, p. 5; "Juden und Polen wurden verurteilt: Schnellgericht schickte 18 Angeklagte nach Nummer Sicher," *LZ,* 17 July 1940, p. 5.

68. Adolf Kargel, "Die Stadt Alexandrow und ihre Juden: Eine geschichtliche

und kulturgeschichtliche Betrachtung zu diesem Thema: die Juden im ehemaligen Polen," *LZ,* p. 7.

4. The Ghetto Will Endure

1. Rtg., "Dramatischer Zwischenfall in der Zirkus: Ein 21jähriger Stallbursche verletzt/Dompteur und Zirkusdirektor retten ein junges Menschenleben," *LZ,* 2 August 1940, p. 5.

2. A.U., "Judenbau forderte ein Menschenleben: Einsturz einer Wohnung in der Gartenstraße[.] Ein Toter, drei Verletzte," *LZ,* 9 August 1940, p. 5.

3. Adolf Kargel, "Wo sich die Körper im gesunden Spiel regen: Eine aufschlußreiche Besichtigungsfahrt zu zahlreichen Litzmannstädter Sport- und Badeplätzen," *LZ,* 1 August 1940, p. 5.

4. "Strahlende Augen glücklicher Sieger: Wieder mehrere Gebiets- und Obergaumeistertitel—Schwimmerwettkämpfe am Vormittag im Hallenbad—Endkämpfe in Anwesenheit des Gauleiters," *LZ,* 19 August 1940.

5. Kargel, "Wo sich die Körper im gesunden Spiel regen," p. 5. "Wo das Seebad Litzmannstadt entsteht," *Die Zeit im Bild: Bildbeilage der "Litzmannstädter Zeitung,"* 25 August 1940.

6. Fred, "Ein Vormittag im Quellenpark: Eine grüne Oase im grauen Häusermeer," *LZ,* 8 August 1940, p. 5.

7. A. K., "Sommer-Sonntag: Erholung in heimatischer Landschaft," *LZ,* 6 August 1940, p. 5.

8. USHMM RG-05.008M, Reel 1, File 32, pp. 124–125: Bericht über die Tätigkeit der Ernährungs- u. Wirtschaftsstelle Getto vom 1. bis 31. August 1940, dated 3 September 1940, signed Biebow.

9. The loan was in fact proffered by October, as noted in USHMM RG-05.008M, Reel 1, File 32, p. 182: Tätigkeitsbericht der Gettoverwaltung in der Zeit vom 1. bis 31. Oktober 1940, dated 3 November 1940.

10. APL GV 29362, pp. 124–125: An den Hern Regierungspräsidenten, Litzmannstadt, 0231/B/A, 15 October 1940. In a further effort to reduce the deficit, backed by the recommendation of a local finance office inspector, Biebow also urged at the least a scaling back of the ghetto's tax obligations to the city. See APL GV 29234, pp. 212–213: 0231/B.Wz., Aktennotiz, Ernährungs- und Wirtschaftsstelle Getto, 25 October 1940, initialed B[iebow]. APL 29234, pp. 200–201: Biebow, Akten-Notiz, 11 November 1940.

11. APL PSZ 1072, p. 61: Bekanntmachung No. 123, 20 September 1940.

12. USHMM RG-05.008M, Reel 3, File 51, p. 92: Monatsbericht der Stadt Litzmannstadt, October 1940.

13. On use of the term in this context, see Christopher R. Browning, *The*

Path to Genocide: Essays on Launching the Final Solution (New York: Cambridge University Press, 1992), pp. 28–56 (first reference to the term, p. 30).

14. USHMM RG-05.008M, Reel 3, File 51, pp. 92–93: Monatsbericht der Stadt Litzmannstadt, October 1940.

15. Sitzungsprotokoll. Betr.: Verwaltung und Unterstützung des Gettos in Litzmannstadt, 24 October 1940, signed von Herder, in *Dokumenty i materiały do dziejów okupacji niemieckiej w Polsce,* ed. A. Eisenbach, vol. 3, *Getto Łódzkie,* pt. 1 (Warsaw: Centralna żydowska Komisja Historyczna, 1946), pp. 102–104.

16. Material für die Behördenbesprechung am 28.8.40 [20 August 1940] beim Herrn Reg.-Präsidenten, ibid., pp. 96–98. Staatliche Kriminalpolizei, Kriminalpolizeistelle Litzmannstadt, Niederschrift über eine Besprechung am 23.10.40 [23 October 1940] zwischen der Gettoverwaltung und der Kriminalpolizei, signed, Im Auftrage: Dr. Zirpins, ibid., pp. 100–101.

17. Christopher R. Browning, with contributions by Jürgen Matthäus, *The Origins of the Final Solution: The Evolution of Nazi Jewish Policy, September 1939–March 1942* (Lincoln: University of Nebraska Press, 2004), p. 155.

18. APL SV 31866a: announcement titled "Unterstützungsaktion," 30 October 1940, signed Rumkowski.

19. APL SV 31866a: "Betr.: Lebensmittelzuteilung als Vorrat für die Wintermonate: Dezember, Januar und Februar 1940/41," 14 November 1940, signed Ch. Rumkowski.

20. By the end of October shipments of flour to the ghetto had been halted owing to the displeasure of the Germans over what they considered the too rapid consumption of reserves of delivered flour and the lack of fuel to support the operation of ghetto bakeries. USHMM RG-05.008M, Reel 1, File 32, p. 183: Tätigkeitsbericht der Gettoverwaltung in der Zeit vom 1. bis 31. Oktober. 1940, dated 3 November 1940. USHMM RG-05.008M, Reel 3, File 51, p. 94: Monatsbericht der Stadt Litzmannstadt, October 1940.

21. APL SV 31866a: Rumkowski to the City Health Department, 23 November 1940.

22. APL PSZ 1094, pp. 78–79.

23. Ibid., pp. 78–92.

24. Ibid., pp. 80–81.

25. Ibid., pp. 79–81.

26. Ibid., p. 81.

27. Ernährungs- u. Wirtschaftsstelle Getto, Aktennotiz, 2 September 1940, in Eisenbach, *Dokumenty i materiały,* vol. 3, pt. 1, p. 99. USHMM RG-05.008M, Reel 1, File 32, pp. 126–127, 151: Ernährungs- u. Wirtschaftsstelle Getto, Bericht über die Tätigkeit der Ernährungs- u. Wirtschaftsstelle Getto

vom 1. bis 31. August 1940 [from 1 to 31 August], dated 3 September 1940, signed Biebow; Tätigkeitsbericht der Ernährungs- u. Wirtschaftsstelle Getto für die Zeit vom 1. bis 30.9.40 [from 1 to 30 September], dated 1 October 1940, signed Biebow.

28. APL GV 30305, pp. 33–34: Ernährungs- und Wirtschaftsstelle An die Lagerverwaltung z.H. des Herrn Straube, indicating signatures of Biebow and Straube, 28 October 1940.

29. APL GV 29244, p. 86: Lager Hermann-Göring-Straße 39, Tätigkeitsbericht bis 30. November 1940, signed Straube.

30. ŻIH Lodz 136: Gettoverwaltung, Bericht, 12 November 1940; inspection report, signed Quay, Stadtoberinspektor, 23 November 1940, copy. APL GV 30305, pp. 16, 28, 32: Biebow to Straube, 3 December 1940; Ribbe to Straube, 7 December 1940; Lagerverwaltung, Hermann-Göring-Straße 39, Monatsbericht, February 1941.

31. Quoted in Laurence Rees, *The Nazis: A Warning from History* (New York: New Press, 1997), pp. 154–155.

32. ŻIH, Lodz 136: W. Neumann, K.II/5, Bericht, Betrifft: Veränderung der Gettobegrenzung, 4 October 1940, copy.

33. APL PSZ 1147, pp. 6, 9: Szoszana F., "Sen," *Kol Hechazit,* 21 November 1940.

34. APL PSZ 1147, pp. 16–18: Edmond Fleg, "Chodź z nami!" ("Klaudiusz i Marietta"), *Kol Hechazit,* 21 November 1940.

35. APL PSZ 1147, pp. 13–16: "Ilu nas jest?" *Kol Hechazit,* 21 November 1940.

36. "1000 Jahre Regensburger Domspatzen: Vom Schwarzen Meer zur Ostseee/Kreuz und quer duch unsern Kontinent, aber immer mit Schulstunden!" *LZ,* 13 November 1940.

37. "Der Solocellist Tibor de Machula: Das zweite volkstümliche Konzert in der Sporthalle zu Litzmannstadt," *LZ,* 20 November 1940, p. 6.

38. "Wir wollen ein Volk der Musik werden!" *LZ,* 21 November 1940, p. 6. Internal reference indicates that the opening took place on 19 November.

39. Officially titled the Reichsminister für Wissenschaft, Erziehung, und Volksbildung.

40. "Reichsminister Rust besucht unsere Schulen," *LZ,* 22 November 1940, p. 5.

41. "Afen im 'Erziehungsinstitut' des Münchner Zoo: Orang-Atans, die aus voller Kehle singen/Eine enzigartige Intelligenz-Prüfstätted für Affen," *LZ,* 14 December 1940.

42. "Löwen und Tiger überwintern bei uns: 'L. Z.'-Besuch bei einem 'abgebrannten' Zirkusbesitzer und seinen Gästen," *LZ,* 6 December 1940, p. 6.

43. Late that autumn just such a theme had found expression in a local theatrical production of a work by Josef-Maria Frank, *Jungle,* dramatizing the life of a European doctor who had fled to the tropics. See R., "Josef-Maria Franks Kolonialstück Dschungel," *LZ,* 10 December 1940, p. 6.

44. "Wir freuen uns, Litzmannstadt kennezulernen: Filmkünstler besuchen zum erstenml unsere Stadt/L. Z.-Gespräch mit Brigitte Horney und Ivan Petrovich," *LZ,* 1 December 1940, p. 4. "Zur heutigen Erstaufführung in Litzmannstadt. *Feinde:* Ein Film vom Deutschen Volkstumskampf im Osten," *LZ,* 30 December 1940, p. 7.

45. "3600 Wohnungen wurden völlig erneuert: Zweitausnnd Handwerker im Großeinsatz/Besuch im 'Wolhynienviertel' im Litzmannstädter Norden," *LZ,* 26 November 1940, p. 5.

46. "Der Mann, der Litzmannstadt entwanzt: 'Jüdische Erbschaftswanzen für deutsche Kultur untragbar!'/Bisher 10,000 Wohnungen vergast," *LZ,* 7 November 1940, p. 5.

47. APL GV 29361, pp. 96–98: Gettoverwaltung 027/B/A to Dr. Marder, 11 December 1940; Quay, Stadtoberinspektor, report for presentation to Bürgemeister Dr. Marder, 4 December 1940.

48. APL 29361, pp. 98–99: Quay, report for Dr. Marder, 4 December 1940.

49. *The Chronicle of the Łódź Ghetto, 1941–1944,* ed. Lucjan Dobroszycki, trans. Richard Lourie, Joachim Neugroschel et al. (New Haven: Yale University Press, 1984), entry for 12 January 1941, pp. 6–7.

50. APL GV 29364, p. 197: 027/B/A to Polizeipräsidium z. Hd. Inspektor König, 11 November 1940.

51. APL GV 29361, p. 99: unsigned listing dated 2 December 1940.

52. APL GV 30305, p. 31: Ribbe to Straube, 7 December 1940.

53. APL GV 31298, p. 55: untitled memo, Gettoverwaltung 027/B/A, 6 December 1940, accompanying approval by Marder.

54. "Es beginnt bereits zu weihnachten," *LZ,* 13 December 1940, p. 5. "Der 'Weihnachtsbaum für alle,'" *LZ,* 19 December 1940.

55. SS Brigadeführer Karl Wilhelm Albert succeeded SS Brigadeführer Johannes Schäfer, whose tenure as Police President ended on 30 June 1940. SS-Obergruppenführer Heinz Beckerle served as Police President from 24 September to 20 November 1939. Stanisław Nawrocki, *Policja hitlerowska w tzw. Kraju Warty w latach 1939–1945* (Poznań: Instytut Zachodni, 1970), pp. 104, 165.

56. "Kampf und Sieg der Polizei in Litzmannstadt: Mit 100 Mann began es/ Schutzpolizei im Kampf gegen Winterkälte, Juden und Verbrechertum," *LZ,* 6 November 1940, p. 5.

57. "Bericht über das erste Jahr fruchtbaren Aufbaus: Bürgermeister Dr.

Marder auf der Jahresfeier der Stadtverwaltung/Einführung der Rathsherren am 10. Januar," *LZ,* 21 December 1940, pp. 5–7.

58. YIVO RG241/No. 800, p. 25. USHMM RG-15.008M, Reel 168, File 868: Todesfälle nach Todesursachen im Jahre 1940.

5. The Ghetto and the City of the Future

1. On January 12 the chroniclers recorded a temperature of 10 degrees (Celsius) below zero. *The Chronicle of the Łódź Ghetto, 1941–1944,* ed. Lucjan Dobroszycki, trans. Richard Lourie, Joachim Neugroschel et al. (New Haven: Yale University Press, 1984), entries for 12 and 23 January 1941, pp. 3, 15.

2. Shlomo Frank, *Togbukh fun lodzher geto* (Buenos Aires: Tsentral-Farband fun Poylishe Yidn in Argentine, 1958), entry for 5 January 1941, p. 18.

3. Ibid., entry for 18 January 1941, p. 23.

4. Ibid., entry for 6 January 1941, p. 18.

5. Ibid., entry for 7 January 1941, p. 18.

6. Joseph Zelkowicz, "A Little Organization," winter 1941, reproduced in Isaiah Trunk, *Łódź Ghetto: A History,* ed. and trans. Robert Moses Shapiro (Bloomington: Indiana University Press in association with the United States Holocaust Memorial Association, 2006), pp. 144–146.

7. Ibid., p. 124. The phenomenon is mentioned often in Josef Zelkowicz's account of his own participation in the inspection of ghetto residences. See Josef Zelkowicz, *In Those Terrible Days: Notes from the Lodz Ghetto,* ed. Michal Unger, trans. Naftali Greenwood (Jerusalem: Yad Vashem, 2002), pp. 60, 74–75, 106.

8. Leon Hurwitz [Hurwicz], diary excerpt reproduced in Trunk, *Łódź Ghetto,* pp. 146–147. Zelkowicz, *In Those Terrible Days,* pp. 66–67.

9. On the carpenters' strike, see especially Zelkowicz, *In Those Terrible Days,* pp. 205–232; *Chronicle,* entry for 23 January 1941, p. 14.

10. Christopher Browning with contributions from Jürgen Matthäus, *The Origins of the Final Solution* (Lincoln: University of Nebraska Press and Yad Vashem, 2004), pp. 155–156. It is noted that deliveries rose again in March and April, followed in June by at least the acknowledgment on the part of the central authorities in Posen that the food situation had to be improved. Assurance that necessary steps would be undertaken, however, proved illusory. Ibid., p. 157.

11. APL GV 29244, p. 58: Bericht der Lagerverwaltung am Baluterring f. den Monat Dezember [19]40 to Gettoverwaltung Zentrale, 3 January 1941.

12. APL GV 29244, pp. 69–70: Gettoverwaltung Abt. Holzarbeitung, 31 December [19]40.

13. APl GV 29244, pp. 47–49: Monatsbericht für den Monat Februar 41

(stamp indicating report of Lagerverwaltung, Gettoverwaltung, Baluter Ring), 28 February 1941.

14. *Chronicle,* entries for 1 and 5 March 1941, pp. 22–23, 30.

15. Frank, *Togbukh,* entry for 13 March 1941, pp. 52–53.

16. *Chronicle,* entry for 6 March 1941, p. 31.

17. Ibid., entry for 1 March 1941, p. 22.

18. USHMM RG 05.083M, Reel 93, File 283, pp. 99–100.

19. *Chronicle,* entry for 1 March 1941, pp. 22–23.

20. On the chronology of the unit's presence and activities in Łódź, see Stanisłwaw Nawrocki, *Policja hitlerowska w tzw. Kraju Warty w latach 1939–1945* (Poznań: Instytut Zachodni, 1970), pp. 171–172; and Christopher R. Browning, *Ordinary Men: Reserve Police Battalion 101 and the Final Solution in Poland* (New York: Harper Collins, 1992), p. 39. Nawrocki indicates the unit arrived in Łódź on 22 June 1940 and "returned to Hamburg" on 7 April 1941. It guarded the ghetto from 28 November 1940 to 31 March 1941.

21. Frank, *Togbukh,* entry for 9 January 1941, p. 19.

22. Ibid., entry for 16 January 1941, p. 22.

23. Ibid., entry for 13 March 1941, p. 53. *Chronicle,* entry for 10–24 March 1941, p. 34.

24. APL SV 31866a, p. 20: Gesundheitsamt 500 Dr. N./F. to Polizeipräsident Litzmannstadt, Betr.: Getto, 27 February [194]1. APL SV 31866a, p. 4: St. A. 500/1/4, to Leiter des Gesundheitsamtes Herrn Dr. Nieberding, signed Benthin, 14 March 1941.

25. APL SV 31866a, p. 20: Gesundheitsamt 500 Dr. N./F. to Polizeipräsident Litzmannstadt, Betr.: Getto, 27 February [194]1.

26. Werner E. Hecht, "Ein Filmdokument—der Jude ohne Maske: 'Der ewige Jude'—Das Filmwerk von Wesen und Art des Judentums/Eine eindringliche Mahnung," *LZ,* 19 January 1941, p. 5. In the same vein, see Werner E. Hecht, "Der ewige Jude: Ein dokumentarischer Film über das Judentum," *LZ,* 16 January 1941, p. 3. H. Grohmann, "Das Judentum als rassenbiologische Frage: Die geistige Struktur des Judentums als rassisches Merkmal," *LZ,* 24 January 1941, p. 5.

27. Niels Gustschow, "Stadtplanung im Warthegau 1939–1944," in *Der "Generalplan Ost": Hauptlinien der nationalsozialistischen Planungs- und Vernichtungspolitik,* ed. Mechthild Rössler and Sabine Schleiermacher (Berlin: Akademie Verlag, 1993), pp. 234, 241, 245–248.

28. "Die Neugestaltung von Litzmannstadt: Wie unsere Stadt unter nationalsozialistischer Führung nach und nach ein neueres Gesicht erhält," *LZ,* 20 October 1940, p. 5.

29. APL GV 29361, pp. 75–77: B[iebow] to Bürgermeister u. Stadtkämmerer

Dr. Marder, Betr.: Dienstgebäude in der Moltkestr, 211. Bezug: Bericht des Rechnungsprüfungsamts, 21 April 1941. The move to the new headquarters was to begin at 8 AM on 21 May 1941. GV PSZ 29215, p. 35 [535]: Gettoverwaltung to Transport-Abt., 20 May [19]41, signed Czarnulla.

30. "Einführung des neuen Oberbürgermeisters: Gestern führte der Gauleiter und Reichsminister Pg. Ventzki in sein Amt des Oberbürgermeisters ein," *LZ,* 9 May 1941, p. 3. Photograph of Ventzki appears here and in "Neuer Oberbürgermeister von Litzmannstadt: Gauamtsleiter der NSV., Pg. Werner Ventzki, Posen, wurde zum Oberbürgermesiter unserer Stadt ernannt," *LZ,* 7 May 1941, p. 5; and "Der zweite Tag des Gauleiterbesuchs bei uns," *LZ,* 10 May 1941, p. 5. A brief biography of Dr. Karl Marder appears under the title "Bürgermeister und Stadtkämmerer Dr. Marder: Anderthalb Jahre erfolgreicher Arbeit im Dienst der Stadtverwaltung von Litzmannstadt," *LZ,* 7 May 1941, p. 5.

31. APL AmL GV 28677, pp. 198–199: Verkehrs-u. Nachrichtenamt O12 H/Z, Vermerk, 12 July 1941.

32. APL AmL GV 28677, pp. 215–226: filming log, 2–26 September 1941. Bundesarchiv-Filmarchiv Berlin, Magazin-No. 3578: "Aus Lodz wird Litzmannstadt."

33. Frank, *Togbukh,* entry for 21 March 1941, pp. 58–59.

34. From "The Chronology of the Ghetto's Industry," in *Łódź Ghetto: Inside a Community under Siege,* ed. Alan Adelson and Robert Lapides (New York: Penguin Books, 1989), pp. 77–78.

35. *Chronicle,* entry for 14 April 1941, pp. 47–48.

36. Ibid., entry for 10 May 1941, p. 53. *The Diary of Dawid Sierakowiak: Five Notebooks from the Łódź Ghetto,* ed. Alan Adelson, trans. Kamil Turowski (New York: Oxford University Press, 1996), entry for 1 May 1941, pp. 85–86.

37. *Chronicle,* entry for 10–24 March 1941, p. 35.

38. Ibid., entry for 20 April 1941, pp. 49–50.

39. A. Volf Yasni, *Di geshikte fun di yidn in Lodz in di yorn fun der daytscher yidn-oysrotung* (Tel-Aviv: I. L. Peretz Library, 1960), p. 401.

40. Cited ibid., pp. 401, 403–404.

41. *The Warsaw Diary of Adam Czerniakow: Prelude to Doom,* ed. Raul Hilberg, Stanislaw Staron, and Josef Kermisz, trans. Stanislaw Staron and the staff of Yad Vashem (New York: Stein and Day, 1979), p. 237.

42. Cited in Adelson and Lapides, *Łódź Ghetto,* pp. 146–147.

43. Frank, *Togbukh,* entry for 21 May 1941, p. 103.

44. Ibid., entry for 8 July 1941, p. 133.

45. Ibid., entries for 22 and 26 May 1941, pp. 103, 105.

46. Ibid., entry for 15 July 1941, pp. 136–137.

47. YIVO RG 241/No. 800, pp. 23, 26.

48. Frank, *Togbukh,* entry for 17 May 1941, p. 98.

49. USHMM-RG.05.008M, Reel 10, Kriminalpolizeistelle Litzmannstadt, File 25, pp. 1–8, 134–135: Der Aelteste der Juden in Litzmannstadt-Getto, Vorstand d. Ordnungsdienstes to Kriminalpolizei, Sonderkommando Getto, 15, 19, 23, 26, 27, 30, and 31 December 1940, 1 January 1941; note of Krim.-Oberassistent, K. II/5, 2 January 1940[1]; Bescheinigung, Krim.-Oberassistent W. Neumann, 2 January 1940. RG-15.083M, Reel 4, File 17, pp. 100–101: Rumkowski to Geheime Staatspolizei, 26 May [194]1; S. Hertzberg, Zentralgefängnis to Aeltesten der Juden, 25 May 1941. USHMM RG-15.083M, Reel 4, File 20, p. 93: Rumkowski to Geheime Staatspolizei, 16 April 1943; Der Aelteste der Juden in Litzmannstadt Kohlen-Abteilung to Zentralsekretariat Bałuter Ring, 29 March 1943.

50. On this, see Dan Diner, *Beyond the Conceivable: Studies on Germany, Nazism, and the Holocaust* (Berkeley: University of California Press, 2000), pp. 133–134.

51. *Chronicle,* entry for 9 May 1941. Frank, *Togbukh,* entry for 10 May 1941, pp. 94–95.

52. *Chronicle,* entry for 10 May 1941, p. 53.

53. Frank, *Togbukh,* entry for 12 June 1941, pp. 112–114. See also the photograph of Rumkowski's encounter with Himmler in Adelson and Lapides, *Łódź Ghetto,* opposite p. 386.

54. Dr. Marder to Regierungspräsident, 4 July 1941, in A. Eisenbach, *Dokumenty i materiały do dziejów niemieckiej w Polsce,* vol. 3, *Getto Łódzkie,* pt. 1 (Warsaw: Centralna Żydowska Instytut Historyczny, 1946), pp. 177–179. Marder was here making, on the city's behalf, a bid to replace these losses and outlays by drawing payment from ghetto resources, an ongoing effort that failed to meet with the approval of the Regierungspräsident. See also Browning, *Origins of the Final Solution,* pp. 154–155.

55. Eisenbach, *Dokumenty i materiały,* vol. 3, pt. 1, p. 184: Biebow, "Einsiedlung weiterer Juden ins Getto," 3 June 1941.

56. Ibid., pp. 197–200: Der Oberbürgermeister von Litzmannstadt, Gettoverwaltung, to Regierungspräsident, 24 September [19]41, signed Ventzki. USHMM RG-05.008M, Reel 1, File 32: Der Oberbürgermeister, Gettoverwaltung, to Regierungspräsident, 25 September 1941. Browning, *Origins,* 330–332. Florian Freund, Bertrand Perz, and Karl Stuhlpfarrer, "Das Getto in Litzmannstadt (Łódź)," in *"Unser einziger Weg ist Arbeit": Das Getto in Łódź 1940–1944,* ed. Hanno Loewy and Gerhard Schoenberner (Vienna: Löcker Verlag, 1990), pp. 26–27.

57. *Chronicle,* entry for "the month of September 1941," p. 76. YIVO, RG

241/No. 1049 (Film 117): "Album Presented to Rumkowski on the Eve of Rosh Hashanah, 5702, September 1941," greeting, p. 18.

58. *Chronicle,* entry for "The month of September 1941," pp. 76–78. YIVO RG 241/No. 800, pp. 878–879 [internally numbered pp. 8–11]: Table, "Eingesiedelete im Jahre 1941, aus dem Altreich, Wien, Prag, Luxemburg und aus Leslau und Umgebung."

59. ŻIH Pamiętnik 302/115, Sz. Rozenstein, entry for 28 September 1941, p. 118.

60. YIVO RG 241/No. 800, pp. 878–879 [8–11]: Table, "Eingesiedelete im Jahre 1941." Age profile based on count of those born in 1890 or earlier. On the experience of removal and departure from Prague, see Oskar Rosenfeld, *In the Beginning Was the Ghetto: Notes from Łódź,* ed. Hanno Loewy and trans. Brigitte M. Goldstein (Evanston: Northwestern University Press, 2002), Notebook A, pp. 3–12.

61. The quotations and summary of conditions in the discussion that follows are from Rosenfeld, *In the Beginning,* pp. 12–26. On the sleeping arrangements, see also APL PSZ 1099, p. 202: Oskar Singer, "Zum Problem Ost und West," pt. 12, 26 June 1942: "Most people had to sleep on the floor. There was not sufficient room for everybody to lie down and stretch out. One hadn't closed one's eyes for eight whole days. . . . People were," quite simply, "at the end of their strength. They just wanted to *stretch out* and sleep." APL PSZ 1101, pp. 26–27: Bernard Heilig, "Die ersten sieben Monate in Litzmannstadt-Getto: Flüchtige Eindrücke und Bilder," unpublished ms.

62. Rosenfeld, *In the Beginning,* pp. 16, 25–26.

63. YIVO RG 241/No. 800, pp. 890–891 [32–33]: Table, "Todesfälle unter den Eingesiedelten Aus Altreich, Wien, Prag, und Luxemburg, X. 1941–VI. 1942."

64. ŻIH 302/115, diary of Sz. Rozenstein, entry for 9 November 1941, p. 140.

65. Trunk, *Łódź Ghetto,* pp. 307–310.

66. APL PSZ 1101, p. 23: Heilig, "Die ersten sieben Monate in Litzmannstadt-Getto."

67. APL PSZ 1101, pp. 1, 2, 5–6 [11–14]: Alicja de Bunon, "Durch's Fenster gesehen. . . . oder die letzte Blaue!"

68. Ibid., pp. 2, 5–6 [12, 13, 14].

69. Ibid., pp. 11, 13, 16–18 [16–19]. See also APL PSZ 1099, p. 202: Singer, "Zum Problem Ost und West."

70. Oberbürgermeister [Werner] Ventzki, "Der Führer befiehlt die Neugestaltung Litzmannstadt: Der künftigen Entwicklung unserer Stadt ist

nunmehr der Weg bereitet," *LZ,* 1 November 1941. "Die Neugestaltung von Litzmannstadt: Glückwünsch des Gauleiters zum Führererlass/Beauftragung des Oberbürgermeisters," *LZ,* 15 November 1941.

71. "Litzmannstadt der Zukunft gewinnt Gestalt: Arbeit, Kultur und Wehrhaftigkeit sind der künftigen frohen und gesunden deutschen Bevölkerung," *LZ,* 27 November 1941. See also *Chronicle,* p. 21, n. 31.

72. Ibid.

73. Ibid.

6. Banishment

1. Shlomo Frank, *Togbukh fun Lodzher geto* (Buenos Aires: Tsentral-farband fun Poylishe Yidn in Argentine, 1958), entry for 2 January 1942, p. 218.

2. *The Chronicle of the Łódź Ghetto, 1940–1944,* ed. Lucjan Dobroszycki, trans. Richard Lourie, Joachim Neugroschel et al. (New Haven: Yale University Press, 1984), entry for 20 December 1941, pp. 96–97.

3. Ibid., entry for 1–5 January 1942, pp. 111–113.

4. Ibid., pp. 111–112.

5. Ibid.

6. Ibid., entry for 7 January 1942, p. 116.

7. Ibid., entry for 10–13 January 1942, p. 119.

8. Ibid., entry for 1–5 January 1942, pp. 107–108.

9. Ibid., entry for 14–31 January 1942, 124–125.

10. Frank, *Togbukh,* entry for 14 January 1942, pp. 227–228.

11. *Chronicle,* entries for 10–13 and 14–31 January 1942, pp. 120–121, 124.

12. APL PSZ 1238, p. 62: Hinda Bendkowska to the Ausweisungs-Kommission, 11 January 1942.

13. APL PSZ 1238, p. 66: Temar Braun to the Ausweisungs-Kommission, 16 January 1942.

14. APL PSZ 1238, p. 47: Szmul Abram Ackermann to Police Precinct 1, 22 January 1942.

15. APL PSZ 1238, p. 45: Josef Ajnreder to the Ausweisungs-Kommission, 21 January 1942.

16. APL PSZ 1238, p. 43: Szmul Hersch Ajlenberg to the Ausweisungs-Kommission, 21 January 1942.

17. *Chronicle,* entry for 14–31 January 1942, p. 124.

18. APL PSZ 382, pp. 3–6, 8–9, 11, 15, 79: Order Service log, 20–24 January and 17 February 1942.

19. Frank, *Togbukh,* entries for 14–17 January 1942, pp. 227–230.

20. Only weeks before, at the end of December, in a ceremony held in the ghetto, Rumkowski was married to Regina Weinberger, a young attorney from Łódź. *Chronicle,* entries for 26–28 and 29–31 December 1941, pp. 101–103.

21. APL PSZ 1090: "Praca Jest Naszym Drogowskazem," Imponujące Wystawa w Rocnicę Wytworni Sukien i Bielizny, 17 January 1942. APL PSZ 1108, p. 29: series marked "Wäsche und Kleider[,] 1 Jahr." APL PSZ 1090, pp. 70–71.

22. APL PSZ 1090: "Praca Jest Naszym Drogowskazem," Imponujące Wystawa w Rocnicę Wytworni Sukien i Bielizny, 17 January 1942. APL PSZ 1108, p. 29: series marked "Wäsche und Kleider[,] 1 Jahr." APL PSZ 1090, pp. 70–71.

23. "Speech by Chaim Rumkowski," 17 January 1942, reproduced in *Łódź Ghetto: A Community under Siege,* ed. Alan Adelson and Robert Lapides (New York: Penguin, 1989), p. 207.

24. Operating under the authority of Higher SS and Police Leader Wilhelm Koppe, acting in concert with Gauleiter Greiser of the Warthegau, SS-Hauptsturmführer Herbert Lange, the first of the camp's commanders, directed a team of executioners assembled from men of the Security Police, reinforced by some one hundred men recruited from the Litzmannstadt Schutzpolizei. Shmuel Krakowski, "The Historical Outline of the Camp in Chełmno-on-Ner," in *Chełmno Witnesses Speak,* ed. Łucja Pawllicka-Nowak, trans. Juliet D. Golden and Arkadiusz Kamiński (Konin and Łódź: Council for the Protection of Memory of Combat and Martyrdom in Warsaw and District Museum in Konin, 2004), pp. 8–11.

25. "Als Totengräber im Vernichtungslager: Augenzeugenbericht über die Ermordung von Juden und Zigeunern in der Gaswagenstation Chełmno am Ner vom 5. bis zum 19. Januar 1942, mitgeteilt von 'Szlamek,' der von dort fliehen konnte [aufgezeichnet von Hersz Wasser]," in Ruta Sakowska, *Die zweite Etappe ist der Tod: NS-Ausrottungspolitik gegen die polnischen Juden, gesehen mit den Augen der Opfer,* Publikationnen der Gedeknkstätte Haus der Wannsee-Konferenz, ed. Wolfgang Scheffler and Gerhard Schoenberner, vol. 3 (Berlin: Edition Hentrich, 1993), p. 179. Ruta Sakowska, "About an Account by Szlamek, a Chełmno-on-Ner Runaway," in Pawlicka-Nowak, *Chełmno Witnesses Speak,* pp. 98–100.

26. Sakowska, *Die zweite Etappe,* pp. 179–180. A third early escapee from Chełmno, Michał Podchlebnik, would survive the war. For his account, see Pawlicka-Nowak, *Chełmno Witnesses Speak,* pp. 119–124.

27. Sakowska, *Die zweite Etappe,* pp. 180–182.

28. See ibid., p. 184, n. 2. After providing his account, Szlamek made his way

from Warsaw to relations in the ghetto in Zamość. There, in April 1942, he was caught up in a deportation to the death camp at Bełżec, where he was killed. Sakowska, "About an Account by Szlamek," p. 100.

29. See Israel Gutman, "Introduction: The Distinctiveness of the Łódź Ghetto," in Isaiah Trunk, *Łódź Ghetto,* trans. and ed. Robert Moses Shapiro (Bloomington: Indiana University Press in association with the United States Holocaust Memorial Museum, 2006), pp. l, li. *Chronicle,* introduction, pp. xx–xxii. Sakowska, *Die zweite Etappe,* p. 156.

30. *Chronicle,* pp. 133, 139, entry for "The Month of March, 1942." See also APL GV 29252, pp. 62–64: monthly statistics on disease, hospital admissions, deaths, and births supplied by Rumkowski, 3 February 1942, 1 March 1942, 1 April 1942.

31. *Chronicle,* p. 139, entry for "The Month of March, 1942."

32. Ibid., pp. 133–134.

33. APL GV 30733, p. 8: Bertram v. Hobe, "Bertram v. Hobe Modelle Kleider Sport" to Oberbügermeister von Litzmannstadt, Getto-Verwaltung, 11 February 1942.

34. APL GV 30733, p. 4: Gebrüder Nehrling Kleider- und Blusenfabrik to Oberbürgermeister, Getto-Verwaltung, Litzmannstadt, 17 March 1942.

35. Raul Hilberg, *The Destruction of the European Jews,* vol. 1 (New York: Holmes & Meier, 1985), p. 263.

36. Ibid. Biebow to Geheime Staatspolizei, Kommandant Fuchs, 4 March 1942, in A. Eisenbach, *Dokumenty i materiały do dziejów okupacji niemieckiej w Polsce,* vol. 3, *Getto Łódźkie,* pt. 1 (Warsaw: Centralna Żydowska Komisja Historyczna, 1946), pp. 243–244.

37. Eisenbach, *Dokumenty i materiały,* pp. 244–245.

38. APL PSZ GV 29246, p. 51: Monatsbericht der Auftrangsüberwachungs-Abteilng f. März 1942 [Monthly Report of the Department for the Monitoring of Orders for March 1942], dated 14 April 1942, signed Schuster.

39. *Chronicle,* p. 141, entry for 1 April 1942.

40. Ibid., pp. 141–142.

41. Ibid., pp. 141–143.

42. Ibid., p. 139, entry for "The Month of March, 1942."

7. Departure, Worry, and Disappearance

1. "Die Staffel 'Quer durch Litzmannstadt'—ein voller Erfolg," *LZ,* 30 March 1942.

2. Oskar Rosenfeld, *In the Beginning was the Ghetto: Notebooks from Łódź,* ed.

Hanno Loewy, trans. Brigitte M. Goldstein (Evanston: Northwestern University Press, 2002), Notebook B, pp. 36–37.

3. ŻIH Lodz 138: Zum Anruf von Herrn Biebow! 4 April 1942, 027/2/Ri/Po, copy.

4. *The Chronicle of the Łódź Ghetto, 1941–1944,* ed. Lucjan Dobroszycki, trans. Richard Lurie, Joachim Neugroschel et al. (New Haven: Yale University Press, 1984), entry for 10–14 April 1942, p. 145. Janusz Gulczyński, *Obóz śmierci w Chełmnie nad Nerem* (Konin: Wojcwódzki Ośrodek Kultury w Konine, 1991), p. 41.

5. Ian Kershaw, "Improvised Genocide? The Emergence of the 'Final Solution' in the 'Warthegau,'" *Transactions of the Royal Historical Society,* 6th ser., 2 (1992): 70–72. Greiser to Himmler, 1 May 1942, reproduced in *Faschismus-Getto-Massenmord: Dokumentation über Ausrottung und Widerstand der Juden in Polen während des zweiten Weltkrieges,* ed. Tatiana Berenstein, Artur Eisenbach, Bernard Mark, and Adam Rutkowski (Frankfurt am Main: Röderberg Verlag, 1960), p. 278.

6. Peter Witte, Michael Wildt, Martina Voigt et al., eds., *Der Dienstkalendar Heinrich Himmlers 1941/42* (Hamburg: Hans Christians Verlag, 1999), pp. 398–400 and 400, n. 41. Gulczyński, *Obóz śmierci,* p. 61.

7. Witte et al., *Der Dienstkalendar Heinrich Himmlers 1941/42,* pp. 398–400.

8. ŻIH Lodz 138: Getto-Verwaltung, Betr.: "Umsiedlung von Juden," 20 April 1942, copy, notated as signed by Biebow.

9. *Chronicle,* p. 149, entry for 18–20 April 1942. Oskar Rosenfeld, *Wozu noch Welt: Aufzeichnungen aus dem Getto Lodz,* ed. Hanno Loewy (Frankfurt am Main: Verlag Neue Kritik, 1994), p. 66.

10. Rosenfeld, *Wozu noch Welt,* p. 67.

11. *Chronicle,* entry for 29 and 30 April 1942, p. 156.

12. Ibid.

13. Ibid., entry for 6 May 1942, p. 162. This was the first of two entries both dated 6 May.

14. Ibid. Of the twenty originally exempt translators, by 6 May three had died without being replaced.

15. Ibid., entries for 6 and 17 May 1942, pp. 161–163, 175.

16. Ibid., entry for 17 May 1942, p. 175.

17. Ibid., entry for 9–11 May 1942, p. 168.

18. APL PSZ 1288, p. 508: Dr. Oskar Fantl to the Resettlement Commission, 3 May 1942.

19. APL PSZ 1288, p. 80: Jula Appel to Amt für Eingesiedelte, n.d.

20. APL PSZ 1288, p. 10: Sophie Abraham to Resettlement Commission, 4 May 1942.

21. APL PSZ 1288, p. 542: To the Resettlement Commission, unsigned letter on behalf of Rosa Freitag, 3 May 1942.

22. *Chronicle,* entry for 29 and 30 April 1942, pp. 156–157.

23. Ibid., p. 157.

24. Rosenfeld, *In the Beginning,* p. 104. Rosenfeld, *Wozu noch Welt,* p. 131.

25. APL GV 29201, pp. 390–392: Versand d. Ordnungsdienstes, Zusammenfassung der Tagesmeldungen v. 1.–31.5 1942, dated 2 June 1942, signed Leon Rosenblatt. *Chronicle,* entry for Tuesday, 12 May 1942, p. 171.

26. APL PSZ 1099, pp. 32–34: commentary of Oskar Singer.

27. Rosenfeld, *In the Beginning,* pp. 103–104.

28. *Chronicle,* entries for Monday, 4 May 1942, and Thursday, 7 May 1942, pp. 160, 164. Rosenfeld, *In the Beginning,* Notebook E, p. 104.

29. *Chronicle,* p. 160, entry for Monday, 4 May 1942.

30. Ibid., p. 161, entry for Wednesday, 6 May 1942.

31. Ibid., p. 159, entry for 1 May 1942.

32. Ibid., pp. 163–164, entry for 6 May 1942.

33. G. K., "Eine Anlage, die eine Zukunft vor sich hat," *LZ,* 8 May 1942.

34. Adolf Kargel, "Die Pflanzen, die unter Naturschutz stehen," *LZ,* 15 May 1942.

35. "Ich reise übers grüne Land!" *LZ,* 12 May 1942.

36. *Chronicle,* entry for 20 and 21 May, 1942, p. 181.

37. ŻIH File 302/3, pp. 260–261: Shlomo Frank, Łódź ghetto, entry for 26 May 1942.

38. *Chronicle,* pp. 181–182, entry for 20 and 21 May 1942.

39. Ibid., p. 183, entry for 20 May 1942.

40. Ibid., pp. 180, 182–184, entries for 18 and 20 May 1942. By 20 May some four thousand persons from Brzeziny were reported to have reached Łódź. Ibid., entry for 20 May 1942, p. 182.

41. Ibid., p. 180, entry for 18 May 1942.

42. Ibid.

43. Ibid., p. 185, entry for 22 and 23 May 1942.

44. Ibid., p. 190, entries for 30 and 31 May 1942.

45. APL GV 29667, pp. 158, 160: to Getto-Verwaltung in Litzmannstadt, Betr. Evakuierung nichtarbeitsfähiger Juden, Erfassung von Vermögenswerte, 18 May 1942, and attached Verzeichnis der bei der Räumung der Judenwohnungen sichergestellten Vermögenswerte (Evakuierung am 9. Oktober 1941).

46. APL GV 29666: 027/1/Lu/Po to Stadtsparkaße Litzmannstadt, Betr.: Devisenverkauf/Sonderkonto 12300: 6 June 1942 (p. 179), 10 June 1942 (p. 165), 23 June 1942 (p. 24). APL GV 29667: 027/1/Lu/Po Betr.: Devisenverkauf/Sonderkonto 12300, 14 July 1942 (p. 46). APL GV 29669: 027/1/Lu/Po to Stadtsparkaße Litzmannstadt, 1 September 1942 (p. 158).

47. One listing for compensation as *Zusatz-Gefahrenzulage* for the period from 15 April to 30 June 1942 for ten such indicated employees notes that they were granted individually daily supplements of RM4, amounting to RM2,781.99. APL GV 29667: Gettoverwaltung Personalstelle, 9 and 10 July 1942. In reference to the dirty nature of sorting goods meriting additional pay, see APL/GV 29666: Aktenvermerk 97/42, Betr.: Sonderaktion/Sonderzulage für Amtsboten Seidel und Fenner, 12 June 1942, signed Biebow.

48. APL GV 29666: Aktenvermerk 97/42, Betr.: Sonderaktion/Sonderzulage für Amtsboten Seidel und Fenner, 12 June 1942, signed Biebow.

49. APL GV 29666, p. 158: Receipt *(Quittung)*, stamped "paid": 22 May 1942; further stamped "Enclosure" *(Anlage)*, 23 May 1942.

50. APL GV 29667, p. 39: Stadtsparkaße Litzmannstadt to Oberbuergermeister von Litzmannstadt—Gettoverwaltung, 6 June 1942.

51. APL GV 29666, p. 188: Stadtsparkaße Litzmannstadt to the Ghetto Administration, 22 June 1942.

52. APL/GV 29667, pp. 155–156: B[iebow] to Buchhaltung im Hause, 22 June 1942; Betr.: Sonderkonto 12300, 30 June 1942; B[iebow] to Buchhaltung Herrn Genewein, 10 June 1942.

53. APL GV 29667, p. 158: Amtskommissar Chodecz to Getto-Verwaltung in Litzmannstadt, 18 May 1942.

54. APL GV 29667, p. 156: B[iebow] to Buchaltung, Herr Genewein, Betr.: Sonderkonto 123200: 10 June 1942. Betr.: Sonderkonto 12300, 30 June 1942.

55. APL GV 29667, pp. 158–159: Amtskommisar Godetz (Chodecz) to Getto-Verwaltung in Litzmannstadt, 18 May 1942; Verzeichnis der bei der Raeumung der Judenwohnungen sichergestellten Vermoegenswerte, Amtskommisar Chodecz, 4 April 1942.

56. APL GV 29668, pp. 94, 95: Quittung Stadtsparkaße Litzmannstadt, Zur Gutschrift auf Kto. No. 12300, 10 August 1942; Einnahmebescheinigung to N.S.V. Ortsgruppe Pabianice-Ost, 8 August 1942.

57. APL GV 29667, pp. 55–56, 61: F. W. Ribbe to Singer Sewing Machine Company, 8 July 1942; Singer Sewing Machine Company, Litzmannstadt, to Buergermeister Stadt Lentschuetz, 21 April 1942; Singer Sewing Machine Company Litzmannstadt to Buergermeister in Poddembitze, 11 June 1942.

58. APL GV/29668, pp. 113, 113–114, 115–116: Regierungshauptkasse, Duesseldorf, to Geheime Staatspolizei, Litzmannstadt, 13 July 1942, and Gestapo, Litzmannstadt, to Gettoverwaltung, 25 July 1942; Die Gerichtskasse, Litzmannstadt, Justizinspektor, to Gestapo, Litzmannstadt, 24 June 1942, and Gestapo, Litzmannstadt, to Gettoverwaltung, 25 July 1942.

59. APL GV 29666, pp. 137, 140: Litzmannstaedter Elektrischische

Zufuhrbahnen Aktiengesellschaft to Geheime Staatspolizei, Rechnungen, 19 and 26 May 1942.

60. Bahnhof, Pabianice, to Gestapo Litzmannstadt, 26 May 1942, reproduced in Berenstein et al., *Faschismus-Getto-Massenmord*, p. 395.

61. Deutsche Reichsbahn Vorstand des Verkehrsamts AA 3 to Geheime Staatspolizei, Litzmannstadt, 19 May 1942, with accompanying notation: II B 4 Weiter an die Ghettoverwaltung in Litzmannstadt zur Bezahlung des Betrages an die Reichsbahn; Nachweis der in der Zeit von 4.5–15.5.42 abgefertigten Juden, reproduced in Berenstein et al., *Faschismus-Getto-Massenmord*, pp. 280–281.

62. "Fernschreiben des stellvertrenden Leiters der deutschen Gettoverwaltung in Lodsch, Luchterhandt, an das Wirtschaftsamt in Posen über den Abtransport von 370 Waggons Kleidung, 27 May 1942," in Berenstein et al., *Faschismus—Getto—Massenmord*, p. 396.

63. APL/GV 29668: Transport firm billings for Gettoverwaltung in Litzmannstadt, Sondereinsatz: Rechnung No. 166, 5 June 1942 (p. 144); No. 485, 19 June 1942 (p. 122); and No. 535, 10 July 1942 (p. 123).

64. APL GV 29669, pp. 192–193: Rechnung No. A.406/VII and No. A.1459/VII, Adjutantur d. Reichstatthalter, Posen, 6 July and 20 July 1942.

65. APL GV 29668: Likörfabrik und Weingrosshandlung Helmuth Ring, Rechnung fuer die Gettoverwaltung Litzmannstadt, 17 July [19]42 (p. 118), and payment slip number 197471, 10 August 1942 (p. 117).

66. Gerda Zorn, *"Nach Ostland Geht Unser Ritt": Deutsche Eroberungspolitik und die Folgen. Das Beispiel Lodz* (Cologne: Röderberg im Pahl-Rugenstein Verlag, 1988), p. 125. ŻIH Łódź 138: An die Einkaufsabteilung Herrn Hämmerle, 23 May 1942.

67. APL GV 29669, p. 184: Der Reichskommissar für die Festigung deutschen Volkstums, Voksdeutsche Mittelstelle—Umsiedlung—Einsatzstab Litzmannstadt Gesundheitsabteilung, Betrifft: Desinfektionsarbeiten: Rechnung 12 August 1942.

68. YIVO RG 241/No. 895: Josef Zelkowicz, "Inem lager fun altshik," 17 August 1943 [p. 3]. Isaiah Spiegel, *Ghetto Kingdom: Tales of the Łódź Ghetto*, trans. David H. Hirsch and Roslyn Hirsch (Evanston: Northwestern University Press, 1998), p. 98.

69. Arieh Ben-Menachem, *With a Camera in the Ghetto* (Tel-Aviv: Ghetto Fighters' House and Hakibbutz Hameuchad Publishing House, 1970), pp. 103–104.

70. On Rosenfeld's early writings, see Hanno Loewy, "Editor's Introduction," in Rosenfeld, *In the Beginning*, pp. xiv–xv.

71. Ibid., pp. 44, 67, Notebooks B and D, entries listed as *"Face of the Ghetto,* June 1942," and 8 June [1942].

72. Ibid., Notebook D, entries for 27 June 1942, p. 75. See also Rosenfeld, *Wozu noch Welt,* entry for 27 June 1942, p. 105.

73. Rosenfeld, *In the Beginning,* p. 75, Notebook D, entry for 27 June 1942.

74. Ibid., pp. 74–75, Notebook D, entry for 27 June 1942. Rosenfeld, *Wozu noch Welt,* p. 105.

75. See Loewy's comment in Rosenfeld, *In the Beginning,* p. 294, n. 5.

76. *Chronicle,* p. 209, including n. 70, entry for 22 June 1942. The address of Wendel's bureau was shared by the Litzmannstadt bureau of the Reichspropagandaamt. See APL GV 31254, p. 11: Der Reichsstatthalter, Reichspropagandaamt, Zweigstelle Litzmannstadt to Biebow, 1 July 1942.

77. *Chronicle,* pp. 169, 169n., 209–210, including n. 70, entries for 9–11 May and 22 June 1942. Rosenfeld, *In the Beginning,* Notebook H, pp. 305, n. 12, and 307, n. 13. Also Rosenfeld, *Wozu noch Welt, Heft* H, pp. 314–315, nn. 12 and 13, Notebook H. APL GV 31254, p. 29: Bescheinigung, Biebow, 28 April 1942. APL GV 31254, p. 544: Biebow to Ältesten der Juden, 5 May 1942. APL GV 31254 [page number illegible]: Prof. Emanuel Hirschberg to Gettoverwaltung, 19 May 1942. APL GV 31254, p. 28: Biebow to Ältesten der Juden, Betr. Lebensmittelzuteilung für die Mitarbeiterinnen des Professor Hirschberg, 28 April 1942. APL GV 31254, p. 26: Biebow to Ältesten der Juden, Betr.: Lebensmittelzuteilung fur die Mitarbeiterinnen des Prof. Hirschberg, 7 May 1942.

78. APL GV 31254, p. 8: Reichsministerium fuer Volksaufklaerung und Propaganda, Der Generalreferent fuer Ausstellungen und Messen to Reichspropagandaamt Wartheland Zweigstelle Litzmannstadt, 26 June [19]42 [Abschrift].

79. APL GV 31254, pp. 5–6: 027/2/Ri/R, to Reichstatthalter, Reichspropagandaamt, z. Hd. Herrn Gissibl, Litzmannstadt, 27 August 1942, signature faint, with handwritten notation "Herrn Biebow zur Kenntnisnahme" and initialed B[iebow]. See also GV 31254, p. 3: Biebow to Reichspropagandaamt, Litzmannstadt, 1 December 1942, Betr.: Getto-Ausstellung.

80. *Chronicle,* p. 210, entry for 22 June 1942.

81. Rosenfeld, *In the Beginning,* pp. 306–307.

82. See APL PSZ 1124, p. 3.

83. On Rosenfeld's novella and his performance criticism, see Loewy, "Editor's Introduction," in Rosenfeld, *In the Beginning,* pp. xvi, xiii–xvi.

84. Rosenfeld, *In the Beginning,* Notebook 13, p. 79; and Rosenfeld, *Wozu noch Welt,* Notebook 13, p. 109.

85. Rosenfeld, *In the Beginning,* p. 79, Notebook 13.

86. Ibid., p. 80.

87. Biographical notations by Loewy, ibid., p. 290, n. 2.

88. Ibid., p. 80, Notebook 13.

89. Ibid.

90. YIVO RG 241/858, O[skar] R[osenfeld], Kulturhaus-Konzerte. Symphonie-Konzert, 1 July 1942.

91. Rosenfeld, *In the Beginning*, p. 81, Notebook 13.

92. YIVO RG 241/858: O[skar] R[osenfeld], Kulturhaus-Konzerte. Symphonie-Konzert, 1 July 1942.

93. Recall the title of a work by Judith Miller, *One, by One, by One: Facing the Holocaust* (New York: Simon and Schuster, 1990).

8. "Give Me Your Children"

1. S., "Unsere Kleinsten feierten ein Kinderfest: Auf der Spielwiese tummelten sich Mädel und Buben/Manche Überraschung erfreute," *LZ,* 25 June 1942. "So Turnen unsere Kleinen auf der Spielwiese," *LZ,* 26 June 1942.

2. "Fröhliches Kinderglück im Sonnenschein: In den Parks von Litzmannstadt laden viele Plätze unsere Kleinen zum Tummeln ein," *LZ,* 15 June 1942.

3. "Badefreuden winken," *LZ,* 8 July 1942.

4. In considering this, I have found Elaine Scarry's commentary on "injuring-as-substantiation" in war, on the body and sacrifice, on the biblical focus on the centrality of numbers in generational increase and decline, and on the importance of laying claim to a land of much interest. Elaine Scarry, *The Body in Pain: The Making and Unmaking of the World* (New York: Oxford University Press, 1985), pp. 137–138, 185–205.

5. Account of Heinz May in K. M. Pospieszalski, "Niemiecki nadleśniczy o zagładzie Żydów w Chełmnie nad Nerem," *Przegląd Zachodni* 18, no. 3 (May–June 1962): 102. See also Łucja Pawlicka-Nowak, ed., *Chełmno Witnesses Speak,* trans. Juliet D. Golden and Arkadiusz Kamiński (Konin: Council for the Protection of Memory of Combat and Martyrdom in Warsaw and District Museum in Konin, 2004), account of H. May, p. 159, and testimony of Andrzej Miszcak, p. 141. Głowna Komisja Badania Zbrodni przeciwko Narodowi Polskiemu—Instytut Pamięci Narodowej, Ob 271, t. III, pp. 208–209: witness statement, Czesław Urbaniak, 5 July 1945.

6. Accounts of May and Misczak in Pawlicka-Nowak, *Chełmno Witnesses Speak,* pp. 158–161, 141. Glowna Komisja, Ob 271, t. I, pp. 70–71: witness statement, Aleksander Wózniak, 16 June 1945; Ob 271, t.II, p. 115: statement of Jozef Czuprynski, 25 June 1945.

7. Account of May in Pawlicka-Nowak, *Chełmno Witnesses Speak,* p. 160.

"Testimony by Walter Piller," ibid., p. 185. Affidavit of Rudolf Höss, cited in Richard Rhodes, *Masters of Death: The SS-Einsatzgruppen and the Invention of the Holocaust* (New York: Knopf, 2002), p. 259. The mill's provenance is not altogether certain, but we do know that in the summer of 1942 one was requested from the Łódź ghetto. It is perhaps a mark of the confidence, if not to say the brazenness, of the Gettoverwaltung, accomplice to the crime, that in July 1942 it delivered to Rumkowski a query regarding the availability of such "a bone grinder." The request went so far as to indicate that the mill was being sought for the Sonderkommando Kulmhof (Chełmno). See Ribbe to Eldest of the Jews, Litzmannstadt, 16 July 1942, in *Dokumeny i materiały do djieow okupacji niemeickiej w Polsce*, ed. A. Eisenbach, vol. 3, *Ghetto Lodzkie*, pt. 1 (Warsaw: Centralna Żydowska Komisja Historyczna, 1946), p. 279.

8. APL PSZ 1099, p. 124: Oskar Singer, "Der Tag in Fragmenten. Zu Kapiteln von frueher."

9. "Swit ('dawn' in Polish) purported to be broadcasting clandestinely within occupied Poland, but in fact it was a British-sponsored service broadcasting from facilities near London." Robert Moses Shapiro, "Diaries and Memoirs from the Lodz Gheto in Yiddish and Hebrew," in *Holocaust Chronicles: Individualizing the Holocaust through Diaries and Other Contemporaneous Personal Accounts* (Hoboken, N.J.: KTAV Publishing House, 1999), p. 114, n. 31.

10. Shlomo Frank, *Togbukh fun Lodzher geto* (Buenos Aires: Tsentral-farlag fun Poylishe Yidn in Argentine, 1958), entry for 9 July 1942, pp. 289–290.

11. Ibid., entry for 20 July 1942, pp. 292–293.

12. *The Chronicle of the Łódź Ghetto, 1941–1945,* ed. Lucjan Dobroszycki, trans. Richard Lourie, Joachim Neugroschel et al. (New Haven: Yale University Press, 1984), entry for Sunday, 26 July 1942, p. 230.

13. Ibid., and p. 230, n. 76.

14. ŻIH Łódź 138: Gettokommissariat, Bericht, Betrifft: Lagerberichteerstattung an den Inspekteur der Sicherheitspolizei und des SD, July 28, 1942, copy. Lagebericht, Gestapo in Litzmannstadt, 2 July 1942, excerpt in Tatania Berenstein, Artur Eisenbach, Bernard Mark, and Adam Rutkowski, *Faschismus—Ghetto—Massenmord: Dokumentation über Ausrottung und Widerstand der Juden in Polen während des zweiten Weltkrieges* (Frankfurt am Main: Röderberg-Verlag, 1960), p. 292.

15. See Dan Diner, *Beyond the Conceivable: Studies on Germany, Nazism, and the Holocaust* (Berkeley: University of California Press, 2000), pp. 133–135.

16. *Chronicle,* entry for 1 June 1942, pp. 194–195. APL PSZ 1091: transcript of speech, dated 31 May 1942.

17. *Chronicle,* entry for Tuesday, 21 July 1942, p. 226, and Thursday, 23 July 1942, p. 228, both credited to B[ernard] O[strowski].

18. USHMM RG-083M, Reel 168, File 867, p. 63: Statistical Tables,

"Waisenhaus: Zöglinge nach Alter und Geschlecht I.–VIII. 1942 [January–August 1942]"; "Im Arbeitsressorts beschäftigte Zöglinge nach Alter."

19. USHMM RG-15.083M, Reel 168, File 867, pp. 5[1], 53: Statistical Tables, "Kinderkolonien[,] Bewegung, Kinder anch Jahrgängen und Geschlecht[,] VIII. 1940–IX. 1942 [August 1940–September 1942]"; "Arbeitsstellen der Kinder 31.VII. 1942 [31 July 1942]."

20. USHMM RG-15.083M, Reel 4, File 19, p. 231: Die Insassen des Greisenheims II, Gnesenerstraße 26, to Rumkowski, 12 July 1942. Printed in part in a stylized poster-style format not reproduced here.

21. *Chronicle,* entry for 28 August 1942, pp. 244–245.

22. Oskar Rosenfeld, *In the Beginning Was the Ghetto: Notebooks from Lodz,* ed. Hanno Loewy, trans. Brigitte M. Goldstein (Evanston: Northwestern University Press, 2002), Notebook E, entry for 27 August [1942], p. 118.

23. ŻIH File 302/299, pp. 7–8: Dziennik Ireny Hauser, entry for 19 August [1942].

24. ŻIH File 302/299, pp. 8, 11–12: Dziennik Ireny Hauser, entries for 19 and 20 August [1942].

25. Janusz Gumkowski, Adam Rutkowski, and Arnfrid Astel, *Briefe aus Litzmannstadt* (Cologne: Friedrich Meddelhauve Verlag, 1967), pp. 72–75.

26. Josef Zelkowicz, *In Those Terrible Days: Notes from the Łódź Ghetto,* trans. Naftali Greenwood (Jerusalem: Yad Vashem, 2002), p. 251. *Chronicle,* entry for 1 September 1942, p. 248, credited to Zelkowicz.

27. *Chronicle,* p. 249. Zelkowicz, *In Those Terrible Days,* entry for 1 September 1942, p. 251.

28. Zelkowicz, *In Those Terrible Days,* pp. 251–254. *Chronicle,* entry for 1 September 1942, pp. 248–249. On the pushing of children from windows, see testimony of Dr. Donat Szmulewicz-Stanisz, in Jerzy Lewiński, *Proces Hansa Biebowa* (Warsaw: PRS, 1999), p. 107, and of Bronyka Szyldwach, in *Preserved Evidence: Ghetto Lodz,* ed. Anna Eilenberg-Eibeshitz, vol. 1 (Haifa: H. Eibeshitz Institute for Holocaust Studies, 1998), pp. 256–257.

29. Note the exchange in Lewiński, *Proces Hansa Biebowa,* p. 67.

30. Testimony of Aleksander Klugman, ibid., pp. 139–140.

31. Testimony of Szyja Teitelbaum, ibid., p. 112.

32. Testimony of Hersz Janowski, ibid., p. 111.

33. *Chronicle,* entry for 1 September 1942, p. 249.

34. *Chronicle,* entry for 2 September 1942, p. 249.

35. Rosenfeld, *In the Beginning,* Notebook E, entry for 4 [September] [1942], p. 121. Oskar Rosenfeld, *Wozu noch Welt Aufzeichnungen aus dem Getto Lodz,* ed. Hanno Loewy (Frankfurt am Main: Verlag Neue Kritik, 1994), entry for 4 [September] [1942], p. 148.

36. Zelkowicz, *In Those Terrible Days,* p. 264.

37. Ibid., pp. 264–265.

38. Ibid., p. 265.

39. Ibid., p. 266.

40. Ibid., pp. 267–268.

41. Ibid., p. 268. *Chronicle,* pp. 250–251.

42. Zelkowicz, *In Those Terrible Days,* pp. 268–269.

43. Ibid., p. 269.

44. Ibid., pp. 270–271.

45. Ibid., p. 273.

46. Ibid., pp. 274–275.

47. Ibid., p. 276. The account in the *Chronicle* refers to Rumkowski's address as having taken place at 4:00 PM. *Chronicle,* entry for 14 September 1942, p. 250.

48. Zelkowicz, *In Those Terrible Days,* p. 276.

49. Ibid., p. 277.

50. Ibid., pp. 277–278.

51. Ibid., p. 278.

52. Ibid.

53. Ibid., p. 279.

54. Ibid.

55. Ibid., p. 280.

56. Ibid.

57. Ibid., p. 282.

58. Ibid., p. 281.

59. Ibid., pp. 280–283.

60. Ibid., pp. 280–282.

61. Ibid., p. 281.

62. Ibid., p. 283.

63. Ibid., pp. 282–283.

64. In addition, elsewhere the Nazis proved equally capable of carrying out evacuations without engaging the direct cooperation of the councils. See Yehuda Bauer, *Rethinking the Holocaust* (New Haven: Yale University Press, 2001), pp. 77–78.

65. In other ghettos, however, such attempts were made, though with very limited success. See Dov Levin, "The Fighting Leadership of the Judenräte in the Small Communities of Poland," in *Patterns of Jewish Leadership in Nazi Europe, 1933–1945: Proceedings of the Third Yad Vashem International Historical Conference,* ed. Yisrael Gutman and Cynthia Haft (Jerusalem: Yad Vashem, 1979), pp. 134, 136–142. Leni Yahil, *The Holocaust: The Fate of European Jewry,* trans. Haya Galai (New York: Oxford University Press), pp. 471–472.

66. Quoted in *Fotoamator* (1998), dir. Dariusz Jabłoński, Apple Film Productions, English version trans. Alina Skibińska and Wolfgang Jöhling.

67. Zelkowicz, *In Those Terrible Days*, p. 286.

68. Ibid., p. 287.

69. Ibid., p. 288.

70. Ibid., pp. 288–289.

71. Ibid., p. 286. On the theme of wishful halting of time, see also Bernard-Henry Lévy, *War, Evil, and the End of History* (Hoboken, N.J.: Melville House, 2004), pp. 224–225.

72. Zelkowicz, *In Those Terrible Days*, p. 289.

73. Ibid., p. 300.

74. Ibid., p. 301.

75. Ibid.

76. Testimony of Matithiahu Jakubowicz, cited in Eilenberg-Eibeshitz, *Preserved Evidence*, p. 261.

77. Ibid. Zelkowicz, *In Those Terrible Days*, pp. 349–351.

78. Zelkowicz, *In Those Terrible Days*, p. 302.

79. Ibid., p. 303.

80. Ibid., p. 307.

81. Oskar Singer, *Im Eilschritt durch den Gettotag. . .* , ed. Sascha Feuchert, Erwin Leibfried, Jörg Recke et al. (Berlin: Philo, 2002), p. 137. Zelkowicz, *In Those Terrible Days*, pp. 307–308.

82. Isaiah Trunk, *Łódź Ghetto: A History*, ed. and trans. Robert Moses Shapiro (Bloomington: Indiana University Press, 2006), pp. 244–245. Yakov Nirenberg, "Di geshikte fun lodsher geto," in *In di yorn fun yidishn khurbn* (New York: Farlag Unser Tsait, 1948), p. 270. Rosenfeld, *In the Beginning*, Notebook H, entry for 12 July [1943], p. 196.

83. Zelkowicz, *In Those Terrible Days*, pp. 343–344.

84. APL Aml GV 28677, p. 256: Betreff: Dokumentarfilm von Litzmannstadt, shooting log for 5 Sept. 1942. The public was also informed of the filmmakers' arrival; see "Der Litzmannstädter Dokumentarfilm," *LZ,* 5 Sept. 1942.

85. Bundesarchiv—Filmarchiv, Berlin, Mag. No. 3578: *Aus Lodz wird Litzmannstadt.*

86. G. K., "Jede Minute verkehren 3 Straßenbahnzüge: Litzmannstadts überaus starker Verkehr/Besondere Disziplin ist sehr notwendig," *LZ,* 5 September 1942.

87. Ilse Schneider, "Litzmannstädter Kleinkunstbühnen," *LZ,* 5 September 1942.

88. G. K., "Nationaltheater des Ostens," *LZ,* 5 September 1942. "Eröffnungsvorstellung im Theater," *LZ,* 5 September 1942.

89. Trunk, *Łódź Ghetto*, pp. 245–246.

90. Frank, *Togbukh*, pp. 308–309.

91. Ibid., p. 309.

92. Ibid., p. 310.

93. Ibid., p. 312.

94. Ibid., p. 317.

95. Ibid., pp. 317–318.

96. Ibid., p. 314.

97. Zelkowicz, *In Those Terrible Days,* pp. 356–358.

98. Ibid., pp. 359–361.

99. Ibid., pp. 375–379.

100. Moshe Pulawer, *Geven iz a geto* (Tel Aviv: Y. L. Peretz-Bibliotek, 1963), p. 19. Dawid Sierakowiak, too, writing on 6 September noted with bitterness: "Laments and shouts, cries and screams have become so commonplace that one pays almost no attention to them. What do I care about another mother's cry when my own mother has been taken from me!? I don't think there can be ample revenge for this." *The Diary of Dawid Sierakowiak: Five Notebooks from the Łódź Ghetto,* ed. Alan Adelson, trans. Kamil Turowski (New York: Oxford University Press, 1996), p. 221.

101. Zelkowicz, *In Those Terrible Days,* p. 348.

102. Ibid., pp. 347–349. Rozka Winogracka, in Eilenberg-Eibeshitz, *Preserved Evidence,* p. 276.

103. Rosenfeld, *In the Beginning,* entry for 12 September [1942], p. 128.

104. Testimony of Rozka Winogrocka, in Eilenberg-Eibeshitz, *Preserved Evidence,* pp. 277–278. She was finally able to break away and survived by hiding inside a mattress (pp. 278–281).

105. Sara Zyskind, *Stolen Years,* trans. Marganit Inbar (Minneapolis: Lerner Publishing, 1981), pp. 94, 103. Testimony of Elchanan Eibeshitz, Etka Krishow, and Irka Schuster, in Eileberg-Eibeshitz, *Preserved Evidence,* pp. 264, 271, 275. See also Trunk, *Łódź Ghetto,* p. 245.

106. Pulawer, *Geven iz a geto,* p. 20.

107. Rozka Winogrocka, in Eilenberg-Eibeshitz, *Preserved Evidence,* p. 279.

108. Pulawer, *Geven iz a geto,* pp. 71–72.

109. Ibid., p. 20.

110. Trunk, *Łódź Ghetto,* pp. 247–248, 287.

111. APL PSZ 465, pp. 16, 30[?], 31, 33, 23, 35, 36: L.DZ.214 G/K/42, Do Referatu Opiekunczego, 15 [17] September 1942, and attached inventories of personal belongings left behind by families and individuals resettled from residences along Marysinska and Marynarska streets.

112. Gettoverwaltung 027/2/Lu/Po, F. W. Ribbe to Städt. Gesundheitsamt, 21 September 1942, and reply of Amtsarzt, Städt. Gesundheitsamt, 24 September 1942, reproduced in Eisenbach, *Dokumenty i materiały,* vol. 3, pt. 1, p. 232.

113. APL Aml GV 28677, pp. 258–259: film log for 13 September [19]42. Bundesarchiv-Filmarchiv Berlin, Mag. No. 3578, *Aus Lodz wird Litzmannstadt.*

114. "Freude und Erholung durch die Partei: Vierhundert Kinder waren Gäste der NS-Volkswohlfahrt im Erzhausen-Tagheim," *LZ,* 20 September 1942.

115. G. K., "Unsere Mutter sind heute ganz auf Draht: Mutterschule des Deutschen Frauenwerks/eine vorbildliche Einrichtung im Werden," *LZ,* 18 October 1942.

116. Adolf Kargel, "Der Hort unserer germanischen Bodenkunde: Ein Gang durch das heute zu eröffende Museum für Vorgeschichte am Deutschlandplatz," *LZ,* 26 September 1942. In June, Kargel had reported on the discovery of these artifacts in Erzhausen, referring to the unearthing of a child's rattle made of clay and bronze. He indicated too that the excavations had drawn crowds of interested spectators. A. K., "Die Ausgrabungen im Stadtteil Erzhausen: Urnengräber aus der Zeit der germanischen Einwanderung in unser Gebiet freigelegt," *LZ,* 20 June 1942.

117. Helmut Lemcke, "'Frauen sind doch bessere Diplomaten': Erstauffuhrung des ersten deutschen Farbgroßfilms in Litzmannstadt im 'Casino,'" *LZ,* 26 September 1942. On the recent improvements to the cinema house, see "Litzmannstädter Kulturstätte öffnet wieder: Ufa-Theater 'Casino' spielt nach der Neugestltung am 1. August 'Die große Liebe,'" *LZ,* 1 August 1942; G. K., "Das Lichtspieltheater als eine Kulturstätte: Festliche Wiedereröffnung des wirksam neugestatlteten Ufa-Theaters 'Casino,'" *LZ,* 2 August 1942.

118. On Genewein and his photo series, see Floran Freund, Bertrand Perz, and Karl Stuhlpfarer, "Bildergeschichten—Geschichtsbilder," in *Unser einziger Weg ist Arbeit,*" ed. Hanno Loewy and Gerhard Schoenberner (Vienna: Löcker Verlag, 1990), pp. 50–58; Frances Guerin, "Reframing the Photographer and His Photographs: *Photographer* (1995)," *Film & History* 32, no. 1 (2002): 43–54.

119. Jüdisches Museum Frankfurt, Farbfotos Genewein, II, 58.

120. Adolf Kargel, "'Ich will den Menschen von heute gestalten!' Vom Schöpferglück des Kunstschaffenden/'L.Z.'-Besuch bei der Bildhauerin M. Kronig," *LZ,* 7 October 1942.

121. Dr. Kurt Pfeiffer, "Gelungener Opernstart in Litzmannstadt: Erfolgreicher Aufführung von Humperdincks Märchenoper 'Hänsel und Gretel,'" *LZ,* 7 November 1942.

122. Ibid. See also *Haensel and Gretel: The Story of Humperdinck's Opera,* authorized edition of Metropolitan Opera Guild, Inc., adapted by Robert Lawrence and illustrated by Mildred Boyle (New York: Grosset & Dunlap, 1938), pp. 23–27, 36–37.

123. Ibid.

9. Who Shall Live and Who Shall Die?

1. On 19 January 1943 the *Chronicle* indicated that there were 87,164 residents in the ghetto. *The Chronicle of the Łódź Ghetto, 1941–1944,* ed. Lucjan Dobroszycki, trans. Richard Lourie, Joachim Neugroschel et al. (New Haven: Yale University Press, 1984), entry for 19 January 1943, p. 314.

2. O[skar] R[osenfeld], "The Look of the Ghetto, June 1943," *Chronicle,* entry for Friday, 9 July 1943, p. 356.

3. See *Chronicle,* p. 43, n. 57.

4. This discussion is suggested by my reading of Elaine Scarry, *The Body in Pain: The Making and Unmaking of the World* (New York: Oxford University Press, 1985), pp. 192–193.

5. W.W., "Ein geschichtlicher Abschnitt erreicht," *LZ,* 1 January 1943.

6. See Scarry, *Body in Pain,* pp. 192–193.

7. "Proklamation des Führers: Unser Sieg," *LZ,* 25 February 1943, p. 1.

8. Oskar Rosenfeld, *In the Beginning Was the Ghetto,* ed. Hanno Loewy, trans. Brigitte M. Goldstein (Evanston: Northwestern University Press, 2002), Notebook G, entry for 25 February [1943], p. 160. On the clandestine circulation within the ghetto of reports via radio and newspapers, see Andrea Löw, *Juden im Getto Litzmannstadt: Lebensbedingungen, Selbstwahrnehmung, Verhalten* (Göttingen: Wallstein Verlag, 2006), pp. 448–453. Dawid Sierakowiak, *The Diary of Dawid Sierakowiak: Five Notebooks from the Łódź Ghetto,* ed. Alan Adelson, trans. Kamil Turowski (New York: Oxford University Press, 1996), entries for 11 November 1942 and 25 February 1943, pp. 229, 251.

9. Rosenfeld, *In the Beginning,* Notebook G, entry for 5 March 1943, p. 162.

10. APL PSZ 1086, p. 26: Tageschronik No. 41, Tagesbericht, 25 February 1943.

11. By the end of October, according to the *Chronicle,* the paper goods *ressort* was making ready to produce "a big collection" of "several million" toys of the "most modern" and "inventive" design. APL PSZ 1083, p. 37: Tageschronik No. 179, Tagesbericht, 31 October 1942. *Chronicle,* entry for 31 October 1942, p. 280.

12. APL PSZ 1094, pp. 201–203, 208: Res[s]ort Papierniczy, unsigned report, 12 January 1943.

13. Ibid., pp. 204, 208.

14. Ibid., pp. 203–204.

15. APL PSZ 1108: see images 11–302–1; 11–302–2; 11–302–3; 11–302–4; 11–302–5; 11–302–6; 11–302–7; 11–302–8; 11–302–9; 11–302–10; 11–306–4; 11–306–5; 11–306–6; 11–1272–3; 11–1272–5; 36–1201–4; 36–1201–5; 36–1207–1; 36–1207–3; 36–1207–4; 36–1207–5; 36–1206–2; 36–1206–3; 36–1206–4; 36–1206–5; 36–1206–6; 36–1206–9; 36–1207–1; 36–1207–3; 36–1207–4; 36–1207–5; 36–1207–6; 37–1272–

2; 37–1272–4; 37–1275–1; 37–1275–5; 38–1201–3; 56–1890–1; 56–1890–2; 56–1890–3; 56–1890–4; 56–1890–5. APL PSZ 838, pp. 9–11, 15–19: "Wäsche- u. Kleider Abt.: Reproduktion," marked "Litzmannstadt-Getto 1942."

16. On this, see Dan Diner, *Beyond the Conceivable: Studies on Germany, Nazism, and the Holocaust* (Berkeley: University of California Press, 2000), pp. 128, 134, 136.

17. Rosenfeld, *In the Beginning*, Notebook G, pp. 301–302, n. 11. The Supreme Control Chamber, or HKK (Höchste Kontrolkammer), came into being on 6 December 1940 and subsequently (2 November 1942) was attached to the ghetto's Central Labor Office.

18. Isaiah Trunk, *Łódź Ghetto: A History*, ed. and trans. Robert Moses Shapiro (Bloomington: Indiana University Press, 2006), pp. 118 (on the low quality of products delivered), 119 (quoting Tabaksblat).

19. Trunk, *Łódź Ghetto*, p. 111.

20. Josef Zelkowicz, report dated 8 July 1943, reproduced ibid., pp. 135–137.

21. Trunk, *Łódź Ghetto*, pp. 114–117.

22. Rosenfeld, *In the Beginning*, Notebook H, entries for 9 March and 28 May [1943], pp. 178, 192. On the scarcity of Vigantol, ibid., Notebook G, entry for 17 March [1943], p. 163.

23. YIVO RG 241/No. 899: "Drei Jahre Ordnungsdienst: Gründungsfeier am Sonntag," 28 February 1943.

24. USHMM RG-15.083M, File 347, p. 57: Rumkowski to Vostand des Ordnungsdienstes—z. H. des Herrn Komm Rosenblatt.

25. Rosenfeld, *In the Beginning*, Notebook G, entry for 1 January 1943, p. 155.

26. Ibid., entry for 23 February [1943], p. 159.

27. Ibid., Notebook H, entry for 8–9 July [1943], p. 195.

28. USHMM RG-02.146: Genia Bryl [Jean Beller], ed. Sheila Beller, "If My Heart Didn't Break Then," unpublished memoir, p. 69.

29. Lucille Eichengreen with Rebecca Cahmi Frommer, *Rumkowski and the Orphans of Łódź* (San Francisco: Mercury House, 2000), pp. 80–82.

30. Rosenfeld, *In the Beginning*, Notebook H, entry for 6 May [1943], p. 189.

31. USHMM RG 15.083M, Reel 111, File 345, p. 137: Der Aelteste der Juden, Gericht: Urteil [judgment], 19 July 1943; Urteil [judgment on appeal], 24 September 1943. *Chronicle*, entry for 24 September 1943, pp. 384–385. Jakub Poznański, *Dziennik z łodzkiego getta* (Warsaw: Dom Wydawniczy Belloona and Żydowski Instytut Historyczny, 2002), entry for 12 October 1943, p. 117.

32. Rosenfeld, *In the Beginning*, Notebook 16, "My Two Neighbors," 4 August 1943, p. 219.

33. Ibid.

34. Ibid., pp. 222–223.

35. O[skar] R[osenfeld], in *Chronicle*, entry for 7 August 1943, p. 367.

36. Sierakowiak, *Diary*, entry for 30 March 1943, pp. 264–265, 268.

37. Shmuel Krakowski, "The Historical Outline of the Camp in Chełmno-on-Ner," in *Chełmno Witnesses Speak*, ed. Łucja Pawlicka-Nowak (Konin: Council for the Protection of Memory of Combat and Martyrdom in Warsaw and District Museum in Konin, 2004), p. 14. Greiser to Himmler, 19 March 1943, and Himmler to Greiser, 20 March 1943, ibid., pp. 202–203.

38. Greiser to Himmler, 19 March 1943, and Himmler to Greiser, 20 March 1943, ibid., pp. 202–203. Brandt to Kaltenbrunner, 29 March 1943, in *Eksterminacja Żydów na ziemiach Polskich w okresie okupacji hitlerowskiej: Zbiór dokumentów*, ed. T. Berenstein, A. Eisenbach, and A. Rutkowski (Warsaw: Żydowski Instytut Historyczny, 1957), p. 326. "Testimony by Walter Piller," in Pawlicka-Nowak, *Chełmno Witnesses Speak*, p. 180.

39. "Sheets of Paper—Letters of the Chełmno-on-Ner Camp Prisoners," dated 2 April 1943, and "April 1943 (not later than 7th)," in Pawlicka-Nowak, *Chełmno Witnesses Speak*, pp. 87–88.

40. Krakowski, "Historical Outline of the Camp in Chełmno-on-Ner," p. 14.

41. A.K., "Die Störche sind wieder da!" *LZ*, 12 April 1943. A. K., "Fledermäuse im Park," *LZ*, 12 May 1943.

42. "Ein Besuch beim geflügelten Moorochsen von Lentschutz: Hundert Vogelarten hausen im Lentshützer Moor/Von B. von Henström, Leiter des Reichsbundes für Vogelschutz E. v.," *LZ*, 24 June 1943.

43. G. K., "Siebzig Neueingänge in unserem Tierpark: Neugruppierungen verbessern die Übersicht/Die Tiere fühlern sich wohl bei uns," *LZ*, 22 April 1942.

44. Oe., "'Kirschgarten' für die Litzmannstädter," *LZ*, 13 May 1943.

45. G. K., "Gefährliches Unkraut," *LZ*, 17 May 1943.

46. "Eine ganze Stadt treibt Liebesübungen: Vom Oberbürgermeister bis zu den Jüngsten—alles turnt und schwimmt mit," *LZ*, 14 May 1943.

47. "Eigene Krankenhäuser betreuen die Umsiedler in den Lagern: Die ärtzliche Versorgung wird heute schon zum größten Teil durch Ärzte aus den eigenen Reihen der Umsiedler sichergestellt," *LZ*, 11 April 1943.

48. G. K., "Unseren Kranken stehen beste Einrichtungen zur Verfügung: LZ-Besuch in einem städischen Krankenhauses/Vorbildliche Einrichtungen stehen zur Verfügung/Deutsche Ordnung eingekehrt," *LZ*, 28 March 1943.

49. "Das Strandbad Erzhausen wurde eröffnet: Ideale Erholungstätte für Tausende/Ansprache von Oberbürgermeister Ventzki," *LZ*, 17 May 1943. "Volkssportfest in Erzhausen," *LZ*, 17 May 1943. "Strandbad Erzhausen mit Volksfest eröffnet," *LZ*, 18 May 1943.

50. G. K., "Warthegau steht in der Geburtenfreudigkeit an der Spitze:

Großkundgebung mit Reichsgesundheitsführer Dr. Conti/Die günstige Gesundheitsbilanz unseres Volkes in diesem Kriege," *LZ,* 24 May 1943.

51. G. K., "Die Trauung—ene Akt von innerer Würde: Das Trauzimmer im Standesamt entspricht den vom Führer dafür gegebenen Richtlinien," *LZ,* 25 May 1943.

52. "Kunst als Kraftborn/Große Kunstausstellung München 1943," *LZ,* Beilage, 27 June 1943.

53. G. K., "Ausstellung 'Wunder des Lebens' eröffnet: Öberregierungsrat Dr. Bradfisch nahm die Eröffnung vor/Der erste Rundgang," *LZ,* 9 September 1943. See also Dieter Kuntz, ed., project director Susan Bachrach, *Deadly Medicine: Creating the Master Race* (Washington, D.C.: United States Holocaust Memorial Museum, 2004), pp. xiv, 1, 40–41. In the summer of 1943, SS-Stürmbannführer Dr. Otto Bradfisch, since spring 1942 director of the Litzmannstadt Gestapo, assumed the position of acting Oberbürgermeister in Werner Ventzki's absence. Stanisław Nawrocki, *Policja hitlerowska w tzw. Warty w latach 1939–1945* (Poznań: Instytut Zachodni, 1970), pp. 124, 128, 281. *Chronicle,* p. xl. Gerda Zorn, *"Nach Ostland geht unser Ritt": Deutsche Eroberungspolitik und die Folgen. Das Beispiel Łódź* (Cologne: Röderberg Verlag, 1988), p. 96.

54. G. K., "Eine Ausstellung, die jeden von uns angeht! 'Der gläserne Mensch' in der Sporthall/Einblicke, die man sonst nicht bekommt," *LZ,* 8 September 1943.

55. On the efforts of the Gettoverwaltung senior management to shelter its employees from military service, see, for example, APL GV 29299, pp. 196–202: 027/2/Ri/Po to Rüstungskommando in Litzmannstadt, 25 June 1942; Biebow to Rüstungskommando Litzmannstadt, 25 June 1942; 027/2/Lu/Ri to Wehbezirkskommando Litzmannstadt, 30 May 1942.

56. Gettoverwaltung, Biebow, to Oberbürgermeister Ventzki, 19 April 1943; Ventzki, Aktenverkmerk, 23 April 1943, in A. Eisenbach, *Dokumenty i materiały do dziejów okupacji niemieckiej w Polsce,* vol. 3, *Getto Łódzkie,* pt. 1 (Warsaw: Centralna Żydowska Komisja Historyczna Łódź, 1946), pp. 245–248.

57. APL SV 31866a, p. 106: St. A. 500, Stadtmedizinalrat to Oberbürgermeister Ventzki, 24 April 1943.

58. Reference to this translation of the term in *Chronicle,* entry for Wednesday, 6 October 1943, p. 393.

59. Oskar Singer, *"Im Eilschritt durch den Gettotag. . . ,"* ed. Sascha Feuchert, Erwin Leibfried, Jörg Recke et al. (Berlin: Philo, 2002), pp. 222–223, 225. See also Eichengreen, *Rumkowski and the Orphans of Łódź,* pp. 75–77.

60. Singer, *"Im Eilschritt,"* p. 224.

61. Eichengreen, *Rumkowski and the Orphans of Łódź,* pp. 76–77. Singer, *"Im Eilschritt,"* pp. 222–223.

62. In the original with the insertion of a bracketed exclamation point after the word "Garden." Singer, *Im Eilschritt*, p. 215.

63. "'Das sind meine Freunde!' 'Und was tut man nicht alles für treue Freunde!'" ibid., pp. 215–216.

64. Rosenfeld, *In the Beginning*, Notebook H, entry for 12 July[1943], p. 196.

65. Ibid., entries for 12 April and 12 May [1943], pp. 183, 189.

66. APL PSZ 1086, pp. 200–202: Tageschronik No. 144, Tagesbericht, 9 June 1943. Programm der Revue des Ordnungsdienstes, Litzmannstadt-Getto, June 1943, pt. 2, reproduced in Julian Baranowski, *The Łódź Ghetto, 1940–1944/ Łódźkie Getto 1940–1944* (Łódź: Archiwum Państwowe w Łodzi & Bilbo, 1999), p. 59.

67. APL PSZ 1086, p. 194: Tageschronik No. 141, Tagesbericht, 6 June 1943.

68. Trunk, *Łódź Ghetto*, pp. 212–213.

69. O[skar] R[osenfeld], "The Look of the Ghetto, June 1943," *Chronicle*, entry for Friday, 9 July 1943, pp. 356–357.

70. O[skar] R[osenfeld], "The Look of the Ghetto, June 1943," *Chronicle*, entry for Friday, 9 July 1943, p. 356.

71. Josef Zelkowicz, report, 6 August 1943, reproduced in Trunk, *Łódź Ghetto*, pp. 359–361.

72. Ibid., p. 359.

73. O[skar] R[osenfeld], "Krankheit und Ernährung," in APL PSZ 1086, pp. 217–218: Tageschronik No. 155, Tagesbericht, 20 June 1943.

74. On the relentless and painful sensitizing of the body under duress, see Scarry, *Body in Pain*, pp. 54–55, 57, 207, 269.

75. Poznański, *Dziennik*, entry for 1 September 1943, p. 104.

76. Rosenfeld, *In the Beginning*, Notebooks G and H, entries for 24 October [1942], 3 November [1942], 8–9 July [1943], 12 July [1943], pp. 144–146, 194–196. Josef Zelkowicz, *In Those Terrible Days: Notes from the Lodz Ghetto*, ed. Michal Unger (Jerusalem: Yad Vashem, 2002).

77. APL PSZ 1093, pp. 213–214: "Bałucki Rynek." This anonymous report, composed in Polish, was preserved in the archive as a fragment. It contains the opening pages of what its author intended as a description of activity on the square during the course of a single day, from dawn to dark. Internal reference within the document to a ghetto population then numbering 83,000 suggests that the account dates from the early autumn of 1943, possibly 3 October, when there arrived "a seemingly endless procession of potato wagons, rolling one after another toward Bałut Market and from there to the vegetable storage lots." *Chronicle*, entry for 30 September 1943, p. 388. O[skar] R[osenfeld], "Sketches of Ghetto Life: The First Days of October, 1943," ibid., entry for 6 October 1943, p. 393.

78. APL PSZ 1093, pp. 213–214: "Bałucki Rynek."

79. Ibid.

80. O[skar] R[osenfeld], "Sketches of Ghetto Life: The First Days of October, 1943," in *Chronicle*, entry for 6 October 1943, p. 393. O[skar] R[osenfeld], "Sketches of Ghetto Life: Yom Kippur in the Ghetto Year, 1943 (5704)," ibid., entry for 11 October 1943, pp. 395–396.

81. Ibid.

82. hd., "Schon vor 350 Jahren Juden unerwünscht: Wie einst Welun räumen mußten/Eine königl. Urkunde, die Aufenthalt untersagte," *LZ*, 9 October 1943. The article appeared on Yom Kippur.

83. Kn., "Wo die Juden niemals landen konnten: Ein alt beliebter Sommeraufenthalt der Litzmannstädter/Die Gondeln auf der Linda," *LZ*, 8 August 1943.

84. G. K., "Wilhelm Raabe kannte den Geist der Juden: Ein überaus treffende Schilderung der jüdischen Haltung gegenüber der Gastnation," *LZ*, 11 September 1943.

85. "'Kulturbilder' sus dem Lodscher Getto: Eine vielsagende jüdische Selbstanklage/Organisiertes jüdisches Verbrechertum," *LZ*, 22 September 1943.

86. hd., "Schon vor 350 Jahren Juden unerwünscht."

87. Cited and commented on in Raul Hilberg, *The Destruction of the European Jews*, rev. ed, vol. 3 (New York: Holmes and Meier, 1985), pp. 1015–1016.

88. Otto Kniese, "LZ.-Nachtfahrt zu unserem entferntest wohnende Leser: Zeitungsarbeiten, an die viele nie denken/Im Wettstreit mit der östlichen Weite/Mittler zwischen Einzelhof und Außenwelt," *LZ*, 28 November 1943.

89. Rosenfeld, *In the Beginning*, Notebook 17, "Night Work in the Ghetto— Lecture for the Archive," and Notebook J, "Encyclopedia of the Ghetto," pp. 212–213, 229–231.

90. Ibid., Notebook J, entry for 28 November [1943], p. 228.

91. Ibid., entry for 27 December [1943], p. 241.

92. Ibid., section titled "Chanukah in the Ghetto, 1943," dated 28 December 1943, pp. 242–243.

10. Numbered Are the Days

1. "Der Sieg dem Volke, das ihn verdient! Neujahrsaufruf des Führers/ nationalsozialistische Kraft gegen die Weltverschwörer," *LZ*, 1–2 January 1944, p. 1.

2. Ibid.

3. Georg Keil, "Unser Heimatstadt schwingt im Rhythmus des Alltags: Unermüdlich schaffende Frauen/Mütterlichkeit im männlichen Werte/ Besinnliche Stunden unserer Jugend mit Hausmusik," *LZ*, 1–2 January 1944.

4. Adolf Kargel, "Ein steinernes Buch der Geschichte von Litzmannstadt: Friedhöfe unserere Stadt wandeln sich in Parks/Der Hitler-Jugend Park wäre fast ein Friedhof geworden," *LZ*, 1–2 January 1944. A. K., "Die Ratsherren begehen das Friedhofgelände an der Sulzfelder Straße/Beratung vor der Neugestaltung," *LZ*, 8 January 1944.

5. *The Chronicle of the Łódź Ghetto, 1941–1944, ed.* Lucjan Dobroszycki, trans. Richard Lourie, Joachim Neugroschel et al. (New Haven: Yale University Press, 1984), entry for Saturday, 8 January 1944, pp. 428–429.

6. Introduction to *Chronicle*, pp. lx–lxi. Isaiah Trunk, *Łódź Ghetto: A History*, trans. and ed. Robert Moses Shapiro (Bloomington: Indiana University Press, 2006), pp. 248–250. Florian Freund, Bertrand Perz, and Karl Stuhlpfarrer, "Das Getto in Litzmannstadt (Łódź)," in *"Unser eigener Weg ist Arbeit": Das Getto in Łódź 1940–1944,* ed. Hanno Loewy and Gerhard Schoenberner (Frankfurt: Löcker Verlag, 1990), p. 30.

7. Trunk, *Łódź Ghetto*, pp. 248–251. Introduction to *Chronicle*, pp. lxi–lxiii. T. Berenstein, A. Eisenbach, and A. Rutkowski, eds., *Eksterminacja żydów na ziemiach polskich w okresie okupacji hitlerowskiej: Zbiór dokumentów* (Warsaw: Żydówski Instytut Historyczny, 1957), document no. 180: Pohl to Himmler, 9 February 1944; no. 181: Greiser to Pohl, 14 February 1944, pp. 342–344.

8. APL GV 29299, pp. 196–202: 027/2/Ri/Po to Rüstungskommando in Litzmannstadt, 25 June 1942; Biebow to Rüstungskommando Litzmannstadt, 25 June 1942; 027/2/Lu/Ri to Wehrbezirkskommando Litzmannstadt, 30 May 1942. Frank Stier, *Kriegsauftrag 160: Behelfsheimbau im Getto Litzmannstadt (Łódź) und im KZ-Außenlager Königs Wusterhausen durch das Deutsche Wohnungshilfswerk* (Berlin: Verlag Willmuth Arenhövel, 1999), p. 50. Freund, Perz, and Stuhlpfarrer, "Das Getto in Litzmannstadt," p. 30.

9. APL PSZ 1083 p. 374, reverse of p. 374, and following summary titled "Die Rede des Amtsleiters Biebow vom 7. Dezember 1943 Gehalten im ehemmaligen Kulturhaus Schneidergasse 1."

10. ŻIH Łódź 39, pp. 269–273: Informationsbericht, Stadtoberinspektor Quay to Oberbürgermeister, 1 April 1944.

11. Głowna Komisja Badania Zbrodni przeciwko Narodowi Polskiemu—Instytut Pamięci Narodowej [GKBZPNpNP-IPN], Ob 271, t. I, pp. 176–177: Protokol Przesluchania Swiadka, Rudolf Kramp, 1.7.1945. Gestapo officer Walter Piller, second in command to Bothmann during this second phase of the camp's operation, indicated that the ghetto supplied a steam-powered clothing shredder as well. "Testimony by Walter Piller," 19 May 1945, in *Chełmno Witnesses Speak*, ed. Łucja Pawlicka-Nowak, trans. Juliet D. Golden and Arkadiusz Kamiński (Konin: Council for the Protection of Memory of Combat and Martyrdom in Warsaw and District Museum in Konin, 2004), p. 185.

12. "Testimony by Simon Srebrnik," 29 June 1945, in Pawlicka-Nowak, *Chełmno Witnesses Speak*, pp. 125–126. Piller, who arrived in the spring of 1944 to assume his duties as Bothmann's second in command, observed the construction of the furnaces, describing them as follows: "Both furnaces had the same dimensions (therefore were the same size), and were made of fireproof bricks. At the top it was rectangular, about eight meters long and five to six meters wide, and narrowed toward the bottom to a depth I estimate to be about seven to eight meters deep. About a meter to a meter and a half above the foundation made of fireproof brick there was a fire-grate made of train rails. The ash passed through that grate and was sucked out through an airshaft running at an angle towards the top. The shaft was so large that, in a slight crouching position, one could reach the grate (foundations)." He additionally noted that "the furnaces were fueled with pinewood delivered in sufficient quantities by truck from a nearby clearing." "Testimony by Walther Piller," 19 May 1945, ibid., pp. 184–185.

13. A. K., "Reise vom Tor der Welt zum Ausfalltor nach dem Osten," *LZ*, 18 April 1944.

14. A. K., "Die Hamburger Gäste besichtigten gestern Litzmannstadt," *LZ*, 19 April 1944.

15. G. K., "Geländespiel als Auftakt der Sommerarbeit in der HJ," *LZ*, 19 April 1944.

16. "Staffellauf durch Litzmannstadt," *LZ*, 15 March 1944.

17. Advertisement, *LZ*, 30 April and 1 May 1944. Adolf Kargel, "Frohmachende zirzensische Kunst/ Premiere bei Althoff," *LZ*, 4 May 1944.

18. *Chronicle*, entry for Tuesday, 16 May 1944, pp. 488–489. The *Chronicle* makes no mention of the ultimate fate of the child's parents.

19. Oskar Rosenfeld, *In the Beginning Was the Ghetto: Notebooks from Łódź*, ed. Hanno Loewy, trans. Brigitte M. Goldstein (Evanston: Northwestern University Press, 2002), Notebook K, entry for 3 May [1944], p. 268.

20. Cited ibid., following the entry for 17 May 1944, p. 273.

21. APL PSZ 1096, III/172, 31 May 1944, pp. 187–188: "Refleksje na temat życia gettowego."

22. Rosenfeld, *In the Beginning*, Notebook K, entry listed as "Twenty-eighth to twenty-ninth" [of May 1944], p. 275. At the beginning of March 1944 a total of 1,600 ghetto workers were deported and "sent to the munitions factories in slarżysko and Częstochowa (Radom district)." Trunk, *Łódź Ghetto*, pp. 253–354.

23. Rosenfeld, *In the Beginning*, Notebook K, p. 275.

24. Henuschi was the pet name of Rosenfeld's wife, Henriette, then residing in England. Ibid. and editor's introduction, p. xvii.

25. Ibid., entry for 3 June [1944], p. 276. On Rosenfeld's occasional use of English, see editor's introduction, ibid., p. xxxi.

26. Trunk, *Łódź Ghetto*, pp. 251–252. Introduction to *Chronicle*, p. lxiii. Greiser telegram to Himmler, 9 June 1944, in Berenstein, Eisenbach, and Rutkowski, *Eksterminacja Żydów*, p. 345.

27. AL PSZ 1087, pp. 336–337: section initialed O.R. [Oskar Rosenfeld].

28. APL PSZ 1087, pp. 338–339: Tageschronik No. 166, Tagesbericht, 15 June 1944.

29. *Chronicle*, entry for 16 June 1944, pp. 504–505.

30. Ibid.

31. Ibid., entry for 17 June 1944, p. 505.

32. Ibid., entry for 21 June 1944, p. 512.

33. Ibid., entry for 23 June 1944, pp. 513–514.

34. Ibid., entry for 19 June 1944, pp. 510–511.

35. Ibid., entry for 26 June 1944, observation by P[eter] W[ertheimer], p. 517.

36. Ibid., entry for 24 June 1944, pp. 514–515.

37. Ibid., entry for 2 July 1944, p. 519.

38. YIVO RG 1400, Box M7, Folder 16, p. 479: Yakov Hiller, "Diary of Łódź Ghetto," entry for 4 July 1944.

39. Ibid., p. 476.

40. Ibid., p. 477.

41. Ibid., entry for 8 July 1944, pp. 487–488.

42. *Chronicle*, entry for 13 July 1944, pp. 524–525.

43. Rosenfeld, *In the Beginning*, "June 27, 1944, Outsettlement, Last Stage," Notebook 20, p. 288. Still, even though in doing so they faced the loss of their rations, many families did initially attempt to hide away rather than face deportation. APL PSZ 1087, p. 352. O[skar] R[osenfeld], "Kleinter Getto-Spiegel," Tagesbericht, 20 June 1944.

44. *Chronicle*, entry for 26 June 1944, p. 516.

45. Ibid.

46. Ibid., entries for 26 June 1944 and Friday, 7 July 1944, pp. 516, 521.

47. O[skar] R[osenfeld], ibid., entry for Monday, 3 July 1944, pp. 520–521.

48. O[skar] R[osenfeld], ibid., entry for Thursday, 13 July 1944, p. 525.

49. YIVO RG 1400, Box M7, Folder 16, p. 478: Hiller, "Diary," entry for 4 July 1944, p. 478.

50. Julian Baranowski, *The Łódź Ghetto/Łódzkie Getto* (Łódź: Archiwum Państwowe w Łodzi & Bilbo, 1999), pp. 100–101. Trunk, *Łódź Ghetto*, pp. 257–258.

51. *Chronicle*, entry for 15 July 1944, pp. 526–527.

52. Ibid., entry for Monday, 17 July 1944, p. 528.

53. Ibid., entry for Tuesday, 18 July 1944, p. 529.

54. Ibid., entry for Wednesday, 19 July 1944, p. 530.

55. Ibid., entry for Monday, 24 July 1944, p. 534. The deception was con-

firmed by a surviving member of the Chełmno Waldkommando. Mordka Żurawksi, who testified "that eight to ten people from each transport were forced to write letters to their families, notifying them that they were staying in Leipzig or Munich together with other Jews, and that they were doing fine. . . . [T]hose who wrote letters were not put to death in the vans. They were led near the crematoriums and shot in the head." "Testimony by Mordka Żurawksi of 1945," 31 July 1945, in Pawlicka-Nowak, *Chełmno Witnesses Speak*, p. 133.

56. On the background to the diary's discovery and its use of entries in multiple languages, see especially Hanno Loewy and Andrzej Bodek, eds., *"Les Vrais Riches"—Notizen am Rand: Ein Tagebuch aus dem Ghetto Łódź (Mai bis August 1944)*, trans. Esther Alexander-Ihme, Ardrzej Bodek, Irgard Hölscher, and Ronen Reichmann (Leipzig: Reklam Verlag, 1997), pp. 5–8, 33–34.

57. Ibid., pp. 30–31.

58. Ibid., entry for 20 June 1944, p. 47.

59. Ibid., reproduction of original handwritten entry for 16 July 1944, p. 16 [page number in the original text].

60. Ibid., reproduction of original handwritten entry for 11 July 1944, p. 13 [page number in the original text].

61. Ibid., reproduction, passage inserted between entries for 7 and 15 July 1944, p. 15 [page number in the original text].

62. Loewy and Bodek, *"Les Vrais Riches,"* entry for 29 July 1944, p. 94. Rosenfeld, *In the Beginning*, section titled *"Little Ghetto Mirror, July 8, 1944: Apocalypse or Redemption,"* pp. 280–281.

63. Rosenfeld, *"Little Ghetto Mirror,"* in *In the Beginning*, p. 280.

64. Ibid., p. 281.

65. Ibid.

66. Loewy and Bodek, *"Les Vrais Riches,"* entry for 3 August 1944, p. 99.

67. Jakub Poznański, diary entry for 2 August 1944, in *Łódź Ghetto: Inside a Community under Siege*, ed. Alan Adelson and Robert Lapides (New York: Penguin Books, 1989), p. 442.

68. Ibid., p. 443. Yakov Nirenberg, *In di yorn fun yidishn khurbn* (New York: Farlag Unser Tsait, 1948), p. 293.

69. Poznański, diary entry for 2 August 1944, p. 443.

70. Ibid.

71. Ibid., diary entry for 4 August 1944, pp. 443–444.

72. Ibid., p. 444.

73. Ibid.

74. Ibid. According to Yakov Nirenberg, some two thousand were expected to appear for deportation on 4 August, but only 150 did, many of the latter already under arrest. Nirenberg, "Di geshikte fun Lodzher geto," in *In di yorn*, p. 291.

75. Poznański, diary entry for 4 August 1944, p. 444.

76. A. Eisenbach, *Dokumenty i materiały do dziejów okupacji niemieckiej w Polsce,* vol. 3, *Getto Łódzkie,* pt. 1 (Warsaw: Centralna Żydowska Komisja Historyczna, 1946), p. 269: Der Oberbürgermeister von Litzmannstadt, Betr.: Verlagerung des Gettos, 4 August 1944.

77. Poznański, diary entry for 10 August 1944, in Adelson, *Łódź Ghetto,* p. 446.

78. Ibid., entry for 12 August 1944, p. 447.

79. Announcement no. 425, reproduced in Adelson, *Łódź Ghetto,* p. 448.

80. Ben Edelbaum, *Growing Up in the Holocaust* (Kansas City: by the author, 1980), pp. 180–182. Sara Zyskind, *Stolen Years* (Minneapolis: Lerner Publications, 1981), p. 176.

81. Yisroel [Israel] Tabaksblat, *Khurban Lodzh: 6 yor natsi ghenem* (Buenos Aires: Tsentral-farband fun Poylishe Yidn in Argentine, 1946), p. 176.

82. Reproduced in Adelson, *Łódź Ghetto,* p. 459.

83. See photograph, ibid., p. 463.

84. Tabaksblat, *Kurban Lodzh,* p. 177. Irena Liebman in Adelson, *Łódź Ghetto,* p. 459.

85. Nirenberg, "Di geshikte," p. 291.

86. Ibid., p. 292.

87. *Chronicle,* entry for 30 July 1944, p. 536. Arnold Mostowicz, *With a Yellow Star and a Red Cross: A Doctor in the Łódź Ghetto,* trans. Henia Reinharz and Nochem Reinharz (London: Valentine Mitchell, 2005), p. 124. Nirenberg, "Di geshikte," p. 293.

88. Rosenfeld, *In the Beginning,* Notebook H, entry for 22 April [1943], p. 186. Trunk, *Łódź Ghetto,* p. 397. Stroop report, 16 May 1943, reproduced in *A Holocaust Reader,* ed. Lucy S. Dawidowicz (New York: Behrman House, 1976), p. 120.

89. Trunk, *Łódź Ghetto,* pp. 395, 397.

90. Ibid., p. 397.

91. Arnold Mostowicz, interviewed in *Fotoamator* (1998), dir. Dariusz Jabłoński, Apple Film Productions, trans. Alina Skibińska and Wolfgang Jöhling.

92. Irena Liebman in Adelson, *Łódź Ghetto,* p. 459.

93. USHMM RG-02.146: Genia Bryl [Jean Beller], "If My Heart Didn't Break Then," p. 79.

94. Jakub Poznański, diary entry for Thursday, 31 August 1944 (here recalling as well events of the previous Monday), in Adelson, *Łódź Ghetto,* p. 457. Jakub Poznański, *Dziennik z łódzkiego getta* (Warsaw: Dom Wydawniczy Bellona, 2002), p. 209.

95. Jakub Poznański, diary entry for 28 August 1944, in Adelson, *Łódź Ghetto,* pp. 456–457. Poznański, *Dziennik,* pp. 208–209.

96. See photograph attributed to Henryk Ross in Loewy and Schoenberner, *"Unser eigener Weg ist Arbeit,"* p. 258. See also photographs in Pinchas Schaar, "Mendel Grossman: Photographic Bard of the Lodz Getto," in *Holocaust Chronicles: Individualizing the Holocaust through Diaries and Other Contemporaneous Personal Accounts,* ed. Robert Moses Shapiro (Hoboken, N.J.: KTAV Publishing House, 1999), pp. 136–137, 139–140.

97. Schaar, "Mendel Grossman," pp. 128–129.

98. Quoted in Shmuel Huppert, "King of the Ghetto: Mordechai Ḥaim Rumkowksi, the Elder of Lodz Ghetto," *Yad Vashem Studies* 15 (1983): 150. Also noted and discussed in Michal Unger, *Reassessment of the Image of Mordechai Chaim Rumkowski,* Search and Research—Lectures and Papers no. 6 (Jerusalem: Yad Vashem, 2004), p. 45.

99. Rumkowski is thought to have left on one of the last transports, departing on either 28 or 29 August. Baranowski, *Łódź Ghetto/Łódzkie Getto,* pp. 100–101. Tabaksblat, *Kurban Lodzh,* p. 177. Andrea Löw, *Juden im Getto Litzmannstadt: Lebensbedingungen, Selbstwahrnehmung, Verhalten* (Göttingen: Wallstein Verlag, 2006), p. 482. Trunk, however, states that the date was 30 August (*Łódź Ghetto,* p. 266).

100. Rosenfeld, *In the Beginning,* "Remembrances (As Manuscript for Author Only)," Notebook 15, pp. 207–208.

101. The destination of the train bearing Rumkowski, like all others that departed the ghetto in August 1944, was Auschwitz-Birkenau. During the course of the month some 67,000 Jews were sent there to be murdered. Only a small number, admitted to the camp as laborers, would survive. Trunk, *Łódź Ghetto,* p. 267. Rumkowski was not among them. Accounts speak of his having been brutally tormented in Birkenau by Jewish prisoners, and either killed outright by their hand or in the end shot by a German from the SS. A similarly gruesome torment is said to have befallen the chief of the ghetto police, Leon Rozenblat. See Löw, *Juden im Getto Litzmannstadt,* p. 483. Michael Checinski, "How Rumkowski Died," *Commentary* 67 (May 1979): 63–65. Reference to Rumkowski's creative ingenuity is drawn from a comment by Rosenfeld, who, speaking of the ghetto's "inventive spirit," took note of "achievements demanded out of nothing, and reached." Rosenfeld, *In the Beginning,* Notebook G, entry for 5 March 1943, p. 161.

102. USHMM RG-05.008M, SV, Reel 1, File 66: Niederschrift über die Dezernentensitzung, 23 August 1944, p. 52.

103. USHMM RG-05.008M, SV, Gesundheitsamt, Reel 6, File 71, p. 142: Arbeitsplan für die Räumung und Verwertung des Gettogebietes, 24 August 1944.

104. Ibid., p. 141.

105. USHMM RG-05.008M, SV, Gesundheitsamt, Reel 6, File 71, p. 136: Der Amtsartzt I.V., intitialed B, Medizinaldirektor to Ernährungs- und Wirtschaftsamt, Litzmannstadt, Betrifft: Zuteilung von Lebensmittelzulagen an Ansteckungsgefährdete bei der groben Reinigung des Gettos, 26 August 1944.

106. USHMM RG-05.008M, SV, Gesundheitsamt, Reel 6, File 71, p. 140: Dr. Marder to Oberbürgermeister, 25 August 1944. The Medical Department was eager to get started; a medical officer, requesting of the Police President clearance for essential disinfection personnel to enter the zone, noted that "every delay entails a longer stay for the Jewish Arbeitskommando." USHMM RG-05.008M, SV, Gesundheitsamt, Reel 6, File 71, p. 138: Gesundheitsamt to Polizeipräsidenten Litzmannstadt, 28 August 1944.

107. Bendet Hershkovitsch, quoted in Trunk, *Łódź Ghetto,* p. 268.

108. Ibid., pp. 266, 268, including in part Trunk's citation from Hershkovitsch.

109. Bendet Hershkovitsch, quoted ibid., p. 268.

110. Ibid.

111. Ibid.

112. USHMM RG-05.008M, SV, Gesundheitsamt, Reel 6, File 71, pp. 144, 151: Gesundheitsamt to stellvertretenden Amtsarzt im Hause. Betrifft: Grobreinigung des Gettos, 31 August 1944; Gesundheitsamt to Getto-Verwaltung Litzmannstadt, 4 September 1944. The Medizinalrat appears to suggest that the flies, originating in the ghetto, had grown so numerous as to result in an increase in their number in a city hospital.

113. USHMM RG-05.008M, SV, Gesundheitsamt, Reel 6, File 71, p. 151: Gesundheitsamt to Getto-Verwaltung Litzmannstadt, 4 September 1944.

114. APL SV 31866a, pp. 166–167, 206: Gesundtheitsamt to Getto-Verwaltung Litzmannstadt, 25 September, 1944; Gesundheitsamt, Zahnärtzliche Abteilung to Oberbürgermeister Dr. Bradfisch über Herrn Steadtrat Dr. Wiedenbrüg, 10 October 1944.

115. APL SV 31866a, pp. 173, 180–184: Lieferung der vom Krankenhaus I, Richterstr. 7 nach dem Blauter Ring gebrachten sauberen Wäsche, lists marked I, II, III, V [Kinderwäsche], VI, 21, 22, and 25 September 1944.

116. Testimony of Dr. Michał Eliasberg, in Jerzy Lewiński, *Proces Hansa Biebowa* (Warsaw: PRS, 1999), pp. 127–128. Testimony of Abram Rosenblum, ibid., p. 114.

117. Testimony of Dr. Michał Eliasberg, ibid., p. 127. On the incident, see as well Testimony of Dr. Leon Szykier, ibid., pp. 93, 98; and Poznański, *Dziennik,* entry for 2 September 1944, p. 211. Poznański indicates that the incident had taken place at 36 Łagiewnicka Street. So does the testimony of Szlama Uberbaum, ibid., p. 110, and GKBZpNP-IPN: Ob 271, t. IV, p. 177: statement of Rudolf Krampf (Protokol Przesluchania Swiadka), 1 July 1945.

118. Poznański, *Dziennik,* entry for 2 September 1944, p. 211.

119. Shmuel Krakowski and Ilyta Altman, "The Testament of the Last Prisoners of the Chelmno Death Camp," *Yad Vashem Studies* 21 (1991): 110–113. (In this testimony the family name was given as Mendelson rather than Mandels.) Rudolf Kramp, a staff member of the Getttoverwaltung, recalled accompanying the transport taking the family to Chełmno. GKBZpNP- IPN: Ob 271, vol. 4, p. 177: statement of Rudolf Kramp (Protokol Przesluchania Swiadka), 1 July 1945.

120. Testimony of Szlama Uberbaum, in Lewiński, *Proces Hansa Biebowa,* p. 110; testimony of Leon Szykier, ibid., pp. 93–94.

121. GKBZpNP-IPN Ob 271, t. I, p. 14: statement of Henryk Kruszczynski (Protokol Przesluchania Swiadka), 9 June 1945, p. 14.

122. GKBZpNP-IPN Ob 271, t. I, p. 14: statement of Henryk Kruszczynski, 9 June 1945, p. 14.

123. GKBZpNP-IPN Ob 271, t. II, pp. 109–109R: statement of Franciszek Kazmierski (Protokol Prezesluchania Swiadka), 25 June 1945.

124. ŻIH, Łódź 138: Bescheinigung, 14 August 1944.

125. "Testimony by Szymon Srebrnik," 29 June 1945, in Pawlicka-Nowak, *Chełmno Witnesses Speak,* p. 126.

126. See Dominick LaCapra, *Writing History, Writing Trauma* (Baltimore: Johns Hopkins University Press, 2001), pp. 131, 140 n. 27.

127. Łucja Pawlicka-Nowak, "Archaeological Research in the Grounds of the Chełmno-on-Ner Former Extermination Center," in *Chełmno Witnesses Speak,* p. 58. "Testimony by Walter Piller," ibid., pp. 185–186.

128. GKBZpNP-IPN Ob 271, t. III, pp. 279–280: statement of Jozef Grabowski (Protokol Przesluchania Swiadka), 12 July 1945.

129. "Testimony by Bruno Israel," 29 October 1945, in Pawlicka-Nowak, *Chełmno Witnesses Speak,* p. 199.

130. "Testimony by Walter Piller," ibid., p. 184. Oberwachtemeister Bruno Israel, a member of the Bothmann Sonderkommando, however, briefly indicated that the dismantling took place in December 1944. "Testimony by Bruno Israel," 29 October 1945, ibid., p. 198.

131. GKBZpNP-IPN Ob 271, t. I, pp. 13–14: statement of Henryk Kruszcynski (Protokol Przesluchania Swiadka), 9 June 1945.

132. "Die letzte kleine Abendmusik in unserer Musikschule," *LZ,* 31 August 1944.

133. Dr. H. Fiechtner, "Die Zwischenbilanz der Oper: Ein Rückblick von Dr. H. Fiechtner," *LZ,* 19 September 1944.

134. Wolf Delhaes, "300 000 Litzmannstädter erlebten 572 Vorstellungen," *LZ,* 26 October 1944.

135. W. D., "Litzmannstädter Bühnenkünstler kamen zum Ein[satz]," *LZ,* 20

September 1944. Also see local notice under the heading "Reichsmusikammer," *LZ*, 3 September 1944, advising music teachers to report to the Musikschule for "important instructions" relating to their integration into the wartime labor force.

136. "Film-Theater" announcement, *LZ*, 16 January 1945.

137. "Fünf Jahre deutscher Aufbau im Warheland: Aus dem Rechenschaftsbericht des Gauleiters und Reichsstatthalters," *LZ*, 8 November 1944.

138. Johannes Moeller, "Noch deutsche Ostfroschung?—Nun erst recht!" *LZ*, 21 November 1944.

139. "Der Gauleiter Sprach zu den Rußland-Deutschen im Wartheland: Eine bedeutsame Arbeitstagung in der Gauhauptstadt/Danktelegramm an den Reichsführer SS Himmler," *LZ*, 12 December 1944, p. 1.

140. "Adele Proesler spricht vor Schulen," *LZ*, 1 July 1944. E. G., "Deutsche Märchen erzählt," *LZ*, 8 July 1944.

141. Amtl. Bekanntmachungen, "Gültig im Reichsgau Wartheland! Verteilung von Bienenhonig an deutsche Kinder bis zu zehn Jahren," *LZ*, 20 September 1944.

142. "Reges vorweihnachtliches Wirken der Partei in Litzmannstadt," *LZ*, 17 December 1944.

143. Gü, "Reges vorweihnachtliches Wirken der Partein in Litzmannstadt," *LZ*, 17 December 1944.

144. Gü, "Ein Postamt hat einen Weihnachtsschalter," *LZ*, 15 December 1944.

145. APL AmL GV 28677, p. 356: Stadtauskunft Litzmannstadt, Vermerk, 5 July 1944. See also a later notice, dated 9 September 1944, confirming that the film had been placed in the hospital cellar and indicating that, packed into "21 rolls and 21 boxes," its length 4,779 meters, it would have had a running time of "at least 3 hours." APL AmL GV 28677, p. 365: typed memorandum, 23 September 1944 (on reverse of Ufa letter dated 23 August 1944).

146. APL AmL GV 28677, p. 364: Universum-Film Aktiengesellschaft, Abteilung Ufa-Wirtschaftsfilm to Oberürgermeister, Verkehrs- und Nachrichtenamt, Litzmannstadt, 23 August 1944.

147. APL AmL GV 28677, p. 366: Der Oberbürgermeister—ooo, Betr. Dokumentaarfilm Litzmannstadt, 30 September 1944, and accompanying handwritten note.

148. APL AmL GV 28677, pp. 367–368: M/D. to Universum-Film-Aktiengesellschaft, Abteilung Ufa-Wirtschaftsfilm, in reference to correspondence of 23 August 1944; An die Universum-Film-Aktiengesellschaft—Abteilung Ufa-Wirtschaftsfilm, 28 October 1944.

149. "Kriegsbedingter Wechsel in der Führung der Stadtverwalltung," *LZ*, 10 December 1944.

150. "Führerwechsel im Polizeipräsidium," *LZ,* 3 November 1944. Nawrocki, *Policja Hitlerowska,* p. 165.

151. USHMM RG-05.008M, Reel 1, File 66, pp. 89, 92: Niederschrift über die Dezerrnentensitzung, 13 December 1944.

152. Bericht, Räumung der Stadt Litzmannstadt, Oberbürgermeister von Litzmannstadt, Trautwein, 13 March 1945, in *Die Räumung des "Reichsgaus Wartheland" vom 16. bis 26. Januar 1945 im Spiegel amtlicher Berichte,* ed. Joachim Rogall (Sigmaringen: Jan Thorbecke Verlag, 1993), p. 47.

153. Ibid, pp. 47, 49, 51.

154. Ibid., p. 48.

155. Ibid., p. 52.

156. Ibid., pp. 48–49, 51–53.

157. Pawlicka-Nowak, *Chełmno Witnesses Speak,* p. 74.

158. Ibid., p. 77.

159. "Testimony by Szymon Srebrnik," 29 June 1945, ibid., pp. 128–129; "Testimony by Mordka Żurawski of 1945," 31 July 1945, ibid., pp. 133–134; "Testimony by Mordka Żurawski of 1950," 30 January 1950, ibid., pp. 137–138; "Testimony by Bruno Israel," 29 October 1945, ibid., p. 200.

160. Poznański, *Dziennik,* entries for 15–18 January 1945, pp. 261–263.

161. Ibid., entries for 19–20 January 1945 and Notebook 13, p. 264.

Epilogue

1. Hannah Arendt, *Eichmann in Jerusalem,* rev. and enl. ed. (New York: Viking Press, 1964). Isaiah Trunk, *Judenrat: The Jewish Councils in Eastern Europe under Nazi Occupation* (New York: Macmillan, 1972). Raul Hilberg, "The Ghetto as a Form of Government," *Annals of the American Academy of Political and Social Science* 450 (July 1980): 98–112. Dan Diner, *Beyond the Conceivable: Studies on Germany, Nazism, and the Holocaust* (Berkeley: University of California Press, 2000), pp. 121–122. Dov Levin, "The Fighting Leadership of the Judenräte in the Small Communities of Poland," in *Patterns of Jewish Leadership in Nazi Europe, 1933–1945: Proceedings of the Third Yad Vashem International Historical Conference,* ed. Yisrael Gutman and Cynthia Haft (Jerusalem: Yad Vashem, 1979), pp. 133–147. Aharon Weiss, "The Relations between the Judenrat and the Jewish Police," in Gutman and Haft, *Patterns of Jewish Leadership,* pp. 201–217.

2. Hilberg, "The Ghetto as a Form of Government," p. 103. Raul Hilberg, "The Judenrat: Conscious or Unconscious 'Tool,'" in Gutman and Haft, *Patterns of Jewish Leadership,* p. 38. Diner, *Beyond the Conceivable,* pp. 134, 136.

3. Hilberg, "The Ghetto as a Form of Government," p. 108. Diner, *Beyond the Conceivable,* pp. 124, 129, 134.

4. On the pitfalls of such rational calculations, see Diner, *Beyond the Conceivable*, pp. 131–137.

5. Hilberg, "The Judenrat: Conscious or Unconscious 'Tool,'" p. 39.

6. On the difficulties of perception, see Yisrael Gutman, "The Concept of Labor in Judenrat Policy," in Gutman and Haft, *Patterns of Jewish Leadership*, p. 162. Israel Gutman, "Introduction: The Distinctiveness of the Łódź Ghetto," in Isaiah Trunk, *Łódź Ghetto: A History*, trans. and ed. Robert Moses Shapiro (Bloomington: Indiana University Press, 2006), p. liii. Yehuda Bauer, "Conclusions," in Gutman and Haft, *Patterns of Jewish Leadership*, pp. 401–402. Gustavo Corni, *Hitler's Ghettos: Voices from a Beleaguered Society, 1939–1944*, trans. Nicola Rudge Iannelli (London: Arnold, 2003), pp. 297–300. Walter Laqueur, *The Terrible Secret: The Suppression of Truth about Hitler's "Final Solution"* (Boston: Little, Brown, 1980).

7. Gutman, "Introduction," in Trunk, *Łódź Ghetto*, pp. li, 423, n. 73.

8. Ibid., pp. li, lii.

9. Ibid., pp. li, 423, n. 73.

10. Friedrich Hielscher, *Fünfzig Jahre unter Deutschen* (Hamburg: Rowohlt, 1954), pp. 360–363. Yehuda Bauer, *Rethinking the Holocaust* (New Haven: Yale University Press, 2001), pp. 80–81. Diner, *Beyond the Conceivable*, pp. 126–127. Gutman, "Introduction," in Trunk, *Łódź Ghetto*, p. xlix.

11. Gutman, "Introduction," in Trunk, *Łódź Ghetto*, pp. lii–liii. Corni, *Hitler's Ghettos*, p. 299. Diner, *Beyond the Conceivable*, p. 123.

12. Hilberg, "The Ghetto as a Form of Government," pp. 103, 109. Diner, *Beyond the Conceivable*, pp. 123, 134, 136.

13. On the prospect of "a miracle" that would save the ghetto, see Arnold Mostowicz, *With a Yellow Star and a Red Cross: A Doctor in the Łódź Ghetto*, trans. Henia Reinhartz and Nochem Reinhartz (London: Valentine Mitchell, 2005), p. 124. On Rumkowski's fantasy of being at the head of a remnant safely exiting the ghetto, see Oskar Rosenfeld, *In the Beginning Was the Ghetto: Notebooks from Łódź*, ed. Hanno Loewy, trans. Brigitte M. Goldstein (Evanston: Northwestern University Press, 2002), entry for 12 May 1943, p. 189.

14. Trunk, *Judenrat*, p. 413. Mostowicz, *With a Yellow Star*, p. 124.

15. Gutman, "The Concept of Labor in Judenrat Policy," pp. 171–172.

16. On the topic of setting fire to small ghettos and attempting to escape to the forests, with limited success, see Levin, "The Fighting Leadership of the Judenräte in the Small Communities of Poland," pp. 134, 136–142. On setting fires and rushing the perimeter in the Bialystock ghetto, see Leni Yahil, *The Holocaust: The Fate of European Jewry*, trans. Haya Galai (New York: Oxford University Press), pp. 471–472.

17. Trunk, *Łódź Ghetto*, pp. 394–395. Corni, *Hitler's Ghettos*, pp. 310–311. Gutman, "Introduction," in Trunk, *Łódź Ghetto*, p. lvii. Bauer, "Conclusions,"

in Gutman and Haft, *Patterns of Jewish Leadership,* p. 398. Dov Levin, "The Fighting Leadership of the Judenräte in the Small Communities of Poland," in Gutman and Haft, *Patterns of Jewish Leadership,* pp. 136–142. Bauer, "Conclusions," in Gutman and Haft, *Patterns of Jewish Leadership,* p. 404; Shmuel Krakowski, "The Opposition to the Judenräte by the Jewish Armed Resistance," in Gutman and Haft, *Patterns of Jewish Leadership,* p. 199.

18. Mostowicz, *With a Yellow Star,* pp. 125–126.

19. Ibid., p. 118.

20. See the discussion in Trunk, *Judenrat,* pp. 570–573.

21. Bauer, "Conclusions," in Gutman and Haft, *Patterns of Jewish Leadership,* p. 395.

22. Jan Waszczyński, "Z problematyki odpowiedzialności karnej za zbrodnie popełnione na Żydach w Łódźi (1939–1945)," in *Dzieje żydów w Łodzi (1820–1944),* ed. Wiesława Puś and Stanisława Liszewski (Łódź: Wydawnictwo Universitetu Łódźkiego, 1991), pp. 360–361. Jerzy Lewiński, *Proces Hansa Biebow* (Warsaw: PRS, 1999), pp. 230–239.

23. Wasczyński, "Z problematyki odpowiedzialności karnej," pp. 361–362, 365–366.

24. Ibid., pp. 359–360, 366. Gerda Zorn, *"Nach Ostland geht unser Ritt": Deutsche Eroberungspolitik und die Folgen. Das Beispiel Lodz* (Cologne: Röderberg im Pahl-Rugenstein Verlag, 1988), pp. 138–139, 149–150, 187. Of the men of the Sonderkommando in Chełmno, commandant Bothmann committed suicide following his arrest; Walter Piller, his second in command, was sentenced to death by a Polish court. A handful of other men attached to Bothmann's team faced trial decades later, receiving limited terms of imprisonment. Wasczyński, "Z problematyki odpowiedzialności karnej," p. 362.

25. Bundesarchiv-Filmarchiv Berlin, Mag.-Nr. 3578: "Aus Lodz wird Litzmannstadt."

26. Wilm von Elbwart, *Stadt im Sommerwind,* 2nd ed. (Breslau: Gauverlag Niederschlesien, 1944), pp. 7, 10–11, 18–22, 26–27, 50–58, 66–77, 144–156.

27. Ibid., pp. 132–134, 140–142.

28. JMF: Genewein Series II 24, II 28, II 40, II 41, II 42, [II] 43, II 46, II 48, II 58. See also Hanno Loewy and Gerhard Schoenberner, eds., *"Unser einziger Weg ist Arbeit": Das Getto in Łódź 1940–1944* (Vienna: Löcker Verlag, 1990), pp. 74–77. Florian Freund, Bertrand Perz, and Karl Stuhlpfarrer, "Bildergeschichten—Gesichtsbilder," ibid., pp. 50–58. See also Frances Guerin, "Reframing the Photographer and His Photographs: *Photographer* (1995)," *Film and History* 32.1 (2002): 43–54.

29. See Loewy and Schoenberner, *"Unser einziger Weg ist Arbeit,"* pp. 68, 72, 91, 110, 112, 115–117, 119, 122–123, 125, 128, 139.

30. Łucja Pawlicka-Nowak, "Archaeological Research in the Grounds of the

Chełmno-on-Ner Former Extermination Center," in *Chełmno Witnesses Speak,* ed. Łucja Pawlicka-Nowak, trans. Juliet D. Golden and Arkadiusz Kamiński (Konin: Council for the Protection of Memory of Combat and Martyrdom in Warsaw and The District Museum in Konin, 2004), pp. 54–58 and accompanying photographs of recovered articles.

31. See the discussion in Elaine Scarry, *The Body in Pain: The Making and Unmaking of the World* (New York: Oxford University Press, 1985), pp. 281–326, esp. p. 292, and Scarry, *On Beauty and Being Just* (Princeton: Princeton University Press, 1999), pp. 25–26. See *The Union Prayer Book for Jewish Worship,* ed. The Central Conference of American Rabbis, rev. ed. pt. 2 (Cincinnati: The Central Conference of American Rabbis, 1950), p. 350.

32. On the theme of transgression, and on the imagery of the overflowing and ebbing of waters and the purifying of remains, see Georges Bataille, *Erotism: Faith and Sensuality,* trans. Mary Dalwood (San Francisco: City Lights Books, 1986), pp. 66–67, 100, 104.

Acknowledgments

In the researching and writing of this work I have been fortunate to bene-fit from the assistance of many individuals whose knowledge, professional skill, critical interest, and patience proved indispensable to me in the gathering of my evidence, the formulation of my ideas, and the successful completion of my task. I am especially indebted to those associated with several archival institutions in Europe and in the United States that play such a vital role in organizing and preserving the invaluable historical record that is the lifeblood of scholarship on the Holocaust. In particular, I wish to thank the staff of the YIVO Institute for Jewish Research in New York, where I began my initial exploration of the documentation on the subject of the Łódź ghetto. At the Jüdisches Museum in Frankfurt, Mi-chael Lenarz kindly allowed me to view close-up the museum's remarkable collection of color images of the ghetto, and later assisted greatly in facili-tating the reproduction of some of these images in this volume. Also dur-ing the early phase of my work, the staff of the Jewish Historical Institute in Warsaw generously provided help in exploring the topic and in gather-ing evidence. At the Polish State Archive in Łódź, Julian Baranowski and his fellow archivists were instrumental in facilitating my search of origi-nal documents from the vast ghetto administrative collections in the ar-chive's possession. These materials remain an essential resource for all who wish to explore original research on this topic. In addition, the Institute für Zeitgeschichte in Munich kindly supplied microfilmed copies of the *Litzmannstädter Zeitung*. In Washington, the archive of the United States Holocaust Memorial Museum offered invaluable help in providing access to microfilmed copies of additional ghetto materials from the State Archive in Łódź. For her assistance in the acquisition of further images available in the museum's photo archive, I thank Caroline Waddell. Among those who, along the way, shared with me their interest in the topic of the Łódź ghetto, I express my special appreciation to Zofia Snawadzka, Lucie Cytryn-Bialer, and Michael Lee. At Harvard University Press my editor, Joyce Seltzer, lent invaluable support. She believed in the work from the start and brought to it the full range of her outstanding knowledge and skill. I am fortunate indeed to have the privilege of working with her. In addition, her assistant, Jennifer Banks, was a steady and reliable presence, patiently helping in the final preparation of the manuscript. To the anonymous readers who lent their critical expertise to a review of the manuscript in its final stages, I remain indebted for their valuable insights and suggestions. I also thank Illinois Wesleyan University, which, in addition to providing sabbatical leave, facilitated my research through its program of Artistic and Scholarly Development Grants. To the university's Ames Library, and most especially Tony Heaton, I owe thanks for helping me gather numerous sources by way of interlibrary loan. In addition to my parents, I thank most particularly Li-Lin Tseng, who, during the writing of this work, was my indispensable friend and interlocutor. Over the course of our many conversations, her unfailing interest, critical insights, and warm support were crucial. Finally, I am pleased to dedicate this book to the memory of Marcia L. Kahn. For the example of her passion for history, and for the encouragement she provided me in pursuing my research when I was young, I am forever grateful. Her intellectual legacy is a gift I recall with deepest appreciation and fondness.

Index

Administration of Łódź, 2, 15, 32–34, 35, 305–306, 307

Administration of the ghetto, 27–29, 58, 64–68, 70, 72–73, 95–96, 122, 143, 252, 259, 267–268; autonomy of, 83; costs of, 63, 92–93; duties and procedures for, 74–75; failure of, 79; institutional supervision, 63; mismanagement and corruption in, 238–239, 240, 246; by municipal German planners, 61; through banking institutions, 175–176

Agudah movement, 14

Albert, Karl Wilhelm, 111, 306, 318

Anti-Semitism, 119–120, 227; exploitation, 58; harassment, 30, 57; hatred, 118, 132, 262–263; humiliation, 11–12, 59, 184–185, 267, 296; persecution, 313; in political parties, 4; racial exclusion, 141; restrictions on Jewish doctors, 14; stereotypes of Jews, 7, 11; verbal threats, 4. *See also* Violence against Jews

Architecture of Łódź, 4–5. *See also* Modernization and renovation of Łódź

Arendt, Hannah, 311

Armbands, Star of David, 23, 26, 89, 90, 139, 321

Arts and entertainment in Łódź, 229–230, 303; ballet, 302; cinema, 106–107, 120, 229, 302; exclusion of Jewish artists from, 52; music, 53, 104–105, 124, 221, 229, 230–231, 248, 302; opera, 52; theater, 32–34, 112, 124, 221, 248, 273, 302

Arts and entertainment in the ghetto of Łódź, 114; music, 125, 145, 188, 189–191, 256; theater, 125, 188–189, 256–257

Arts and entertainment in the Jewish community of Łódź, 2, 5, 6

Auschwitz, Poland, 7

Auschwitz death camp, 293, 300, 316

Austria, 134

Baltic states, 24, 25, 30, 111

Bałut Market/Bałuty district, 5, 6, 22, 43, 51, 52, 54–55, 68, 70, 73, 74, 75, 83, 116, 117, 126, 130, 131, 134, 161, 162, 172, 176, 222, 259–261, 262, 267, 272, 276, 277, 283, 295, 299

Bandler, Rudolf, 190–191

Bangert, Walter, 120, 121

Berlin, Germany, 132, 133, 141

Biebow, Hans, 64–65, 66, 131, 229, 276–277; cleanup of the ghetto after deportations and, 226; closure of ghetto hospitals and, 204; confiscation and sale of Jewish property and, 110, 176, 179; deportation of Jews from the ghetto and, 160, 278; deportation of Jews to the ghetto and, 132; evacuation of the ghetto and, 276–277, 287–288; factories and workshops in the ghetto and, 76, 101, 116, 235; on the failings of Jews, 270; financial affairs of the ghetto and, 93–94; food supplies for the ghetto and, 95–96, 155–157; Jewish exhibition and, 185, 186–187; liquidation process and, 252; modernization of Łódź and, 122; mortality rates in the ghetto and, 155; personal behavior after liquidation of the ghetto, 299–300; physical attack on Rumkowski, 276–277, 284, 296, 299; Rumkowski and, 83, 84, 233, 295; survey of the ghetto population by, 283; transfer of control over the ghetto, 269–270; trial and execution of, 204, 317–318; waste removal operations and, 79–80, 81

Black market, 137–138, 140, 144, 199, 238, 240

Bloody Thursday assault, 49, 51

Bothmann, Hans, 180, 246, 247, 269, 272, 301–302

Bradfisch, Otto, 251, 266–267, 276, 277, 287, 288–289, 305, 318

Catholic church, 54–55

Cemeteries: in the ghetto of Łódź, 28, 39, 40, 57, 73, 145; Jewish, in Łódź, 5, 21, 57

Chanukah, 265

Charitable agencies, 14

Chełmno death camp, 151–152, 162, 194, 198, 269, 284, 314, 321–322; burning and disposing of corpses at, 195, 272, 300–302, 313–314; efficiency of, 313; escapes from, 152–153; evacuation of, as Soviets approach, 307; expansion of operations, 180, 272–273; Jewish property confis-

cated at, 176, 301; Jewish workforce at, 301; killing of Jewish workers at, 308–309; misinformation about conditions at, 161; planned dissolution of, 246–247; Sonderkommando unit, 160, 179, 180, 269, 272, 301, 308; use of gas vans, 152

Children, German, 54, 192–193, 194, 230, 231, 236, 270, 304–305; day camps for, 227; orphaned, 247

Children, Jewish, 114, 120, 133, 192, 193, 299; brought to the ghetto of Łódź, 172–173, 174, 193; care facilities for, 95; conditions in the ghetto for, 115, 120, 139, 185, 205, 206, 215–216, 217, 261, 279, 284–285; death of, in the ghetto, 78, 118, 222, 223, 225, 308; departure from Łódź, 26; deportation of, 191, 193, 196–197, 199, 203, 204, 205, 206, 207, 208, 209, 211, 212, 213, 214, 215, 218–220, 222, 223–224, 225, 231, 232, 233, 255, 259, 266, 283, 292–293, 308, 314; disinfection of, 134; education of, 21, 71–77, 82, 133–134; during the German invasion of Poland, 8, 9; health concerns for, 19–20; hiding of, to escape deportation, 222, 225; insufficient food for, 128, 136, 254, 261; medical facilities for, 21, 45, 51, 114; murder of, 201–202, 300, 307; playground for, 52, 125; remaining in the ghetto after deportations, 279; summer camps for, 6–7, 82–83, 255; in the workforce in the ghetto, 199–200, 211, 236, 253, 298. *See also* Orphanages in the ghetto of Łódź; Rumkowski, Mordechai Chaim: welfare of children and orphans and

Citizenship, 30

Commerce in Łódź, 2; Jewish, 14, 27, 53

Commerce in the ghetto of Łódź, 27, 259

Concentration camps, 23, 268–269. *See also* Auschwitz death camp; Chełmno death camp

Crime: in the ghetto of Łódź, 101–102, 118, 171; Jewish, in Łódź, 5. *See also* Smuggling

Criminal Police (Kriminalpolizei [Kripo]), 68–69, 93, 96, 111, 118, 129; confiscation of Jewish property and, 96–97; confiscation of weapons by, 129; patrolling of the ghetto boundaries by, 69, 118–119; program of extermination and, 197–198; quarters in the ghetto, 69–70; smuggling and, 102

Curfews: in Łódź, 23; in the ghetto of Łódź, 43, 72, 210, 217, 218, 226, 259

Czechoslovakia, 134

Czerniaków, Adam, 125, 126, 295

Death camps, 4. *See also* Auschwitz death camp; Chełmno death camp

Death in the ghetto of Łódź, 112, 213, 235, 238, 257, 264–265, 294, 313, 318; from cold, 114; from disease, 78, 117, 119, 126, 128, 145, 285, 298; from exhaustion, 145; from heart disease, 128, 156; from hunger and malnutrition, 114, 128, 164, 238, 241, 284, 285, 308; mortality rates, 78, 117, 118, 128, 137, 145–146, 154, 155, 252; by shooting, 119, 128, 172, 204, 213, 222, 223, 316–317; from thirst, 298; of women, 222, 223. *See also* Children, Jewish; Suicide

Death of Jews in Łódź, 8, 39–40; by beating, 22, 23; by shooting, 22, 23, 49, 50

Death of Jews in the provincial ghettos, 201–202, 314

Demographics: of the ghetto, 28, 193, 232; of Łódź, 3, 29, 32, 35–36, 88, 90, 113, 194, 319; of occupied Poland, 24–25. *See also* Population of Łódź; Population of the ghetto of Łódź

Deportation of Jews from Łódź, 24, 25–27

Deportation of Jews from provincial ghettos, 316–317

Deportation of Jews from the ghetto of Łódź, 150, 157, 159, 182–183, 212–213, 228, 235, 238, 259, 278, 315; aided by firefighters, 217–218; aided by the Gestapo and Jewish police, 217–218, 219, 221, 222–223, 280–281; attempts to escape from, 222, 225, 289; to Auschwitz death camp, 316; to Chełmno death camp, 151–154, 161, 163, 179, 218, 272–273, 283, 300; confiscation of personal property prior to, 168–169; effect on ghetto morale, 156, 157, 166, 169, 171–172, 196–197, 203, 205, 207–208, 234–235, 276; exemptions from, 147–149, 164–167, 193, 208, 225, 280–281, 298; expansion of, 162; Ghetto Administration charged for, 178–180; halting of, 302; hiding to escape from, 280, 281, 288, 289, 291, 292, 293, 294, 298, 312; Jewish assistance for, 287; misinformation about, 277–279, 283–284, 290, 314; number of deportees, 157–158, 161–162, 199, 226, 277, 282, 291; physical examinations for, 163–164; quotas for, 143, 207–208, 210, 211, 214, 291, 312; resumed in 1944, 277–282, 286–288, 289–296; roundups and raids, 26, 49–50; of sick and elderly, 148, 200–201, 203, 204–205, 206, 207, 208, 211, 213, 214, 215–216, 218, 219–220, 224, 233; summonses to report for, 146–147, 149–150, 157, 165, 183, 288, 293–294; targeted population for, 161–162, 164, 167–168, 171, 183, 193, 207–208, 209–210, 280; temporary halting of, 157, 160, 161, 196, 226, 282–283; transport fees, 179–180; of undesirable persons, 147, 148, 151, 171; unknown destination and fate of deportees, 151, 158, 175, 201, 212, 231, 277, 280, 283–284, 290, 314; voluntary reporting for, 167, 168, 280, 281, 288, 290, 291, 292, 293, 294, 314; of workers, 284. *See also* Auschwitz death camp; Chełmno death camp

Deportation of Jews to the ghetto of Łódź, 132–133, 134–140, 162, 164, 165, 178–179, 201; from outlying districts, 172–175, 212; targeted population for, 172

Deportation of Poles from Łódź, 3, 24, 25–26

Detention facilities in the ghetto of Łódź, 69, 168, 170, 282; Central Prison, 72, 118, 146, 148, 149, 168, 218, 280, 281, 282–283

Disease in Łódź, 195, 249; communicable, 19, 195; in Jewish orphanages, 20; Jewish rates of, 39–40; Jews blamed for, 36–37, 45, 92, 120, 303

Disease in the ghetto of Łódź, 24, 27, 29, 38, 41, 42, 56, 63, 78, 81, 158, 235, 257, 270, 298; after liquidation, 297; attempts to control, 27, 36–37, 38, 39–42, 44, 46, 55, 82, 119, 226; caused by malnutrition and crowding, 258; epidemics, 94, 133; malnutrition as cause of, 240–241; protection against, 39, 58. *See also specific diseases*

Disinfection: of clothes and belongings, 180; to control disease, 27, 38, 46, 119; of houses, 37, 298; of manufactured products, 37, 67, 108, 298; of outhouses, 119; of persons, 46, 69, 112, 134, 180; of property, 31, 37, 46, 180; of waste removal operations, 46, 69, 81

Dysentery, 78, 81, 117, 119

Eastern Jews, 10, 183, 190, 311

Economy of Łódź, 3, 4, 55, 58

Economy of the ghetto of Łódź, 70, 75, 111, 113, 129, 132, 198; efficiency of, 122, 131–132; underground, 137–138

Education. *See* Children, Jewish: education of

Eichmann, Adolf, 268

Erotic attraction and encounters, 182, 183–184, 243–244, 246, 257

Erzhausen district of Łódź, 1–2, 123, 220, 227, 228, 248, 249

Estonia, 30

Ethnic cleansing, 29. *See also* Liquidation

Ethnic German settlers in Łódź, 2, 3, 24, 29, 30–32, 35–36, 89, 114–115, 122; from the Baltic states, 25, 30; from the Black Sea area, 303–304; boundaries of the ghetto and, 55–56; convalescent home for, 248–249; depicted as brave pioneers, 107; food for, after liquidation of the ghetto, 304; in holding camps, 123; housing for, 47, 107; orphaned children of, 247; in the Polish provinces, 54; property of Jews given to, 297; from Russia, 273; smuggling by, 102; in the Wathegau, 234

Evacuation Committee, 207, 210

Evacuation of Łódź, 306–307; during German air attack, 9; by Jews, 16, 25–26, 30; by Jews fleeing the German invasion, 13; by Poles, 25–26

Exhibitions of Jewish productivity and culture, 185–188

Factories and workshops in Łódź, 2, 3, 5, 13, 14, 35

Factories and workshops in the ghetto of Łódź, 71, 97, 124, 127, 199, 205; closing of, 133; expansion of, 129–130; items for the German military, 131, 133, 155, 198; items for the private sector, 155, 198, 312–313; network of, 75–76; production, 73; raw materials for, 76, 313; resources for, 144; sabotage in, 312. *See also* Workforce in the ghetto of Łódź

Farming and agriculture, 17–19, 25, 30, 151, 167, 278–279, 304

Film documentary of Łódź by Ufa studios, 1–2, 7, 122–124, 219–220, 226–227, 229, 305, 318–319

Financial affairs of the ghetto of Łódź, 27, 74; administration of, 67; banking institutions, 175–177; banking system, 71, 75, 109; bookkeeping department, 75; crisis of, 93–95, 95; donations from abroad and, 64, 67, 93, 197; German control over funds, 64; issuance of ghetto currency, 63–64, 66, 71, 109, 176; monthly budget, 143–144

Firefighting resources in the ghetto of Łódź, 28, 32, 39, 133; deportation exemptions for firemen, 208, 225; deportation of Jews from the ghetto and, 217–218; firebreak surrounding the perimeter of the ghetto, 64, 123

Food and Economy Office, Ghetto Division (later Ghetto Administration/ Gettoverwaltung), 64, 65, 66, 74, 75, 94, 95–96, 97, 99, 110, 113, 121, 122, 131, 155, 156, 163, 306, 318; assistance to the killing center, 271–272; banking institutions and, 176–177; civilian claims on property and transport and, 178–181; cleanup of the ghetto and, 226; confiscated Jewish property and, 175; deportation of Jews and, 160, 225–226, 287; distribution of food by, 239–240; inspection of the ghetto after liquidation by, 297; network of workshops, 198; productionist goals of, 252; survival of the ghetto and, 270; textile industry and, 101, 116

Food supplies for Łódź, 21

Food supplies for the ghetto of Łódź, 27, 28, 57; bread, 21, 44, 77, 98, 117, 124, 206, 217, 240; corruption and, 238–239, 240; cost of, 124; crisis of, 94; dining facilities, 70–71; distribution of, 27, 28, 70–71, 72, 75, 77, 97, 100, 117, 239, 240; for ghetto kitchens, 28; given to newly transferred Jews, 44; insufficiency of, 93, 94, 109, 116, 127; lack of nutrition in, 252; mass demonstration for improved rations, 117–118; payment for, 39, 63, 67; potatoes, 257, 260; prices of, 77; rationing of, 73, 97, 98–99, 100, 109, 117, 118, 125, 127, 136, 146, 155, 157, 163, 239, 240, 242, 252, 280, 288, 291; shortages of, 136–137, 155–157, 240, 252, 276, 279, 289; subsidized meals, 95; supplements to workers, 252–255

Frank, Shlomo, 150, 172, 196, 221

Freedom Square, Łódź, 9, 32

Fuchs, Dora, 42, 130–131, 150, 243, 276, 283

Fulda Conference of Bishops, 54

Generalgouvernement zone, 25, 88, 153

Genewein, Walter, 229, 320–321

German Hygiene Museum, Łódź, 250

German police in Łódź (Schupo), 27, 28, 42, 43, 68, 83–85, 84, 86, 87, 130, 291; auxiliary, 9, 26; final evacuation of the ghetto and, 289, 291; military, 9; transfer of Jews to the ghetto and, 43–44. See also Gestapo (Secret State Police)

Germany: army, 288; defeat of, 291, 307, 312, 316–317; deportation of Jews to the ghetto of Łódź, 134; invasion of Łódź, 9–13, 258; military forces, 67, 71; war economy and production, 3, 71, 131–132, 156, 246, 269, 270, 315

Gestapo (Secret State Police), 213; debts owed by deportees and, 178–179; deportation of Jews from the ghetto and, 161, 221, 222; establishment of hospitals in the ghetto and, 40; food shortage crisis and, 155, 156; intelligence gathering by, 68; pending liberation of Poland and, 291; program of liquidation and, 197; Rumkowski and, 83; survey of the ghetto population by, 283; violence against Jews by, 22; waste removal operations and, 79. See also German police in Łódź

Gettoverwaltung. See Food and Economy Office, Ghetto Division (later Ghetto Administration/Gettoverwaltung)

Ghetto Administration. See Food and Economy Office, Ghetto Division (later Ghetto Administration/Gettoverwaltung)

Ghetto of Łódź: ban on contact with residents of Łódź, 118; ban on movement in and out of, 3, 59, 68–69, 90, 118; boundaries of, 28, 33, 41, 43, 45, 54–55, 57, 60, 61, 62, 73, 316; cleanup operations, after deportations, 226; cleanup operations, after liquidation, 296–299; creation of, 27–28, 29, 36, 37–38, 42, 45, 54, 55, 111, 321, 322; departure of ethnic Germans and Poles from, 45, 46–47; duration of, 95, 97; efficiency of, 320; escapes from, 89, 90; evacuation of, 276; final evacuation of, 286–288, 289–296; illegal residence in, 294; internal divisions in, 238; isolation of, 3, 37, 39, 42, 44, 59, 103, 113, 118, 232; Jews charged for cost of maintaining, 180–181; lice and vermin in, 37, 39, 105, 108, 120, 258, 270, 298; liquidation of, 296; maintenance costs, 270, 271; map of, 48; as means of containing disease, 36–37, 39–42, 44, 55; neutral zone surrounding, 38; photographs of, 229, 320, 321; planned dissolution of, 35, 41, 42, 55, 56, 59, 62, 112, 157, 213, 269, 275–276, 312, 315; plan to become a concentration camp, 268, 269; Polish residents of, 90; population of, 38; resources of, 93–94, 112; routines of,

Ghetto of Łódź *(continued)*
259–261; sealing of, 52, 55, 56, 60, 77, 113, 122, 134; SS control of, 268–270; transfer of city Jews to, 42–44, 45–49, 110, 111; as zone of quarantine, 36, 40, 42, 52, 59. *See also* Rumkowski, Mordechai Chaim

Ghettos of Poland, 311

Goebbels, Joseph, 22

Gonorrhea, 20

Greiser, Gauleiter Arthur, 54, 92, 122, 130, 141, 246–247, 268–269; on German refugees from Russia, 304; Himmler and, 163; on Jews targeted for extermination, 161–162; planned dissolution of the ghetto and, 275–276

Grossman, Mendel, 5, 181, 294

Gypsies, 133, 145, 153

Hallbauer, Wilhelm, 34–35, 36, 55, 88, 120, 121, 123

Health Department of Łódź, 2, 40, 41–42, 46, 252, 298

Health Department of the ghetto of Łódź, 44, 70, 98, 99, 226

Health services in Łódź, 35, 42, 118; hygiene concerns, 88, 105

Health services in the ghetto of Łódź, 27, 41, 42, 56–57, 58, 65–66, 119

Heat and heating in the ghetto of Łódź: delivery of fuel, 28; shortages of wood and coal, 115, 116, 124, 138; wood for, 115, 119

Heydrich, Reinhard, 15, 25

Himmler, Heinrich, 130–131, 161, 162, 163, 246, 263, 268–269, 275–276

Hitler, Adolf, 9, 22, 120, 140, 162, 234, 246; attempted assassination of, 316; goal of total annhililation of the Jews, 263; New Year's address of 1944, 266

Hitler-Jugend-Park in Łódź, 121, 141, 247

Hitler Youth, 2, 92, 121, 124, 159, 249, 304

Horn, Otto, 268

Hospitals in Łódź, 2, 9, 31–32, 112, 249; Jewish, 4, 21

Hospitals in the ghetto, 28, 38, 56, 57, 70, 118, 257, 299; closure of, 203–204, 211,

259; creation of, 40–42; free access to, 77

House of Culture, 143, 188, 190, 256, 257, 269

Housing Department of Łódź, 47

Housing Department of the ghetto of Łódź, 43, 49

Housing in Łódź, 34; renovation of, 2, 121; single-room dwellings, 35, 40

Housing in Łódź owned by Jews, 23; abandonment of, 46; confiscation of, 107–108; disinfection of, 108; given to ethnic German settlers, 36; overcrowding of, 78; plunder of, 12–13, 26

Housing in the ghetto of Łódź, 27, 28, 43, 44, 46, 298; administration of, 28; allocation of residences, 71; disinfection of, 37, 298; for newcomers, 139–140; overcrowding of, 38, 42, 55, 62, 133, 135–136, 140, 257, 258; permits for, 44; supervision of, 70, 71

Hunger. *See* Starvation and malnutrition

Iron Cross, 164, 165, 166

Israel, 103

Jakobson, Stanisław-Szaja, 208, 210, 213–214

Jewish Bund, 291, 314

Jewish community of Łódź, 4, 311, 315; December operation of 1939 and, 25–26; German invasion and, 9–10; Kehilla organization, 14, 15; limited interaction with city representatives, 39; poverty of, 5–6; prewar, 6–7. *See also* Rumkowski, Mordechai Chaim

Jewish Council (Beirat), 23, 213, 239

Jewish Councils, 311

Jewish Elders, 15, 16, 84, 130

Jewish Joint Distribution Committee, 17

Jewish Order Service. *See* Police in the ghetto of Łódź (Jewish Order Service)

Jewish police, 130–131, 203; confiscation of weapons by, 292; deportation of Jews from the ghetto and, 217–218, 221–223, 225, 280–281, 289; influx of Jews to the ghetto and, 134; Rumkowski and, 241–

242; sexual favors asked by, 243; Sonderkommando unit, 93, 126, 180, 233, 246, 247, 260, 301; transfer of Jews to the ghetto and, 50

Jewish question/problem, 22, 88, 186

Killing squads/vans, 3–4, 247
Kripo. *See* Criminal Police (Kriminalpolizei [Kripo])

Labor camps, 268
Latvia, 30
Laws, 30; prohibiting Jewish commerce, 14, 27; prohibiting Jews to own property, 12; regarding armbands, 23; restrictions on Jewish doctors, 14
Liberation by the Soviets: of the ghetto of Łódź, 216, 291–292, 309–310, 312; of Poland, 285–286, 287, 295, 307, 313, 316
Liquidation, 42, 197–198, 246, 252; of the ghetto of Łódź, 157, 196, 213, 246, 276, 292, 294–295, 296, 308, 322; of the ghetto of Warsaw, 295; goal of total annihilation (city without Jews), 2, 3, 14, 29, 32, 49, 61, 62, 89, 90, 119, 194, 196, 220, 233, 234, 262, 263, 264, 266, 303, 313–314, 315, 316, 320, 321; of Jewish businesses in Łódź, 14; of Jewish property, 67; of provincial ghettos, 194; of provincial Jewish communities, 172, 175–177, 211; of sick and elderly, 246
Litzmann, Karl, 53
Łódź/Litzmannstadt without Jews. *See* Liquidation: goal of total annihilation (city without Jews)
Luftwaffe, 159
Luxemburg, 134, 137

Malnourishment. *See* Starvation and malnutrition
Manufacturing in Łódź, 13, 14, 67
Manufacturing in the ghetto of Łódź, 96, 114; disinfection of products, 37, 67, 108; efficiency of, 269; items for the German military, 271; items for the private sector, 235–236, 271; planned exhibit of products, 124; raw materials for,

93, 96, 116, 260. *See also* Factories and workshops in the ghetto of Łódź; Textile industry in the ghetto of Łódź
Marder, Karl, 63–64, 76, 104, 111, 122, 123, 267, 297, 305; on economic viability of the ghetto, 131; escape from justice, 318
Marriage, 233, 246, 257
Medical services in Łódź, 14, 20, 36–37, 249–251, 299
Medical services in the ghetto of Łódź, 38, 45, 240–241; for the indigent, 77; instruments and equipment, 51; staff of doctors, 28
Modernization and renovation of Łódź, 3, 7, 34, 88, 92, 111–115, 120–121, 123, 124, 140–142, 170–171, 194, 220–221, 226–227, 305, 318–319, 321; as Germanification, 33–34, 35, 52, 111, 113, 171, 304; street renewal, 2, 35
Moldenhauer, Johann, 64–65, 76
Museums in Łódź, 228–229, 230

National Socialism, 4, 59, 90, 249
National Socialist Welfare Agency (NSV), 177, 227
Nazi movement/Party, 3, 53, 304, 311, 313, 317, 322
Neftalin, Henryk, 42–43, 50, 283

Order Service. *See* Police in the ghetto of Łódź (Jewish Order Service)
Orphanages in Łódź, 4, 17; food supplies to, 21; Helenówek, 17–20
Orphanages in the ghetto of Łódź, 51–52, 60, 70, 73, 95, 128, 255; children integrated into the workforce, 200; deportation of orphans, 232

Pabianice, Poland, 31, 90, 160, 172–174, 190–191, 201
Palestine, 6, 17, 103
Parks and recreational areas of Łódź, 2, 92, 106, 124, 170–171, 192–193, 220, 247, 267
Pets, 85–88
Pływacki, Leizer I., 14, 16
Poland: German invasion and occupation of, 4, 8–11, 22, 24, 134; government

Poland *(continued)*
　of, 9; resistance in, 317; war crimes
　courts, 318
Police. *See* Criminal Police
　(Kriminalpolizei [Kripo]); German po-
　lice in Łódź; Gestapo (Secret State Po-
　lice); Jewish police; Police in the ghetto
　of Łódź (Jewish Order Service)
Police in the ghetto of Łódź (Jewish Order
　Service), 27, 42, 58, 72, 76, 241–242,
　253–254, 311; carpenters' strike and, 115;
　confiscation of pets by, 85–88;
　confiscation of weapons by, 129; deface-
　ment of cemeteries and, 57; deportation
　exemptions for, 208, 225; deportations
　and, 148, 168, 205, 219, 281–282; mass
　demonstration for improved rations
　and, 118; sale of Jewish property and,
　139; transports into the ghetto and, 50;
　victimization of Jews by, 174, 221; vio-
　lence by, 221, 244; waste removal opera-
　tions and, 79
Pollution, 35
Population of Łódź, 2; birthrate, 303; Ger-
　man, 3, 61, 306; Jewish, 3; Polish, 3, 35,
　55, 65. *See also* Demographics
Population of the ghetto of Łódź, 28, 111,
　171–172, 246, 270, 295; after deporta-
　tions, 158, 199, 232, 233, 291; planned re-
　duction of, 272; registration/surveys of,
　99–100, 207, 283. *See also* Demographics
Posen (Wartheland), 25, 54, 141, 161, 162,
　263, 268
Poznański, Izrael K., 4, 5
Poznański, Jakub, 258, 286, 288, 289, 294,
　309–310
Press and newspapers, 106–107, 123, 263–
　264; coverage of the liquidation of the
　ghetto, 196; in the ghetto, 125–126; Jew-
　ish, 5; misinformation in, 197; verbal
　threats to Jews in, 4
Prison. *See* Detention facilities in the
　ghetto of Łódź
Property of Jews: abandonment of, 44,
　168–170, 226, 301; attempts to recover,
　64; civilian corporate claims on, 177–
　178, 179–180; confiscation and sale of,

12, 13, 14, 28, 29, 66, 67, 68, 69, 72, 74,
　94, 96–97, 100–101, 109–110, 139, 160,
　163, 173–177, 179, 181–182, 185, 269, 271;
　confiscation of, at Chełmno death
　camp, 176, 301; disinfection of, 31, 37,
　46, 180; given to ethnic German settlers,
　297; hiding of, 70, 72, 93, 138; removal
　from the ghetto, 66; sold for food,
　137–138, 144, 169; sold prior to depor-
　tation from the ghetto of Łódź, 147;
　theft of, 101–102; voluntary surrender
　of, 71
Prostitution, 89–90, 147

Raabe, Wilhelm, 262
Rabies, 85, 87
Rail transportation, 6, 154; for deporta-
　tions, 278, 288, 290–291; ethnic German
　settlers, 31; in and out of the ghetto, 117,
　134; overcrowding of trains, 26; station
　in Łódź, 141
Recreation areas of Łódź. *See* Parks and
　recreational areas of Łódź
Reicher, Dr. Edward, 20, 23–24
Rent and tax collection, 58, 71, 95
Resettlement Commission, 143, 147, 150,
　151, 164, 165, 207
Resistance efforts, 311, 317
Ribbe, Friedrich, 160, 226, 318
Rosenfeld, Oskar, 135, 136, 160, 164, 167,
　182, 183, 184, 233, 259, 261, 314; on the
　attractions of women, 243; criticism of
　the Jewish exhibit, 187–188; cultural life
　in the ghetto and, 188, 189–190; on
　death of Jews in the ghetto, 264–265;
　on deportations, 281; on impending
　Allied liberation, 285–286; personal
　life, 244–245, 265; on Rumkowski,
　255–256; on survival of the ghetto,
　274–275
Rozenblat, Leon, 150, 242, 276, 314–315
Rubinstein, Artur, 5
Rumkowski, Mordechai Chaim, 114, 137–
　138, 257, 311; allegations of sexual mis-
　conduct against, 19–20, 243–244;
　Biebow and, 83, 84, 233; black market
　and, 137, 140, 144, 238; boundaries of

the ghetto and, 56, 57, 60; closure of ghetto hospitals and, 204–205; confiscation of pets and, 85–88; deportation of Jews from the ghetto and, 152, 157, 225; education policy, 71–72; evacuation of the ghetto and, 276, 286, 287, 291; failure of, 203, 232, 295–296, 317; finances of the ghetto and, 93; food crisis in the ghetto and, 94–95, 99; food supplement regime, 253–255; Gestapo and, 85; ghetto currency and, 64; ghetto hospitals and, 41; halting of deportations and, 282; Jewish Council (Beirat) and, 23; Jewish exhibition and, 186; Jewish police and, 241–242; joins the deportation, 295–296; knowledge of the fate of deportees, 314–315; as leader of the Jewish community of Łódź, 15–18, 20–21, 23–24, 70, 73, 74–75; Leister and, 16; liquidation of the ghetto and, 294–295; newcomers to the ghetto and, 137–138; office of, 72–73, 74; order to confiscate furs and clothing, 109–110; personality, 14, 16–17, 17–18, 126–127, 210, 317; physical appearance, 15–16, 16, 207–208, 260, 261, 296; physical attack on, by Biebow, 276–277, 284, 299; as president of the labor department, 76–77; public health issues and, 56–57; relations with German rulers, 15, 16, 79, 83–85, 116, 127, 128–129, 130, 131, 144, 203, 211, 237–238, 286; selection of children for deportation by, 219, 255, 314; selection of Jews for deportation by, 143, 151, 210–212, 213, 314; shortages of fuel and, 115; speech to the ghetto regarding deportations, 208, 210–214; strike of carpenters and, 115–116; survival strategy for the ghetto, 124, 125–127, 128–129, 131–132, 133, 232, 237–238, 241–242, 254, 291, 295, 315–316; transfer of Jews to the ghetto and, 42–43, 51; in the Warsaw ghetto, 126–127, 128; waste removal crisis and, 80, 81–82; welfare of children and orphans and, 17, 21–22, 51–52, 60, 82–83, 125, 134, 209, 210–211, 232, 255–256; welfare payments and, 97–98; work policies, 57–58, 75–76,

77–78, 129, 131, 138, 143–145, 198–199, 201, 312, 315

Ryder, Teodor, 189–190

Sabotage, 292, 312
Sanitation in Łódź, 34; sewage systems, 35; waste removal, 27, 28, 121; water supply system, 35, 36, 121
Sanitation in the ghetto of Łódź, 38–39, 72, 135, 138; mandatory regulations for, 119; substandard quality of, 78–82, 138, 297; waste removal, 38, 71, 78–82, 167, 239, 297; water supply system, 39
Schnell, Dr., 41, 44–45, 88
School Department in the ghetto of Łódź, 71–72
Schools in Łódź, 4, 112
Schools in the ghetto of Łódź. See Children, Jewish: education of
Schupo. See German police in Łódź (Schupo)
Security in Łódź, 42, 118, 120
Security in the ghetto of Łódź, 27, 28, 58, 59–60, 70, 72, 73, 143, 213, 259; deportation of Jews from the ghetto and, 168; disinformation and, 197, 198; institutions of, 68. See also police listings
Security Service, 15, 198
Singer, Oskar, 168, 219, 254, 255
Sleep problems, 137, 202–203, 216, 219
Smuggling, 68–69, 72, 102, 118
Social welfare, 21–22, 70, 83, 126, 143
Soviet Union, 2, 17, 35; as ally of Germany, 24; emigrants to Łódź, 304; occupation of Poland, 30, 31. See also Liberation by the Soviets; War
Speer, Albert, 275–276
Sports and athletics in Łódź, 248, 249, 273–274
Spotted fever, 37, 39, 156
Srebrnik, Szymon, 272, 309
SS, 9, 27, 159, 162, 184, 221, 247; attempts to gain control of the ghetto, 267–268, 275; at Chełmno death camp, 308
Stalingrad, 234
Star of David armbands, 23, 26, 89, 90, 139, 321

Starvation and malnutrition, 127, 152, 156, 198, 257–258, 284, 285, 308; physical evidence of, 164, 279

Straube, Hermann, 101, 110

Strength Through Joy, 192

Suicide, 128, 154–155, 167, 173, 202; to escape deportation, 293; of Germans in custody, 318

Swastika, 228

Synagogues, 4–5, 22

Textile industry in Łódź, 2, 3, 4, 6, 13, 14, 58–59

Textile industry in the ghetto of Łódź, 58–59, 64, 66, 109; disinfection of materials and products, 108, 298; exemption of workers from deportation, 156–157; exhibition of products, 150–151; items for the German military, 67, 71, 116, 117, 129–130, 235, 268, 313; items for the private sector, 67, 71; ladies' and men's apparel, 237; number of employees, 271; raw materials for, 101, 116, 235, 260

Trains. See Rail transportation

Tuberculosis, 19, 56, 126, 128, 145, 156, 257, 297; rates of infection and mortality, 39–40

Typhus, 119, 145, 154, 297

Uebelhoer, Friedrich, 88, 92, 111, 122, 151; creation of the ghetto by, 27–28, 29; escape from justice, 318

Underground movement in Łódź, 292

Venereal disease, 20

Ventzki, Werner, 122, 123, 133, 141, 221, 249, 252; escape from justice, 318

Violence against Jews, 118, 211; after the German invasion, 11, 12, 13, 50, 58; assaults, 59–60, 184; beatings by the Gestapo, 22; at Chełmno death camp, 272; during deportation from the ghetto, 169, 172; by Jewish police, 221, 225; organized, 29; stoning, 57; torture, 23, 70, 213; during the transfer to the ghetto, 47–50. See also Anti-Semitism

Volhynia, Poland, 24, 30, 31, 107, 161, 162

Walpurgisnacht, 60–61

War, 234, 304; Allied air attack on Germany, 276; Allied air attack on Poland, 277, 285; Allied landing in France, 316; defeat of Germany, 291, 307, 312, 316–317; defense of Łódź, 306; end of, 305, 317; Soviet air attack on Łódź, 307; Soviet forces, 275, 286, 287, 288, 291–292, 295, 306, 307. See also Liberation by the Soviets

Warsaw, Poland, 9, 22, 213, 285

Warsaw ghetto, 38, 126–127, 128, 153, 162, 292, 295

Warsaw Jewish Council, 209

Warszawski, Dawid, 208, 209, 213–214

Wartheland. See Posen (Wartheland)

Weapons, confiscation of, 129, 292

Weisskopf, Daniel, 292

Welfare agencies in Łódź, 297; Jewish, 4, 9–10, 14, 16, 17; social, 21–22

Welfare agencies in the ghetto of Łódź, 58, 73, 95; day care centers, 279; distribution of payments, 97–98; old-age homes, 70, 73, 95, 98, 154, 200–201, 218; shelters for the poor, 70, 77

Western Jews, 164, 167, 168, 169, 194

White Guard, 217

Wittenberg, Sabina, 292

Women in the ghetto of Łódź: physical appearance of, 182, 183–184, 223, 224; sexual favors given by, 243, 282; shooting of, 222

Workforce in Łódź, 3, 35; disinfection of textiles from the ghetto, 108–109; Eastern Jews in, 9; employed within the ghetto, 111; ethnic German, 301; Jewish, 11–12, 28–29, 40, 41; non-Jewish, 302; Poles in, 3, 41, 301; rations for, 297; restrictions on contact with Jews in the ghetto, 65

Workforce in the ghetto of Łódź, 3, 28–29, 57–58, 59, 64, 111, 131, 198, 313; after liquidation, 298; carpenters' strike, 115–116; categories of workers, 239; children in, 199–200, 211, 232, 236; deportation of workers, 280–281, 284, 286–288; elderly in, 200–201; expansion of, 126; exploitation of, 95; food rations for, 98–99, 109, 116, 127, 155, 200, 201, 205, 240, 252–253, 261; labor activism, 171; labor outside the ghetto, 96; labor system, 66–67, 75, 77–78; liberation and, 309; number of workers, 59, 144; productive capacity of, 252–254; quarantining of, 59; rejection of people unfit for, 283; reliance of Germans on, 129, 198; rest homes for, 254, 255; solidarity of workers, 66; tradespeople and artisans, 66, 71, 75–76, 109, 116–117, 138–139, 200, 235–236, 239, 260, 271, 287–288; weakened state of, 252; workers' movement, 127; workers remaining after deportations, 235. *See also* Factories and workshops in the ghetto of Łódź; Textile industry in the ghetto of Łódź

World Jewry, 103, 120

Yom Kippur, 261
Yugoslavia, 247

Zelkowicz, Josef, 86, 181, 182, 206, 208, 210, 212, 214, 215, 217, 218, 219, 222, 223, 224, 259, 279
Zionism, 14, 19, 103
Zoo in Łódź, 6, 106, 226–227, 247